VARIORUM COLLECTED STUDIES SERIES

# Canon Law, the Expansion of Europe, and World Order

*Also in the Variorum Collected Studies Series:*

**BRIAN TIERNEY**
Rights, Laws and Infallibility in Medieval Thought

**BRIAN TIERNEY**
Church Law and Constitutional Thought in the Middle Ages

**ROBERT FEENSTRA**
Legal Scholarship and Doctrines of Private Law, 13th–18th Centuries

**ROBERT FEENSTRA**
Le droit savant au Moyen Age et sa vulgarisation

**JOHN GILCHRIST**
Canon Law in the Age of Reform, 11th–12th Centuries

**JEAN GAUDEMET**
La doctrine canonique médiévale

**JEAN GAUDEMET**
Droit de l'Eglise et vie sociale au Moyen Age

**ROGER REYNOLDS**
Law and Liturgy in the Latin Church, 5th–12th Centuries

**ADAM VETULANI (Edited by Wacław Uruszczak)**
Institutions de l'Eglise et canonistes au Moyen Age
De Strasbourg à Cracovie

**WALTER ULLMANN (Edited by George Garnett)**
Law and Jurisdiction in the Middle Ages

**KATHERINE FISCHER DREW**
Law and Society in Early Medieval Europe
Studies in Legal History

**JAMES A. BRUNDAGE**
Sex, Law and Marriage in the Middle Ages

**ROBERT SOMERVILLE**
The Papacy, Councils and Canon Law in the 11th–12th Centuries

**KENNETH PENNINGTON**
Popes, Canonists and Texts, 1150–1550

VARIORUM COLLECTED STUDIES SERIES

# Canon Law, the Expansion of Europe, and World Order

James Muldoon

# Canon Law, the Expansion of Europe, and World Order

Routledge
Taylor & Francis Group
LONDON AND NEW YORK

First published 1998 by Ashgate Publishing

Published 2016 by Routledge
2 Park Square, Milton Park, Abingdon, Oxon OX14 4RN
711 Third Avenue, New York, NY 10017, USA

*Routledge is an imprint of the Taylor & Francis Group, an informa business*



**British Library Cataloguing-in-Publication Data**
Muldoon, James.
Canon Law, the Expansion of Europe, and World Order.
(Variorum Collected Studies Series: CS612)
1. Canon law–History. 2. Church history–Middle Ages, 600–1500.
I. Title.
262. 9' 0902

**US Library of Congress Cataloging-in-Publication Data**
Muldoon, James, 1935– .
Canon Law, the Expansion of Europe, and World Order/James Muldoon.
p. cm. – (Variorum Collected Studies Series: 612).
1. Canon law–History. 2. Canonists–Europe–History. 3. International law–Moral and ethical aspects–History. 4. Europe–Foreign relations–Moral and ethical aspects. 5. Indians of South America–Legal status, laws, etc.–Moral and ethical aspects–History.
I. Title. II. Series: Variorum Collected Studies: CS612.
LAW
262. 9' 4–dc21 98–6522
CIP

ISBN 9780860786856 (hbk)

VARIORUM COLLECTED STUDIES SERIES CS612

# CONTENTS


Preface vii–ix

Acknowledgements x

CANON LAW AND EXPANSION

I *Extra ecclesiam non est imperium*: The Canonists and the Legitimacy of Secular Power 553–580
*Studia Gratiana 9. Bologna, 1966*

II A Canonistic Contribution to the Formation of International Law 265–279
*The Jurist 28, no. 3. Washington, D.C., 1968*

III The Contribution of the Medieval Canon Lawyers to the Formation of International Law 483–497
*Traditio 28. New York, 1972*

IV Papal Responsibility for the Infidel: Another Look at Alexander VI's *Inter ceatera* 168–184
*The Catholic Historical Review 64, no. 2. Washington D.C., 1978*

V The Avignon Papacy and the Frontiers of Christendom: The Evidence of Vatican Register 62 125–195
*Archivium Historiae Pontificiae 17. Rome, 1979*

VI John Wyclif and the Rights of the Infidels: The *Requerimiento* Re-examined 301–316
*The Americas 36, no. 3. Berkeley, Calif., 1980*

VII The Development of Group Rights 31–66
*Minority Rights: A Comparative Analysis, Jay A. Sigler. Westport, Connecticut, 1983*

WORLD ORDER

VIII Solórzano's *De indiarum iure*: Applying a Medieval Theory of World Order in the Seventeenth Century 29–45
*Journal of World History 2, no. 1. Honolulu, Hawaii, 1991*

IX The Conquest of the Americas: The Spanish Search for Global Order 65–85
*Religion and Global Order, eds., Roland Robertson and William R. Garrett. New York, 1991*

IRELAND AND AMERICA

X Spiritual Conquests Compared: *Laudabiliter* and the Conquest of the Americas 174–186
*In Iure Veritas: Studies in Canon Law in Memory of Schafer Williams, ed. Steven B. Bowman and Blanche E. Cody, Cincinnati, 1991*

XI The Remonstrance of the Irish Princes and the Canon Law Tradition of the Just War 309–325
*American Journal of Legal History 22. Philadelphia, Pa., 1978*

XII The Indian as Irishman 267–289
*Essex Institute Historical Collections 111, no. 4. Salem, Mass., 1975*

Index 1–6

This volume contains x + 300 pages

# PREFACE

A selection of articles stretching across the full span of a career can, if selected with great care, give the impression of a tightly focused scholarly agenda developed logically over several decades. There are, no doubt, scholarly careers that have followed such a program. Although the articles I have selected for this volume might appear to reflect such a career, in fact, at the outset there was no agenda. The line of research sketched in these articles is really the result of three serendipitous circumstances.

The first such experience was becoming aware of Pope Innocent IV's (1243–54) discussion of the right of all men, Christian and non-Christian alike, to possess lordship and property, what the lawyers term *dominium*. This appeared in a commentary on the *Decretales*, one of the foundation volumes of the canon law. Having published an article dealing with the way in which subsequent canonists developed Innocent IV's ideas about the legitimacy of the *dominium* possessed by non-Christians, the first article in this volume, I found myself at a loss as to what further work could be done on this topic.

The second bit of serendipity occurred when a book salesman sent me a copy of Garrett Mattingly's *Renaissance Diplomacy* (Boston, 1955) for a course in the Renaissance that I was teaching. Mattingly pointed out that the intellectual foundations of the sixteenth-century debate about the rights of the inhabitants of the Americas and the subsequent formation of international law in the seventeenth century 'are obviously implicit in twelfth-century canonists with explicit elaborations in the fourteenth and fifteenth centuries' (p. 284). In other words, early modern discussion of the conquest of the Americas rested on the work of Innocent IV and other canonists. Mattingly led me in turn to the work of James Brown Scott, an ardent advocate of the importance of the morally-based international law thought of the Spanish scholastics of the sixteenth century. Scott's work generated two articles: an analysis of the work of Francisco Vitoria (1480–1546) (chapter II) whose *De Indis* was the most influential scholarly discussion of the rights of native peoples in the face of European overseas expansion; the second article (chapter III), a bibliographical essay on the origins of international law, was written at the suggestion of Professor Edward Pfeifer of St Michael's College, Vermont, where I was teaching at the time. Having heard me discussing some of the issues that Mattingly's and Scott's work on the origins of international law raised, he suggested that a bibliographical article would help to clarify some of the questions involved.

The work of Innocent IV and Vitoria provided a framework for tracing the role of the medieval canon lawyers in developing the language of international law and relations from the thirteenth to the sixteenth century, work reflected in chapters IV, V, and VI. These and other articles led finally to a complete discussion of the role of canonistic thought in the debate about the legitimacy of the conquest of the New World in *Popes, Lawyers, and Infidels* (Philadelphia, 1979).

The third moment of serendipity that contributed to the misleading notion that this work has followed a consistent path from the beginning was my discovery of the work of the seventeenth-century Spanish lawyer and bureaucrat, Juan de Solórzano Pereira (1575–1654) whose *De indiarum iure* was the longest and most complete discussion of the debate about the legitimacy of the conquest of the Americas. Having finished *Popes, Lawyers, and Infidels*, I was at a loss as to my next project. Eventually, Edward M. Peters, Henry Charles Lea Professor of Medieval History at the University of Pennsylvania, suggested examining the Lea collection at the University of Pennsylvania Library for material that would provide a new project. After fending off this sensible suggestion for a year or two, I did as he suggested and found Solórzano's work. His *De indiarum iure* contained much of the same material that Vitoria and the other Spanish scholastics had employed as well as a good deal more historical and ethnographical material, fleshing out the earlier, rather abstract legal discussion of human rights and providing a full-fledged theory of a Spanish and Christian world order. This led to a another book, *The Americas in the Spanish World Order* (Philadelphia, 1994).

The final set of three articles deals with another aspect of European overseas expansion, the way in which English expansion into Ireland provided a model for expansion into the Americas. The English entered Ireland on the basis of a papal bull that authorized them to correct abuses in the Irish Church, a bull that was a forerunner of the papal bulls that authorized the Spanish entry into the Americas in order to preach the faith to the peoples of the New World. Here again, although it is not generally recognized, the canon law tradition played a role in shaping the debate about the legitimacy of conquest.

One theme that emerged in the course of this work was that the medieval canon lawyers were probably the first thinkers to conceive of mankind not simply as a community but as a particular kind of community, a legally-structured one, a concept generally seen as the result of the development of international law from the seventeenth to the twentieth centuries. The intellectual links between medieval and modern thinking on this topic are only now being examined. A second theme is that debates about human rights are not the product of a modern sensibility associated with the Enlightenment but rather are rooted in an older tradition of medieval legal thought that is only now becoming well known. Late twentieth-century debates about human rights and about the responsibility of the world community to enforce a minimum standard of rights in every society echo the generally forgotten treatises of lawyers, canon and Roman, as well as those of philosophers and theologians from the thirteenth to the seventeenth centuries. These writings underlay the development of modern notions of international law and world order. Without Innocent IV, Vitoria, and dozens of other medieval and early modern thinkers, especially canonists, there would be no Grotius, no modern international law, no sense of the world as a legally-structured community. At a time when questions of world order, of human rights and their enforcement by the international community, and of international standards of acceptable behavior have again become the subject of public policy debates, the thought of the canonists and other medieval thinkers on these topics has a special relevance.

JAMES MULDOON

*Camden College of Arts and Sciences,*
*Rutgers University*
*December 1997*

## PUBLISHER'S NOTE

*The articles in this volume, as in all others in the Collected Studies Series, have not been given a new, continuous pagination. In order to avoid confusion, and to facilitate their use where these same studies have been referred to elsewhere, the original pagination has been maintained wherever possible.*

*Each article has been given a Roman number in order of appearance, as listed in the Contents. This number is repeated on each page and is quoted in the index entries.*

## ACKNOWLEDGEMENTS

Grateful acknowledgement is made to the following persons, institutions and publishers for their kind permission to reproduce the studies included in this volume: Fr. Joseph Zucchelli, Pontificio Ateneo Salesiano, Rome (for chapter I); the Managing Editor, *The Jurist*, Washington, D.C. (II); Fordham University Press, New York (III); Robert Trisco, Editor, *The Catholic Historical Review*, Washington, D.C. (IV); Paulius Rabikauskas, S.J., Editor, *Archivum Historiae*, Rome (V); Vincent Peloso, Editor, *The Americas*, Berkeley, California (VI); Greenwood Publishing Group, Inc., Westport, Connecticut (VII); Jerry H. Bentley, Editor, *Journal of World History*, Honolulu, Hawaii, (VIII); Paragon House Publishing, St Paul, Minnesota (IX); Steven B. Bowman (X); the Editor, *American Journal of Legal History*, Philadelphia, Pennsylvania (XI); William T. LaMoy, Editor, *Essex Institute Historical Collections*, Salem, Massachusetts (XII).

# I

## EXTRA ECCLESIAM NON EST IMPERIUM
### The Canonists and the Legitimacy of Secular Power

The problem of legitimacy occupies a major place in both the theory and the practice of contemporary politics. In the wake of the political turmoil which has marked so much of this century's political life politicians and bureaucrats as well as scholars have become very conscious of the need to justify the possession of political power. At the same time, the immediate significance of legitimacy and the technical language often used to discuss it tend to obscure the fact that in every society those who rule must be

(*) I wish to thank Professor Brian Tierney of Cornell University for his advice and guidance in the preparation of this material for my dissertation and in revising it for publication.

able to justify their possession of power. Only where the sheer possession of power, that is force alone, is considered sufficient justification for ruling is the ruler free not to offer some warrant for the power which he possesses and exercises.

At first glance, the problem of legitimacy might seem of little relevance for the medievalist. At most, legitimacy might seem to be a small part of the troubled relationship between Church and State, the usual focus for medieval political analysis. Or, perhaps, the concept of legitimacy might seem too sophisticated a problem for medieval political thinkers. In one sense, legitimacy can be seen in connection with the Church-State problem but in another sense legitimacy forms the core of this relationship as medieval thinkers saw it. Legitimacy, then, is not a small technical aspect of a larger problem. It is fundamental to understanding medieval attempts to justify political power in the framework of Christian society. As for the sophistication of medieval political thought, the failure of scholars to analyze medieval political thought on its own terms has led to a failure to appreciate the contributions of medieval thinkers, especially lawyers, to political thought. Gaines Post rightly observed that « one of the principal errors of modern scholarship on medieval law and institutions has been that of interpreting in accordance with contemporary notions » (1). The concept of legitimacy is a case in point. Although the term legitimacy was not usually employed in medieval discussions of the right of the ruler to rule, medieval thinkers did concern themselves with this question much as modern political thinkers do. The problem must, however, be considered as the medieval thinkers viewed it and not in modern terms.

Perhaps no group was more conscious of this problem than were the lawyers, and among the lawyers the canon lawyers were the

---

(1) « Gierke, it seems to me, is so obsessed with the corporate theory and the desire to make the State a real person superior to moral values and the law, that he feels that otherwise no State exists either in theory or in reality. Indeed, I sometimes think that one of the principal errors of modern scholarship on medieval law and institutions has been that of interpreting in accordance with contemporary notions. I prefer rather to find out if there was a *medieval* conception of the State, just as I prefer to believe that there is a State of the United States even if it is not completely above and outside the citizens, the law, and some morality ». GAINES POST, *Studies in Medieval Legal Thought: Public Law and the State, 1100-1322* (Princeton 1964) 10.

most intimately involved. For the canonists, legitimacy was involved every time a secular ruler was censured by the Church. Did excommunication automatically deprive the ruler's government of its legitimacy? Also, the canonists considered the problem of Christians subjected to non-Christian rulers. Could non-Christians exercise legitimate authority over Christians? Finally, the legitimacy of all authority possessed by non-Christians was discussed. Could infidels legitimately possess and exercise power of any sort? Although various scholars have touched on different aspects of these problems, there has been no attempt to bring together the thought of the canonists on legitimacy (2).

The most extensive discussion of legitimacy by a canonist appears in the writings of Sinibaldo Fieschi, Pope Innocent IV, and several scholars have analyzed this material (3). Innocent's views on legitimacy, important as they are in themselves, become even more significant when placed in the context of the canonistic tradition within which he worked. On the one hand, he continued and expanded the thought of his predecessors concerning legitimacy and related concepts, especially in discussing legitimacy within the context of Christian society. On the other hand, in discussing the legitimacy of power exercised by non-Christians, Innocent's writings show some marked divergences from the major canonistic tradition. The originality of his thought becomes even more clear when compared

---

(2) It cannot be too strongly emphasized that the notion that there is no lawful *dominium* outside the Church was neither the only nor even the preponderant canonistic position. Thus, FIGGIS was wrong when, in discussing the *Somnium Viridarii* (ca. 1376-1377), he declared that the priest's argument « that the dominion of no infidel can ever be really just, and hence war with the Turks is always permissible » is « thorough-going medievalism ». J. N. FIGGIS, *Studies of Political Thought from Gerson to Grotius, 1414-1625*, 2nd ed. (Cambridge 1916) 20-21. For a general survey of the problem of *dominium*, concentrating on the period after 1300, see EWART LEWIS, *Medieval Political Ideas*, 2 vols. (New York 1954) I, 88-108. On Wyclif, see R. L. POOLE, *Illustrations of the History of Medieval Thought and Learning*, 2nd rev. ed. (London 1920) 246-268. On the theological background of the question, see A. GWYNN, *The English Austin Friars in the Time of Wyclif* (London 1940) esp. 35-74, 211-261.

(3) See R. W. and A. J. CARLYLE, *A History of Mediaeval Political Theory in the West*, 6 vols. (London and Edinburgh 1903-1936) V, 323-324; W. ULLMANN, *Medieval Papalism* (London 1949) 128; J. A. CANTINI, *De autonomia judicis saecularis et de Romani Pontificis plenitudine potestatis in temporalibus secundum Innocentium IV*, in: *Salesianum* 23 (1961) 407-480 at 413.

with the views of his famous student, Hostiensis. Although Hostiensis constantly referred to Innocent as *dominus noster* and generally adhered to his master's opinions, on the matter of legitimacy the student and the master parted company. Innocent's views stand out by virtue of their break with the tradition and by the lack of any immediate continuation.

Although the canonists did use various terms which approximate the term legitimacy, their discussion was most generally couched in terms ot the phrase *extra ecclesiam non est imperium.* This phrase was interpreted in several ways and could be taken to mean that there was no legitimate political authority outside of the Church. In keeping with the practical nature of the lawyer's work, the canonists also considered specific situations in which the question of legitimacy arose. Two general kinds of situations attracted canonistic attention. The first concerned legitimacy as it affected Christians dwelling in a Christian society. The particular points at issue were whether legitimacy was conferred by the imperial and royal coronation ceremonies and whether Christians were bound to obey rulers who were under ecclesiastical censure. The second situation concerned the legitimacy of power exercised by non-believers, whether living in Christian society, as in the case of Jews residing in Christian Europe, or in infidel societies.

## I. *Extra ecclesiam non est imperium.*

The notion that no legitimate power existed outside of the Church entered the canonistic tradition by way of Gratian's *Decretum.* In considering the problem of excommunication, Gratian included a letter of St. Augustine which stated that a member of a heretical sect excommunicated by the sect's clergy was not to be readmitted automatically to membership in the orthodox Church (4). Gratian

(4) *Corpus iuris canonici,* ed. EMIL FRIEDBERG, 2 vols. (Leipzig 1879-1881) I, *Decretum,* C. 24 q. 1 c. 39 [title], « Quisquis propter disciplinam ab hereticis excommunicatur, a catholicis non est recipiendus ». *Dictum post* c. 39, « Sed istud Augustini intelligitur dictum non propter sentenciam, cuius potestas nulla est extra ecclesiam, sed in detestatione criminum, que in hereticis, sicut in catholicis, eque sunt punienda. Potest tamen illud Augustini de potestate baptizandi intelligi, non ligandi, aut soluendi, uel cetera sacramenta ministrandi. Baptisma namque siue ab heretico, siue etiam a laico ministratum fuerit, dummodo in unitate catholicae fidei accipiatur, non carebit effectu. Alia uero sacramenta, ut sacri corporis et sanguinis Domini, excommunicationis uel reconciliationis, si ab heretico uel catholico non sacerdote ministrentur,

hastened to add in a *dictum* appended to this statement that Augustine's words should not be interpreted to mean that the excommunication was valid and was being honored by the orthodox Church in the refusal to readmit the person to communion. The reason for the refusal was that the person was obviously a sinner and he must do penance before being readmitted to the Church. The excommunication itself was obviously of no value because « *potestas nulla est extra ecclesiam* », that is, because heretics, cut off from the Church, are cut off from the channel of sacramental and disciplinary power which the Church possesses. Heretics may perform the motions associated with the exercise of such power but their actions lack substance.

In the two generations of canonists which followed the appearance of the *Decretum*, Gratian's *dictum* became a stock phrase in discussion of power. As Fr. Stickler showed in his analysis of the two swords tradition, phrases which originally referred to power within the Church could be and were transformed into statements concerning temporal power (5). In the case of Gratian's statement concerning sacramental power the transformation occurred when *imperium* replaced *potestas* in the writings of later canonists. This change ultimately led to the emergence of three possible political interpretations of the phrase all of which deal with legitimacy but in different ways. The crux of the problem was the definition of *imperium*. *Imperium* originally signified supreme power within the Roman state and specifically included responsibility for declaring war and making law (6). The title *imperator* originally signified a victorious general acclaimed by his troops (7). Medieval understanding of these terms came through Isidore of Seville's *Etymologies*. While recognizing the military roots of *imperator*, the Bishop of Seville also added that the title had been awarded to Augustus « in order to distinguish him from other kings » (8). Gradually other

---

uel nullum, uel letalem habebunt effectum. Unde et ab hominibus fidelibus nullatenus sunt recipienda ».

(5) See A. M. Stickler, *De ecclesiae potestate coactiva materiali apud magistrum Gratianum*, in: *Salesianum* 4 (1942) 2-23; and *Der Schwerterbegriff bei Huguccio*, in: *Ephemerides iuris canonici* 3 (1947) 201-242.

(6) *Oxford Classical Dictionary*, ed. M. Cary (Oxford 1949) 451.

(7) *Ibid.* 450.

(8) Isidore of Seville, *Etymologies*, ed. W. M. Lindsay (Oxford 1911) IX, iii, 4, « Imperatorem autem nomen apud Romanos eorum tantum prius fuit apud quos

definitions for these terms appeared. *Imperium* came to signify the territory ruled by an *imperator* (9). Both definitions of *imperium*, power and the region governed by an *imperator*, remained alive throughout the Middle Ages and they were not always clearly distinguished (10). Given these meanings, the phrase *extra ecclesiam non est imperium* could mean either that there is no empire outside the Church, a limited and specific meaning, or that there is no legitimate power outside of the Church, a broad and sweeping assertion.

Huguccio of Pisa, one of the most important decretists, presented an extensive analysis of legitimacy toward the end of the twelfth century. This discussion summed up the two generations of commentary which had developed since the *Decretum* had appeared. Huguccio offered two interpretations of *extra ecclesiam non est imperium*, one concerned with the Donation of Constantine, the other dealing with the status of the eastern emperor. These interpretations reveal the difficulties caused the canonists by the failure to employ the term *imperium* in a consistent fashion.

According to Huguccio, some canonists described the Donation of Constantine as a public admission by the emperor that the power, *regalia*, which he possessed was not legitimate (11). Constantine obtained legitimacy for his power by granting it to the pope and then receiving it back again from his hands. In Huguccio's opinion, if it was true that Constantine's power received its legitimacy in this way then, logically, there could be no lawful secular power

---

summa rei militaris consisteret, ideo imperatores dicti ab imperando exercitui: sed dum diu dices titulis imperatores fungerentur, senatus censuit ut Augusti Caesaris hoc tantum nomen esset, eoque is distingueretur a ceteris gentium regibus... ».

(9) On the general theory of the empire see: R. FOLZ, *L'idée d'empire en occident du Ve au XIVe siècle* (Paris 1953); A. DEMPF, *Sacrum Imperium* (Munich and Berlin 1929). For the theory of empire as found in the civil lawyers see C. N. S. WOOLF, *Bartolus of Sassoferrato* (Cambridge 1913).

(10) The history of the *imperium* as power has been traced by M. GILMORE, *Argument from Roman Law in Political Thought, 1200-1600* (Cambridge, Mass. 1941). WOOLF, *Bartolus of Sassoferrato*, also dealt with *imperium* as power, but he concentrated on the nature and extent of the empire as a political unit.

(11) « *celestis*... Item et secundum hoc oportet hoc concedere nullum imperatorem rite exercuisse gladium qui illum non acceperat a romana ecclesia presertim... petro concessit iura utriusque imperii que intelligens constantinus in resignatione regalium resignavit beato silvestro gladium ostendens non legitime se usum fuisse gladii potestate enim... ab ecclesia non recepit set in hac questione ego aliter sentio sicut invenies distinctum. et di. 96 duo [c. 10] ». *Summa* ad D. 22 c. 7 (Pembroke MS 72 fol. 131ra).

outside of the Church. Huguccio himself denied this interpretation of the Donation in keeping with his opinion, expressed elsewhere, that the two powers, spiritual and temporal, were separate and the pope had only the spiritual sword (12). Therefore, the pope could not legitimize Constantine's power because temporal authority was outside of the papal sphere of jurisdiction.

Of more immediate interest to his contemporaries was Huguccio's discussion of the status of the eastern emperor. Was the emperor at Constantinople the true emperor or was the German king who also bore the imperial title with papal approval now the true bearer of the title? To resolve this issue, Huguccio began by citing the argument from Roman law that there should be but one emperor (13). Given that assumption, he then proceeded to argue that the ruler at Constantinople could not be the true emperor because he was a schismatic and a heretic. The true emperor must recognize the pope as his superior and the source of his title, something that a schismatic or heretic obviously would not do. By implication, the German king who bore the imperial title must be the sole legitimate emperor because the pope conferred the title upon him. Whithout expressly employing the standard phrase, Huguccio effectively declared that there was not a legitimate emperor outside of the Church.

These two opinions present some difficulties because, while Huguccio admitted the existence of legitimate *imperium* outside of the Church, he denied the legitimacy of the eastern emperor's claim to the imperial title. Examination of Huguccio's conception of the

---

(12) « *Cum ad verum ventum*: usque adventum Christi iura temporalia et pontificalia erant indistincta, quia idem erat imperator et pontifex ut di. XXI cleros (c. 1). Set a Christo distincta sunt iura et officia imperatoris et pontificis et alia sunt attributa imperatori, scilicet temporalia, et alia, scilicet spiritualia, concessa sunt pontifici. Et hoc est factum causa humilitatis servande et superbie vitande, si enim imperator vel pontifex omnia haberet officia de facili superbiret... Et introducitur hoc caput ad ostendendum quod imperator non debet disponere vel iudicare de rebus ecclesiasticis... ». *Summa* ad D. 96 c. 6, STICKLER, *Der Schwerterbegriff bei Huguccio*, 201 n. 1.

(13) « *augustorum*... unus enim solus debet esse imperator. regulariter. ut vii. q. i. in apibus [c. 41]. nec constantinopolitanum credo esse imperatorem set potius hereticum et schismaticum cum ecclesiam romanam non recognoscat caput sibi ». *Summa* ad D. 21 c. 7 (Pembroke MS 72 fol. 130ra). On the question of the two claimants to the imperial title, see W. OHNSORGE, *Das Zweikaiserproblem im früheren Mittelalter* (Hildesheim 1947). On the *translatio imperii*, see P. A. VAN DEN BAAR, *Die kirchliche Lehre der Translatio Imperii Romani* (Rome 1956); and W. GOEZ, *Translatio Imperii* (Tübingen 1958).

empire, however, resolves the apparent contradiction. For Huguccio, the *imperium* was neither the totality of legitimate power nor was it a unique territorial unit. Instead, he used a third meaning, that of an office which existed to protect the papacy. Appointment of a suitable protector was a papal prerogative. Lest it be thought, however, that by making the emperor receive his title from the pope, he was denying the absolute separation of the two powers which he had defended elsewhere, Huguccio explained the origin of this right. The pope, he argued, did not possess the *gladius materialis* by virtue of a divine grant of power (14). The pope did, however, possess secular jurisdiction within Rome and its environs just as many bishops possessed secular power in addition to their spiritual power. In such cases the secular power was derived from some secular ruler who had the right to grant it to a cleric. Huguccio's position suggested that the pope obtained the right to appoint the *patriciatus* after the imperial government was no longer capable of defending the city from attack. Thus, the papacy's right to appoint the emperor ultimately resulted from the breakdown of imperial government in the West and not from any grant of power signified by the two swords.

In spite of the care with which Huguccio delineated the respective spheres of the spiritual and the temporal powers and in spite of the forceful arguments he presented against the opinion that there was no legitimate power outside of the Church, his arguments were soon countered by an equally forceful proponent of the opposing position. Alanus Anglicus, a defender of the most extreme canonistic positions on the nature and extent of papal power, argued that no ruler's power could be considered legitimate unless he believed in the true God and received his power from the Church (15).

---

(14) « *non habet ecclesia gladium materialem in exercitio.* Plures tamen ecclesiae habent gladium materialem quo ad potestatem et prestant auctoritatem exercendi eum in suo patrimonio et maxime ecclesia romana. Et potest delegare talem gladium, licet diffinire vel executionem demandare non possit... ». *Summa* ad C. 33 q. 2 c. 6, STICKLER, *Der Schwerterbegriff bei Huguccio*, 222 n. 2.

(15) « *cursu...* Set veritas est et fides catholica quod pape subest quoad spiritualia et etiam gladium suum habet ab eo, quia ius utriusque gladii est apud papam; quod probatur quia dominus in terris utrumque habuit et utroque usus est ut hic. Set petrum in terris vicarium constituit et omnes petri successores. Ergo et hodie innocentius habet de iure gladium materialem. Quod si negaveris dicas quod principem secularem in hoc sibi vicarium constituit et petri successores. Item petrus dixit domino: ' ecce gladii duo hic '. Ergo et materialis apud petrum fuit. Item si quoad tem-

The key to Alanus' position was his conception of the effect which the coming of Christ had upon the two powers. Before His coming no rulers had legitimate authority, the *ius gladii*, unless they believed in the true God, apparently a reference to the rulers of the Hebrews. The infidel rulers possessed only *de facto* power.

The coming of Christ added a new factor for determining legitimacy, reception of power from the Church. According to Alanus, Christ possessed and exercised the two swords and gave them to Peter and to his successors. The pope then granted the exercise of the material sword to the emperor, and, by implication, to all Christian rulers. Alanus supported his position by asserting the need for a single ultimate source of legitimate power within Christian society. If the pope did not grant the material sword to the emperor, it would mean that he received it directly from God. If this were true then there would be two vicars of Christ on earth, pope and emperor. Since this could not be, because then society would be two-headed and everyone knows that a two-headed animal is a monstrous creation, therefore all legitimate power must flow from the pope. Again, without using the precise words, a canonist argued that *extra ecclesiam non est imperium*.

Alanus' views on legitimacy represented an extreme position and, while not rejected or consciously modified by later commentators, they were not developed further. Instead of discussing legitimacy in terms of the total structure of Christian society, later canonists turned to the *translatio imperii* as a starting point for their analysis of the problem. Innocent III's decretal *Venerabilem* (X. 1.6.34) which included a discussion of the *translatio* forced the canonists to deal directly with the issue of legitimacy as it concerned the legitimacy of the claims of the eastern emperor to be the true emperor. In an argument similar to that employed by his teacher, Huguccio, Innocent III distinguished between the offices of emperor and of German king (16). The German princes elected a king who

poralia imperator pape non subesset, in temporalibus erga ecclesiam peccare non posset. Item unum est ecclesie corpus ergo unum caput tantum habebit vel monstrum erit. Non obitiat [obviat] huic opinioni quod ante fuerunt imperatores quam pape, quia tantum de facto fuerunt et ius gladii non habuerunt, nisi illi tantum qui in verum deum crediderunt. Nec etiam hodie habent infideles principes... » ad D. 96 c. 6 [second recension], A. M. Stickler, *Alanus Anglicus als Verteidiger des monarchischen Papsttums*, in: *Salesianum* 21 (1959) 346-406 at 362.

(16) *Corpus iuris canonici*, II, *Decretales*, 1. 6. 34, « Verum illis principibus ius et potestatem eligendi regem, in imperatorem postmodum promovendum, recogno-

was then to be raised to imperial rank if he was acceptable to the papacy. The imperial office was at the disposal of the papacy because the function of the empire was to protect the papacy from its enemies. The papacy had transferred the *imperium* from Constantinople to the West because the eastern emperor had refused to protect Rome against the Lombards. Charlemagne received the imperial title from the pope because of his willingness to assume the burdens associated with the title. In Innocent's usage, the *imperium* was an office of a specific nature. The title conferred no power or territory upon its holder. In fact, the imperial title only recognized the power actually possessed by Charlemagne in the neighborhood of Rome. Like Huguccio, Innocent denied the legitimacy of the eastern emperor's claim to the imperial title but he did not deny the legitimacy of that ruler's power over those subjects whom he effectively ruled and protected.

The canonists who commented upon *Venerabilem* generally saw the *imperium* as an office within the Church, but an office of much broader significance than that described by Huguccio and Innocent III. Some went so far as to include all legitimate secular power within that office, thus limiting legitimate power to that approved by the Church. Tancred, the author of the standard gloss on *Venerabilem*, argued that the pope had transferred the *regimen mundi*, defined as the *regimen romanae ecclesiae*, from East to West (17). Then adding the Roman law description of the imperial status to this description of the emperor's role in Christian society, Tancred asserted that all kings and nations were subject to his *imperium*. The eastern emperor's claim to imperial status was invalid, apparently because of the failure to defend Rome against the Lombards. Like the king on a chess board the eastern ruler possessed a title

---

scimus, ut debemus, ad quos de iure ac antiqua consuetudine noscitur pertinere; praesertim, quum ad eos ius et potestas huiusmodi ab apostolica sede pervenerit, quae Romanum imperium in personam magnifici Caroli a Graecis transtulit in Germanos ».

(17) « *transtulit*. sic ergo regimen mundi translatum est ad teutonicos nam etiam habent regimen romane ecclesie... et sic patet quod imperium non est apud grecos licet largo nomine appellatur imperator grecarum... sicut rex scottorum dicitur rex. quoniam extra ecclesiam non hic est imperium... est autem imperator ille super omnes reges... et omnes nationes sub eo sunt... ipse enim est princeps mundi et dominus... et omnes provincie... item omnia sunt in potestate imperatoris... » *Comp.* III ad 1. 6. 19 (X. 1. 6. 34), Caius MS 17 p. 162a.

but lacked the power that went with it (18). He was an emperor in name only. To support this argument, the glossator added that *extra ecclesiam non hic est imperium*.

Although Tancred's gloss on *Venerabilem* eventually became the standard commentary, eventually being incorporated in the *Glossa ordinaria*, other decretalists did suggest alternative interpretations which affected the legitimacy of secular power. According to Laurentius Hispanus, any person who gives orders to other men may loosely be termed *imperator*, but only those rulers who have received ecclesiastical approbation are true kings or emperors (19). He added that « *extra ecclesiam nullum credo imperatorem, qui habeat de iure gladium materialem*... » Laurentius' emphasis upon the distinction between *de iure* and *de facto* power makes it clear that Alanus' position was not unique in the canonistic tradition and, although not destined to become standard, it was not destined to be completely overlooked either. Laurentius went on to complete Alanus' argument by providing a concrete illustration of the legitimization of secular power. Choosing an argument that Huguccio had previously rejected, Laurentius declared that Constantine was the first true, that is legitimate, emperor, apparently because he surrendered his power to the pope and then received it back again (20).

---

(18) The comparison, a common one, was *rex scaccariorum*, not *rex scottorum* as found in Caius 17. See G. Post, *Some Unpublished Glosses (ca. 1210-1214) on the 'Translatio Imperii' and the Two Swords*, in: *Archiv für katholisches Kirchenrecht* 117 (1937) 403-429 at 408. Post noted that the phrase *rex scaccariorum* was also written: *rex scotorum*; *rex scaccorum*; *rex francorum*; *rex schacorum*. On the common scribal error of misreading geographical names, see C. Duggan, *Twelfth Century Decretal Collections* (London 1963) 9-11.

(19) « *a grecis transtulit ad Germanos*: Et ita videtur, quod romanus imperator sit verus imperator, non constantinopolitanus. Quare ergo scribit ei papa tanquam imperatori I. de maio. et ob. [1. 33. 6]? Largo vocabulo quilibet potest imperator dici, qui habet, quibus imperet. Unde quicunque est approbatus ab ecclesia sive rex sive imperator et est catholicus, eum credo imperatorem vel regem. Extra ecclesiam nullum credo imperatorem, qui habeat de iure gladium materialem, qui a deo processit... ». *Comp.* III ad 1. 6. 19 (X. 1. 6. 34), S. Mochi Onory, *Fonti canonistiche dell'idea moderna dello Stato* (Milan 1951) 196 n. 2. Mochi Onory identified this gloss as being by Laurentius Hispanus although Post, *Some Unpublished Glosses,* » 407-409, attributed it to an unknown author.

(20) « Unde credo, quod constantinus primo fuit verus imperator rome... ». *Comp.* III ad 1. 6. 19 (X. 1. 6. 34), Post, *Some Unpublished Glosses*, 407-409; Mochi Onory, *Fonti*, 196 n. 2.

II. *The effect of the imperial and royal consecration ceremonies on the legitimacy of secular power.*

As befitted men whose work demanded immediate solutions to concrete problems rather than analysis of theoretical situations, the canonists brought the discussion of legitimacy down to specifics. The focal point of the discussion of legitimacy was the consecration of the ruler which was a part of all royal and imperial coronation ceremonies (21). What precisely did the consecration do? Did it confer legitimacy upon the ruler? Once it is admitted that secular power must be legitimized by the Church then the consecration ceremony becomes crucial to the entire problem because it is the point in the acquisition of power at which representatives of the Church play a significant role. The canonists did not, however, phrase questions concerning the effects of the consecration ceremony in terms of legitimacy. Rather, they tended to ask whether the consecration constituted the ruler or merely confirmed his selection. In spite of the differing ways of formulating the question, however, the result is the same. The canonists were anxious to determine the means by which legitimacy was conferred, if it was conferred at all.

Obviously those canonists who denied the right of the Church to legitimize secular power took the position that the consecration ceremony did not have constitutive effect. Huguccio, for example, denied any ecclesiastical claim to be the source of legitimacy for a secular ruler with the sole exception of the emperor. Even in the case of the imperial consecration the papal role was limited to granting legitimate use of the imperial title and no more (22). Thus, the royal

---

(21) On consecration ceremonies, see: P. SCHRAMM, *Die Krönung in Deutschland bis zum Beginn des Salischen Hauses*, in: *Zeitschrift der Savigny-Stiftung für Rechtsgeschichte, Kan. Abt.* 24 (1935) 184-332; *A History of the English Coronation*, trans. L. C. W. LEGG (Oxford 1937); *Der König von Frankreich*, 2 vols. (Weimar 1939). EDUARD EICHMANN, *Die Kaiserkrönung im Abendland*, 2 vols. (Würzburg 1942). See also F. KERN, *Kingship and Law in the Middle Ages*, trans. S. B. CHRIMES (Oxford 1939) 27-68; and E. H. KANTOROWICZ, *The King's Two Bodies* (Princeton 1954) 318-323.

(22) « *Et digni ipsius Christi i.e. officiis*... Si ergo alicubi inveniatur vel innuatur quod imperator habeat potestatem gladii a papa sic intelligo; i.e. unctionem et confirmationem, quam a papa accipit; et iurat ei fidelitatem. Ante quidem imperator est quoad dignitatem set non quoad unctionem, licet antea non dicatur imperator; et antea habet potestatem gladii et eam exercet ». *Summa* ad D. 96 c. 6, STICKLER, *Der Schwerterbegriff bei Huguccio*, 210-211.

or imperial consecration ceremonies did not constitute, that is legitimize, secular rulers. The author of the *Glossa Palatina*, tersely summarizing Huguccio's position, declared that election by the princes creates the emperor and the pope only confirms this election (23).

The canonists who insisted on the need for ecclesiastical approval of secular power predictably saw the consecration ceremony as the external sign of the Church's power of legitimizing such power. The *Glossa Palatina* presented the argument that the unction which the emperor receives at his coronation, an unction which only a priest can administer, actually makes him emperor (24). The emperor receives the *potestas gladii*, legitimacy for his power, by means of this ceremony (25). As might be expected, Alanus Anglicus maintained this argument and explicitly rejected Huguccio's position (26). Arguing that the Catholic faith required subordination of the secular power to the spiritual, Alanus asserted that the pope must possess both the material and the spiritual swords and that he grants the exercise of the material sword to the emperor. The election in which the German princes purport to choose an emperor is, in this view, only a nomination. Actual appointment of the emperor rests in papal hands.

---

(23) « *Imperator*: ex sola enim electione principum dico eum verum imperatorem, antequam a papa confirmetur... ». *Glossa Palatina* ad D. 93 c. 24, A. M. STICKLER, *'Sacerdotium et Regnum' nei Decretisti e primi Decretalisti. Considerazioni metodologiche di ricerca e testi*, in: *Salesianum* 15 (1953) 575-612 at 589.

(24) « *discrevit*: Argumentum quod imperator potestatem gladii sui non habet a summo pontifice; set cum ex unctione demum sint reges, que a nullo nisi sacerdote haberi potest exemplo davidis et saulis, qui a samuele uncti sunt, liquet omnem principem regnorum a iudice ecclesie confirmationem et executionem consequi... ». *Glossa Palatina* ad D. 10 c. 8, STICKLER, *Sacerdotium et Regnum*, 588.

(25) Other glossators used this same argument, often in the same words: see the *Summa Omnis qui iuste*, ad D. 22 c. 1, MOCHI ONORY, *Fonti*, 110-111, and the *Summa et est sciendum* ad D. 22 c. 1, A. M. STICKLER, *Imperator vicarius Papae*, in: *Mitteilungen des Österreichischen Instituts für Geschichtsforschung* 62 (1954) 165-212 at 203 n. 69.

(26) « *cursu*... Set quoad temporalia nequaquam sec. ug. Verumtamen de voluntate principum qui ex iure consuetudinario eum eligunt posset papa ipsum in temporalibus iudicare et deponere... Secundum eum habet gladium tantum a deo et non a papa (nisi) quantum ad coronationem et confirmationem; ante quam habet totam imperialem iurisdictionem, licet imperator non vocetur. Set veritas est et fides catholica quod pape subest quoad spiritualia et etiam gladium suum habet ab eo, quia ius utriusque gladii est apud papam... » ad D. 96 c. 6 [second recension], STICKLER, *Alanus Anglicus*, 361-362.

The debate over the significance of the coronation ceremonies was ended by Innocent III's decretal *Cum venisset* (X. 1.15.1) which dealt with the effects of various ecclesiastical annointings. The section dealing with the royal consecration carefully defined the differences between the royal and the episcopal annointings with the aim of emphasizing that the royal consecration was not a sacrament but, at most, a sacramental (27). The act of consecration illustrated the superiority of the spiritual power over the temporal. The words of the decretal do not indicate that the act constituted the ruler or in any way affected the legitimacy of his power (28). Innocent III failed to consider the precise nature of the imperial consecration in *Cum venisset*, but in *Venerabilem* which contained Innocent's position on the relation between the papacy and the empire, this gap was filled. In contrast to the royal consecration, the imperial consecration did constitute a ruler but, as Innocent emphasized, this was a special case based on the unique relationship which existed between the papacy and the empire (29). The German princes elected a king of the Germans who was to be advanced to the imperial office if he was acceptable to the papacy. The princes' role was limited to choosing a candidate for the imperial title, a candidate whom the pope could reject as unsuitable. Here, Innocent clearly distinguished between the election of a king which was not a matter for direct papal action and the appointment of an emperor, a direct responsibility of the papacy.

---

(27) KERN, *Kingship and Law*, 40, noted that as late as the eleventh century, royal consecration was counted as a sacrament by Peter Damian and that this view lasted into the twelfth century and can be found in the canonical tradition. KANTOROWICZ, *King's Two Bodies*, 321, stated that Innocent's decretal had little effect outside Rome and that in France and England the tradition of the sacramental nature of the consecration remained.

(28) « In capite vero pontificis sacramentalis est delibutio conservata, quia personam capitis in pontificali officio repraesentat. Refert autem inter pontificis et principis unctionem, quia caput pontificis chrismate consecratur, brachium vero principis oleo delinitur, ut ostendatur, quanta sit differentia inter auctoritatem pontificis et principis potestatem » (X. 1. 15. 1).

(29) « ... quod ius et auctoritas examinandi personam electam in regem et promovendam ad imperium ad nos spectat, qui eum inungimus, consecramus et coronamus » (X. 1. 6. 34).

III. *Obedience to Christian rulers under ecclesiastical censure.*

The canonists did not end the discussion of legitimacy with analysis of the consecration ceremony. Recognizing that legitimacy of power may be lost through its misuse or that a change in the ruler's ecclesiastical status might affect his right to rule, they also discussed the effect of excommunication and of lapse into heresy or schism upon the legitimacy of a ruler's power (30). Here again, the definition of the term *imperium* is important because, as we have already seen, some canonists argued that the eastern emperor lost the *imperium* because he was a heretic or schismatic. This case alone, however, does not explicitly solve the problem of the legitimacy of power held by other schismatic or heretical rulers. The *Decretum* provided several cases which served as focal points of discussion for the problem of legitimacy as it affected the power of rulers who were separated from the Church either because of excommunication or because of heresy or schism. Perhaps the most interesting of these cases concerned the situation of Christian soldiers serving in the Roman army under Julian the Apostate (31). Presumably, these men entered the army during the reigns of Constantine and his sons and then found themselves serving not simply a non-Christian ruler but a man who was an apostate from the Christian faith. According to St. Ambrose, whose statement on the matter Gratian cited, the soldiers remained bound to obey the emperor's orders unless ordered to use their arms against their fellow Christians. Ambrose argued that as soldiers they should continue to serve the Roman people, the lawful duty of soldiers, regardless of Julian's ecclesiastical status. It would appear that to Ambrose the ecclesiastical status of the ruler was not relevant to the legitimacy of his power. Of much greater significance were the ends for which it was being employed.

The glossators who commented upon Ambrose's letter responded in a variety of ways. The author of the *Summa Omnis qui iuste*

---

(30) This topic is obviously closely related to the problem of deposing a ruler. The emphasis here is upon one facet of the overall deposition problem, the effect of the ruler's relation to the body of the Church upon his right to exercise power.

(31) « Iulianus imperator, quamuis esset apostata, habuit tamen sub se Christianos milites, quibus cum dicebat, producite aciem pro defensione reipublicae, obediebatur ei. Cum autem diceret eis, producite arma in Christianos, tunc cognoscebant imperatorem celi ». *Decretum*, C. 11 q. 3 c. 94.

offered two reasons for supporting Ambrose's position. In the first place, Julian had not been formally excommunicated and, therefore, should have been obeyed at least until he was (32). This opinion clearly implies that had Julian been formally excommunicated the Christian soldiers could have properly refused to serve him because he was no longer a legitimate ruler. The second argument which this glossator presented was that the soldiers obeyed Julian as the lesser of two evils. Had they refused to serve there might have been a revival of the persecutions. This argument indicates that Julian's power was in fact illegitimate but that it was necessary to tolerate it. Both of these opinions indicate a tendency to consider power exercised by an excommunicate as illegitimate coupled with a tendency to refrain from acting upon this opinion.

By far the most important chapter of the *Decretum* affecting legitimacy was C. 15 q. 6 c. 3 *Alius* which dealt with the deposition of Childerich III, the last Merovingian king of the Franks. The chapter contained a fragment of a letter written by Gregory VII to justify the action he took against Emperor Henry IV. According to Gregory VII, Pope Zachary had deposed Childerich and freed the Franks from their oaths of allegiance to him so that they might take an oath of fealty to his successor without fear of committing perjury (33). Gratian used the letter to support the argument that the pope could absolve subjects from their oaths of fealty. He did not draw from it any conclusions about either the papal right of deposing secular rulers or the right of the pope to deny legitimacy to secular power.

Following Gratian's lead, the first canonists to gloss this letter focused on the oath itself but, unlike Gratian, they assumed that

---

(32) « *Iulianus* usque *obediebant*... set dici potest quod iste quamvis esset apostata non tamen nominatim erat excommunicatus. vel propter pacem spiritualem in eo fuit toleratum ». *Summa Omnis qui iuste* ad C. 11 q. 3 c. 94 (Leipzig MS 986, fol. 153va-vb).

(33) « Alius item Romanis Pontifex, Zacharias scilicet regem Francorum non tam pro suis iniquitatibus, quam pro eo, quod tantae potestati erat inutilis, a regno deposuit, et Pipinum, Karoli imperatoris patrem, in eius loco substituit, omnesque Francigenas a iuramento fidelitatis absoluit ». *Decretum*, C. 15 q. 6 c. 3. The most recent discussion of the relation between excommunication and deposition in the thought of Gregory VII is: K. F. Morrison, *Canossa: A Revision*, in: *Traditio* 18 (1962) 121-148. Other discussions of the problem are contained in: Carlyle, II, 202-206; Ullmann, *Medieval Papalism*, 176-183; and *The Growth of Papal Government in the Middle Ages*, 2nd ed. (London 1962) 283 and 301-303.

the ruler to whom the oath was given had been excommunicated. According to Rufinus, the basic issue was the nature of the oath, specifically whether it was given to the king in his capacity as a private person or to him in virtue of his office (34). If the oath was given to the ruler as a private individual it was no longer binding if he was excommunicated. An oath given in virtue of office, however, was binding until the ruler was lawfully removed from office. Thus, the ruler's excommunication did not immediately affect the legitimacy of his power.

Rufinus' views remained the core of the decretist discussion of the legitimacy of power held by excommunicates. Huguccio repeated these arguments and implied that excommunication was not meant to deprive a ruler of legitimacy but was meant to serve as a warning that if he did not correct his behaviour he would be deposed. In keeping with his general position on the relation between the two powers, Huguccio placed the responsibility for determining a ruler's fitness on the shoulders of the princes who elected him (35). Excommunication was only part of the overall disciplinary process.

---

(34) « *Alius item Romanus*. Hic sciendum est quod iuramenta fidelitatis fiunt aliquando intuitu personarum, aliquando dumtaxit intuitu dignitatum. Et quidem intuitu personarum, sicut illa, que laicis laici faciunt; contemplatione dignitatum, ut ea, que prelatis ecclesiarum a laicis offeruntur, non utique propter ipsas prelatorum personas, sed propter eas quas ipse persone suscipiunt dignitates. Si quis itaque intuitu persone iuraverit alicui fidelitatem, semper iuramento obligatus ei tenebitur, nisi suus dominus ab ecclesia fuerit anathematizatus: interea enim, scil. dum in excommunicatione dominus fuerit, fidelis etiam non debet servire ei... Si autem intuitu dignitatis quis alteri fidelitatem iuraverit, postquam dominus dignitatem illam canonice perdiderit vel legitime, iuratorum ei deinceps obligatus nequaquam erit, ut notatur ex presenti capitulo. Isti enim regi Francorum iuraverunt Franci intuitu regie potestatis; postquam ergo rex legitime regnum perdidit, iuramenti vinculum absolutum fuit ». Rufinus, *Die Summa Decretorum des Magister Rufinus*, ed. H. SINGER (Paderborn 1902) 350. CARLYLE, II, 206, concluded from this statement that it was « a principle of the canon law » that the excommunication of a ruler *ipso facto* released subjects from their oaths of allegiance. In fact, however, the gloss only required *ipso facto* release if the oath had been given to the ruler in virtue of his person.

(35) « *tam pro suis iniquitatibus quam pro eo quod inutilis*... set numquid papa potest deponere imperatorem vel regem qui non subest imperatori? sic, si de voluntate principum coram eo accusetur et convincatur, et convictus et admonitus nolit satisfacere, tunc debet excommunicare, ut si sic non resipicit recte sententiam depositionis percellitur a papa vel a principibus de voluntate pape... ». *Summa* ad C. 15 q. 6 c. 3, MOCHI ONORY, *Fonti*, 155-156 n. 2. See also ULLMANN, *Medieval Papalism*, 179, where Huguccio's gloss to D. 96 c. 6, which contains the same material

The *Glossa ordinaria* to the *Decretum* repeated the various arguments concerning the effects of excommunication, emphasizing that excommunication did not automatically deprive a ruler of legitimate authority over his subjects. The glossator presented arguments for and against the opinion that excommunication absolved subjects from the obligation of obeying their ruler (36). He did admit, however, that excommunication did free vassals from the penalties attached to failure to obey their lord. This solution to the problem suggests that excommunication was viewed as a temporary disciplinary action rather than total deprivation of legitimacy.

IV. *The legitimacy of power exercised by non-Christians.*

In the early thirteenth century the problem of legitimacy entered a new phase. Until this point, the canonists working with the *Decretum* dealt primarily with legitimacy within Christian society. With the appearance of the new collections of decretals in the late twelfth and early thirteenth centuries, the canonists had new material to work with, material which included a basis for considering the legitimacy of power held by non-Christians. To some extent, the new direction taken by the canonists reflected an increasing awareness of the non-Christian world, not simply in terms of the Moslem threat to Christian Europe but in terms of peoples who posed no direct military threat and who could be dealt with diplomatically.

The decretist discussion of the legitimacy of power exercised by non-Christians had centered on the issue of non-Christians ruling or judging Christians. The underlying justification for denying non-Christians the right to rule over believers came from St. Paul's rebuke to those who sought to air their grievances before pagan

---

as the gloss to C. 15 q. 6 c. 3, is given. Using this gloss, Ullmann argued that Huguccio asserted that deposition followed immediately upon excommunication, but he omitted some significant phrases which affect his view. See STICKLER, *Der Schwerterbegriff bei Huguccio*, 210-211, for the entire text.

(36) « *Obediebant* infra. 15 q. 6 nos sanctorum [c. 4]. et ca. iuratos [c. 5]. contra. ibi enim dicitur, quod si dominus est nominatim excommunicatus, vel haereticus, statim vasallus eius absolutus est a sacramento? Resp. Iulianus adhuc tolerabatur ab ecclesia, ne suscitaret scandalum adversus Christianos. hoc autem verum est, quia excommunicato non tollit obligationem, quia est vasallus obligatus domino, sed tantum effectum obligationis, unde domino absoluto statim tenetur ei obedire ». *Glossa ordinaria in Decretum* (Lyons 1554) ad C. 11 q. 3 c. 94.

judges (37). Appeals to pagan judges disrupted the internal discipinle of the Christian community. The Fourth Council of Carthage repeated this prohibition, adding that the justice or injustice of the case made no difference (38). The Fourth Council of Toledo repeated the theme of the earlier prohibition but made it specifically forbidden for Jews to hold any public office in which they could judge Christians (39). The reason given for this action was that in such offices Jews might harm Christians. In all of these cases the legitimacy of non-Christians ruling or judging Christians was not so much in question as was the prudence of such a situation.

The prohibition against non-Christian judges was translated into contemporary terms by an anonymous Anglo-Norman glossator in the late twelfth century. He argued that the prohibition against entrusting public offices to Jews forbade the paying of homage to them (40). Here again, the issue was not the legitimacy of such power but the prudence of such actions.

The early decretalists repeated with few changes the decretist position on the exercise of power by non-Christians within Christian society. Popes Innocent III and Gregory IX renewed the prohibitions against Jewish officials, adding some words of explanation but not changing the content of the earlier statements. Innocent III declared that it was « irreverent » for non-Christians to exercise power over Christians (41). The decretal did not, however, deny the legitimacy of such power. As a further indication that the propriety and not the legitimacy of such power was being questioned, Innocent's decretal added that any profits which had accrued to

---

(37) I Cor. vi, 1-8. See also CARLYLE, I, 97.

(38) « Catholicus, qui causam suam, siue iustam siue iniustam, ad iudicium alterius fidei iudicis prouocat, excommunicetur ». *Decretum* C. 2 q. 6 c. 32 and *De Pen.* D. 1 c. 7.

(39) « Constituit sanctum concilium, ut Iudei, aut hii, qui ex Iudeis sunt, offitia publica nullatenus appetant, quia sub hac occasione Christianis iniuriam faciunt... Si quis autem hoc permiserit, velut in sacrilegum excommunicatio proferatur, et is, qui subrepserit, publicis cedibus deputetur ». *Decretum* C. 17 q. 4 c. 31.

(40) « elicitas... eos agere. set nec debent Christiani homagia iudeis facere ». Caius MS 676 ad C. 17 q. 4 c. 31 (fol. 141va).

(41) « Officiali vero huiusmodi tamdiu Christianorum communio in commerciis et aliis denegetur, donec in usus pauperum Christianorum secundum providentiam dioecesani episcopi convertatur quicquid fuerit a Christianis adeptus occasione officii sic suscepti, et officium cum pudore dimittat, quod irreverenter assumpsit. Hoc idem extendimus ad paganos » (X. 5. 6. 16).

a non-Christian official were to be confiscated and used for the poor of the diocese, and the official was to be removed from office. Innocent did not deny the legitimacy of any decisions made by the official during his term of office, nor did he insist that the profits of justice be returned to those who had sought justice before non-Christian judges. This continuation of the earlier canonistic tradition by the earlier decretalists emphasized the significance of Innocent IV's approach to the problem of the legitimacy of power exercised by non-Christians.

## V. *Innocent IV and legitimacy.*

When contrasted with the earlier discussions of the legitimacy of power exercised by non-Christians, Innocent IV's treatment of the problem appears as a significant piece of sophisticated political analysis, differing from the previous canonistic discussions in both breadth and scope. Where previous commentators had limited themselves to studying specific situations in which legitimacy was involved, Innocent IV operated within the framework of a theory of government and authority (42).

Innocent III's decretal *Quod super his* (X. 3.34.8), an assertion of the right of the papacy to grant indulgences to crusaders, provided Innocent IV with a starting point for a discussion of legitimacy. *Quod super his* dealt specifically with the problem of those who, having sworn to go on crusade, could not or did not fulfill their vows. In commenting on this decretal, Innocent IV moved the focus of discussion from this specific problem into the realm of morality. On what basis could the crusaders justify their seizure of lands held by the Saracens (43)? The answer to this question came in two parts, an

(42) CANTINI's article on Innocent IV marked the beginning of a series of careful examinations of Innocent's thought on the relation between the two powers. His position has been rejected as too extreme by J. A. WATT, *The Theory of Papal Monarchy in the Thirteenth Century*, in: *Traditio* 20 (1964) 179-317 esp. 250 n. 30; and B. TIERNEY, *The Continuity of Papal Political Theory in the Thirteenth Century. Some Methodological Considerations*, in: *Mediaeval Studies* 27 (1965) 227-245 esp. 229 n. 5.

(43) « *Pro defensione.* Hoc non est dubium, quod licet Papae fidelibus suadere, et indulgentias dare, ut Terram sanctam, et fideles habitantes in ea defendant..., sed nunquid est licitum invadere terram, quam infideles possident, vel que est sua »? INNOCENT IV, *Commentaria in quinque libros decretalium* (Turin 1581) ad 3. 34. 8, fol. 176va-vb.

examination of the right of Christians to retake the Holy Land and a general analysis of the legitimacy of power exercised by non-Christians.

According to Innocent IV, the crusade directed against the Moslem conquerors of the Holy Land was justified because they did not possess it legitimately (44). The pope was the legitimate, that is *de iure*, ruler of the land by virtue of being the heir to the Roman imperial jurisdiction in that region. The Romans had obtained legitimate control over it because they had conquered Palestine in a just war. The Moslems, however, had unjustly deprived the Romans of the Holy Land and, therefore, were a proper target for a crusade raised and encouraged by the papacy. Forestalling the argument that the papacy could only claim imperial jurisdiction over the western half of the Roman empire, the area specifically mentioned in the Donation of Constantine, Innocent IV declared that there were other reasons for justifying such intervention. The most important of these reasons was the fact that the emperor in his capacity as King of Jerusalem could claim the Holy Land. The pope could lawfully assist the emperor in the recovery of what was rightfully his by raising a crusade.

On the broad issue of non-Christians exercising legitimate temporal authority, even over Christians, Innocent IV's position was much less belligerent. According to him, all rational creatures, not only Christians, could legitimately own property and exercise political authority (45). Furthermore, all men have the right to select

---

(44) « Quod autem Papa facit indulgentias illis, qui vadunt ad recuperandam Terram sanctam, licet eam possideant Saraceni, et etiam inducere bellum, et dare indulgentias illis, qui occupant Terram sanctam: quam infideles illicite possident, hoc totum est ex causa, nam iuste motus est Papa, si intendit Terram sanctam que consecrata est... Item Terra sancta iusto bello victa fuit ab Imperatore Romano post mortem Christi, unde licitum est Papae ratione Imperii Romani, quod obtinet, illud ad suam iurisdictionem revocare, quam iniuste expoliatus est, et ab eo, qui non habuit ius spoliandi eum. et haec ro. sufficit in omnibus aliis terris, in quibus Imperatores Romani iurisdictionem habuerunt, licet posset dici, quod hoc iure, scilicet. ratione Imperii non possit, cum ecclesia non habeat Imperium, nisi in Occidentem... sed si non potest facere tanquam Imperator, potest facere ex aliis predictis causis, vel ad minus Imperator potest facere, ut Rex Hierusalem, ad quem regnum illud de iure venit, sicut credimus et credere debemus; ex quo contrarium nobis non constat... ». *Ibid.* See also CARLYLE V, 323-324, and ULLMANN, *Medieval Papalism*, 128.

(45) « ... possessiones et iurisdictiones licite sine peccato possunt esse apud infideles. haec. enim. non tamen pro fidelibus. sed pro omni rationabili creatura facta sunt, ut est pradictum. ipse enim solem suum oriri facit super bonos. et malos. ipse

their own rulers. The pope does not have the right to deprive a non-Christian ruler of his office. At the same time, the pope does possess a general authority over all men, Christian and non-Christian alike, which gives him the right to insure that secular power in the hands of infidels is not used to abuse Christian subjects (46). In the case of lands once held by Christians but now in infidel hands, the pope could not deprive the infidel ruler of his power unless he was using it to persecute Christians under his control (47). Innocent IV's moderate position on the issue of legitimacy is emphasized by his rejection of reckless Christian assaults upon non-Christian rulers. He argued that such rulers should be deprived of their *dominium* over Christians only when there is no other recourse to save Christians from persecution.

Having solved the problems connected with lands where non-Christian rulers have Christian subjects, Innocent IV turned to the question of the land where the subjects became Christians, but the ruler remained a non-believer. Did such a ruler still possess legitimate power over his subjects (48)? The point of departure for resolving this problem was the argument that if Christians could claim the Holy Land because it had once belonged to Christians, why could not infidels claim possession of Italy on the grounds that it

---

etiam volatilia pascit, Matthaei c. 5. circa fin. et 6. et propter hoc dicimus, non licet Papae, vel fidelibus, auferre sua, sive dominia, sive iurisdictiones infidelibus, quia sine peccato possident... ». *Ibid.*

(46) « ... sed bene tamen credimus, quod Papa, qui est vicarius Iesu Christi, potestatem habet non tamen super Christianos sed etiam super omnes infideles... ». *Ibid.*

(47) « ... sed et contra alios infideles, qui nunc tenent terram, in qua iurisdictionem habuerunt Christiani Principes, potest Papa iuste facere praeceptum, et constitutionem, quod non molestent Christianos iniuste, qui subsunt eorum iurisdictioni, immo quod plus est, potest eos eximere a iurisdictione eorum, et dominio in totum... si male tractarent Christianos, posset eos privare per sententiam iurisdictione, et dominio, quod super eos habent. tamen magna causa debet esse, quod ad hoc veniat. debet. enim. Papa eos quantum potest sustinere, dummodo periculum non sit Christianis, nec grave scandalum generetur ». *Ibid.*, fol. 177ra.

(48) « Sed dices, quare non eodem modo licet eis repetere terram istam, scilicet. Italiam, vel alias ubi dominati fuerunt infideles? Respon. quia domini harum terrarum cum populis eorum conversi sunt. fatemur tamen, quod si populi conversi essent, sed domini remanerent infideles, quod Papa bene posset domino infideli dominium et iurisdictionem dimittere super fideles, arg. 1. ad Thimo. 6. in prin. dummodo Christianos non gravaret iniuste. Item propter periculum posset cogi dominus ad recipiendum pretium vel commutationem: saepe. enim. quis amittit res suas sine culpa sua... ». *Ibid.* See also ULLMANN, *Medieval Papalism*, 128-129.

once had been ruled by infidels? The infidels could claim to be the heirs of the last pagan emperors, just as the Christians claimed to have inherited the rights of the Christian emperors in the Holy Land. Innocent replied that there was a fundamental difference between the two examples. In Italy, both the rulers and the subjects had been converted so that the Christian emperors were the true heirs of the pagan emperors. In the Holy Land, however, the Christians were conquered and held in check by force alone. The infidels possessed only a *de facto* power over their subjects, not a legitimate authority. The crusade was designed to restore legitimate government in the Holy Land.

At the same time, Innocent did not encourage the practice of allowing believers to be ruled by non-believers. If the non-Christian ruler posed a threat to his subjects' religion, the pope could remove him from office. The point at issue here was not the theoretical legitimacy of the ruler's power but the practical exercise of that power. Furthermore, the ruler should be encouraged to resign his rights and office in return for payment. Force should be used only as a last resort.

Before any final conclusions can be drawn concerning Innocent IV's views on the legitimacy of power outside of the Church, the letter *Eger cui levia*, often attributed to Innocent, must be examined. J. A. Cantini has denied the authenticity of this letter on several grounds (49). One of his most striking points is that although Innocent IV's genuine writings, especially the commentary on *Quod super his*, admit the existence of legitimate power outside the Church, the arguments contained in *Eger cui levia* deny that possibility and, therefore, this letter does not accurately reflect Innocent's position and cannot be authentic. There are several possible explanations for the contradictions between the two works. The most obvious is that Innocent did write the letter but his failure to include it in his *Register* indicates that he was aware of its contradiction of his views expressed elsewhere. Again, the letter, although not written by Innocent himself, could have been composed by someone conversant with his thought and who intended it as an explication of Innocent's position. In this sense, the letter could be of the school of Innocent IV although not by the master himself.

---

(49) CANTINI, 413.

Such suppositions do not, however, deal directly with the point raised by Cantini. The question remains: does the position on legitimacy of power outside of the Church found in *Eger cui levia* contradict Innocent's known views? According to Cantini, the key words concerning legitimacy are: « (Temporalis regiminis potestas) [.....] *procul dubio* EXTRA ECCLESIAM EFFERRI OMNINO NON POTEST, *cum foris* UBI OMNIA AEDIFICANT AD GEHENNAM A DEO NULLA SIT ORDINATA POTESTAS » (50). Cantini then contrasted this phrase, which he interpreted in terms of *nullum imperium extra ecclesiam*, with the discussion of power found in the commentary on *Quod super his* in which Innocent stated explicitly that non-believers could legitimately own property and govern themselves (51). From the contrast between the two positions, Cantini concluded that *Eger cui levia* must be spurious (52).

Yet, in spite of Cantini's arguments, there still remains some question concerning the authenticity of the disputed letter and, consequently, real questions about Innocent IV's position on legitimacy. By rejecting *Eger cui levia* as unauthentic, Cantini avoided the problems involved in resolving the contradictions. However, in analyzing the letter, Cantini quoted only part of the sentence dealing with legitimacy. The complete sentence is a discussion of the pope's right to judge any Christian, regardless of rank or station in life, clearly a reference to the excommunication of Frederick II (53). The writer of the letter explained that such power should be used *saltem casualiter* and especially in those cases where it can be justified *ratione peccati*. Once judgment is passed, the sinner is cast out of the body of the faithful and « consequently is deprived of the power of temporal government if he had any such power... ». Thus, the Christian ruler who is excommunicated and

(50) *Ibid.*, n. 33. His capitalization.

(51) *Ibid.*

(52) CANTINI's opinion on the authenticity of *Eger cui levia* has been rejected by TIERNEY, *Papal Political Theory*, 232 n. 15.

(53) « Relinquitur ergo Romanum pontificem posse saltim casualiter suum exercere pontificale iudicium in quemlibet Christianum, cuiuscumque conditionis existit, presertim si de ipso alius iustitie debitum nolit reddere vel non possit, maxime ratione peccati, ut peccatorem quemcumque, postquam in profundum viciorum venerit per contemptum, tamquam publicanum et ethnicum haberi constituat et a fidelium corpore alienum sicque saltem per consequens privatum, si quam habebat, temporalis regiminis potestate, que procul dubio... ». E. WINKELMANN, *Acta imperii inedita seculi XIII et XIV* (Innsbruck 1885) 698.

deposed by the pope is deprived of legitimacy of his power because « without any doubt at all [the power of temporal government] cannot be taken outside of the Church ». The letter does not say that legitimate power does not exist outside the Church. It says only that a Christian ruler under ecclesiastical censure loses the legitimacy of his power. As the statement does not deal directly with the status of power exercised by non-Christian rulers it does not actually contradict the views expressed in the commentary on *Quod super his*.

The problem of legitimacy is also to be found in the use made of the Donation of Constantine in *Eger cui levia* and this raises the question of authorship in a fashion not found in the previous statement. In the letter, the Donation was connected with Constantine's resignation of his power to the pope and his reception of it back again, thus legitimizing it (54). There is some difficulty in contrasting this interpretation of the Donation with Innocent's position elsewhere because in his genuine writings Innocent mentioned the Donation only briefly. In *Quod super his* he declared that the pope succeeded to the imperial office only in the West (55). Cantini makes much of the contrast between this limited imperial jurisdiction and the fullness of the imperial power possessed by the papacy indicated in *Eger cui levia*. Even in *Eger cui levia*, however, the description of the Donation does not necessarily mean that there is no legitimate power outside of the Church. In the first place, the letter not only states that Constantine received his power back from the pope, it also says that he might now use it for punishing the wicked and assisting the virtuous. This suggests that before his conversion, Constantine was an evil ruler. With his conversion, however, Constantine became convinced of the need to use his power as it should be used. Furthermore, this version also implies that once Constantine entered the Church it became necessary for him to have his power legitimized

---

(54) « Verum idem Constantinus, per fidem Christi catholice incorporatus ecclesie, illam inordinatam tyrampnidem, qua foris antea illegitime utebatur, humiliter ecclesie resignavit, in cuius resignationis memoriale signaculum et plenum rationis mystice sacramentum relicta ab eo scematis principalis insignia pro venerabili anteriorum patrum similitudine retinemus, et recipit intus a Christi vicario, successore videlicet Petri, ordinatam divinitus imperii potestatem, qua deinceps ad vindictam malorum, laudem vero bonorum, legittime uteretur et, qui prius abutebatur potestate permissa, deinde fungeretur auctoritate concessa ». *Ibid.*

(55) See above, note 44.

in the new, Christian context. Had he remained a pagan, the legitimacy of his power would have depended upon whether or not he used it in accordance with the proper ends of power. In this sense, then, the pope possesses in potency all legitimate power within Christian society (56). The potency is actualized when the power exercised by a Christian ruler is seen by him as coming from the Church. Again, *Eger cui levia* does not deal with the legitimacy of secular power exercised by non-Christians (57).

Just as contrast with the views of earlier canonists underscores the originality of Innocent IV's position on legitimacy, so also does the contrast of his views with those of his successors reinforce this opinion. It appears that Innocent's views on legitimacy were so markedly different from the rest of the canonistic tradition that they were unacceptable to later decretalists. The most obvious illustration of this rejection of Innocent's views on legitimacy can be found in the writings of Hostiensis. In his commentary on *Quod super his*, Hostiensis rejected his master's views without any apparent recognition of the fact that he was contradicting Innocent.

Reverting to the tradition best exemplified by Alanus Anglicus, Hostiensis denied the legitimacy of the power exercised by non-Christian rulers. Without employing the words *nullum imperium extra ecclesiam*, Hostiensis effectively supported the extreme interpretation of the phrase, declaring that non-Christian rulers who recognized the superior *dominium* of the papacy should be tolerated (58). The only reason for extending such toleration was that no one should be forced to accept baptism. On the specific issue of non-Christians ruling Christians, he argued that such power was

---

(56) See TIERNEY, *Papal Political Theory*, 242, for a more complete discussion of the notion that the papacy possesses all power in potency but not in actuality.

(57) It should be pointed out that this argument in no way proves the authenticity of *Eger cui levia*. The aim here is simply to indicate that the aspects of the letter dealt with are not inconsistent with Innocent's other statements on these problems.

(58) « ... unde constanter asserimus quod de iure infideles debent subici fidelibus. non econtra... Concedimus tamen quod infideles qui dominium ecclesie recognoscunt sunt ab ecclesia tolerandi: quia nec ad fidem precise cogendi sunt... Tales etiam possunt habere possessiones et colonos christianos; et etiam iurisdictionem ex tolerantia ecclesie ». HOSTIENSIS, *Lectura quinque Decretalium*, 2 vols. (Paris 1512) ad 3. 34. 8. fol. 124va.

only *de facto dominium*, not *de iure* or legitimate (59). Furthermore, where Innocent IV had counselled acceptance of non-Christian rulers unless they directly threatened their Christian subjects, Hostiensis counselled toleration « lest there be danger to the Christians ». The change in emphasis suggests that for Hostiensis toleration should be extended only where any other policy would cause persecution. Innocent, on the other hand, insisted upon toleration of the non-Christian ruler unless it proved impossible. Hostiensis agreed with his master on only one point in the matter of legitimacy. Like Innocent, he did not encourage Christians to rebel against their non-Christian rulers, prudently advising them to bear patiently with their rulers (60). Here again, Hostiensis responded negatively to any suggestion that infidel power might be legitimate or even tolerable under any but the most extreme conditions.

*Conclusion.*

The development of the notion that outside the Church there was no legitimate power paralleled the evolution of the theory of the two swords described by Stickler. Gratian employed the notion of the material sword to signify the Church's own disciplinary power. The pontificate of Innocent III, however, marked the period in which this limited notion was expanded to include the totality of secular power. The new meaning, combined with the older one, that the two swords were within the Church, gave rise to the theory that all power, spiritual and temporal, was within the Church. The phrase *nullum imperium extra ecclesiam* evolved in the same way. Originally, the words referred to sacramental and disciplinary power within the Church. Gradually the words acquired a political significance and came to include the notion of the legitimacy of secular power as well. It is striking that the transformation from eccle-

(59) « *Pro defensione*... Immo et si male tractent christianos potest eos, privare per sententiam iurisdictione et dominio quod super eos habent. Sed hoc non nisi ex magna causa. debet enim eos quantum potest tolere ne sit periculum Christianis... ». *Ibid.*

(60) « Sed ubi Christiani sub dominio infidelium habitant quibus nec resistere possunt: necesse est quod patientiam habeant: et de facto ipsorum dominium recognoscant ». *Ibid.*

siastical to political significance in the matter of the legitimacy of power also occurred during Innocent III's pontificate.

The transformation of the notion of legitimacy to include temporal power paralleled a similar change in the way in which the canonists conceived the Christian world. Ladner has described this as the transformation of medieval Christian society from *ecclesia* to *christianitas* (61). Fundamentally, *christianitas* referred to a broader, more diversified concept of society, one in which there were several independent Christian kingdoms. The older term had served as long as Christian society could be equated with a universal Christian empire. Around 1200, however, there appeared kingdoms which did not admit, even theoretically, an imperial overlord functioning within an ecclesiastical framework. With this change there arose a need for redefining legitimacy in order to fit the new situation. This need was not met and, as a result, the Church-State conflict of the thirteenth century was acerbated by the application of an older conception of Christian society and its related terminology to an environment in which they did not fit.

One final step concerning the notion of legitimacy of secular power was taken after Innocent III's reign. Until the time of Innocent IV, the canonists concerned themselves only with legitimacy within Christian society. Innocent IV's interest in the broader aspects of the problem and his willingness to recognize the legitimacy of power outside the Church appears to reflect his attempt to begin diplomatic relations with the Mongols in the 1240's in the hope of converting them. For the first time, the papacy attempted to establish contact with a non-Christian power not hostile to it. In order to deal with the Mongols as equals, the papacy would have to recognize them as legitimate rulers. Innocent IV provided a juridical basis for doing just that. The failure of later canonists to follow up Innocent's thought on the subject parallels the failure of the Mongol mission.

---

(61) G. B. Ladner, *The Concepts of 'Ecclesia' and 'Christianitas' and their Relation to the Idea of Papal 'Plenitudo Potestatis' from Gregory VII to Boniface VIII*, in: *Miscellanea Historiae Pontificiae* 18 (Rome 1954) 49-77.

# II

## A CANONISTIC CONTRIBUTION TO THE FORMATION OF INTERNATIONAL LAW

GARRETT MATTINGLY argued in his *Renaissance Diplomacy* that the origins of international law can be traced well before 1625, when Grotius published *On the Laws of War and Peace*.[1] In taking this position, Mattingly was not alone, for scholars had long recognized Grotius' debt to the early sixteenth-century Dominican, Francisco de Vittoria (1480?-1546) and to other members of the Spanish school of legal thinkers. But Mattingly went further, insisting that even sixteenth-century Spain was still not the primary source of the legal ideas which culminated in Grotius' writings. In his opinion, serious attention should be paid to the medieval roots of Vittoria's thought for "Vittoria's basic formulations" on the problems of international law existed in the writings of Thomas Aquinas.[2] That Vittoria, Primary Professor of Sacred Theology in the University of Salamanca, should constantly cite Aquinas and other scholastic theologians, as well as Aristotle and other philosophers, is no surprise. That the roots of his legal thought can be traced to the thirteenth century does, however, cause some surprise. Even the mid-thirteenth century was not far enough back for Mattingly and he suggested that scholars could say little concerning the originality of Vittoria and his successors since "most of the conclusions at which the Spanish school arrived are obviously implicit in twelfth-century canonists with explicit elaborations in the fourteenth and fifteenth centuries. . . ."[3]

Mattingly based his position on a line of research begun by Ernest Nys in the late nineteenth century. Nys pointed to the contributions of late medieval lawyers and diplomats to the

1 Garrett Mattingly, *Renaissance Diplomacy* (Boston, 1955), p. 283.

2 *Ibid.*, p. 284.

3 *Ibid.*

emergence of international law.[4] In the early twentieth century, the Carnegie Institution recognized the role of the Spanish school in the formation of international law by publishing relevant selections from Vittoria and also from his most famous successor, Francisco Suárez (1548-1617) in its series of texts in international law.[5] The writings of both men, filled with citations from medieval theologians, philosophers, and lawyers, illustrate the debt which the Spanish authors owed to their medieval predecessors.

In spite of the availability of the texts, and in spite of the recent interest in sixteenth-century Spanish colonial expansion, scholars have as yet paid little attention to the influence of medieval thought upon the Spanish school.[6] For example, Mattingly's assertion that Vittoria's conclusions were implicit in the canonistic writings of the twelfth century has not been examined. Indeed, Mattingly appears to have made the statement without examining the canonistic tradition. As a result, Mattingly's opinion provides a logical point for beginning an analysis of the role of the canonists in the formation of international law. This analysis will also shed some additional light on the most popular of historical debates, the relation of the Middle Ages to the early modern era.

Vittoria was clearly a transitional figure, seeking to interpret the contemporary Spanish conquest of the Americas in essentially traditional terms. Furthermore, he thought of himself primarily as a priest and theologian, not as a lawyer or political theorist. When discussing the conquest he emphasized that

[4] Ernest Nys, *Les origines de la diplomatie et le droit d'ambassade jusque à Grotius* (Brussels, 1894); *Études du droit international,* 2 vols. (Brussels, 1896).

[5] Franciscus de Victoria, *De Indis et de iure belli relectiones,* ed. Ernest Nys (Washington, 1917; reprinted New York, 1964); Francisco Suárez, *Selections from Three Works,* ed. J. B. Scott, 2 vols. (Washington, 1944).

[6] The basic works on Vittoria remain those of J. B. Scott, *The Spanish Origin of International Law* (Oxford, 1934); and *The Catholic Conception of International Law* (Washington, 1934). His importance can be understood more clearly in the broad context of Spanish thought in the sixteenth century. See Lewis Hanke, *The Spanish Struggle for Justice in the Conquest of America* (Boston, 1949).

> . . . it is not for jurists to settle this question or at any rate not for jurists only, for since the barbarians in question, as I shall forthwith show, were not in subjection by human law, it is not by human, but by divine law that questions concerning them are to be determined. Now, jurists are not skilled enough in the divine law to be able by themselves to settle questions of this sort.[7]

Thus, he began the examination of the legitimacy of the Spanish conquest by warning the reader against narrow, legalistic arguments. Furthermore, he added that even the statements of theologians must be studied with care because of the uniqueness of the problem. The settlement of the issue rested with the priests.[8] For Vittoria, legal arguments concerning the justice of the conquest were relevant only when employed with the clear understanding that the issue was not just simply an abstract legal matter but rather a major moral and spiritual one.

Influence of the canon lawyers which is nevertheless seen upon Vittoria's work appears in three sections of the *De Indis.* These passages deal with three distinct problems associated with the conquest: the problem of *dominium,* that is lawful possession of property and political power; the seven illegitimate titles which the Spanish could assert to the Americas; and finally, the eight legitimate titles which could be asserted. Even in this limited area, however, the canonists comprised only one source from which Vittoria drew. What makes the canonistic material significant is that it provided Vittoria with precedents by which he could support with concrete illustrations the more abstract arguments of the theologians and philosophers.

By beginning the discussion of the Spanish conquest with the problem of *dominium,* Vittoria brought it into a medieval frame of reference, since *dominium* was a major problem in medieval political theory.[9] The issue generally arose over the right of here-

[7] de Victoria, *op. cit.*, trans., 119; text, 222.

[8] *Ibid.*, trans., 120; text, 222.

[9] For a brief, general survey of the problem of *dominium*, concentrating on the period after 1300, see Ewart Lewis, *Medieval Political Ideas,* 2 vols. (New

tics, schismatics, Jews, and Saracens to govern Christians. Vittoria presented numerous authorities, biblical, theological, philosophical, and legal, on the problem of *dominium*. At first glance, the canonists played only a minor role in the argument but their role is significant because Vittoria used canonistic arguments as a foil for philosophical and theological ones.

The crux of the issue of *dominium* was the effect of mortal sin upon the right of an individual to possess property and to exercise political power. Vittoria had asserted that the popular Aristotelian arguments justifying conquest, that some men were natural slaves and therefore legitimately subject to any group of free men were obviously invalid.[10] Assuming the free status of the natives, the arguments had to turn on their right as free men in the state of sin to possess property and power. The problem then was not one of dealing with slaves but with men who were "sinners or were unbelievers or were witless or irrational." [11] Vittoria chose to bring the canonistic tradition into the issue by focusing on Boniface VIII's decretal *Cum secundum leges* (VI, 5, 2, 19).[12] This decretal stated that certain crimes mentioned in the civil law books were punished by depriving the criminal of his possessions. What held good for secular crimes was, according to Boniface VIII, fitting for those who committed the heinous crime of heresy.

To counter this argument and its obvious extension to the inhabitants of America, Vittoria cited the opinion of Thomas Aquinas that heresy and, by implication any other mortally sinful act, did not of itself deprive anyone of legitimate possession of goods.[13] He also cited a number of cases from the Old and New Testaments in which God's own people, with divine approval, obeyed obviously evil rulers. Furthermore, Vittoria ar-

York, 1954), I, 88-108. For the theological background to the problem, see A. Gwynn, *The English Austin Friars in the Time of Wyclif* (London, 1940).

[10] de Victoria, trans., 120; text, 223.

[11] *Ibid.*

[12] *Ibid.*, trans., 123; text 226.

[13] *Ibid.*

gued that a man-made law depriving a criminal of his property might not be just and that in the forum of conscience he could remain the legitimate possessor of those goods.[14] This section of the discussion ended with a very firm declaration of the right of the native population to possess property and lordship.

> From all this the conclusion follows that the barbarians in question can not be barred from being true owners, alike in public and in private law, by reason of the sin of unbelief or any other mortal sin, nor does such sin entitle Christians to seize their goods and lands. . . ." [15]

In the preceding argument, Vittoria clearly opposed what he considered to be a representative canonistic argument which could be used to defend the legitimacy of the Spanish conquest. In rejecting Boniface VIII's position, the Dominican drew heavily on the opinions of the philosophers, especially Aquinas as noted and Cajetan. This indicates that he took seriously his statement mentioned earlier that the problems associated with the conquest were too grave to be treated in a purely legal fashion.

In the discussion of the possible titles to legitimate possession of the Americas which the Spanish could offer, Vittoria made much greater use of canonistic material than in the discussion of *dominium*. Here again this material constituted only a part of the overall weight of authority brought to bear on the issue. Of the seven illegitimate titles to Spanish domination of the Americas which he chose to discuss, three were heavily influenced by the discussion of the canon lawyers. Two of these titles, one resting on the imperial claim to universal temporal jurisdiction, the other resting upon a similar papal claim, provided the bulk of the argument concerning illegitimate titles. The third illegitimate title rested upon the right of the Spanish to punish the natives for their sins.

The argument that the emperor was lord of the world, and therefore of the barbarians who inhabited the Americas, stemmed

[14] *Ibid.*, trans., 124-125; text, 228.
[15] *Ibid.*, trans., 125; text, 229.

from Roman law and had passed into the canonistic tradition. Vittoria cited both the reference from Justinian's *Digest*, the medieval source of the statement, and references to the use of the term among the decretalists.[16] This particular argument was of special interest to Vittoria because King Charles I of Spain was also, by virtue of the imperial election of 1519, Emperor Charles V as well. If the emperor was lord of the world then the Spanish conquest was lawful.

Vittoria's argument concerning the powers of the emperor broke down into two interrelated discussions. The first dealt with his powers before the coming of Christ. The second dealt with the effect of Christ's incarnation upon these powers. At the heart of the argument favoring the emperor's universal lordship lay an analogy from the insect world. Just as there was but one head of a community of bees, so also every human community has but one head.[17] As the human race ultimately comprised a single community, therefore there should be a single universal ruler for this community, at least *de iure* if not *de facto*.

Against this view, Vittoria presented opinions drawn both from the philosophers and from the lawyers. He began by declaring bluntly that the arguments for a universal empire were baseless.[18] Citing Aquinas, he declared that although dominion was ultimately natural, arising from man's political nature, the forms which it actually took were the result of human actions. Therefore, the claim that the emperor possessed universal jurisdiction was based not on natural law but upon human law. To illustrate the process by which political power emerged, he drew upon history as recorded in the Book of Genesis. According to this source, political domination developed as a result of war and of other human activities, so that

> it is manifest that before the coming of Christ no one was vested with world-wide sway by divine law and that the Emperor can

16 *Ibid.*, trans., 130; text, 234.
17 *Ibid.*
18 *Ibid.*, trans., 131; text, 235.

> not at the present day derive therefrom a title to arrogate to himself lordship over the whole earth, and consequently not over the barbarians.[19]

Vittoria next turned to the arguments of those who contended that the coming of Christ, the possessor of all power, spiritual and temporal, provided a basis for an imperial universal jurisdiction. The essence of the argument was that Christ united in Himself all power which had previously been fragmented. At His death, He left two vicars on earth, the pope in spirituals and the emperor in temporals.[20] This argument was supported by biblical and philosophical arguments. No canonists were cited. Here again, however, Vittoria rejected the arguments for a universal empire, this time drawing not only upon biblical and philosophical arguments but upon canonistic material as well. Crucial to his position were the writings of Pope Innocent III which comprised a large part of the canonistic tradition concerning the nature of the empire. Vittoria, citing Innocent III's decretal *Venerabilem* (X, 1, 6, 34), argued that the empire was clearly limited in its jurisdiction.[21] After all, there existed two halves of the empire, Eastern and Western, neither in fact claiming jurisdiction over the other. Furthermore, in another decretal, *Per venerabilem* (X, 4, 17, 34), Innocent III explicitly stated that the King of France was not subject to any superior in temporals. In addition, a glossator on this decretal had declared that the kingdoms of France and Spain were known to be exempt, at least *de facto,* from imperial jurisdiction.[22] As a result of such citations, Vittoria could conclude that "the Emperor was never lord of the whole world" and, therefore, could not claim jurisdiction over the inhabitants of the Americas on that basis.[23]

The next title to Spanish domination of the Americas which Vittoria analyzed rested on the assertion that the pope was lord

19 *Ibid.,* trans., 132; text, 236.
20 *Ibid.,* trans., 132-133; text, 236-237.
21 *Ibid.,* trans., 133; text, 238.
22 *Ibid.*
23 *Ibid.,* trans., 134; text, 238.

of the world and could, therefore, grant the Americas to the Spanish. He began this discussion by referring to the assertion of Hostiensis, one of the most prominent thirteenth-century canonists, that the pope was supreme in temporals.[24] Hostiensis argued that as a result of the pope's jurisdiction in temporal matters, all legitimate power was derived from him. On this basis, the pope could, and according to some of Vittoria's contemporaries did, grant control of the Americas to the Spanish.

To counter this argument, Vittoria again cited several canonists, including Innocent III. The basic counter argument was that the pope's power could not be properly defined in terms of temporal lordship.[25] Also, he pointed out that Innocent III himself had declared the exemption of the King of France from any superior in temporals. This exemption, being unqualified, must therefore include exemption from papal temporal domination as well as from imperial. Hence a Spanish claim to the Americas based on a papal grant was invalid.

A corollary to the argument concerning papal temporal lordship was that, according to some canonists, the failure of non-Christians to recognize papal lordship in temporals was itself sufficient cause for Christians to conquer them.[26] Again, the canonists focused their discussion of this matter on one of Innocent III's decretals, this time *Quod super his* (X, 3, 34, 8), and Vittoria followed their lead. The decretal itself dealt with the oath which each crusader took, but the glossators had extended this opportunity to consider the larger moral issues of the crusades, specifically the question of the right of the crusaders to seize the Holy Land from the Moslems. The most important treatment of this question appeared in Innocent IV's commentary on his predecessor's decretal.[27] Innocent IV main-

[24] *Ibid.*, trans., 134; text, 239.

[25] *Ibid.*, trans., 135; text, 240.

[26] *Ibid.*, trans., 137-138; text, 243.

[27] *Ibid.*, trans., 138; text, 243. This particular reference illustrates the difficulties involved in tracing canonistic influences upon later writers. The text at this point simply refers to "Innocentius in dicto cap. *quod super his*. . . ."

tained that the pope did have the right to raise a crusade and to promise rewards to the crusaders for retaking the Holy Land but not because the Moslems refused to accept the pope as their overlord.[28] Innocent IV went out of his way to emphasize that all rational creatures, not only Christians, possessed the right to govern themselves. The conquest of the Holy Land was lawful because the Moslems had taken it unlawfully from the Christians, its original possessors.[29] Obviously, such arguments could not apply in the case of the Americas because the lands had never belonged to Christians.

Vittoria recognized that Innocent IV's views on this subject, while not totally rejected by other canonists, were not widely accepted. He noted, for example, that Hostiensis, Innocent IV's most famous student who generally followed his master's lead, rejected this position.[30] Hostiensis and others argued that non-

The editor noted that this was from *Decretales,* 3, 34, 8, a letter of Innocent III. In fact, however, the arguments involved are from Innocent IV, *Commentaria in quinque libros decretalium* (Turin, 1581) *ad* 3, 34, 8, fol. 176 va. As more work is done on the canonists, we can expect to find many other cases in which the canonistic influence upon later work has been mislabeled or completely overlooked. On the significance of Innocent IV's commentary on *Quod super his,* see J. Muldoon, "*Extra ecclesiam non est imperium:* The Canonists and the Legitimacy of Secular Power," *Studia Gratiana* 9 (1966), 553-580 at 572.

28 ". . . possessiones et iurisdictiones licite sine peccato possunt esse apud infideles, haec enim. non tamen pro fidelibus. sed pro omni rationabili creatura facta sunt, ut est praedictum. ipse enim solem oriri facit super bonos, et malos. ipse etiam volatilia pascit, Matthaei c. 5. circa fin. et 6. et propter hoc dicimus, non licet Papae, vel fidelibus, auferre sua, sive dominia, sive iurisdictiones infidelibus, quia peccato possident. . . ." (Innocent IV, *Commentaria ad* X, 3, 34, 8, fol. 176 vb).

29 "Quod autem Papa facit indulgentias illis, qui vadunt ad recuperandam terram sanctam, licet eam possideant Saraceni, et etiam inducere bellum, et dare indulgentias illis, qui occupant terram sanctam: quam infideles illicite possident, hoc totum est ex causa, nam iuste motus est Papa, si intendit terram sanctam que consecrata est. . . . Item Terra sancta iusto bello victa fuit ab Imperatore Romano post mortem Christi, unde licitum est Papae ratione Imperii Romani, quod obtinet, illud ad suam iurisdictionem revocare, quam iniuste expoliatus est, et ab eo, qui non habuit ius spoliandi eum. et haec ro. sufficit in omnibus aliis terris, in quibus Imperatores Romani iurisdictionem habuerunt. . . ." *Ibid.*

30 de Victoria, trans., 138; text, 243.

Christians who refused to accept papal supremacy in temporals could be deprived of their property and lordship. At the same time, Vittoria himself, citing the philosophers, especially Aquinas and Cajetan, supported Innocent IV's position. He concluded that

> the allegation of the doctors in question is utterly sophistical, namely, that if the unbelievers recognize the lordship of the Roman Pontiff, war can not be made on them, but that it may if they do not recognize it; for none of them does recognize it.[31]

The last of the illegitimate titles to Spanish possession of the Americas in which the canonistic tradition played a significant role concerned the claim that the sins of the native population justified their conquest by Christians. The key to this argument was whether the sins, or crimes, of the natives violated natural law or positive law.[32] Again, the discussion centered on Innocent IV's commentary on *Quod super his* in which he argued that the pope could require Christians to punish non-Christians for clearly violating the law of nature. Sins which could be considered violations of that law included cannibalism and incest. Yet Vittoria rejected even this comparatively moderate assertion of papal power. He declared firmly that

> Christian princes can not, even by the authorization of the Pope, restrain the Indians from sins against the laws of nature or punish them because of those sins.[33]

Again, he countered the canonistic arguments with other arguments drawn from philosophical and biblical sources. Citing Aquinas, he argued that the pope can act as judge only over Christians because only they have freely submitted themselves to his jurisdiction.[34] Indeed, the pope has no right to deprive even Christians of their property and lordship. This being the

[31] *Ibid.*

[32] de Victoria, trans., 146; text, 252.

[33] *Ibid.*

[34] *Ibid.*, trans., 146-147; text, 252-253.

case, he saw there is no basis for asserting such papal power over non-believers.

The canonists, who played a marked role in Vittoria's discussion of unjust titles to Spanish control of the Americas, played a much smaller role in his discussion of the legitimate titles which followed. Of the seven clearly legitimate titles and the one possibly legitimate title which the Spanish could assert, only four showed traces of canonistic influence. Closer examination indicates that these four titles all dealt with specific aspects of one general problem, the effect of the natives' conversion upon the existing political structure and, moreover, that the basic canonistic materials involved stemmed from a single source, Innocent IV's commentary on *Quod super his*. It is striking that Vittoria, who made extensive use of Innocent IV's commentary, mentioned it explicitly in discussing only one of the four legitimate titles.

The first legitimate title which could be offered by the Spanish, according to Vittoria, rested upon the role of the Spanish in the conversion of the natives to Christianity.[35] The pope could have entrusted the responsibility for the conversion of the native population to the Spanish and forbidden any other European nation to interfere. If the natives hindered the work of conversion, the Spanish could then lawfully go to war against them in order to insure the safety of the missionaries. In this way the Spanish could eventually acquire complete domination of the Americas. In presenting this position, Vittoria cited only biblical and philosophical texts, but the argument is similar to one given by Innocent IV who declared that, although non-believers should not be compelled to accept Christianity, the pope did have the right to insure the safe and free access of Christian missionaries into the lands of non-believers.[36] If the non-believers hindered the mis-

[35] *Ibid.*, trans., 156-157; text, 262-263.

[36] "Item licet non debeant infideles cogi ad fidem, quia omnes libero arbitrio relinquendi sunt, et sola Dei gratia in hac vocatione valeat . . . tamen mandare potest Papa infidelibus. quod admittant predicatores evangelii in terris suae iurisdictionis, nam cum omnis creatura rationabilis facta sit ad Deum lau-

sionaries, the pope could order Christian rulers to punish the offenders.

The next two legitimate titles for Spanish domination of the Americas stemmed from the pope's responsibility to protect Christians, wherever they might live, from persecution. In the first case, the pope could encourage the Spanish to protect the native converts from persecution by their rulers.[37] The Spanish would thus have the duty of assisting their fellow-believers and might then obtain control of the Americas in a just war on these grounds. The second case concerned the need to guarantee that a Christian population had a Christian ruler, even though the existing non-Christian ruler was not interfering with the religious practice of his Christian subjects.[38] Here Vittoria explicitly cited Innocent IV's commentary on *Quod super his* as one source of his views. In both cases, however, Vittoria was drawing upon Innocent IV's commentary in order to discuss the issues raised. Innocent had discussed at some length both the right of the pope to insure the safety of Christian missionaries and also the need or the desirability to provide a Christian ruler for a society in which the population had largely become converts.[39] Innocent also stressed that wherever possible, the removal of a non-believing ruler should be obtained by peaceful means, a point which Vittoria did not make.

The last of these titles having canonistic sources which Vit-

---

dandum, sent. 2. dist. 1. si quaeritur, si ipsi prohibent praedicatores praedicare, peccant, et ideo puniendi sunt. In omnibus autem praedictis casibus. et in aliis, ubi licet Papae eis aliquid mandare, si non obediant, compellendi sunt brachio seculari, et indicendum est bellum contra eos per papam. . . ." (Innocent IV, *Commentaria ad* X, 3, 34, 8, fol. 177 ra).

[37] de Victoria, trans., 158; text, 264.

[38] *Ibid.*, trans., 158-159; text, 264-265. Again, however, the editor assumed that Innocent III was meant when in fact the reference is clearly from Innocent IV's commentary. ". . . fatemur tamen, quod si populi conversi essent, sed domini remanerent infideles, quod Papa bene posset domino infideli dominium et iurisdictionem dimittere super fideles . . . dummodo Christianos non gravaret iniuste. Item propter periculum posset cogi dominus ad recipiendum pretium vel commutionem. . . ." (Innocent IV, *Commentaria ad* X, 3, 34, 8, fol. 177 ra.

[39] de Victoria, trans., 159-160; text, 265-266.

toria presented dealt with the right of the majority of the population to select a ruler acceptable to the majority, even if this action meant the repudiation of an existing ruler. In this case, Vittoria offered the case of a society where the majority of the population had become converts to Christianity but the ruler had not.[40] He argued that the common good of the community might make it necessary to repudiate the existing ruler and to replace him with a Christian. In this way, the King of Spain could be lawfully elected ruler of the American natives and thus obtain a legitimate title to the Americas. This argument was the only one of the four showing canonistic influences which did not rely heavily upon the work of Innocent IV. Instead Vittoria turned to a much older canonistic source, the deposition of Childeric III, the last Merovingian king of the Franks, to illustrate his argument. He argued that the Franks, with papal approval, deposed Childeric and installed Pepin, the father of Charlemagne. Vittoria stressed that the Franks alone were responsible for Childeric's removal and that the pope had only a consultative role.

Vittoria's use of Childeric's deposition to illustrate the manner in which Christian converts could depose a non-Christian ruler throws an interesting light upon his use of canonistic material. The story of Childeric's deposition had been incorporated by Gratian in the *Decretum* (ca. 1140).[41] From this two lines of canonistic commentary emerged, one stressing that the Franks alone actually performed the deposition, the other insisting that the papal role had actually been the determining factor and had not been simply consultative.[42] By accepting the former view,

[40] *Ibid.*, trans., 160; text, 266.

[41] *Corpus iuris canonici*, ed. Emil Friedberg, 2 vols. (Leipzig, 1879-1881), I, *Decretum*, C. 15 q. 6 c. 3.

[42] The view that the pope actually deposed Childeric can be found in the *Glossa ordinaria ad* C. 15 q. 6 c. 3, "*deposuit.* Ergo Papa deponit Imperatorem, ut 96. di. duo et c. si Imperator. . . ." In D. 96 c. 10 (*Duo sunt*) to which the glossator referred, there is the following statement. "*Iudicio.* Zacharias quoque Papa Regem Francorum deposuit, et in locum eius Pipinum substituit, ut infra 15. q. 6 alius." There is a wide range of opinions on the precise roles played by

Vittoria was accepting a minority opinion among the canonists, a view more generally associated with twelfth-century canonists than with their thirteenth- and fourteenth-century successors.

In the final analysis, Vittoria was not, as Mattingly had declared, drawing out conclusions on the nature of Christian relations with the non-Christian world that were implicit in the writings of the twelfth-century canonists. The essence of Vittoria's work was that the issues involved in justifying the Spanish conquest of the Americas were too grave for the lawyers alone to resolve. Throughout his work, Vittoria tended to reject the opinions of the canonists, as for example in discussing the papal claim to universal lordship, or qualified them, as he did with Innocent IV's views on the right of Christians to punish non-believers for their sins. Furthermore, although Vittoria cited several canonists, the real source of most of the canonistic material he employed appears to have originated in Innocent IV's commentary on *Quod super his*.

Of greater significance than the issue of Vittoria's debt to the canonists, however, is the obvious importance which he placed upon the canonists. The canonistic material which Vittoria used was an integral part of his entire discussion, even if it served largely as a foil for the philosophers and theologians. The canonists may have been too narrow in outlook to deal adequately with the complex issues of the Spanish conquest but their arguments had to be answered. Furthermore, the canonists did provide precedents that served to illustrate the problems which Vittoria analyzed.

Finally, Vittoria's use of the canonists underscored anew the relationship between the Middle Ages and the early modern period, a relationship which Mattingly emphasized. Without attempting to join in that popular historical debate about the relationship between the medieval period and the succeeding period, one can say that Vittoria's use of canonistic material illus-

the popes and the Frankish nobles in this deposition but, as yet, there is no thorough study of the different opinions and their relation to the overall problem of the relation between the pope and secular rulers.

trates one aspect of the relationship. Vittoria took from medieval thought what he could use in his attempt to resolve new problems, using some of the material directly, modifying and qualifying other material, but always recognizing that previous writers had concerned themselves with the problems that interested him and always recognizing the debt which he owed them.

# III

## THE CONTRIBUTION OF THE MEDIEVAL CANON LAWYERS TO THE FORMATION OF INTERNATIONAL LAW*

Scholars have been aware of the contribution of the medieval canon lawyers to the formation of international law ever since the pioneering work of Ernest Nys during the last two decades of the nineteenth century. Since then, historians of international law and relations generally have given at least a ritual nod of recognition to the work of the canonists in their discussions of the precursors of Hugo Grotius (1583-1645), whose *De jure belli ac pacis*, published in 1625, is generally considered the foundation of international law. Recent research in canonistic sources, however, has suggested a need to reconsider the work of the canonists as it affected the pre-Grotian period of development. Furthermore, as most of the previous work dealing with the role of the canonists has dealt with them only peripherally, canonistic writings dealing with international law have not been fully appreciated and deserve more extensive examination.

Consideration of the canonists' role in shaping international law has generally come in connection with one of three major topics. The first of these was the study of Grotius' relation to the work of his predecessors and especially his debt to several sixteenth-century philosophers and lawyers who had grappled with some of the issues which he was to study in the *De jure belli ac pacis*. The second approach was by way of research into the theory of the just war, research often inspired by the twentieth-century peace movement. The final approach has been through the study of the justifications for the Spanish conquest of the Americas presented by sixteenth-century Spanish philosophers and theologians.

Of all the students of the pre-Grotian development of international law, Ernest Nys (1851-1920), a Belgian professor of law and judge, made by far the greatest contribution to the field. His work also reveals the greatest familiarity with canonistic sources. Nys' writings laid down the guidelines for future scholarly analysis of the pre-Grotian period. In his opinion, the fundamental difference between Grotius and his predecessors was that they treated the basic issues pertaining to international law in a 'fragmentary manner,' while the great Dutch legist treated these issues systematically.[1] Nys traced

---

* I wish to thank St. Michael's College for a grant from the Faculty Research Fund which enabled me to complete the research for this paper, and I wish to express my appreciation to my colleagues, Edward J. Pfeifer and George Olgyay, for their advice and assistance.

1 *Les origines du droit international* (Brussels-Paris 1894) iv. See also his *Études de droit international et de droit politique* (2 vols.; Brussels 1896, 1901) and *Le droit international* (3 vols.; Brussels 1912). A convenient summary of Nys' views on the pre-Grotian origins of international law can be found in his introduction to Vitoria's *De Indis et de jure belli relectiones* (Washington, D.C. 1917; reprinted New York 1964) 55-100.

the failure of medieval lawyers and philosophers to consider more broadly the implications of their preliminary work in international law to two interconnected causes. In the first place, according to Nys, the medieval lawyers were generally engaged in recovering Roman law and codifying customary law, neither of which considered international law in any coherent fashion. In the second place, the medieval thinkers never succeeded in separating the elements of international law from natural law. As a result, the materials for creating at least a rudimentary international law remained widely scattered throughout Roman and canon law during the Middle Ages.[2] These scattered pieces were brought together only in the sixteenth century and, according to Nys, not by the canonists but by scholastic philosophers and theologians. He pointed to two Spanish philosophers, Francisco Vitoria (ca. 1480-1546) and Francisco Suárez (1548-1617) as the first writers to attempt the synthesis of the materials for creating international law.[3]

According to Nys, Vitoria and Suárez drew upon the canonistic tradition in their discussion of two important aspects of international law, the theory of the just war and the question of the legitimacy of secular power exercised by non-Christians. Although he cited a number of canonists who contributed to this tradition, he placed special emphasis on the writings of Innocent IV († 1254) and of Hostiensis († 1271) because their respective opinions on the legitimacy of secular power *extra ecclesiam* were at the root of the canonistic discussion of questions relating to international law. For example, much of the just-war theory rested on the assumption that Christians had the right to conquer infidel peoples because the power exercised by infidel rulers over their subjects was illegitimate. Nys observed that although the issue of legitimacy had arisen in connection with the crusades, the classic positions on the subject were taken in the mid-thirteenth century by Innocent IV and Hostiensis. Innocent IV recognized the legitimacy of secular power held by infidels while Hostiensis did not.[4] All later discussion of the relations between Christians and infidels drew upon the arguments which these canonists advanced.

Nys indicated the development of various aspects of the just war and legitimacy questions in the writings of later canonists. One of the most important of these was Paulus Vladimiri (*ca.* 1370-1435), who represented the King of Poland in his struggle with the Grand Master of the Teutonic Knights for possession of Lithuania. In 1415, at the Council of Constance, Vladimiri presented a series of arguments which consisted largely of an attack on Hostiensis' teachings concerning the illegitimacy of secular power in infidel hands.[5] The knights had justified their conquest on the grounds that they had lawfully deprived the pagan Lithuanians of their lands because infidels could not legitimately possess secular power.

In Nys' opinion, this canonistic tradition culminated in Vitoria's *De Indis*. This work, though first published in 1557, had formed the substance of his lectures at the University of Salamanca some years before his death. The core of the *De Indis* was a rejection of the position taken by Hostiensis and an affirmation of the legitimacy of secular power in infidel hands.[6] According to Nys, Grotius' work cannot be properly understood unless the spadework ac-

---

[2] Nys, *Origines* 7.
[3] *Ibid.* 11.
[4] *Ibid.* 144.
[5] *Ibid.* 150.
[6] *Ibid.* 154-55.

complished by his predecessors is recognized.[7] Yet, in spite of this obvious invitation to further study of the pre-Grotians, Nys' volumes remain the most extensive general study of the early development of international law, even though Arthur Nussbaum has rightly criticized Nys' writings as poorly organized and lacking adequate documentation.[8]

The lack of documentation in Nys' writings was remedied somewhat when A. Vanderpol published a small volume of excerpts concerning the theory of the just war drawn from the writings of medieval and early-modern canonists, philosophers, and theologians.[9] Vanderpol published these excerpts in connection with his work in the world peace movement, but the volume supplements Nys' work because it includes segments from the writings of Innocent IV, Hostiensis, Vitoria, and other authors whom Nys had cited. Although Vanderpol is open to the charge that he failed to appreciate fully the significance of the material which he presented and that he shaped his interpretation of its meaning to fit his own pacifism, nevertheless his volume provided a number of important canonistic sources not readily available.[10]

The most important aspect of Vanderpol's work for the student of the canonistic contribution to international law was the discussion of what he called the 'Three Errors of the Canonists.'[11] The errors involved were the opinions that: infidels could not possess legitimate secular power; the pope was the true temporal ruler of the world; the emperor was the true temporal ruler of the world. Vanderpol presented the opinions of Innocent IV and of Hostiensis on these topics in order to prove that the Hostiensian opinion, although the most well-known, was not in fact the only canonistic opinion on these issues. He also indicated how Vitoria later used these classic positions in the *De Indis*.[12]

The third pioneer in the study of the pre-Grotians, Thomas E. Holland, Regius Professor of Civil Law at Oxford, concentrated on Grotius' debt to the sixteenth-century civilians who had discussed various aspects of international law. Holland devoted his inaugural lecture, given in 1874, to the work of Alberico Gentili (1552-1608), whose writings had a marked influence on Grotius.[13] In Holland's opinion, although Grotius did admit his debt to Gentili, he did so 'in words which hardly suggest its full extent.'[14] Holland attributed to Gentili 'the general scheme of the immortal work of Grotius' and argued that the works of both men 'rest upon the same conception of natural law.'[15] Gentili's significance was not limited to this, however, because he also linked two distinct traditions, 'the practical discussions of the Catholic theologians' and 'the theory of natural law which had been mainly worked out by the Protestants.'[16] These two traditions also found their way into Grotius' work. In another essay, Holland cited a number of canonists who had

---

[7] *Ibid.* 159.

[8] Arthur Nussbaum, *A Concise History of the Law of Nations* (rev. ed. New York 1954) 293-94.

[9] A. Vanderpol, *Le Droit de guerre d'après les théologiens et les canonistes du moyen-âge* (Paris-Brussels 1911).

[10] Robert Regout, *La doctrine de la guerre juste* (Paris 1935) 301.

[11] Vanderpol, 151.

[12] *Ibid.* 155.

[13] Thomas E. Holland, *Studies in International Law* (Oxford 1898) 1-39.

[14] *Ibid.* 2. [15] *Ibid.* [16] *Ibid.* 22.

made significant contributions to the formation of international law by their discussions of the just war. In his opinion, they 'spun a web of fine distinctions, which at last amounted to a considerable body of doctrine.'[17] Like Nys and Vanderpol, Holland placed special emphasis on the roles played by Innocent IV and Hostiensis in the development of the canonistic tradition.[18]

All three of these pioneering scholars recognized that the medieval canonists did make a contribution, a minor one perhaps but a real one nonetheless, to the tradition which culminated with the publication of Grotius' *De jure belli ac pacis*. Not being primarily interested in the canonists, however, none of these scholars clearly distinguished the work of the canonists from that of the theologians and philosophers. Furthermore, none attempted to analyze in detail the interplay among the views of the canonists, theologians, and philosophers. For example, even Vanderpol does not appear to have been aware of the extent to which Vitoria's arguments against the theory of universal papal domination were largely derived from Innocent IV's commentary on the decretal *Quod super* (X, 3, 34, 8), although his volume contained the relevant extracts from the works of both men.[19]

In spite of the obvious deficiencies in these early efforts to trace the origins of international law, Nys, Vanderpol, and Holland pointed the way for a reconsideration of the pre-Grotian period of development. In the task of placing Grotius' work in its proper historical context, examination of the canonistic tradition could have been expected to play a significant role. Yet, this was not to be. As A. J. Carlyle, a contemporary of Nys and Vanderpol and a scholar who did recognize the potential value of canonistic sources, indicated, the vast amount of unpublished canonistic material made the study of this material extremely difficult.[20] As a result, references to the pre-Grotian period of legal development in the scholarly literature of international law were based almost entirely on the work of Nys, Vanderpol, and Holland. Standard texts, such as Oppenheim's *International Law*, began to include some brief mention of the pre-Grotians. Oppenheim, for example, argued that although Grotius fully deserved the title 'Father of the Law of Nations,' his work was based on a long tradition of which the canonists were a part.[21]

Although the canonistic contribution to the formation of international law did not receive the attention that Nys and others had indicated that it deserved, other aspects of the pre-Grotian period of development did attract scholarly attention. Interest centered on the issue of whether Grotius or one of his predecessors truly deserved the title 'Father of International Law.' This phase of the study of the pre-Grotian development of international law was associated with the career of James Brown Scott (1866-1943), an official of the Carnegie

---

[17] *Ibid.* 44.

[18] *Ibid.* 44, 56. It should be noted, however, that Holland's references to the canonists are filled with minor errors which suggest that his knowledge of the sources must have been slight. For example, he refers to 'the title *De Homocidio* in the sixth book of the Decretals' when in fact it is in the fifth and last book.

[19] Vanderpol, 154-55.

[20] R. W. and A. J. Carlyle, *A History of Mediaeval Political Theory in the West* (6 vols.; Edinburgh and London 1903-1936) II viii.

[21] L. Oppenheim, *International Law: A Treatise* (2 vols.; 2nd ed. London and New York 1912) I 54-55, 83-84, 86.

Endowment for Peace.[22] He served as director of the Endowment's Division of International Law, editor (1907-1924) of its publication *The American Journal of International Law*, and general editor of its series of texts, *Classics of International Law*. Under Scott's direction, both the *Journal* and the series of texts dealt extensively with the pre-Grotian theorists of international law and relations. Scott himself strongly opposed what he considered to be the general opinion that Grotius deserved the title 'Father of International Law.' In a public letter announcing the beginning of the *Classics* series, Scott made his position quite clear.

> International law is not, therefore, a creation of Grotius, although he was its first and its greatest expounder. We look beyond Grotius and see that the international law of today is rooted in a more remote past. We know, too, that Grotius was the culmination of a quiet and unsuspected development, not the sole figure in international law. . . .[23]

As a result, the *Classics* series was designed to include not only the 'masterpieces of Grotius . . . but the works of his leading predecessors and successors' as well.[24] By predecessors, however, Scott meant, for the most part, the scholastic philosophers and the civilians of the sixteenth and early-seventeenth centuries. The only clearly medieval work to appear in the series was John of Legnano's *Treatise on War, Reprisals, and Duels*, written ca. 1360.[25]

While the editors were preparing the texts for the *Classics* series, *The American Journal of International Law* published several articles on the pre-Grotian period, none of which added significantly to the earlier work of Nys, Vanderpol, and Holland. Perhaps the most important of these articles was one in which Nys himself presented his views on the pre-Grotians to an English-speaking audience.[26] The other articles tended to be general surveys of pre-Grotian developments. The authors generally noted that the canonists did contribute to the development of international law but they added nothing new to the discussion. Two authors chose to consider in more detail than Holland had done Gentili's influence on Grotius.[27] The emphasis was upon Grotius's immediate predecessors, and neither author added significantly to the analysis of Grotius' sources. The overall effect of these articles was to arouse interest in the problem of the pre-Grotian development of international law and to provide a convenient introduction to it for English-speaking scholars.

---

[22] On Scott's life and career, see: G. A. Finch, 'James Brown Scott, 1866-1943,' *American Journal of International Law* [AJIL] 38 (1944) 183-217; and F. R. Coudert, 'An Appreciation of James Brown Scott,' *ibid.* 37 (1943) 559-61.

[23] Letter to Dr. Robert S. Woodward, President of the Carnegie Institution, AJIL 3 (1909) 701-07 at 703.

[24] J. B. Scott, Preface to Vitoria, *De Indis* p. 6.

[25] John of Legnano, *Tractatus de bello, de represaliis et de duello*, ed. T. E. Holland (Oxford 1917).

[26] Ernest Nys, 'The Development and Formation of International Law,' AJIL 6 (1912) 1-29, 279-315. See also Amos Hershey, 'The History of International Relations During Antiquity and the Middle Ages,' *ibid.* 5 (1911) 901-33; and 'History of International Law Since the Peace of Westphalia,' *ibid.* 6 (1912) 30-69; G. E. Sherman, 'The Nature and Sources of International Law,' *ibid.* 15 (1921) 349-60.

[27] T. W. Blach, 'Albericus Gentilis,' AJIL 5 (1911) 665-79; F. F. Abbott, 'Alberico Gentili and his Advocatio Hispanica,' *ibid.* 10 (1916) 737-48.

III



Although Scott had hoped that publication of the classic texts in international law would further stimulate interest in the early history of international law, this did not occur. One reason for this failure was that the texts appeared over a long period of time. For example, the volume on Vitoria appeared in 1917 while that containing Suárez's writings appeared in 1944. Thus, Scott's goal of providing 'the texts in convenient from for scientific study' proved difficult to achieve.[28] Furthermore, the series broke little new ground since it consisted of reprints of older printed texts with an English translation added.

The one pre-Grotian figure who did receive a good deal of attention was Vitoria. This resulted from Scott's campaign to promote the view that Vitoria, not Grotius, deserved the title 'Father of International Law.' The argument, which Scott espoused in several books and articles, was that the Spanish scholastic philosophers, specifically Vitoria and Suárez, were the true founders of international law. Taken to an extreme, as Scott did, this argument reduced Grotius to the level of a popularizer, albeit a great one.

> And [wrote Scott] as a popularizer the services of Grotius to international law should never be overlooked. The modern law of nations of which Victoria was the expounder, Suárez the philosopher, and Grotius the systematizer, is the contribution of what we may call, and indeed must call, the Spanish School of International Law. For if Grotius was not a Spaniard by blood, he was a Spaniard in his conception of international law, and so far as the basic principles of his system are concerned, he was indubitably a member of the Spanish School.[29]

Scott's work, supported by numerous references to Nys and Vanderpol, suggests that his own work is a continuation of that of his predecessors.[30] This impression, however, is somewhat misleading as Nys certainly did not view Grotius simply as a popularizer of his predecessors' ideas. In the Introduction to the edition of Vitoria's writings in the *Classics* series, Nys clearly indicated his view of Grotius' relationship to his predecessors, a view which stressed Grotius' creative role.

> . . . the man of genius who is called the founder of a science merely brings together its already existing elements; he confines himself to uniting its *disjecta membra* and breathing into them the breath of life. Such was the role of Hugo Grotius and such was the effect produced by his treatise *De jure belli ac pacis*. . . .[31]

What is most striking at first glance about Scott's work is its quantity. His enthusiastic adoption of Vitoria propounded in such 'stately volumes published by such a high authority within the framework of an impressive series' seems to have intimidated his readers.[32] These volumes consist for the most part of lengthy paraphrases from Vitoria's writings linked together by paragraphs

---

[28] Preface to Vitoria, *De Indis* p. 5.

[29] J. B. Scott, *The Spanish Conception of International Law and of Sanctions* (Washington, D.C. 1934) 51. Scott's other works include: *The Spanish Origin of International Law* (Washington, D.C. 1928); *The Catholic Conception of International Law* (Washington, D.C. 1934); *The Spanish Origin of International Law: Francisco de Vitoria and his Law of Nations* (Oxford 1934).

[30] See for example, *Spanish Origin* (1934) 71, 118.

[31] Vitoria, *De Indis* 55.

[32] Nussbaum (*cit. supra* n. 8) 304.

which praise his great achievements in the formation of international law. Rather than analyzing Vitoria's ideas in order to determine their origins or, for that matter, to determine the precise nature of the relationship between Vitoria and Grotius, Scott assumed his subject's importance and then proceeded to praise him in glowing terms. What interested Scott was not the source of Vitoria's ideas but what he considered their end product. For example, in his opinion, the idea of the League of Nations was rooted in Vitoria's work.[33] Scott's emphasis on what he believed to be the modern applications of Vitoria's ideas appears to have been connected with his work in the Carnegie-sponsored segment of the world peace movement. Vitoria was, therefore, significant for his supposed contribution to the modern peace movement.[34]

James Brown Scott's decision to focus his attention on Vitoria had a major impact on the direction which the study of the pre-Grotians was to take. Looked at another way, his decision determined the direction which study of the pre-Grotians did not take. For the most part he became the standard authority concerning the pre-Grotian development of international law. His opinion that Vitoria was the real 'Father of International Law' became widespread and references to Scott's work tended to replace references to Nys, Vanderpol, and Holland, whose works were overlooked. The effect of Scott's work can be seen clearly in the succeeding editions of J. L. Brierly's standard text on international law. In the first edition, published in 1928, Brierly asserted that 'Grotius . . . is more generally and on the whole rightly regarded as the founder of international law.'[35] Furthermore, the text contained only a few references to the pre-Grotians. Later editions devoted more space to Grotius' predecessors and contained a revised evaluation of their significance and of Grotius' place in the development of international law.

> Few books [wrote Brierly in 1955] have won so great a reputation as the *De jure belli ac pacis* but to regard its author as the 'founder of international law' is to exaggerate its originality and to do less than justice to the writers who preceded him: neither Grotius nor any other single writer, can properly be said to have 'founded' the system.[36]

Even scholars who rejected Scott's enthusiastic praise of Vitoria recognized that his work did focus attention on Grotius' forerunners and served to rescue them from oblivion.

Although Scott's work did not arouse a great deal of scholarly interest in the pre-Grotians, it did lead a number of scholars, generally Catholic, to espouse the view that modern international law was rooted in medieval Catholic principles. The role of denominational differences in influencing scholarly judgments concerning the merits of the pre-Grotians had been suggested by T. E. Holland. Pointing to what he considered a marked difference between Catholic and Protestant approaches to the problem of international law before Grotius, he argued that:

---

33 Scott, *Spanish Origin* (1934) 98.

34 It might be noted here that several of the authors discussed indicated a debt to the Carnegie Endowment. These include John Eppstein, Lewis Hanke, and Jean Moreau-Reibel.

35 J. L. Brierly, *The Law of Nations* (Oxford 1928) 19.

36 *Ibid.* (5th ed. 1955) 36.

> Two attempts were made to answer the questions which arose in the sixteenth century. On the one side, a series of Catholic casuists, amongst whom Vitoria and Soto were the most eminent.... The Catholic attempt ended where it began, in a slight development of casuistry. On the other side, a long series of Protestant writers have succeeded in extricating from theology, and, to a certain extent, from ethics, the rules which are accepted as binding between State and State.[37]

Nys also pointed to religious differences which hindered scholarly discussion of the pre-Grotians and quoted with approval the opinion of one writer who said that from

> these few observations you will have no difficulty in perceiving the extreme injustice of the manner in which, down to our own time, it has been customary to speak of the scholastic jurists. . . . The fact is, that ever since the Reformation the prejudices of Protestants against Roman Catholics have been so vehement as to deprive them of the power of forming a dispassionate opinion of their works, even if they had been acquainted with them, which they rarely were.[38]

The Catholic scholars sought to follow Scott's lead and to publicize further the role of medieval Catholic thinkers in the formation of international law.

The most influential figure among the Catholic scholars who worked on the pre-Grotians was Herbert F. Wright (1892-1945), whose doctoral dissertation at the Catholic University of America consisted of an edition of Vitoria's *De jure belli relectio*.[39] He also provided revised texts of Vitoria's writings for he *Classics* series. While admitting a debt to Nys and Vanderpol, Wright's views on Vitoria's significance were more like those held by Scott.[40] In his opinion, 'A careful scrutiny of Grotius' chief work, *De jure belli ac pacis*, shows that he agrees with nearly every proposition laid down in Vitoria's *De jure belli*, although he does not always cite him.'[41] Furthermore, Wright asserted that 'Grotius' direct indebtedness to Vitoria may be greater than has hitherto been recognized.'[42] The key to Vitoria's significance in Wright's opinion lay in the fact, noted previously by Vanderpol, that he 'was one of the most vigorous opponents of three errors commonly found in extremist writers on civil and canon law who preceded him.'[43] These errors were the denial of *dominium* to infidels, the assertion that the pope was the universal temporal sovereign, and the opinion that the emperor was the universal temporal sovereign. Like Scott, Wright also stressed the modernity of Vitoria's ideas, emphasizing superficial similarities with twentieth-century practices but never really examining his own premises.[44]

---

[37] Holland (*cit. supra* n. 13), 20.

[38] James Lorimer, *The Institutes of the Law of Nations* (1883) I 71, quoted in Nys, Introduction to *De Indis*, p. 99.

[39] Herbert F. Wright, *Francisci de Victoria: De iure belli relectio* (Washington, D.C. 1916).

[40] *Ibid.* 17, 21. [41] *Ibid.* 20. [42] *Ibid.* 21. [43] *Ibid.* 17.

[44] See H. F. Wright, 'International Law: Old Wine in New Bottles,' *Catholic World* 132 (1931-1932) 513-21; 'Catholic Founders of International Law,' *Records of the American Catholic Historical Society of Philadelphia* 45 (1934) 119-43. See also his 'The Divorce of Henry VIII,' *American Catholic Quarterly Review* 44 (1919) 556-65; 'Origin of American Aborigines: A Famous Controversy,' *Catholic Historical Review* 3 (1917-1918) 257-75; and 'St. Augustine and International Peace,' *Thought* 6 (1931) 399-416.

Several other scholars entered the lists on behalf of the Catholic origins of international law. One writer stressed Grotius' supposed Catholic leanings.[45] Another attempted to trace the roots of Vitoria's thought to the writings of Thomas Aquinas.[46] The author did not provide examples of direct borrowing from Aquinas by Vitoria, but, rather, he simply showed that Vitoria's views were consonant with those of Aquinas. Yet another author, elaborating on Scott's views, traced many of the doctrines of modern international law to Vitoria, including 'the idea behind the League of Nations.'[47] The climax of this effort to show the Catholic roots of modern international law came with the publication of a volume designed to encourage Catholics 'to appreciate the wealth of their inheritance — ignored by too many Catholics — and incline them to a more vigorous participation in the Apostolate of Peace. . . .'[48] Here again, the work of the early figures in the field, especially Vanderpol, was used as a basis for a work of popularization. The author made no attempt to examine more deeply the sources of the medieval tradition.

The writings of these Catholic authors shared several important characteristics. Each stressed the role of medieval Catholic thought in the shaping of modern international law, and each stressed the leading role played by James Brown Scott in the study of pre-Grotian international law. In addition, none of them made any serious attempt to analyze precisely the relationship between Vitoria and Grotius or between Vitoria and his predecessors. Finally, several of these writers sought to link Vitoria and the late-medieval Catholic tradition of international law with the twentieth-century peace movement. This enthusiastic but uncritical acceptance of Scott's views was to some extent apparently due to Scott himself not being a Catholic. In a review of one of Scott's books, Wright declared that it 'need not be surprising then that the best book on the Catholic conception of international law should be written by a Protestant.'[49] Being a Protestant, Scott was viewed as being more acceptable to the scholarly public on this issue than a Catholic scholar, who might be accused of denominational chauvinism. This kind of reverse prejudice seems to have kept Wright and others from examining Scott's work critically.

The last area of scholarship which reflected, and to a large extent still reflects, Scott's views was the study of sixteenth-century Spanish imperialism. While the study of international law has taken new directions and while Catholic scholars no longer feel forced to prove the medieval Catholic origins of modern concepts, the study of colonialism and imperialism has sparked a wave of in-

---

[45] Max G. Rupp, 'Hugo Grotius and his Place in the History of International Peace,' *Catholic Historical Review* 4 (1924-1925) 358-66. See also A. H. Chroust, 'Hugo Grotius and the Scholastic Natural Law Tradition,' *New Scholasticism* 17 (1943) 101-33.

[46] Nicolaus Pfeiffer, 'The Doctrine of International Law According to Francis de Victoria O.P.,' *Catholic Historical Review* 6 (1926-1927) 185-224. See also G. F. Benkert, *The Thomistic Conception of an International Society* (Washington, D.C. 1942).

[47] C. H. McKenna, 'Francisco de Vitoria: Father of International Law,' *Studies* 21 (1932) 635-48 at 647.

[48] John Eppstein, *The Catholic Tradition of the Law of Nations* (Washington, D.C. 1935) xviii. For a similar point of view by an author who was not a Catholic, see: R. F. Wright, *Medieval Internationalism: The Contribution of the Medieval Church to International Law and Peace* (London 1930).

[49] H. F. Wright, in *New Scholasticism* 9 (1935) 369-70 at 369.

terest in the effects of expansion upon European society. Interest in Spanish history, strong in American historical circles since the nineteenth century, climaxed in 1934 with the appearance of the final volume of R. B. Merriman's *Rise of the Spanish Empire.* This was also the year in which Scott published his final volume on the Spanish scholastic philosophers. This coincidence reflected the beginning of a significant change in the study of Spanish imperialism, a change hinted at in Merriman's final volume and one which gave a new impetus to Scott's ideas. Merriman was essentially in the tradition of the great narrative historians who recreated the past from the sources and who concentrated on political history. In this last volume, however, he noted briefly the significant development of international law in the sixteenth century, citing Vitoria and Suárez as important figures in the development. He even cited a Spanish author's opinion that Vitoria was 'one of the precursors of the League of Nations.'[50]

After the conclusion of Merriman's work scholars began to take notice of the legal and philosophical arguments which the Spanish had used to justify the conquest. The two most important scholars in this area, J. H. Parry and Lewis Hanke, reflected Merriman's influence. Parry's small volume on the theoretical basis for the Spanish Empire broke new ground in the discussion of the pre-Grotians by tracing Vitoria's ideas to the older Dominican theologian John Major (1469-1550).[51] Parry argued that Vitoria must have been aware of his Scottish confrere's arguments rejecting any papal or imperial claims to universal temporal jurisdiction.[52] Major also rejected the theory that infidels could not possess true *dominium.* Parry recognized that the views which Major rejected were those associated with Hostiensis' earlier work. Thus Parry paved the way for proving what so many scholars had assumed on flimsy evidence, namely that there was a direct link between medieval theories of international relations and Grotius' modern theories.[53]

The most complete discussion of the ideas which underlay the Spanish conquest of the Americas appeared in Lewis Hanke's volume *The Spanish Struggle for Justice in the Conquest of America*, in which he traced the core of the justifications back to Hostiensis.[54] At the same time, however, being primarily interested in the Spanish attempt to 'make Christian precepts prevail in the relations between peoples,' Hanke devoted most of his attention to the application of these theories by the Spanish and devoted little space to their source.[55] Even Vitoria received comparatively little attention. For those in-

---

[50] Salvador de Madariaga, *Spain* (New York 1930) 48, cited in R. B. Merriman, *Rise of the Spanish Empire* (4 vols.; New York 1918-1934; reprinted New York 1962) IV 484. Madariaga gives no indication in the text as to the source of this opinion, but in a bibliographical note at the end he cites the *Classics* edition of Vitoria's *De Indis*, suggesting the possibility that he was influenced by Nys' views. See *Spain* 484.

[51] J. H. Parry, *The Spanish Theory of Empire in the Sixteenth Century* (Cambridge 1940) 19.

[52] *Ibid.* 19-20.

[53] Parry has not essentially changed his views concerning the importance of Vitoria and the other pre-Grotians. See his *The Spanish Seaborne Empire* (New York 1966) 138-39, 142.

[54] Lewis Hanke, *The Spanish Struggle for Justice in the Conquest of America* (Philadelphia 1949; reprinted Boston 1965) 28.

[55] *Ibid.* 1.

terested in Vitoria's contribution, Hanke suggested that they consult the works of 'such experts as . . . the late James Brown Scott.'[56]

The overall effect of James Brown Scott's work was to block serious examination of the pre-Grotian development of international law and relations. His massive volumes and numerous articles on all facets of international law seem to have discouraged further study. Furthermore, since his views on Vitoria in particular were widely cited, not only by Catholic apologists but by respected scholars in the fields of international law and history, criticism of Scott's work may have seemed *lèse majesté*. Finally, and perhaps most important, the writers who drew upon Scott's work were not primarily interested in the pre-Grotian history of international law, as, indeed, Scott himself had not been. For all of these reasons, study of the pre-Grotians did not advance beyond the work of Nys, Vanderpol, and Holland. If anything, study of the pre-Grotian period took a backward step because of Scott's misguided enthusiasm for the Spanish philosophers and theologians.

In the years following World War II, however, the situation changed markedly. In the first place, Scott's work has been strongly criticized. In the second place, there has been increasing interest in the medieval canonists and some attention has been focused on canonistic materials which relate to international law. As a result of these developments, scholars are beginning to pave the way for a re-evaluation of the pre-Grotian growth of international law with increased emphasis upon the canonists' role.

The seeds of the criticism of Scott's work can be found in the reviews of his volumes as they appeared. One reviewer of the *Catholic Conception of International Law* noted that Scott might be charged with having 'been led in his enthusiasm for his subject to use phrases which ascribe too great relative importance to the contribution of Vitoria and Suárez. . . .'[57] At the same time, however, the reviewer hesitated to judge the author too harshly, arguing that 'one need not be too critical of details in a work that is marked by the high idealism of Dr. Scott.'[58]

The criticism flowered in an attack which Arthur Nussbaum leveled in his *Concise History of the Law of Nations*. Nussbaum devoted two appendices to the attack. He devoted one to the historiography of international law and one to Scott's views on the Spanish scholastics and the influence of Scott's work. The tone of the criticism was strong, not to say polemical. At the same time, however, in the text itself, Nussbaum dealt extensively with the pre-Grotian development of international law, and he dealt sympathetically with the significance of Vitoria and Suárez. The target of the attack was Scott's misunderstanding of the significance of the Spanish writers. While admitting that Grotius' work was the result of an evolutionary process, he also argued firmly that Grotius deserved the title '"founder" or "father" of international law' because his *De jure pacis ac belli* 'initiated the doctrine of modern international law. . . .'[59]

According to Nussbaum, Scott simply did not understand the writings of the Spanish authors whom he praised so highly.[60] Nussbaum blamed Scott and his translators for mistranslating or misunderstanding a number of terms

---

[56] *Ibid.* 151.

[57] C. G. Fenwick, AJIL 29 (1935) 183-84 at 184.

[58] *Ibid.* [59] Nussbaum 113. [60] *Ibid.* 301.

employed by Vitoria and Suárez so that in translation their works sound modern when in fact they were traditional. For example, Scott 'and his translators, invariably render *jus gentium* as "law of nations" or as "international law," although Vitoria and Suárez used this term 'in the ancient and medieval sense of universal or quasi-universal law.'[61] The same can be said of Scott's use of the terms *civitas, respublica, gens, natio,* and other words and phrases. He interpreted these words in such a way as to suggest modern usage rather than in the way that the authors understood them. Finally, Nussbaum declared that Scott's attempt to see in Vitoria's writings such modern concepts as the mandate system of the League of Nations indicated 'a naïveté which is truly disarming' on his part.[62]

In discussing Vitoria's work, Nussbaum argued that Scott and his followers had in fact underestimated the real significance of that work. In his opinion, 'Vitoria's claims as an anticipant of international law can be supported for better reasons' than the 'verbal grounds' which Scott offered.[63] Finally, Nussbaum argued that Ernest Nys' work was of much greater value in appreciating the significance of the Spanish writers. He himself used Nys' works in preference to Scott's as a guide to the pre-Grotians. As a result, Nussbaum was able to point to yet another weakness in Scott's work, his failure 'to trace the theories of the two Spaniards back to their medieval predecessors, except for the customary references to St. Augustine and Thomas Aquinas, . . . [giving] them a wrong appearance of originality.'[64] Thus Nussbaum brought the study of the pre-Grotians full circle, rejecting Scott's work as superficial and misleading and insisting on following' Nys' lead.[65]

The work of reconsidering the entire question of the medieval contribution, especially that of the canonists, to the formation of international law had already begun, even before Nussbaum suggested the need for doing it. Robert Regout had already raised two major points concerning previous study of the medieval contribution to international law. In the first place, he argued that Vanderpol's volume of texts, the most convenient source for examples of canonistic thought relating to international law, was badly flawed. In his opinion, Vanderpol's selection of texts and his interpretation of them was heavily influenced by his own ardent pacifism.[66] Furthermore, Regout argued that medieval thinking on relations between peoples included more than the theory of the just war. Ultimately, medieval thought on international relations rested on the notion of a universal society comprising all men.[67] He indicated that Innocent IV, among other medieval writers, recognized the existence of such a society and that Vitoria and Suárez developed this concept in their works. In turn, Grotius incorporated this tradition in *De jure belli ac pacis*.[68]

Regout's argument that the medieval writers possessed a conception of an international society received its fullest development in a long article by Jean Moreau-Reibel. Moreau-Reibel reconsidered the pre-Grotian development of inter-

---

[61] *Ibid.* 298. [62] *Ibid.* [63] *Ibid.* 80-81. [64] *Ibid.* 297.

[65] It should be noted that Nussbaum's views on the significance of Vitoria and Suárez and the polemical tone of his criticism of Scott were in turn criticized as being too extreme. See the review by J. L. Kunz, AJIL 50 (1956) 448-49. Ironically, one reviewer of the first edition (1947) declared that 'Victoria and Suarez are masterly portrayed in the restricted space of some fifteen pages.' See A. V. Freeman, AJIL 43 (1949) 603-05 at 603.

[66] Regout, 9-10, 301. [67] *Ibid.* 59-60. [68] *Ibid.* 15.

national law, tracing the growth of the conception of a 'société interhumaine.'[69] Looked at in this fashion, the medieval debate concerning the legitimacy of power in the hands of infidels, a debate centered on the commentaries of Innocent IV and Hostiensis, becomes of great significance. If the Hostiensian view that legitimate power existed only in the hands of Christians prevailed, then there could be no international law and no international society.[70] Given the importance played by the discussion of power *extra ecclesiam* in the writers of the sixteenth century, Moreau-Reibel was able to conclude that 'if Vitoria and Suarez have created a work, it is because the way had been prepared by the canonists.'[71] This work then climaxed in Grotius' volume.[72]

In dealing specifically with the canonists, Moreau-Reibel emphasized that the lawyers of the fourteenth and fifteenth centuries provided the link between Innocent IV and Hostiensis on the one side and Vitoria on the other. These lawyers, especially Johannes Andreae († 1348) and Paulus Vladimiri, expanded and refined the rudimentary canonistic discussion of international law. Johannes' contribution lay in his discussion of alliances between Christian and infidel nations.[73] Vladimiri's role, in Moreau-Reibel's opinion, was even greater. Following Nys' evaluation of Vladimiri's significance, and taking advantage of a new edition of the Polish lawyer's writings, he asserted that Vladimiri had provided a 'synthèse magistrale' of the canonistic materials relating to international law.[74] Here again, the heart of the discussion was the question of legitimate power *extra ecclesiam*, with Vladimiri's refutation of Hostiensis' views playing a vital role. Finally, according to Moreau-Reibel, Vitoria belongs in this tradition because he drew upon it to assert the possibility of legitimate power in infidel hands.[75]

The major contribution of Regout and Moreau-Reibel to the discussion of the origins of international law was their emphasis upon the need to study the issue in a much broader context than had been done previously. In addition, both authors indicated the need to study canonistic thought as a whole from the thirteenth to the sixteenth centuries on the issues relating to international law. Moreau-Reibel even added to Nys' list of canonistic sources on these issues.

In the period since Moreau-Reibel's essay was published, several studies have appeared which indicate the kind of work that can be done. By far the most important work concerning the role of the medieval canonists in the pre-Grotian period is Stanislaus Belch's edition of Paulus Vladimiri's writings together with a lengthy commentary on Vladimiri's work and its significance. Belch's two volumes deserve a much fuller treatment than can be given here. At this point, the most important aspect of his work is his evaluation of Vladimiri's place in the development of international law. In his opinion,

> it cannot be denied that Vladimiri made an important contribution to the development of ideas that were later reviewed by one who was the founder of modern international

---

[69] Jean Moreau-Reibel, 'Le droit de société interhumaine et le jus "gentium": Essai sur les origines et le développement des notions jusqu'à Grotius,' *Académie de droit international, Recueil des cours* 77 (1950) 481-597 at 524.

[70] *Ibid.* 523-24.

[71] *Ibid.* 514.

[72] *Ibid.* 486.

[73] *Ibid.* 524.

[74] *Ibid.* 531.

[75] *Ibid.* 532.

> law, Francesco [sic] Vitoria, and in consequence Vladimiri should be placed among those learned men who are the originators of that law.[76]

Belch verges on calling Vladimiri the 'Father of International Law' but never quite does. The key problem in evaluating Vladimiri's influence on later writers, especially those influenced by the canonistic tradition, is, as Belch admits, that 'none of these authors quotes or refers to Vladimiri so that there is no direct evidence that any of them knew his works.'[77] Belch suggests, however, that Vitoria may have known of the Polish canonist's writings because Vladimiri presented his arguments at the Council of Constance and Vitoria had studied the Council's proceedings.[78]

The major criticism of Belch's work is that he tried to make Vladimiri's significance out to be greater than it actually was. This is especially true in his attempt to find a possible link between Vladimiri and Vitoria. Yet, although this enthusiasm for Vladimiri recalls Scott's enthusiasm for Vitoria, there is a fundamental difference. Belch, a finer scholar than Scott, recognized that if it is admitted that the concept of legitimate power existing outside the Christian Church is a fundamental element of the development of international law, then Innocent IV 'should be regarded as the founder of the doctrine of the rights of infidel nations, however imperfect and incomplete this doctrine might be.'[79]

Interestingly enough, although Innocent IV's role in the development of international law has been recognized since Nys' day, his views have been overshadowed by the contrary opinions of his student, Hostiensis. Two recent articles have discussed various aspects of Innocent's views. The first dealt with the canonistic tradition of power *extra ecclesiam*, tracing the concept as it developed in the canonists up until its fullest statement in Innocent IV's commentaries.[80] The second article demonstrated that Vitoria's arguments for and against the legitimacy of the Spanish conquest of the Americas were largely based on Innocent's commentaries even though Vitoria does not appear to have been aware of their origin.[81]

## Conclusion

The study of the pre-Grotian phase of legal development has gone in a circular fashion. The work of James Brown Scott deflected scholars away from the course charted by Nys, Vanderpol, and Holland and into fruitless paths in order to discover the origins of international law. The work of Regout, Moreau-Reibel, and Belch has put the search back into the paths outlined at the turn of the century.

---

[76] Stanislaus Belch, *Paulus Vladimiri and His Doctrine Concerning International Law and Politics* (2 vols.; The Hague 1965) I 742.

[77] *Ibid.* [78] *Ibid.* 751. [79] *Ibid.* 75.

[80] J. Muldoon, '*Extra ecclesiam non est imperium*: The Canonists and the Legitimacy of Secular Power,' *Studia Gratiana* 9 (1960) 553-80.

[81] J. Muldoon, 'A Canonistic Contribution to the Formation of International Law,' *The Jurist* 28 (1968) 265-79.

A major danger in the recent work, however, has been the attempt, especially in Belch's volumes, to discover a chain of direct influence from Innocent IV to Vladimiri to Vitoria to Grotius. It might be better, at least at this stage of research, to assume that the writers in the canonistic tradition from Innocent IV to Vitoria represent various abortive attempts to create from the canonistic elements a rudimentary international law. Innocent IV, Vladimiri, and Vitoria share one important characteristic which supports this view. Each man was personally interested in European contacts with infidel societies.[82] The early contacts never flourished and the problems of the theoretical issues involved, especially the problem of the legitimacy of secular power in infidel hands, were forgotten in the press of more urgent matters.

Whenever interest in infidel societies revived, however, the arguments of Innocent IV and Hostiensis came readily to hand as a basis for considering the legitimacy of secular power as held by infidels and, therefore, the possibility or impossibility of peaceful relations with infidel societies. Thus, it would seem that the writings of the canonists from Innocent IV to Vitoria should be combed for references to the problems associated with international law and relations. Furthermore, the papal letters dealing with Spanish and Portuguese overseas expansion should be examined with a view to determining the possibility that these letters contain a coherent political and legal doctrine of international relations.[83] Luis Weckman's attempt to explain Alexander VI's bulls in terms of a doctrine of papal suzerainty over unclaimed islands has several obvious weaknesses.[84] The close links between the papacy and the canonists which have received so much scholarly attention in recent years suggest the need to consider the possibility that papal views on European expansion were influenced by canonistic opinions on the rights of infidels. A series of articles by Charles-Martial de Witte has opened new vistas on this issue by providing a full list of bulls dealing with Portuguese expansion and by suggesting that historians reconsider the history of this expansion in terms of the papal role in it.[85]

One final point remains to be mentioned. At first glance, the development of international law and relations might seem far removed from the canonists' major interests and, therefore, interesting but peripheral. In reality, however, the opposite is true. The issue of whether or not legitimate secular power exists *extra ecclesiam* is one more aspect of that most fundamental question in medieval political thought, the problem of *dominium*, and, as such, central to the study of medieval political thought and practice.

---

[82] Innocent IV's sponsorship of an embassy to the Mongols is often forgotten. See Christopher Dawson, *The Mongol Mission* (London and New York 1955).

[83] Several of the most important bulls are available in F. G. Davenport, *European Treaties Bearing on the History of the United States and its Dependencies to 1815* (4 vols.; Washington, D.C. 1917-1919; reprinted Gloucester, Mass. 1967) I.

[84] Luis Weckman, *Las Bulas Alejandrinas de 1493 y la teoría política del papado medieval* (Mexico City 1949). Weckman's bibliography, though extensive, does not include the works of Nys, Vanderpol, or Scott.

[85] Charles-Martial de Witte, 'Les bulles pontificales et l'expansion portugaise au XV$^{e}$ siècle,' *Revue d'histoire ecclésiastique* 48 (1953) 683-718; 49 (1954) 438-61; 51 (1956) 415-53, 809-36; 53 (1958) 5-46 and 443-71.

# IV

## PAPAL RESPONSIBILITY FOR THE INFIDEL: ANOTHER LOOK AT ALEXANDER VI'S *INTER CAETERA*

Pope Alexander VI's bull *Inter caetera* is one of the few papal letters generally known to an audience of more than a few medievalists or a handful of ecclesiastical historians.[1] The picture of one of the more lurid figures to occupy the See of Peter calmly dividing the entire non-western world between the Portuguese and the Castilians never fails to elicit a smile. On a more serious level, the vision of a pope whose control over the traditional Christian nations was minimal, whose political interest was in the centralization of the Papal State, and who, on the eve of the Reformation, condemned Savonarola, seeming to divide up the world between two small European powers is a pathetic parody of the power wielded by Innocent III, Innocent IV, or even Boniface VIII.

Yet, in spite of the reputation of Alexander VI, his bull *Inter caetera* is not without intrinsic interest. Even though he may have been a disgrace to the office which he held, nevertheless, the papacy was an institution that did not depend on the vagaries of personality to function. The distinction between person and office was long understood so that even the poorest of popes was limited in the harm he could do because of the institutional structures which bounded him on all sides. A bull such as *Inter caetera,* for example, reflected not simply

[1] There are actually three bulls involved, two beginning *Inter caetera,* the first dated May 3, 1493, the second dated the following day, and one beginning *Eximiae devotionis,* dated May 3, 1493. The second *Inter caetera* and *Eximiae devotionis* essentially restated the first *Inter caetera* and it is this bull which is cited throughout this paper unless otherwise specifically stated. The bulls are available in various editions, the most convenient being that of Frances G. Davenport, *European Treaties Bearing on the History of the United States and its Dependencies to 1648* (4 vols.; Washington, D.C., 1917-1937; reprinted, Gloucester, Massachusetts, 1967), I, 56-78.

Alexander's view of the papal role in the world, but, rather, a conception of papal responsibility for mankind rooted in the tradition of canon law that formed the intellectual framework within which the pope's curia operated.

In recent years there have been two important attempts to understand *Inter caetera* within the context in which it was written.[2] Both have stressed that the bull was only one of the many which dealt with the problem of awarding to Christian rulers dominion over other peoples, often, but not always, non-Christians. What has not been given adequate attention is the fact that these papal letters were rooted in the canon law tradition. Underlying any position taken in a papal document was a long line of legal thinking which could be used to support and to justify the position taken. The creative aspect of any papal statement lay in the choice which the pope and his legally trained staff made between conflicting legal traditions when deciding upon a course of action.

Although *Inter caetera* is commonly described as the bull which divided up the world, this popular view is in error. Rather, it is a statement on the nature of Christian-infidel relations and on the responsibility of the pope to protect the infidels and to convert them to Christianity. In a general sense, it is a statement on ecclesiology, de-

[2] The most extensive discussion of this kind, and one which provided an excellent introduction to the literature concerning *Inter caetera,* is the series of articles by Charles-Martial de Witte, "Les bulles pontificales et l'expansion portugaise au XV$^{e}$ siècle," *Revue d'histoire ecclésiastique,* XLVIII (1953), 683-718; XLIX (1954), 438-461; LI (1956), 415-453, 809-836; LIII (1958), 5-46, 443-471. The essence of de Witte's position is that *Inter caetera* was only one in a long series of papal bulls dealing with the crusading movement and can only be understood in that context. Luis Weckman's *Las Bulas Alejandrinas de 1493 y la teoría política del papado medieval* (Mexico City, 1949) was an earlier attempt to place *Inter caetera* both in the context of earlier papal letters and in a context of legal theory. Although Weckman's argument that papal claims to control of unclaimed regions was rooted in the Donation of Constantine cannot be accepted, he was correct in seeking the legal tradition that influenced Alexander VI in drawing up the bull. Neither de Witte nor Weckman addressed himself to what contemporary canon lawyers were saying on the issues involved in *Inter caetera.* Since the appearance of the work of de Witte and Weckman, there has developed an extensive literature on the relationship between the medieval colonizing experience and the early modern, suggesting that the medieval experience can be seen in the development of colonizing institutions of the sixteenth and seventeenth centuries just as the medieval experience of contact with non-European peoples is reflected in *Inter caetera:* see especially Charles Verlinden, *The Beginnings of Modern Colonization* (Ithaca, New York, 1970); and Joshua Prawer, *The Crusaders' Kingdom. European Colonialism in the Middle Ages* (New York, 1972).

scribing the extent of the pope's role both within the formal church structure and also outside of that structure. The problem was not a new one in 1493, so that when Alexander sought to determine how the infidel societies which Columbus encountered should be treated, he was forced to consider what had already been written on this subject by earlier popes and lawyers. The result, as presented in *Inter caetera,* was a position thoroughly grounded in two and one-half centuries of canonistic thinking on the problem.

The problem of Christian relations with non-Christians appeared in the canonical collections of the earliest materials. In the period from the appearance of Gratian's *Decretum* (*ca.* 1140) to the publication of the *Decretales* (1234), the age of the greatest collections, the non-Christian world was seen in an essentially adversary relationship to the Christian world.[3] The non-Christian was the schismatic, heretic, Jew, or Saracen, each of whom posed a threat to the Christian world. For the most part, the canonists of this period discussed the non-Christian world in terms of the just war which could be waged against such people.

Only in the mid-thirteenth century did the canonists begin to give serious consideration to the possibility of peaceful relations with non-Christian societies. The appearance of the Mongols on the eastern fringes of Europe seems to have sparked reconsideration of the status of the infidel and his relation to the Christian world. Although the Mongols obviously posed a severe military threat to Europe and could have easily been categorized as invaders against whom a just war of defense could be waged, nevertheless they were not so treated. Instead, in one of the most imaginative papal diplomatic initiatives of the Middle Ages, Innocent IV sent the Dominican friar John of Plano Carpini to treat with the Mongol Khan.[4] The Dominican went armed with two letters from Innocent to the Khan. In the first, which was primarily doctrinal in nature, the pope declared that he was responsible for spreading the word of God everywhere and he requested that the Khan give John of Plano Carpini freedom of movement throughout the Mongol empire.[5] In the second, alluding to his role as univer-

[3] On the early development of papal and canonistic thinking on Christian relations with non-Christians, see James Muldoon, "*Extra ecclesiam non est imperium:* The Canonists and the Legitimacy of Secular Power," *Studia Gratiana,* IX (1966), 553-580.

[4] See Christopher Dawson (ed.), *The Mongol Mission* (London and New York, 1955).

[5] Innocent IV, *Dei patris immensa,* March 5, 1245, in *Monumenta Germaniae Historica, Epistolae saeculi XIII e regestis Pontificum Romanorum,* Vol. II, sel. G. H.

sal judge, Innocent called upon the Mongols to stop ravaging the borders of the Christian world lest the wrath of God fall upon them.[6]

Although the Mongol mission eventually came to naught, Innocent IV's conception of papal responsibility for the infidel and his conception of Christian-infidel relations entered the mainstream of legal thinking because Innocent was also one of the leading canonists of the thirteenth century. In a commentary on the decretal *Quod super his,* a letter of Innocent III on crusading vows, Innocent IV took the opportunity provided by this decretal to discuss the legitimacy of the entire concept of the crusade. While arguing that war to regain lands once held by Christians and presently held by Moslems was legitimate, he denied that Christians have the right to invade infidel lands simply because they are held by infidels.[7] Having accepted the legitimacy of infidel *dominium,* Innocent IV then went on to explain that this rejection of any claim to universal jurisdiction in the temporal sphere did not mean that there were no claims that Christians could press to dominate infidels. He pointed out that the pope was responsible to God for the spiritual well-being of all men, Christians and non-Christians alike. In terms recalling the image of Christ as the Good Shepherd, Innocent argued that Christ's injunction to the apostles "Feed my sheep" applied to all men, baptized or not, because "the infidels are sheep of Christ . . . although not of the flock of the Church."[8] Underlying this conception of Christ's flock was Christ's statement that there were other sheep that He had who were not as yet in the fold but that one day there would be one flock and one shepherd.[9] The infidel, in this view, is a member of the Church, at

Pertz, ed. C. Rodenberg (Berlin, 1887), pp. 72-73 (hereafter cited as *MGH*). See also Dawson, *op. cit.,* pp. 73-75.

[6] Innocent IV, *Cum non solum,* March 13, 1245, *MGH,* pp. 74-75; Dawson, *op. cit.,* pp. 75-76. It is interesting to note that the Mongol Khan asserted, in response to Innocent IV's claims to universal responsibility, a similar claim of his own. See George Vernadsky, *The Mongols and Russia* (New Haven, 1953), pp. 92-99.

[7] " possessiones et iurisdictiones licite sine peccato possunt esse apud infideles. haec. enim. non tamen pro fidelibus. sed pro omni rationabili creatura facta sunt, ut est praedictum. ipse enim solem oriri facit super bonos et malos. ipse etiam volatilia pascit . . et propter hoc dicimus, non licet Papae vel fidelibus, auferre sua, sive dominia sive iurisdictiones infidelibus, quia sine peccato possident. . . ." Innocent IV, *Commentaria in quinque libros decretalium* (Turin, 1581), *ad* 3.34.8, fol. 176$^{v}$.

[8] "Item alibi, pasce oves meas, etc. . . omnes autem tam fideles, quam infideles oves sunt Christi per creationem, licet non sint de ovili ecclesiae. et sic per predicta apparet, quod Papa super omnes habet iurisdictionem, et potestatem de iure, licet non de facto. . . ." *Ibid.*

[9] John 10:16.

least potentially, and is deserving of papal interest in his spiritual well-being.

Having outlined a theory of papal responsibility for the infidel, Innocent IV went on to explain the practical applications of the theory. In the first place, the pope is to seek the conversion of the infidels, but they are not to be forced to accept baptism. Should an infidel ruler forbid the entry of missionaries, however, the pope could call upon Christian rulers to protect the missionaries so that he could fulfill his responsibility for ensuring the preaching of the Gospel throughout the world. In the second place, the pope who judges Christians according to the laws of the Church is also the ultimate judge of all non-Christians according to the laws appropriate to them. For example, he may judge Jews according to the law of Moses and infidels according to the law of nature.[10] Innocent was careful to point out that the infidels did possess their political power and their goods legitimately. They could not be deprived of these simply because they were infidels. On the other hand, his opinion makes it quite clear that under certain circumstances Christians could deprive infidels of goods and political power because the spiritual order is ultimately superior to the temporal.

This theoretical discussion of the manner in which Christians should initiate contacts with infidels in seeking to carry out the papal responsibility of preaching the Gospel obviously paralleled the stages of Innocent IV's Mongol mission. John of Plano Carpini went first to instruct the Khan in Christian doctrine and to warn him that he was sinning against the law of nature by invading the lands of Christians who had done him no wrong.

Innocent's views on Christian-infidel relations were not without opposition within canonistic circles. His pupil Hostiensis took the opposite position, concluding his commentary on *Quod super his* with the opinion that "infidels ought to be subjected to the faithful, not the reverse."[11] In arguing this way, Hostiensis erased the distinction be-

[10] ". . . unde per potestatem, quam habet Papa, credo, quod si gentilis, qui non habet legem nisi naturae, si contra legem naturae facit, potest licite puniri per Papam, arg. Gen. 19. ubi habes, quod sodomitae, qui contra legem naturae peccabant, puniti sunt a Deo. . . . Item Iudaeos potest iudicare Papa, si contra legem evangelii faciunt in moralibus. si eorum prelati eos non puniant, et eodem modo si haereses circa suam legem inveniant, et hac ratione motus Papa Greg. et Inn. mandaverunt conburi libros talium, in quo multae continebantur haereses, et mandaverunt puniri illos, qui praedictas haereses sequerentur. . . ." Innocent IV, *ad* 3.34.8, fol. 176$^v$.

[11] " . . . unde constanter asserimus quod de iure infideles debent subici fidelibus.

tween spiritual domination and temporal which was at the heart of Innocent IV's commentary.

The debate over the relation between Christian and non-Christian societies in the legal literature for the next two and one-half centuries moved between these two poles. All agreed that as universal shepherd, the pope was responsible for Christian and infidel alike. The lawyers differed on the ways in which this responsibility was to be implemented. During the fourteenth century the discussion of such relations and the responsibility of the pope for the salvation of the infidels was for the most part a minor aspect of legal thinking because it was not a matter of immediate concern. Contact with representatives of the peaceful non-Christian world was minimal and there were no papal initiatives in this sphere to attract the interest of lawyers. John of Legnano, whose *On War, Reprisals, and the Duel* (*ca.* 1360) was the first treatise devoted to the problem of the law of war, repeated the Innocentian position concerning the rights of the infidels and the responsibility of the pope for them, but in a purely academic way. His chief interest was clearly the law of war as it affected the wars in Italy.[12] This treatise and the important commentaries on the *Decretales,* such as the lengthy one of Joannes Andreae which presented a wide range of opinions on disputed passages, made the opinions of Innocent IV and Hostiensis readily available to the students of the law, arming them in the event of another opportunity such as had been presented by the Mongol Mission.[13]

Although the general discussions of war and its legitimacy treated the issue of war with the infidels, other than the Moslems, as a remote matter during the fourteenth century, the writers of *consilia,* legal opinions on specific questions, did occasionally treat the problem. For example, Oldratus de Ponte (d. 1335) in a *consilium* on the

---

non econtra. . Concedimus tamen quod infideles qui dominium ecclesie recognoscunt sunt ab ecclesia tolerandi: quia nec ad fidem precise cogendi sunt. . . . Tales etiam possunt habere possessiones et colonos christianos; et etiam iurisdictionem ex tolerantia ecclesie." Hostiensis, *Lectura quinque Decretalium* (2 vols.; Paris, 1512), ad 3.34.8, fol. 124$^{v}$.

[12] "Et iste est Papa. Et hic non solum super fideles, immo etiam super infideles habet iurisdictionem. . Sic igitur Papa de iure habet iurisdictionem super infideles, licet non de facto. Hinc est quod si gentilis, habens solum legem naturae, peccat contra legem naturae, puniri possit per papam." Giovanni da Legnano, *Tractatus de Bello, de Represaliis et de Duello,* ed. T. E. Holland (Oxford, 1917), p. 92.

[13] Ioannes Andreae, *In tertium Decretalium librum Nouella Commentaria* (Venice, 1581), *ad* 3.34.8, fol. 172$^{v}$-173$^{r}$.

legitimacy of the wars against the Moslems in Spain developed Innocent IV's opinion on the relation of the pope to the infidels, drawing it out even further. Oldratus argued that the war itself was legitimate because the Saracens were always either attacking or planning to attack the Christians.[14] Furthermore, following the opinion of Hostiensis, he denied that the Saracens possessed *dominium* because since the coming of Christ only Christians have possessed it.[15] As a result, wars against infidels were always justified if their purpose was the expansion of the faith. To support this argument he drew upon Biblical pastoral imagery which had not previously been used in this regard. Quoting the Eighth Psalm, he stated that "the sheep, and the cattle, and the wild beasts of the fields" are subject to Christ and, therefore, to His Vicar.[16] The sheep are the Christians, while the cattle and the wild beasts of the fields are the Saracens and, presumably, all other non-Christians because he included idol worshipers among the wild beasts. In addition to this pastoral imagery, a logical extension of Innocent's imagery, Oldratus went on to argue that the Saracens were rightly called beasts because they were the descendants of Ishmael and it is well known that all his offspring were unsurpassedly wicked.[17] The Christian Church he described as Sarah, the faithful wife of Abraham. The Saracens and other non-Christians were the offspring of Hagar, the servant who was subject to Sarah.[18]

The extension of Innocent's arguments reinforced the conception of the non-Christians' subjection to the Christians. In the first analogy, the responsibility of the Church to convert and to tame the wild beasts of the fields paralleled the domination over animals given to Adam in Genesis.[19] In the second analogy, the patriarchal power of

[14] "Sed quod contra Sarracenos illos bellum sit licitum, probatur sic. quia aut ipsi impugnant Christianos: et tunc non est dubium. . . Aut ipsi non impugnant, et adhuc dico, quod bellum debet eis inferri, quia uerisimile est, quod quandoque ipsi opportunitatem habebunt, oppugnabunt, et persequentur Christianos, et ecclesiam. . . " Oldratus de Ponte, *Consilia, seu Responsa, et Questiones Aureae* (Venice, 1571), consilium 72, fol. 27$^r$.

[15] ". . .et ideo dicit Host. quod hodie non est iurisdictio, nec dominium, nec honor, nec potestas poenes infideles: nam per aduentum Christi translata sunt in Christianos. transfertur enim regnum de gente in gentem propter iniustitias suas. . . ." *Ibid.*, fol. 27$^v$.

[16] *Ibid.*

[17] *Ibid.*

[18] *Ibid.*

[19] "Et licet istae bestiae, quo ad pastum Petro non uideantur commissae, sunt tamen pedibus eius subiectae, quo ad dominium, et potestatem." *Ibid.*

the pope, in this case the new Abraham, extended not only to his children by Sarah, but also to his children by Hagar. In the long run, Oldratus denied Innocent IV's distinction between spiritual and temporal jurisdiction over infidels. His position reduced itself to the argument that as pope responsible for the well-being of all men he is justified in using force to achieve that end.

In another *consilium* Oldratus moderated some of the fierceness of his views on Christian relations with non-Christians. Again following Hostiensis, he argued that non-Christians ought not be exiled from Christians' lands if they live at peace with the Christians and accept the lawful rule of their Christian prince.[20] In his opinion, a policy of kindness toward them was better suited to leading them to the Church than a policy of harshness. As he pointed out, Jews and pagans, being already numbered among the members of Christ's flock, must be treated with respect.

In the early fifteenth century the opportunity to use this stored legal knowledge increased as European society expanded at either end. In the East, the kings of Poland fought with the Teutonic Knights for control of the pagan Lithuanians. In the West, Castilian and Portuguese seamen explored the west coast of Africa and discovered or rediscovered the island chains of the Atlantic. In both cases, the problem of the right of the Christians to conquer the peoples they encountered became a major legal issue. Because both situations pitted two Christian principalities against each other for domination of a region inhabited by non-Christians, the need arose for a judgment in these cases as to which, if indeed either, Christian principality had the right to control the lands under dispute. Both disputes were eventually debated at general councils, that over Lithuania at Constance and that over the Canaries at Basel. While Stanislaus Belch recently attempted to prove that the Polish position which was argued by Paulus Vladimiri at Constance played a role in shaping the development of

[20] "Illa uidetur probabilior sententia, quod princeps absque legitima causa pacificos Iudaeos, sarracenos, et alios paganos de terris suis non possit expellere. . . Expellere ergo tales absque ratione contra praecepta charitatis aperte est. . pagani, et Iudaei inter oues Christi computantur creatione, gubernatione et redemptione ex parte Christi. . . Unde et papa super eos potestatem habet, sicut super oues, quas ei inter alia commisit Christus. Io. ulti. pasce oues meas, non distinguens inter has, et illas. Cum ergo papa eos pascere debeat et uerbo, et exemplo, et humanitate non rebelles, non ergo debet eos impugnare, nec permittere, ut laedantur. . . infidelibus non terroribus. non asperitatibus, non uiolentiis sunt trahendi ad fidem, neque expulsionibus, sed blanditiis, et muneribus, ut integra sit forma iustitiae, et libertas arbitrij." *Ibid.*, consilium 263, fol. 126$^{v}$.

theories of Christian-infidel relations, there is no demonstrable connection between his writings and later work on the problem.[21] The material on the Canary Islands presented at Basel, however, clearly fits into the chain of legal thinking that influenced Alexander VI on the rights of infidels. This difference came in part at least because the debate over Lithuania represented a debate over a frontier which was closing while the Canaries represented a small part of a frontier that was just opening.

The expansion of the Iberian kingdoms overseas was originally part of the reconquest of the peninsula itself from the Moslems. As such, the general theory of the just war of recuperation could be and was applied to justify much of this expansion. Even the Portuguese capture of Ceuta on the coast of North Africa in 1415 could be justified in this way. The discovery of lands which were not controlled by Moslems and whose inhabitants did not pose any military threat to Europe required another justification. The papacy's involvement in the debate sprang from two sources. In the first place, the efforts of the Portuguese and Castilians to oust the Moslems had benefited from papal bulls authorizing crusading tithes and other benefits for the kings of those countries. Any further expansion would similarly benefit from papal blessing. In the second place, both of these kingdoms claimed jurisdiction over the Canaries. The pope was the logical choice to determine their respective claims. In addition, popes of the fifteenth century appear to have been increasingly conscious of their universal responsibilities. Martin V, for example, indicated that his interest in Portuguese expansion and discovery of infidel peoples stemmed from his responsibility for "the care and governance of the universal flock."[22] In another letter he spoke of the pope's role as universal father whose only desire was to bring the infidels into the Lord's flock.[23]

[21] Stanislaus Belch, *Paulus Vladimiri and His Doctrine Concerning International Law and Politics* (2 vols.; The Hague, 1965). A more recent edition provides not only the Latin text but English and Polish translations as well: see Ludwik Ehrlich, *Works of Paul Wladimiri* (3 vols.; Cracow, 1968).

[22] Martin V, *Ab eo qui humani sumens,* March 26, 1419, in João Martins da Silva Marques, *Descobrimentos portugueses* (2 vols.; Lisbon, 1944, 1949), I, 251.

[23] ". . . Romanus Pontifex . . habens super Orbis Ecclesias et monasteria universa, aliaque loca religiosa, plenitudinem potestatis, privilegiis, more Pastoris, suae providentiae oculis universum Orbem terrarum, et nationum in illo degentium, qualitates paterna consideratione discutiens et examinans diligenter, ex injuncto sibi Apostolatus officio singulorum salutem appetans, et exquirens, quaedam ex locis huiusmodi

The pontificate of Eugenius IV (1431-1447) saw a sharp increase of interest in the status of the infidel. In the first place, the Portuguese were anxious to maintain the impetus of their overseas expansion. The second source of interest in the infidels came from Eugenius' own heightened conception of the papal responsibility for all men, perhaps resulting from his battle with the conciliar forces. Sometime in 1433 or 1434 he banned further European expansion in the Canaries at the request of a bishop of the islands who reported that a Portuguese raiding party had attacked a village of Christian converts on one of the islands.[24] The ban was to protect the islands held by both the Christians and the infidels. Furthermore, his letters dealing with the situation on the islands suggest some knowledge of the actual situation there. The letters not only contain general statements about the need to create one flock and one shepherd, perhaps a cliché by this time; they also express an awareness of the conditions of life in the islands.[25] Apparently drawing upon explorers' descriptions of the islands, Eugenius pointed out that these people obviously lived accord-

---

pro reductione Infidelium ad ovile Dominicum, ad fastigia Ecclesiasticae dignitatis attolit. . ." Martin V, *In eminenti*, June 2, 1420, *ibid.*, p. 253. There is an extensive literature about the phrase *plenitudo potestatis* and its meaning. In this case the meaning seems to restrict the *plenitudo* to spiritual affairs although in the period from the twelfth to the fourteenth centuries the phrase often seemed to imply a plenitude of power in both secular and spiritual matters. Walter Ullmann has argued that the papacy asserted its possession of the plenitude of power in both spheres: see his *The Growth of Papal Government in the Middle Ages* (2nd ed.; London, 1962) and *Principles of Government and Politics in the Middle Ages* (London, 1961). Other scholars have interpreted the phrase differently, generally recognizing that various writers used it differently and that it must be understood within specific contexts. For more recent work, see Brian Tierney, "The Continuity of Papal Political Theory in the Thirteenth Century: Some Methodological Considerations," *Mediaeval Studies*, XXVII (1965), 227-245; J. A. Watt, *The Theory of the Papal Monarchy in the Thirteenth Century* (New York, 1965); and Robert Benson, "Plenitudo Potestatis: Evolution of a Formula from Gregory IV to Gratian," *Studia Gratiana*, XIV (1967), 193-218. For the concept as it developed in the late Middle Ages, see M. J. Wilks, *The Problem of Sovereignty in the Later Middle Ages* (Cambridge, 1963); and William D. McCready, "Papal *Plenitudo Potestatis* and the Source of Temporal Authority in Late Medieval Papal Hierocratic Theory," *Speculum*, XLVIII (October, 1973), 654-674.

[24] The problem of the Canary Islands is discussed in detail in my article, "A Fifteenth-Century Application of the Canonistic Theory of the Just War," *Proceedings of the Fourth International Congress of Medieval Canon Law* ("Monumenta Iuris Canonici," Series C. Subsidia 5 [Vatican City, 1976]), pp. 467-480.

[25] Eugenius IV, *Et si cunctis*, September 29, 1434, in D. J. Wölfel, "La Curia Romana y la Corona de España en la defensa de los aborígenes Canarios," *Anthropos*, XXV (1930), 1011-1083 at 1038.

ing to the law of nature, and he justified papal interest in them and jurisdiction over them by noting that the pope could judge them according to that law.[26] At the same time, he also recognized that the Canarians required not only spiritual assistance but very practical instruction as well. He requested that "men skilled in using the various mechanical arts" be sent out, presumably to teach the natives.[27] Some time later another letter pointed out that the natives were unskilled in manual crafts and required instructors who could teach them.[28]

These letters reflect Eugenius' twofold interest in the inhabitants of the Canaries. In the first place he was anxious to convert them to Christianity and to raise their cultural level. In the second he was anxious to protect them from European raiders. His letters even suggest a rudimentary conception of the "White Man's Burden" more generally associated with the nineteenth century. He was interested not simply in uplifting the natives spiritually but in assisting them to develop their social and cultural level as well. The Portuguese attack on peaceful Christian inhabitants of the islands served as a reminder to Eugenius that even conversion to Christianity would not of itself necessarily protect the natives from Europeans.[29]

[26] ". . . intelleximus licet in Insulis predictis quedam de Lancellot nuncupata et nonnulle alie circum adiacentes insule quarum habitatores et incole solam legem naturalem imitantes nullam antea fidelium aut hereticorum sectam nouerant a paucis citra temporibus diuina cooperante clemencia ad orthodoxam catholicam fidem sint reducte pro eo tamen [tantum?] quod labente tempore in quibusdam alijs e predictis insulis gubernatores ac defensores idonei qui illarum habitatores et incolas in spiritualibus et temporalibus ad rectam fidei obseruanciam dirigerent ac eorum res et bona grate tuerentur defuerunt. . . ." Eugenius IV, *Creator omnium rerum,* January 13, 1435, *ibid.*, p. 1044.

[27] " cum decenti et oportuna aliarum personarum comitiua personaliter transire in breui desideret et proponat ac pro huiusmodi ipsius transitu faciendo et ecclesiarum ornamentis ac vno congruo nauigio ad alias insulas visitandas ac personis in artibus mechanicis instructis qui eosdem Canarios in illis instruant et informent ac ferro et aliis metallis opportunis emendis necnon ecclesijs edificandis. ." Eugenius IV, *Ad ea ex,* December 28, 1433, *ibid.*, p. 1034.

[28] ". . . ad hoc quod ipsarum insularum habitatores et incole qui ueluti nimium grossi et materiales alicuius de qua ante indigenciam suscipere possent artis exercicium penitus ignorant in artificibus et ministerialibus opibus eciam pro ipsius fidei exaltacione necnon christiane professionis corroboracione instrui possent assignarentur ex inde fidei et professionis predictarum propagacio cum multiplici salutis animarum augmento succederent euidenter." Eugenius IV, *In excelso,* January 12, 1435, *ibid.*, p. 1043.

[29] Being Christians, the Canarians should have been protected by the laws of war governing conflicts between Christian armies which forbade the enslaving of fellow

Events in 1436 forced Eugenius to consider carefully the extent to which the pope could interpose the spiritual power between infidels and Christians. In that year King Edward I of Portugal requested that Eugenius restrict the ban on further European penetration in the islands to the islands occupied by Christians. The request, as presented by King Edward, was based on zeal for the welfare of the natives. He described them as lacking even the simplest forms of social organization, any knowledge of metal working, and any kind of literature.[30] Given papal approval, the king would bring the natives under Portuguese control, convert them to Christianity, and give them "civil laws and the means to live in a polity."[31] King Edward's outline of the reasons motivating his request suggests the same mixture of spiritual and socio-cultural reasons for overseas expansion that seems to have struck Eugenius. In addition, the king observed ominously that while the Portuguese could be expected to obey the papal ban if it continued, nevertheless other men, less noble and less God-fearing, would not be deterred by papal fulminations.[32] Lacking a fleet to patrol the waters around the islands, Eugenius could only excommunicate slavers and others who sought to exploit the natives.

King Edward's letter appears to have perplexed Eugenius. In order to resolve the dilemma of providing adequate protection for the natives without at the same time compromising their rights, he resorted to asking opinions from theologians and canonists before drafting an answer. Only the opinions of two canonists have been found and they are not very revealing. Both men discussed the question in terms of

---

Christians. The invaders seem to have made no distinction, however, between Christian and infidel Canarians, and enslaved both indiscriminately. On the law of war, see M. H. Keen, *The Laws of War in the Late Middle Ages* (London and Toronto, 1965), pp. 12-13.

30 "Has indomiti silvestres fere homines inhabitant qui nulla religione coagulati, nullis denique legum vinculis irretiti, civili conversacione neglecta, in paganitate veluti pecudes vitam agunt. Iis navale comercium, literarum exercicium, genus aliquod metali aut numismatis nullum est." De Witte, *op. cit.*, XLVIII (1953), 715.

31 ". . . parata navium et galiarum armatarum classe de consenssu et mandato serenissimi regis Eduardi domini et fratis sui ad prefatas insulas Canarie misit ut primum eos ipsos paganos ad fidem christianam et devocionem corone Portugalie convertisset, leges eciam civiles et politicum vivendi modum eisdem traderet." *Ibid.*, p. 716.

32 ". . . tum quia primus ipse incepit preffatas insulas subigere, magis certe animarum illarum insularum paganorum salutis gracia quam private utilitatis que nulla erat, unde rei tam pie, que auxilio pocius et directorio Sanctitatis Vestre digna fuit, eadem Sanctitati ultro inpedimento esse non debuit. . ." *Ibid.*

the general theory of the just war and based their arguments heavily on Innocent IV's commentary on *Quod super his*.[33] The most striking element of the opinions is the argument presented by Antonio Rosselli that the infidels, being the descendants of Hagar and Ishmael, are the responsibility of the pope who clearly enjoys a patriarchal power over them.[34] In doing this, he explicitly extended Oldratus de Ponte's use of this analogy to all infidels, an action which could be used to justify Christian domination over the Canaries.

Eugenius' official response to the Portuguese request in the bull *Romanus pontifex* (September 15, 1436) steered a careful line through the conflicting theoretical and practical aspects of the problem. He agreed to lift the ban on entry into the infidel-occupied islands in order that the Portuguese might undertake the work of conversion.[35] He took no explicit note of the other points of Edward's letter, but it must be assumed that he considered the lifting of the ban as the lesser of two evils. He could expect that the Portuguese in their desire to retain their license to operate on these islands would prevent slavers and other European raiders from entering them. The mutual interest of the pope and the king in the spiritual and temporal well-being of the natives would serve to protect the natives and to improve their lot. The need to protect not only them but also the missionaries who were sent to them would necessitate the use of Christian arms, an action supported by Innocent IV's argument and by the view of the pope as the heir of Abraham's patriarchal power.

Eugenius IV appears to have considered the complexities of Christian-infidel relations more thoroughly than any of his successors was to do. His careful analysis of the situation in the Canaries and the distinction which he appears to have made between just wars

[33] These commentaries were discovered and discussed briefly by de Witte, *ibid.*, pp. 700-702. They are also discussed at greater length in my article, "A Fifteenth-Century Application of the Canonistic Theory of the Just War," pp. 471-477.

[34] "Set per saram significatur sancta mater ecclesia et per agar amallam significatur illa amalla maledicta in qua secta manomecti que ab ea traxit originem significatur ex qua ista inproba secta manometi originem ducit. . . . Et ideo facta ecclesia que per saram ut dixi significatur. iurisdictionem habet in hanc amallam et sectam paganorum non quidem eos ad fidem compellendo set exortando. . . ." Vatican Library, cod. lat. ms. 1932, fol. 121ʳ.

[35] "Nos igitur . . prefatas Cannerie insulas, illis exceptis que antea per christianos possidebantur, auctoritate apostolica et de plenitudine potestatis nobis desuper tradite tibi concedimus in conquestam et eas, postquam in tuam ditionem redigeris et ad fidem converteris, tibi subiicimus per presentes, ita ut ad te et tuos successores perpetuo spectare debeant et pertineant pleno iure. . . ." de Witte, *op. cit.*, XLVIII (1953), 718.

against the Moslems and the need of the pope to employ the secular arm to protect infidels from Christians does not appear in the papal letters issued between Eugenius' death and Alexander VI's *Inter caetera*. Nicholas V, for example, in the bull *Romanus pontifex* (January 8, 1455), blended the themes of papal responsibility to gather all the Lord's sheep into the fold with that of the justice of the wars against the Moslems and infidels, making no distinction between the two groups. Both Moslems and infidels he defined as "enemies of Christ" and he authorized the Portuguese to seize their goods and to reduce them to slavery.[36]

In the realm of legal thinking, there also appears to have been a lack of further development of the problem of Christian-infidel relations during the middle and late fifteenth century. The opinions of Innocent IV, John of Legnano, and Oldratus de Ponte continued to be cited but neither the Lithuanian nor the Canary Islands situation appears to have entered the mainstream of legal thinking. For the most part, the lawyers continued to discuss the issue of relations between Christians and non-Christians in terms of Jews living in Christian Europe or in terms of the wars with the Moslems.

The voyages of Columbus and the subsequent publicizing of his discoveries made the question of the rights of the infidels a matter of immediate interest to European rulers and their lawyers. The discovery of the Americas also added another bone of contention between the Portuguese and Castilians. When Alexander VI was asked to resolve the problem of what rights the Portuguese and the Castilians had with regard to the newly discovered lands, he was in effect being asked to continue the role which his predecessors had played for more than two centuries with regard to the rights of Christians who discover infidel lands and also to attempt a resolution of the long-standing Portuguese-Castilian conflict.

Alexander's solution to the problems raised by Columbus' voyage is reminiscent of the solution which Eugenius IV gave to the Portuguese in 1436. The line of demarcation itself was a comparatively simple

[36] "Nos, premissa omnia et singula debita meditatione pensantes, ac attendentes quod cum olim prefato Alfonso Regi quoscunque Sarracenos et paganos aliosque Christi inimicos ubicunque constitutos, ac regna, ducatus, principatus, dominia, possessiones, et mobilia ac immobilia bona quecunque per eos detenta ac possessa invadendi, conquirendi, expugnandi, debellandi, et subjugandi, illorumque personas in perpetuam servitutem redigendi. . . ." Nicholas V, *Romanus Pontifex*, January 8, 1455, in Davenport, *op. cit.*, pp. 13-20 at 16; translation, p. 23.

issue because it was based upon theories of papal responsibility and power and it is of no interest here. What is important is the line of argument which the pope took in order to justify drawing the line and assigning spheres of responsibility. At the beginning of *Inter caetera,* Alexander described the natives in terms obviously drawn from Columbus' own reports. He says that they were "living in peace . . . going unclothed, and not eating flesh . . . these very people . . . believe in one God, the Creator in heaven, and seem sufficiently disposed to embrace the Catholic faith and be trained in good morals."[37] Although peaceful, the Indians clearly lived in a primitive state, if not like the animals of the fields, not like that found in Europe either. The stated aim of the Castilians, according to Alexander, had been "to bring under your sway the said countries and islands with their residents and inhabitants, and to bring them to the Catholic faith."[38] This motivation when joined to the obviously primitive state of the Indians required the Castilians to "appoint to the aforesaid countries and islands worthy and God-fearing, learned, skilled, and experienced men to instruct the aforesaid inhabitants and residents in the Catholic faith, and to train them in good morals."[39] In return for carrying out these obligations, Alexander forbade "all persons of no matter what rank . . . to dare, without your special permit or that of your aforesaid heirs and successors, to go for the sake of trade or any other reason whatever to the said islands and countries after they have been discovered and found by your envoys or persons sent out for that purpose."[40] This final aspect of the bull presumably was

[37] ". certas insulas remotissimas, et etiam terras firmas, que per alios hactenus reperte non fuerunt, invenerunt, in quibus quamplurime gentes, pacifice viventes, et, ut asseritur, nudi incedentes, nec carnibus vescentes, inhabitant; et, ut prefati nuntii vestri possunt opinari, gentes ipse in insulis et terris predictis habitantes, credunt unum Deum Creatorem in celis esse, ac ad fidem Catholicam amplexandum et bonis moribus imbuendum satis apti videntur. . . ." Alexander VI, *Inter caetera,* May 3, 1493, *ibid.*, pp. 58-61 at 58-59; translation, p. 62.

[38] *Ibid.*, p. 59; translation, p. 62.

[39] "Et insuper mandamus vobis in virtute sancte obedientie, ut, sicut etiam pollicemini et non dubitamus pro vestra maxima devotione et regia magnanimitate vos esse facturos, ad terras et insulas predictas viros probos et Deum timentes, doctos, peritos, et expertos, ad instruendum incolas et habitores prefatos in fide Catholica et bonis moribus imbuendum, destinare debeatis, omnem debitam diligentiam in premisis adhibentes. . . ." *Ibid.*, pp. 59-60; translation, p. 63.

[40] ". . . ac quibuscumque personis, etiam cujuscumque dignitatis, status, gradus, ordinis, vel condictionis, sub excommunicationis late sententie pena, quam eo ipso, si contrafecerint, incurrant, districtius inhibentes, ne ad insulas et terras predictas, post-

based on the realistic view that papal refusal to allow European rulers the right to govern infidel lands in return for promises to convert the natives and to raise them to a European standard of social and political life would not prevent anyone from raiding such lands, enslaving the natives, or establishing colonies.

While Alexander did not mention the letter of Edward I to Eugenius IV, the six decades of exploration between 1436 and 1493 made it clear that no European ruler would be deterred from overseas expansion by papal bans. Furthermore, the natives of the Americas were, at first glance at least, on a primitive level of existence and would not be able to protect themselves against Europeans bent on conquest. Faced with authorizing an orderly settlement of the great contemporary colonial rivalry, or leaving expansion to those whom Edward I had described as seeking only their personal gain, Alexander and his aides chose to authorize orderly expansion based on the high motives expressed by the parties involved. As the lesser of two evils, the Castilians were authorized to control the Americas as the Portuguese had been authorized to govern the Canaries.

*Inter caetera* was not, then, an assertion of long-dead papal claims to world domination but rather a carefully worded statement which balanced the rights of the infidels, the papal responsibility for preaching the Gospel, and the political realities of aggressive expansionism. It would appear that Alexander basically accepted Innocent IV's views on the right of infidels to *dominium*. At least he did not argue that the mere fact of the natives being infidels would justify conquest. Instead, the granting of the Americas to the Castilians was based on the argument that the natives require protection and that the pope, in the absence of any other authority capable of providing this protection, was required by the nature of his vicariate of Christ to provide the protection. The best means to do this was to authorize the Portuguese and the Castilians to be responsible for the exercise of this papal responsibility in specific regions.

In the long run, the papal policy failed or, to be more exact, was outflanked when the warring Iberian kingdoms signed the Treaty of Tordesillas (June 7, 1494) which ended their long-standing war by mutual agreement. With the existence of peace between the two par-

---

quam per vestros nuntios seu ad id missos invente et recepte fuerunt, pro mercibus habendis vel quavis alia de causa, accedere presumant, absque vestra ac heredum et successorum vestrorum predictorum licentia speciali." *Ibid.*, p. 60; translation, p. 83.

ties there was no longer any possibility of the pope being able to influence the colonial administrative policies of one kingdom by threatening to withdraw papal approval for conquest and to authorize the other kingdom to assume the responsibility for protecting the natives. Although there were some later papal bulls concerned with expansion, they only had the effect of confirming what the Portuguese and Castilians had already agreed to do.[41]

In spite of the failure of the papacy to influence colonial policy in the sixteenth century and later by possession of a generally recognized power to award or withdraw a protectorate over infidel peoples, the legal tradition continued to include the materials which underlay *Inter caetera* and the other bulls which reflect opinions of the nature of Christian-infidel relations. As recent scholarship has indicated, the Spanish writers, such as Francisco Vitoria and Bartolomé de las Casas, who wrote against the excesses of the Spanish conquerors in the Americas, rooted their arguments in the medieval legal tradition.[42] In addition, the flourishing school of early writers on international law up to and including Hugo Grotius appears to have drawn more heavily on this tradition than has been generally recognized.[43] The very conservative nature of the law as an institution tended to preserve these arguments well beyond the point at which we might have expected that they would have faded away to be replaced by other, more up-to-date legal formulations. That any attempt was made in the sixteenth century to protect the non-Christian world from the worst excesses of European expansion was in large part due to the efforts of the lawyers from the time of Innocent IV to develop a rational policy of relations with infidel societies.

[41] See for example, the bulls *Ea quae* of Julius II, January 24, 1506, and *Praecelsae devotionis* of Leo X, November 3, 1514, *ibid.*, pp. 107-117.

[42] On Vitoria's use of the canonistic tradition in his *De Indis*, see James Muldoon, "A Canonistic Contribution to the Formation of International Law," *The Jurist*, XXVIII (1968), 265-279. For Las Casas, see Kenneth Pennington, "Bartolome de Las Casas and the Tradition of Medieval Law," *Church History*, XXXIX (June, 1970), 149-161. On the whole issue of the Castilian attempt to rule Latin America within a legal framework, see Lewis Hanke, *The Spanish Struggle for Justice in the Conquest of America* (Philadelphia, 1949).

[43] See James Muldoon, "The Contribution of the Medieval Canon Lawyers to the Formation of International Law," *Traditio*, XXVIII (1972), 483-497.

V

# THE AVIGNON PAPACY AND THE FRONTIERS OF CHRISTENDOM: THE EVIDENCE OF VATICAN REGISTER 62

*Summarium.* — Convenit inter omnes *Reg. Vat. 62,* quod litteris constat nec ab uno pontifice maximo missis nec temporis ordine servato transcriptis, ceteris registris dissimillimum esse. Eius enim magna pars litteras a quattuor pontificibus saec. XIV, nempe a Clemente V, Ioanne XXII, Benedicto XII, Clementeque VI, missas continet, qui se sollicitos praebebant erga populos non christianos. His in litteris tria praeprimis tractata sunt: quo modo Christiani se defenderent a Turcis, quo modo Christiani, qui in vera fide non perseveraverunt, cum Ecclesia occidentali coniungerentur, quo modo pagani — e. gr. Lituani et Tartari —, qui terras inter septentrionem et orientem extra Europam christianam incolunt, et incolae insularum Fortunatarum in partibus Africae ad veram fidem traducerentur. In hac elucubratione exponitur huiusmodi litteras in *Reg. Vat. 62* propterea collectas fuisse eoque spectavisse, ut demonstraretur, quo modo pontifices Avenionenses munus suum versus gentes ad fines extremos Christianitatis sitas intellexissent: ut auctor opinatur, pontificum Avenionensium plurimum interfuit ut Christiani bene ab hostibus defendi possent, utque qui extra Ecclesiam versantur ad fidem veram converterentur. His enim in rebus pontifices Avenionenses non aliter se gesserunt ac pontifices maximi saeculi tertii decimi. *

---

* I wish to express my appreciation to Rutgers University for granting me two sabbaticals that enabled me to work continuously on this manuscript and to the American Philosophical Society for providing me with a grant that enabled me to visit the Vatican in order to examine Vatican Register 62 in October 1974.

The following abbreviations are used currently:

*Acta Ioannis XXII* = *Acta Ioannis XXII (1317-1334)* (Pontificia Commissio ad redigendum codicem iuris canonici orientalis, Fontes, ser. 3, v. 7, pt. 2), ed. ALOYSIUS L. TĂUTU, Rome 1952.

*Acta Benedicti XII* = *Acta Benedicti XII (1334-1342)* (Pont. Comm.... orientalis, Fontes, ser. 3, v. 8), ed. ALOYSIUS L. TĂUTU, Rome 1958.

DÉPREZ, GLÉNISSON, MOLLAT = *Clément VI: Lettres closes, patentes et curiales se rapportant à la France,* ed. É. DÉPREZ, J. GLÉNISSON and G. MOLLAT, 3 v., Paris 1910-1961.

DÉPREZ and MOLLAT = *Clément VI: Lettres closes, patentes et curiales intéressant les pays autres que la France,* ed. É. DÉPREZ and G. MOLLAT, Paris 1900-1961.

GAY = JULES GAY, *Le pape Clément VI et les affaires d'Orient, 1342-1352,* Paris 1904.

MOLLAT (MOLLAT, *Lettres communes*) = *Jean XXII: Lettres communes analysées d'après les registres dits d'Avignon et du Vatican,* ed. G. MOLLAT, 16 v. in 17, Paris 1904-1947.

MOLLAT, *The Popes at Avignon* = G. MOLLAT, *The Popes at Avignon, 1305-1378,* trans. Janet Love, London 1963.

RAYNALDUS = ODORICO RINALDI (Raynaldus), *Annales ecclesiastici,* 38 v., Lucca 1738-1759.

VIDAL = *Benoît XII: Lettres communes analysées d'après les registres dits d'Avignon et du Vatican,* ed. J.-M. VIDAL, 3 v., Paris 1903-1911.

VIDAL and MOLLAT = *Benoît XII: Lettres closes et patentes intéressant les pays autres que la France,* ed. J.-M. VIDAL and G. MOLLAT, 2 v., Paris 1913-1950.

WADDING = LUKE WADDING, *Annales Minorum,* 32 v., 3rd ed., Quaracchi-Florence 1931-1964.

## INTRODUCTION

Petrarch's famous description of the papal court of Avignon continues to dominate the popular image of the fourteenth century papacy[1]. The picture of place hunting and worse forms of corruption that the poet provided takes on an especially grim significance in the light of the subsequent crises through which the papacy passed in the next two centuries. The Great Schism, the conciliar movement and finally the Protestant Reformation seem to flow inexorably from the wickedness which Petrarch described[2]. The only logical goal was to prune the luxuriant growth of the papacy as the conciliarists desired or to eliminate it completely as the Protestant reformers wished.

A major obstacle to a balanced evaluation of the papacy in the fourteenth and fifteenth centuries has been the mass of still unpublished material that remains in the papal archives from the pontificates of these centuries[3]. Despite the efforts of the scholars of the French School in Rome, the letters from these years have not been completely calendared, much less published in scholarly editions. Many of the letters that have appeared in print can only be found scattered through old histories such as those by Raynaldus and Wadding or in various document collections such as those which Theiner published in the nineteenth century[4]. The result is that the picture of the papacy as the papacy saw itself in these centuries has yet to be written.

As the materials from the reigns of the various popes at Avignon have become available, the picture of the Avignon papacy has gradually undergone revision. One area of papal activity in this period that has attracted scholarly attention in modern times has been

---

[1] Petrarch's dim view of Avignon was based in part on his failure to obtain a suitable position at the papal court: MORRIS BISHOP, *Petrarch and His World*, Bloomington (Indiana) 1963, pp. 304-319.

[2] Nineteenth and early twentieth century historians often saw this progression in stark terms. Examples of this include: MANDELL CREIGHTON, *A History of the Papacy* (5 v., new ed., London 1892) 1: p. 50; and ALEXANDER C. FLICK, *The Decline of the Medieval Church* (2 v., London 1930) 2: pp. 466-475. Much recent scholarship has shifted from the problem of institutional breakdown and the discontinuity of the medieval and the early modern experience to emphasis upon the role of individuals who bridged the two historical periods. Among the most important of these new works are two books by JAROSLAV PELIKAN, *Obedient Rebels: Catholic Substance and Protestant Principle in Luther's Reformation*, New York 1964; and *Spirit Versus Structure: Luther and the Institutions of the Church*, New York 1968.

[3] For a brief introduction to the problems involved in dealing with the papal registers in this period and to the literature concerning the registers, see LEONARD E. BOYLE, *A Survey of the Vatican Archives and of its Medieval Holdings*, Toronto 1972, esp. pp. 103-131.

[4] ODORICO RINALDI (Raynaldus), *Annales ecclesiastici*, 38 v., Lucca 1738-1759; LUKE WADDING, *Annales Minorum*, 32 v., 3rd ed., Quaracchi-Florence 1931-1964; AUGUSTIN THEINER, *Vetera Monumenta Poloniae et Lithuaniae*, 4 v., Rome 1860-1864.

papal interest in foreign missions. In order to counter the unflattering portrait of the popes at Avignon as primarily interested in raising money and engaging in political intrigue, some modern scholars have emphasized that these popes gave much more attention to the traditional religious responsibilities of the office than has been generally recognized, especially by critics of the papacy. Ludwig Pastor, for example, argued that emphasis upon the negative aspects of the Avignon period has led to the creation of « a very partial picture » of papal activity in these decades « wherein the noble efforts of these much-abused pontiffs for the conversion of heathen nations become almost imperceptible in the dim background »[5]. Professor Mollat's evaluation of the religious zeal of these popes is even stronger. « In conclusion, the religious activities of the Avignon popes stand out in the zeal with which they put down heresy, reformed the religious orders and brought the knowledge of the Gospel to distant lands »[6].

As research into the Avignon papacy continues, this era appears less and less as an aberration in the history of the papacy. More and more, the popes of Avignon can be seen as fitting within the mainstream of papal development during the Middle Ages[7]. The seventy-five years of the Avignon papacy appear to have been a continuation of the style and the aims of the thirteenth century papacy, not a break with them. Even the fact that the popes lived at Avignon was not such a break with the past as was once believed. Between 1100 and 1304 « the popes spent one hundred and twenty-two [years] away from Rome and eighty-two in Rome »[8]. While Avignon was further away from Rome than the Italian cities to which various popes retired, it was not as far away as Lyons where both Innocent IV (1243-1254) and Gregory X (1271-1276) lived and held coun-

5 LUDWIG PASTOR, *The History of the Popes*, trans. F. J. Antrobus, H. F. Kerr, E. Graf, E. F. Peeler (40 v., various eds., London 1938-1961) 1: p. 60.

6 G. MOLLAT, *The Popes at Avignon, 1305-1378*, trans. Janet Love, London 1963, p. 344. This translation from the ninth French edition did not include the extensive bibliographies found in the original. The most recent French edition contains revised and expanded bibliographies: *Les papes d'Avignon*, 10th ed., Paris 1965.

7 « L'histoire de ce pontificate [Clement VI] nous montre par un contraste saisissant, comment se continuent, dans l'Église occidentale, les rêves orientaux, qui font, en quelque sorte, l'âme commune de la chrétienté latine, — et quels obstacles leur opposent les rivalités commerciales, politiques, dynastiques. Dans cette cour brillante d'Avignon, si éloignée des temps heroïques de Grégoire VII et d'Urban II, le poids toujours croissant des intérêts et des ambitions terrestres ne fait pas disparaître l'idéal traditionnel ». JULES GAY, *Le pape Clément VI et les affaires d'Orient, 1342-1352*, Paris 1904, p. 169. Mollat pointed out that the centralization of papal government that had begun under Gregory VII « reached its climax in the fourteenth century », indicating that the Avignon popes were not so very far removed from the spirit of Gregory VII and his immediate successors as has sometimes been believed: MOLLAT, *The Popes at Avignon*, p. 335.

8 L. GAYET, *Le Grande Schisme d'Occident*, Florence 1889, p. 3; cited in MOLLAT, *The Popes at Avignon*, p. XII.

cils [9]. The city of Rome was often in turmoil that encouraged the popes to leave for a more peaceful location where the work of the papacy could be carried on without interference [10]. The policy of holding church councils beyond the Alps as a means of bringing papal concerns directly to distant ecclesiastical and secular officials also meant that popes had positive reasons for leaving Rome over long periods of time. This practice was rooted in the efforts of the reforming popes of the eleventh and twelfth centuries to assert direct papal control over the Church everywhere [11].

Intellectually, the popes of the fourteenth century were also continuators, not innovators. In keeping with the traditions of the thirteenth century papacy, legal training or interest in canon law played a major role in shaping the popes of the Avignon period. Innocent VI (1352-1362) had been a noted professor of law before his election [12]. Two other popes, Clement V (1305-1314) and John XXII (1316-1334), added collections of decretals, the *Clementinae* and the *Extravagantes Johannis Papae XXII*, to the body of canon law [13]. In so doing, they were following in the footsteps of the great canonist-popes of the thirteenth century. Innocent III (1198-1216) had begun the practice of officially sponsoring collections of papal decretals for the use of students and practitioners of the law in order to keep them abreast of current papal thinking. Gregory IX (1227-1241)

---

9 HORACE K. MANN, *The Lives of the Popes in the Middle Ages* (18 v., London 1902-1932) 14: pp. 69-80; 15: pp. 382-387 and 412-419. In addition, see the more recent study by DENO J. GEANAKOPLOS, *Emperor Michael Palaeologus and the West, 1258-1282*, Cambridge, Mass. 1959, pp. 258-276.

10 The conditions in Rome that encouraged the popes to live elsewhere are described in FERDINAND GREGOROVIUS, *History of the City of Rome in the Middle Ages*, trans. Annie Hamilton (8 v. in 13, London 1894-1902; reprint ed., New York 1967), v. 6. A more recent, but briefer, description is found in PETER PARTNER, *The Lands of St. Peter*, Berkeley 1972, pp. 297-365.

11 « Le programme grégorien ... comporte avant tout la centralisation ecclésiastique sans laquelle l'autorité du Saint-Siège ne peut s'exercer avec efficacité. Pour réaliser la réforme et pour faire respecter les décrets pontificaux par les évêques, par les clercs, par les laïques, il est indispensable de resserrer les liens qui unissent à Rome les diocèses de la chrétienté.

« Avant 1075, deux rouages permettaient à la papauté d'agir sur les églises locales: les conciles généraux ou provinciaux et les légats envoyés par le pontife romain dans les différents pays pour préparer ou surveiller l'application des décisions apostoliques. Grégoire VII va utiliser cette double institution, mais en la fortifiant et en la perfectionnant, en même temps, qu'il s'efforcera d'affaiblir le pouvoir des primats, métropolitains, évêques ». AUGUSTIN FLICHE, *La réforme grégorienne* (2 v., Louvain Paris, 1924-1925) 2: p. 205.

12 G. LE BRAS, C. LEFEBVRE and J. RAMBAUD, *L'âge classique 1140-1378, Sources et Théorie du Droit* (Histoire du Droit et des Institutions de l'Église en Occident, v. 7), Paris 1965, p. 40; MOLLAT, *The Popes at Avignon*, p. 45.

13 As one recent work has described it: « Le temps d'Avignon avait été celui des juristes; ils sont partout à la Curia et partout ils imposent leur esprit plus encore que leurs idées ». PAUL OURLIAC and HENRI GILLES, *La période post-classique (1378-1500): La problématique de l'époque; les sources* (Histoire du Droit et des Institutions de l'Eglise en Occident, v. 13, part 1), Paris 1971, p. 87; see also, LE BRAS, pp. 15, 252-256; MOLLAT, *The Popes at Avignon*, pp. 7, 17.

issued a major collection of papal decisions, the *Decretales*, in 1234, and Boniface VIII (1294-1303) added the *Liber Sextus*, a small collection of decretals from the pontificates of the thirteenth century, including his own [14].

In addition to the canonist-popes, the papal court also included large numbers of legally-trained staff members who helped to shape the style of the papacy. During the thirteenth century, the legally trained popes and curial staff stressed the juridical nature of the papal office. The pope became the *iudex omnium* and the decretal, or judicial decision, became the most common expression of papal opinion. The papal court became increasingly a place where litigants came seeking justice. As a result, the administration of justice became increasingly bureaucratic. Formula books emerged which enabled clerks to treat common problems in a standard fashion [15]. The clearest evidence for the increasing judicial and administrative activity of the papacy is the increasing number of letters dispatched by successive popes. The series of registers known as the Vatican Registers contains 47 volumes for all of the thirteenth century popes while the pontificate of John XXII alone has over fifty volumes of registers and the 77 volumes from the pontificate of Clement VI (1342-1352) contain over 86,000 items [16].

By continuing to employ and develop the institutional structure inherited from the thirteenth century pontiffs the Avignon popes automatically cast themselves in the same role that their predecessors had assumed. As a result, although it is common to view these popes as the antithesis of the reforming popes of the Gregorian era, it is important to realize that they saw themselves as continuing in that tradition. John XXII and Benedict XII (1334-1342) have reputations as reformers of ecclesiastical abuses [17]. In secular affairs, several of these popes sought to mediate the Hundred Years War between France and England in the same manner as Innocent III had earlier tried to mediate between John and Philip Augustus [18]. Clement VI continued the papal practice of transferring the overlordship of lands held by heretics, schismatics or infidels to secular

---

14 LE BRAS, pp. 133-154, 222-251.

15 For the development of the papacy's administrative practices, see GEOFFREY BARRACLOUGH, *Papal Provisions: Aspects of Church History, Constitutional, Legal and Administrative, in the later Middle Ages*, Oxford 1935, pp. 99-100; and PETER HERDE, *Beiträge zum päpstlichen Kanzlei- und Urkundenwesen im dreizehnten Jahrhundert*, Kallmünz 1961, pp. 101-176.

16 BOYLE, p. 105.

17 MOLLAT, *The Popes at Avignon*, pp. 17, 33; see also, BERNARD GUILLEMAIN, *La politique bénéficiale du pape Benoît XII, 1334-1342*, Paris 1952; and C. SCHMITT, *Un pape réformateur et défenseur de l'unité de l'Église. Benoît XII et l'Ordre des Frères-Mineurs (1334-1342)*, Quaracchi-Florence 1959.

18 EDOUARD PERROY, *The Hundred Years War*, trans. W. B. Wells, London 1951, pp. 84, 88, 90-94, 106, 116; HELEN JENKINS, *Papal Efforts for Peace under Benedict XII, 1334-1342*, Philadelphia 1933.

rulers who promised to reform the state of the Church in such lands or to impose Christianity, a practice that went back to the Gregorian reform [19].

Finally, the popes at Avignon continued the efforts which earlier popes had begun to reconcile the schismatic churches of the East with Rome, to preach the Gospel to the infidels of Asia, and to free the Holy Land from the Moslems. Such aspects of the Avignon papacy's activities tend to be overlooked, lost in the great amount of attention given to the internal European problems which faced these popes. In the sphere of missionary activity the fourteenth century popes attempted to follow the lead of their thirteenth century predecessors by asserting the universal nature of the papal mission. The fourteenth century papal registers contain numerous letters dealing with these topics. The emperors and patriarchs of Constantinople, the kings of Armenia and Georgia, and other schismatics continued to receive letters and embassies from the West. The Mongol khans also continued to exchange letters and embassies with the West during the fourteenth century. The Christian rulers of Europe continued to receive appeals from the popes to return to the work of the crusade.

The desire of the popes at Avignon to play the kind of dominant role in European society that their immediate predecessors had played appears clearly in an unusual register of papal letters compiled toward the end of the Avignon period of papal history. Strictly speaking, Vatican Register 62 is not a true papal register, that is, it does not contain letters from one pontificate arranged chronologically [20]. Instead, it contains letters from several pontificates, the vast majority from the reigns of Clement V, John XXII, Benedict XII, and Clement VI. The letters all concern a common theme, the relations of the papacy with the frontiers of European Christianity. The unknown compiler of the volume headed it simply: « Here begin the titles of the letters or other writings from the reigns of Clement V, John XXII, Benedict XII, and Clement VI, which dealt with business of the Tartars, the lands of *outre-mer*, infidels and heretics » [21].

---

19 The best known cases of this during the Gregorian era consisted of the papal blessing of William the Conqueror's invasion of England in 1066 and the papal grant of Ireland to Henry II of England in 1155. Concerning the place of this papal power *New Catholic Encyclopedia* (15 v., New York 1967) 1: p. 306; and *The Alexandrine de 1493 y la Teoría Política de Papado Medieval*, Mexico City 1949. Weckmann has re-stated his views in two shorter and more accessible pieces: *Alexandrine Bulls*, in *New Catholic Encyclopedia* (15 v., New York 1967) 1: p. 306; and *The Alexandrine Bulls of 1493: Pseudo-Asiatic Documents*, in *First Images of America*, ed. FREDI CHIAPPELLI (2 v., Berkeley 1976) 1: pp. 201-210.

20 BOYLE, p. 107, n. 14.

21 « Incipiunt Rubrice litterarum seu scripturarum tangentium de negotiis Tartarorum partium ultramarinarum et infidelium ac scismaticorum tempore felicis recordationis Clementis v. Iohannis xxii. Benedicti xii. et Clementis vi. per eos missarum et receptarum ». Vatican Archives, *Vatican Register* (*RV*) *62*, fol. 1*r.

The register consists of 5 parts. At the beginning (folios 1*-4*) there is a brief introduction to the volume and a table of contents which lists the letters under topical headings. The main body of the volume (folios 1-97) consists of 191 letters or parts of letters relating to the theme of papal concern with the peoples of the frontier. There are 3 letters from the registers of Clement V (folios 1-4), 33 letters from those of John XXII (folios 5-28), 17 of Benedict XII's letters (folios 29-35), and 138 letters (folios 40-97) from the registers of Clement VI. The third section (folios 100-124) contains a lengthy criticism of erroneous doctrines and practices attributed to the Armenian Church which Benedict XII compiled as part of an attempt to reconcile the schismatic Armenians with Rome [22]. The last two sections contain letters from the East to various popes. There are seven letters (folios 126-139) from Byzantine Emperors and 3 letters (folios 139-143) from the king of Armenia.

The compiler did not identify himself, nor did he indicate when or why he compiled the volume. Because the fourth section contains letters addressed to Innocent VI (1352-1362), the volume must have been compiled some time in the later years of his pontificate or after. One scholar suggested that it may have been compiled in the reign of Urban V (1362-1370), perhaps after the pope returned to Rome in October 1367 and where he remained until August of 1370 [23]. Another possibility is that it was compiled during the years 1377-1378 when Gregory XI had returned to Rome. The register is associated with the return to Rome because it was customary for the curia to carry only some volumes of the registers from earlier pontificates with the popes as they moved from place to place [24]. Vatican Register 62 may have been compiled in connection with the papal return to Rome in order to provide Urban V or Gregory XI with a guide to what his predecessors at Avignon had done with regard to the borderlands of Europe. Urban himself had a strong interest in reunion with the eastern church which culminated in the short-lived reunion which he negotiated with John V Paleologus when that emperor visited Rome in October 1369 [25]. Any pope who planned to remain in Rome would need basic working files, copies of actions

22 « Rubrice plurimorum articolorum erroneorum quos Armeni tenere dicuntur ». *Ibid.*, fol. 120v.

23 GAY, pp. 8-9.

24 BOYLE, pp. 7-8. The number of this volume in the series of Vatican Registers is irrelevant to the question of when it was compiled because the enumeration of the volumes as they presently stand came only long after the individual volumes were compiled. *RV 62* stands between the last register of Clement V (*RV 61*) and the first register of John XXII (*RV 63*), a location that is clearly not indicative of when it was compiled.

25 MOLLAT, *The Popes at Avignon*, p. 58; OSKAR HALECKI, *Un empereur de Byzance à Rome*, Warsaw 1930; reprint ed., London 1972.

which his predecessors had taken, until the complete collection of registers could be brought to Rome[26].

A second reason for compiling this register may have been to encourage a pope who planned to return to Rome, or who had actually returned, to reassert the universal mission of the papacy which was especially linked with the city of Rome. Seen in this way, the letters were compiled to remind the pope that the sense of universal responsibility that had marked the great pontificates of the thirteenth century had not died in Avignon and should be renewed in conjunction with the return to Rome.

Although the compiler did not identify himself, the very existence of a volume of letters such as this indicates that he would have been an important member of the papal staff. He mentioned at various places in the register that he compiled the volume by examining the copies of letters which were kept in the chests that contained the papal files[27]. This indicates a person of some position within the court. In addition, the fact that he could arrange for the copying of letters indicates something about his standing.

The recipients of the letters found in Vatican Register 62 comprised a broad cross-section of secular and ecclesiastical figures. The major Christian rulers, the emperor of Constantinople, the kings of Armenia, Georgia, England, France, Castile, Portugal, Aragon and Poland, along with members of their families, were represented. Other letters went to potential converts such as the Mongol khans and the dukes of the Lithuanians. The attempt to undertake yet another crusade brought letters to the leaders of Genoa and Venice whose assistance was vital to the success of any plan to halt the Turkish drive to the west. Finally the register contains a number of letters to missionaries, generally Franciscans and Dominicans, working in various parts of the world.

Vatican Register 62 provides an interesting insight into the way in which the frontiers of Europe appeared to a member of the papal court about the middle of the fourteenth century. The compiler clearly selected the documents which he included according to some principles of selection. He did after all indicate that he did not include all the relevant documents which related to the theme, only some of them. Because of this unique insight into the world view of the Avignon papacy that this register provides, it is curious that it has not received much attention. Its existence has long been known. Raynaldus cited it in his continuation of Baronius' *Annales Eccle-*

---

26 Concerning proposals to return the papacy to Rome, see MOLLAT, *The Popes at Avignon*, pp. 154-160.

27 « Ideo supradicte littere de dicto coffro hic sunt posite. Est etiam sciendum quod in dicto coffro sunt alie multe littere ... ». *RV 62*, fol. 4*r-4*v. « Supradicte littere sunt extracte de Archivo ecclesie Romane et fuerunt reposite in quodam coffro ». *Ibid.*, fol. 139r. For a brief discussion of these chests, see GAY, p. 10.

*siastici* in the seventeenth century, as did Luke Wadding in his history of the Franciscans. They cited it, however, only as a source which contained papal letters that were also available in the original registers. Early in the twentieth century, Jules Gay used the register as part of a study of the eastern policy of Clement VI. He observed, correctly, that the register only provided a partial list of letters from Clement's reign that concerned the East, so that he moved from this register to a broader study of Clement's policy [28].

The present study will look at Vatican Register 62 as an integral whole which reflects the papal conception of its responsibilities toward those who lived along the frontiers of Christendom and those who were outside the Church. This is by no means a complete study of the Avignon papacy's relations with those who were not members of the Latin Church. Much more research will have to be done before such a study can be written. The present work is a contribution toward the writing of that larger work.

# I

## PAPAL RESPONSIBILITY FOR ALL MEN

### 1. The Theory of Universal Papal Responsibility

The letters in Vatican Register 62 expressed the papacy's conception of its role in the world with a body of phrases that had a long history. The ideas which these phrases expressed had received their most famous exposition in Boniface VIII's *Unam sanctam* issued in 1302 [1]. Their use in the fourteenth century was not due to a desire to rehabilitate Boniface's memory or to an intention to criticize Philip the Fair. It was due to the legal training of the popes and their staffs. When papal officials drafted letters they naturally drew from the same intellectual wells from which Boniface VIII had drawn. In his turn, Boniface had drawn on a body of ideas and a special language for expressing those ideas that had emerged in the wake of the Gregorian reform movement. The form in which Boniface had expressed these ideas had been created in the early decades of the thirteenth century as canon lawyers came

[28] GAY, p. 10.

[1] The basic introduction to Boniface VIII's intellectual formation is JEAN RIVIÈRE, *Le problème de l'église et de l'état au temps de Philippe le Bel*, Louvain and Paris 1926. The best full-length study of Boniface VIII in English remains T. S. R. BOASE, *Boniface VIII*, London 1933. For a convenient introduction to the literature of the conflict between the pope and the king of France, see *Philip the Fair and Boniface VIII* (European Problem Studies, ed. CHARLES T. WOOD), 2nd ed., New York 1971.

to dominate the papacy. The language of the papacy was increasingly the language of the canonists.

The guiding theme of the Gregorian movement was the unity of the Church. The Church was one body, the body of Christ, with one head, Christ, whose vicar, the pope, acted for Him in this world. From this theological analogy came the papal claim to be the chief judge and universal ordinary of the Church. In this way, a theological concept was translated into an administrative reality[2]. During the thirteenth century, the canonist-popes brought the development of the papacy as a juridical institution to its peak. The result was the perfection of the papal administrative and bureaucratic structure which implemented the decisions of the pope acting as judge.

The success of the papacy in gaining control over the episcopate and its partial success in gaining control over secular rulers blinded the popes to changes that were occurring within European society. Intellectually, the papacy had opposed its ideology of ecclesiastical unity under the pope to the competing ideology of a universal empire under one emperor[3]. The intensity with which this battle was fought during the thirteenth century caused the papacy to concentrate its efforts on this ideological conflict to the exclusion of other political developments. Because the papal-imperial controversy occurred at the same time as the canonistic expression of the papacy's role was being formulated, the political language of the papal court considered only universal political claims, not provincial ones[4].

---

[2] The stress that the Gregorian reform movement placed on ecclesiastical unity is clearly illustrated in the *Dictatus papae,* a document from the pontificate of Gregory VII. The text of the *Dictatus papae* is available in a number of collections of documents; for example, *The Crisis of Church and State, 1050-1300,* ed. Brian Tierney, Englewood Cliffs, New Jersey 1964, pp. 49-50. Two convenient introductions to the literature of the Gregorian reform movement are: *The Gregorian Epoch: Reformation, Revolution, Reaction?* (Problems in European Civilization, ed. Schafer Williams), Boston 1964; and *The Investiture Controversy* (European Problems Studies, ed. Karl F. Morison), New York 1971.

[3] The development of papal legal and political thought during the twelfth and thirteenth centuries has been widely studied in recent years. At the heart of the modern debate lies the question of what the popes and the canon lawyers thought was the right relationship between the spiritual and the temporal powers. Two useful introductions to the literature, both by Brian Tierney, are: *Some Recent Works on the Political Theories of the Medieval Canonists*: Traditio 10 (1954) 594-625; and *The Continuity of Papal Political Theory in the Thirteenth Century: Some Methodological Considerations*: Mediaeval Studies 27 (1965) 227-245. Much of the scholarly debate about the papacy's aims has centered on the work of Walter Ullmann who has argued that the papacy sought the creation of a theocratic Christian state. For an extensive and highly critical analysis of Ullmann's views, see Francis Oakley, *Celestial Hierarchies Revisited: Walter Ullmann's Vision of Medieval Politics*: Past & Present, no. 60 (August 1973) 3-48.

[4] During the thirteenth century, some lawyers began to recognize the independence of kings from the emperor or from any other secular ruler. Such a king was a *rex imperator in regno suo.* On the development of this concept, see Gaines Post, *Studies in Medieval Legal Thought,* Princeton 1964, pp. 453-482; and Helmut G. Walther, *Imperiales Königtum, Konziliarismus und Volkssouveränität. Studien zu den Grenzen des mittelalterlichen Souveränitätsgedankens,* Munich, 1976, pp. 65-111.

As a result of the papal failure to grasp the nature of the shift in European politics that was taking place toward the end of the thirteenth century, Boniface VIII could only respond to the limited claims of Philip the Fair in the language of universal responsibility which had been developed in the struggle with the Holy Roman Empire. *Unam sanctam* therefore missed the point of the French king's challenge. It contained a re-statement of papal views about the nature of the Church and the relationship between the spiritual and temporal powers that did not respond to the claims that the French were making[5]. Philip the Fair was not challenging Boniface for domination of Christian society, he was seeking the more limited goal of sovereignty in France.

When Boniface began *Unam sanctam* with the assertion that there is but « one holy, catholic and apostolic Church », he inadvertently admitted that he did not grasp the problem facing him. The remainder of *Unam sanctam* developed the implications of the opening statement, employing the legal language that had been developed by the canonists of the preceding century. Boniface went on to explain that « outside the Church there is no salvation », a point which was irrelevant to Philip's interests. In fact Philip would no doubt have agreed with the statement, as he could have agreed with the statement that the Church forms the mystical body of Christ and that there is « one God, one faith, one baptism ». Boniface supported these arguments about the fundamental unity of the Church with a number of standard references drawn from the Bible, comparing the Church to Noah's ark and to the seamless cloak which Christ wore[6].

From the unity of the mystical body of Christ flowed the pope's authority. Christ, the Head of the Body, gave responsibility for the care of His people, the remaining parts of His body, to Peter and

---

5 On the debt of *Unam sanctam* to the legal thought of the preceding century, see JAMES MULDOON, *Boniface VIII's Forty Years of Experience in the Law*: The Jurist 31 (1971) 449-477. The text of the bull can be found in TIERNEY, *The Crisis*, pp. 188-189.

6 « Unam sanctam ecclesiam catholicam et ipsam apostolicam urgente fide credere cogimur et tenere ... extra quam nec salus est ... 'Una est matri suae, electa genetrici suae', quae unum corpus mysticum repraesentat, cuius caput Christus Christi vero Deus. In qua unus Dominus, una Fides, unum baptisma. Una nempe fuit diluvii tempore arca Noe, unam ecclesiam praefigurans ... Pro anima enim, id est pro se ipso, capite simul oravit et corpore, quod corpus unicam scilicet ecclesiam nominavit, propter sponsi, fidei, sacramentorum et caritatis ecclesiae unitatem. Haec est tunica illa Domini inconsutilis, quae scissa non fuit, sed sorte provenit. Igitur ecclesiae unius et unicae unum corpus, unum caput, non duo capita, quasi monstrum. Christus videlicet et Christi vicarius Petrus, Petrique successor, dicente Domino ipsi Petro: 'Pasce oves meas'. Meas, inquit, et generaliter, non singulariter has vel illas, per quod commisisse sibi intelligitur universas. Sive ergo Graeci sive alii se dicant Petro eiusque successoribus non esse commissos: fateantur necesse se de ovibus Christi non esse, dicente Domino in Ioanne, unum ovile et unicum esse pastorem ». *Corpus iuris canonici*, ed. E. FRIEDBERG (2 v., Leipzig, 1879-1881) 2: *Extravagantes communes*, 1.8.1., *Unam sanctam.*

his successors. Then, lest the point not be completely clear, Boniface VIII switched to the well known analogy of the shepherd and the flock. The pope's responsibility for the souls of men made him the shepherd while the Christian community formed the flock. Boniface added that no one who professed to be a Christian could truly deny his subordination to the pope who took the place of Christ on earth. As a result, he argued, those like the Greeks who rejected papal supremacy were not really members of the Church although they falsely claimed to be Christians.

In the last half of *Unam sanctam* Boniface drew a series of conclusions about the relations between the spiritual and the temporal powers which he derived from the unity of the Church. Here again, he used a very traditional set of images and arguments to prove the correctness of his opinions about the nature of the papal relationship with the kingdom of France.

When at the request of Philip the Fair Clement V revoked the acts of Boniface VIII, he was careful not to reject the principles on which Boniface acted, only some of the conclusions. The letter *Meruit* which Clement issued concerning *Unam sanctam* simply stated that Boniface's bull had in no way changed the relation that should exist between the papacy and the French[7]. The basic statements about the nature of the Church, the unity of Christian society, and the impossibility of salvation *extra ecclesiam* remained valid because these principles had been the basis on which earlier popes had dealt with Philip's predecessors.

Therefore, when the popes at Avignon found it necessary to explain the nature of the Church to schismatics and infidels along the frontiers of Europe they continued to use the language that Boniface had used. When for example, John XXII wrote to the Georgians in 1321 about the nature of the Church in order to secure their reunion with Rome, his letter restated many of the general themes found in *Unam sanctam* together with many of the biblical images which Boniface had used. In the letter the pope stressed the unity of the Church, a unity from which the schismatic Georgians had severed themselves. The true Church had but one head, Christ, whose vicar, the pope, acted for Him on earth[8]. Responding to the

---

[7] « Hinc est, quod nos regi et regno per definitionem et declarationem bonae memoriae Bonifacii Papae VIII. praedecessoris nostri, quae incipit: 'Unam sanctam', nullum volumus vel intendimus praeiudicium generari. Nec quod per illam rex, regnum et regnicolae praelibati amplius ecclesiae sint subiecti Romanae, quam antea exsistebant; sed omnia intelligantur in eodem esse statu, quo erant ante definitionem praefatam tam quantum ad ecclesiam, quam etiam ad regem, regnum et regnicolas superius nominatos ». *Ibid.*, 5.7.2., *Meruit*.

[8] Originally the pope was described as the Vicar of Peter, but during the twelfth century this term was gradually replaced by the term Vicar of Christ: MICHELE MACCARRONE, *Vicarius Christi. Storia del Titolo Papale*, Rome 1952; see also, WALTER ULLMANN, *The Growth of Papal Government in the Middle Ages*, 2nd ed., London 1962, pp. 428-430.

argument that the schismatic church could exist under its own patriarch, John XXII used the same analogy that Boniface had used in a similar context in *Unam sanctam.* If a schismatic church claimed such independence it would be equivalent to arguing that the body of Christ had two heads. Expanding on the biblical references which Boniface had employed, John XXII reminded the Georgians that all men spring from the one Adam and were redeemed by the one Christ. Schism amputates a limb of this body which leads to the spiritual death of the schismatic community, just as an amputated limb dies when cut off from the rest of a human body[9].

Although no other letter recorded in Vatican Register 62 contained as many of the phrases found in *Unam sanctam* as did John XXII's letter to the Georgians, these phrases do appear scattered through the remaining letters. The most widely repeated image was that of the Church as the flock of Christ and the pope as the terrestrial shepherd. The schismatic rulers of the East often received letters with this image as part of the papal policy of seeking reunion. Benedict XII reminded the King of Armenia that the pope is « the universal Pastor of the Lord's flock », representing Christ « whose sheep are committed to our care »[10]. Papal responsibility even extended to « those who had wandered away from the flock », meaning schismatics and infidels, as well as those within the church[11].

---

9 « Nempe orthodoxorum neminem credimus non latere, unum esse in terris caput tantummodo ex quo totum corpus contexitur militantis ecclesiae, rerum id exigente natura, que corpus si habuerint duo capita iudicat monstruosum ... unus Adam deputatus ad opus et custodiam paradysi unam est sortitus uxorem unum dominum Iesum Christum in iustitia et veritatis sinceritate creatum eiusdem unum in terris vicarium et unicam eius sponsam ecclesiam prefigurans ... qui ecclesiam scindunt occidunt animas parvulorum. Deinde salutis archam tantum unam fuisse legimus ... quod in ovili suo unus tantum debeat esse pastor ... Unde schismaticos et ab unitate corporis Ecclesiae per inobedientiam recedentes notans vitandosque insinuans ait: Nemo vos seducat ... ipse Christus sit pastor ecclesie atque caput ... ut quo caput ibat membra se itura sperarent, ne corpus peregrinantis ecclesie propter corporalem ipsius absentiam videatur acephalum remanere sibi successorem vicarium substituit specialem ». John XXII, *Cum simus,* October 15, 1321: *RV 62,* fols. 5v-6r; *Acta Ioannis XXII (1317-1334)* (Pontificia Commissio ad redigendum codicem iuris canonici orientalis, Fontes, ser. 3, v. 7, pt. 2), ed. ALOYSIUS L. TĂUTU, Rome 1952, no. 46 (pp. 89-93) at p. 89-90; MOLLAT, *Lettres communes,* no. 16093. Innocent IV had sent the same letter to the king of the Bulgarians in 1245: Innocent IV, *Cum simus,* March 21, 1245, *Acta Innocentii PP. IV (1243-1254)* (Pont. Comm... orientalis, Fontes, ser. 3, v. 4, pt. 1), ed. T. T. HALUŠČYNSKYJ and M. M. WOJNAR, Rome 1962, no. 20, pp. 43-48.

The texts of the letters contained in *RV 62* are written here as they appear in the register. There are often minor differences between the way the texts read in *RV 62* and in modern editions. Where there are several printed editions of a letter contained in *RV 62,* the most recent edition is cited here unless otherwise indicated.

10 « ... porro quia nos tamquam pastor universalis gregis dominici oves dominicas cure nostre commissas ... ». Benedict XII, *Quamvis dilecti filii,* August 1, 1341: *RV 62,* fols. 34r-35v at fol. 34v; *Acta Benedicti XII (1334-1342)* (Pont. Comm. ... orientalis, Fontes, ser. 3, v. ), ed. ALOYSIUS L. TĂUTU, Rome 1958, no. 55, pp. 114-116; *Benoît XII (1334-1342): Lettres closes et patentes intéressant le pays autres que la France,* ed. J.-M. VIDAL and G. MOLLAT (2 v., Paris 1913-1950), no. 3149.

11 « ... premissis igitur per eundem militem apostolatui nostro expositis, nos qui summi et eterni pastoris qui pro suis ovibus animam posuit vices licet immeriti ge-

Even the infidels could not claim exemption from papal jurisdiction. The image of the flock was capable of extension to them. As John XXII informed the Tartars, the pope was responsible for every « single human being outside the Holy Roman Church ... and for leading the ignorant and those who had wandered from the flock into the fold »[12]. Although Boniface VIII had not mentioned papal responsibility for the souls of infidels in *Unam sanctam*, as a canonist he knew that the image of the flock had been extended to include them by Pope Innocent IV. In a commentary which he wrote in his capacity as a canon lawyer, Innocent IV pointed out that Christ had spoken to the apostles of other sheep which He had which were not of this flock, a statement which the pope took to mean that those outside of the Church were also the sheep of Christ for whom His vicar was responsible[13]. In his capacity as pope, Innocent IV wrote to the Mongols asserting his responsibility for their salvation in terms derived from the conception of the pope's powers which he had developed as a canonist[14]. Later canonists incorporated this extension of the image of the flock to include infidels in the mainstream of canonistic thinking.

Other letters of the Avignon popes repeated the argument that salvation cannot be found outside of the Church, as Boniface VIII had argued. Both schismatics and infidels were informed that unless they entered the fold assigned to Christ's flock they would not be

---

rimus, oves ipsas extra ovile dominicum oberrantes, in illud reduci, ne faucibus dyaboli qui tamquam leo rugiens circuit querens quos devoret ... ». Benedict XII, *Nuper*, January 17, 1337: *RV 62*, fol. 29v; *Acta Benedicti XII*, no. 15, pp. 28-29 at p. 28; VIDAL and MOLLAT, no. 1199.

12 « Unde nos qui licet immeriti prefato beato Petro succedimus, et in regno mundi vice fungimur celestis pastoris, et domini animarum exigente officii nostri debito tenemur et totis desideriis affectamus omnem humanam creaturam extra sanctam Romanam ecclesiam existentem, fideique christiane insciam et deviam ab eadem dominici gregis inducere, ac reducere, in ovile unire et reconciliare penitus ecclesie prelibate ... ». John XXII, *Salvator noster*, October 1, 1333: *RV 62*, fols. 27²v-28v at fol. 28r [there is an error in the pagination, fol. 27 is counted twice]; *Bullarium Franciscanum*, ed. J. H. SBARALEA and CONRAD EUBEL (8 v., Rome 1759-) 5: no. 1039d, pp. 558-559 at p. 558; MOLLAT, *Lettres communes*, no. 63875.

13 « ... possessiones et iurisdictiones licite sine peccato possunt esse apud infideles. haec enim non tam pro fidelibus sed pro omni rationabili creatura facta sunt, ut est praedictum. ipse non solum solem suum oriri facit super bonos et malos. ipse etiam volatilia pascit, Matthaei. c. 5 circa nu. et 6. ... omnes autem tam fideles, quam infideles oves sunt Christi per creationem, licet non sint de ovili ecclesiae et sic per praedicta apparet quod Papa super omnes habet iurisdictionem, et potestatem de iure, licet non de facto ... ». Innocent IV, *In Quinque Libros Decretalium ... Commentaria Doctissima*, Turin 1581, 3.34.8., *Quod super his*. Concerning the development of papal and canonistic thinking about the rights of infidels, see JAMES MULDOON, « *Extra ecclesiam non est imperium* ». *The Canonists and the Legitimacy of Secular Power*: Studia Gratiana 9 (1966) 553-580.

14 Innocent IV, *Dei patris*, March 5, 1245, and *Cum non solum*, March 13, 1245, *Epistolae saeculi XIII e regestis pontificum Romanorum selectae*, ed. G. H. PERTZ and C. RODENBERG (3 v., Berlin 1883-1894) 2: nn. 102, 105, pp. 72-73, 75. English translations of these letters are available in *The Mongol Mission*, ed. CHRISTOPHER DAWSON, New York 1955; reprinted as *Mission to Asia*, New York 1966, pp. 73-76.

saved. The Armenians, for example, received a letter from John XXII reminding them that reunion with Rome was essential because « the union of all men in the unity of the orthodox faith » was absolutely necessary for salvation [15]. Benedict XII later reminded the same people that membership « in the Lord's flock, of which there is but one shepherd » was essential because outside of it « there is no grace nor any salvation for any man » [16]. Even in the letters of Clement VI which generally reflected a more pragmatic approach to the problems of dealing with those outside of the Church, the theme of papal responsibility for all men derived from the essential unity of all men under Christ was repeated. In his dealings with the Armenians he also stressed the need for the schismatics to return to « holy mother Church, outside of which there is no grace nor any salvation » [17]. Other letters to the Byzantine emperor contained the same theme [18].

The responsibility which the pope bore because of his vicariate of Christ required that he emulate Christ's efforts to make converts. As Clement VI noted, Christ « selected disciples whom he then sent throughout the entire world to preach the gospel to all men » [19]. Combining the theme of the flock of Christ with that of the Church's universal mission, John XXII was able to inform the Georgians that the pope acted for Christ, the Good Shepherd, caring for and feeding

---

15 « ... et nos quidem qui ... salutem animarum in cunctis nationibus divinitus humilitatis nostre cure commissis, accuratius exquirentes, ad unitatem omnium in orthodoxe fidei veritate, sine qua salus esse non potest et in ecclesiasticorum consonantia rituum desideranter afficimus ... ». John XXII, *Salvator noster*, November 22, 1321: *RV 62*, fols. 21r-21v at fol. 21r; *Acta Ioannis XXII*, no. 54, pp. 105-107 at p. 105; Mollat, *Lettres communes*, no. 16118.

16 « ... seque veraciter in ovili dominico cuius est unus pastor et extra quod non est alicui gratia neque salus ... ». Benedict XII, *Quamvis dilecti filii: RV 62*, fol. 34v; *Acta Benedicti XII*, p. 115.

17 « Sicut ut credimus memoria tua tenet iam dudum percepto quod Catholicon et ecclesia armenorum in fide catholica quam tenet docet et predicat sancta Romana mater ecclesia extra quam nulli est gratia nulli salus aliqualiter vacillabat ... ». Clement VI, *Sicut ut credimus*, September 14, 1351: *RV 62*, fols. 95v-96v at fol. 95v; WADDING 8: pp. 60-62 at p. 60; *Clément VI. Lettres closes, patentes et curiales intéressant les pays autres que la France*, ed. É. DÉPREZ and G. MOLLAT, Paris 1900-1961, no. 2498.

18 « ... volentes indubie et tenere quod si tu ac Grecorum clerus et populus reiecta infectione illius execrandi et damnandi scismatis quod eos damnabiliter a sacrosancta Romana ecclesia matre omnium fidelium et magistra divisit per unionem salutarem deo placabilem ... unam esse catholicam et apostolicam ecclesiam quam ipse dominus Iesus Christus in seipso lapide angulari fundavit et eius magisterium principi apostolorum beato Petro videlicet cui licet insufficientibus meritis successimus in apostolatus dignitate commisit, vos sub eodem ovili, extra quod non est alicui gratia neque salus, reducere curaretis ... ». Clement VI, *Magnificentie*, October 21, 1343: *RV 62*, fols. 44r-44v at fol. 44v; RAYNALDUS, ad ann. 1343, no. 12 (*Munificentiae*); *Clément VI. Lettres closes, patentes et curiales se rapportant à la France*, ed. E. DÉPREZ, J. GLÉNISSON and G. MOLLAT (3 v., Paris 1910-1961), no. 466.

19 « ... destinamus exemplo eius instructi qui pro salute humani generis de supernis celorum ad yma descendens discipulos quos elegit in universum orbem transmisit omni creature evangelium predicare ... ». Clement VI, *Quia corporali*, August 31, 1343: *RV 62*, fols. 51r-52r at fol. 51r; DÉPREZ, GLÉNISSON, MOLLAT, no. 340.

all of His sheep without making any distinctions among them as to whether they were actually members of the Church or not [20]. The goal of the continuous missionary endeavor was « to gather the various peoples of the earth who desire to dwell in the house of the Lord into a single people acceptable to Christ in the observance of the faith » [21].

The heavy emphasis which these letters placed on the unity of the Church led to increased stress on the pope's role in the Church. The universal mission which Christ had assigned to the popes required the development of the tools necessary to implement the mission. As a result, the strong language which the thirteenth century canonists had employed to describe the powers of the papacy was repeated in the letters of the popes at Avignon. The pope bore the *plenitudo potestatis*, the fullness of power that Christ Himself possessed [22]. He held the power to bind and loose, the power of the keys. These descriptions of the powers of the papacy undercut whatever claims to ecclesiastical independence that any eastern patriarch might claim. The patriarch of Constantinople or the Catholicos of the Armenian Church was as much a subordinate of the pope as any European bishop was. Here again, the letters of the fourteenth century popes reflect the language which the canonists had developed in the struggle to dominate the administrative structure of the western Church. Having brought the bishops of the West under papal domination, it was logical to insist that the reconciliation of the schismatics required the similar subordination of eastern bishops to the pope. Increasingly, the ultimate test of membership in the true Church was recognition of papal supremacy, the external symbol of unity.

---

[20] « ... hunc itaque suarum ovium pastorem substituens universalem in terris earundem pascendarum curam indistincte commisit eidem ... ». John XXII, *Cum simus*: *RV 62*, fol. 6r; *Acta Ioannis XXII*, p. 90.

[21] « ... variasque gentium nationes sub eiusdem observantia fidei in unum acceptabilem Christo populum congregatas in domo domini habitare ». John XXII, *Exultamus*, June 1, 1324: *RV 62*, fols. 14r-16r at fol. 14v; *Acta Ioannis XXII*, no. 76, pp. 149-155 at p. 151; Mollat, no. 20322.

[22] « Nec omittamus quod ipsa sacrosancta Romana ecclesia summum et plenum primatum et principatum super universalem catholicam ecclesiam obtinens quam se ab ipso domino in beato Petro apostolorum principe seu vertice, cuius Romanus pontifex est successor cum potestatis plenitudine recepisse veraciter et humiliter recognoscit ... ». John XXII, *Salvator noster: RV 62*, fol. 21v; *Acta Ioannis XXII*, p. 107. « ... quod solus pontifex Romanus habet plenitudinem potestatis quam beatus Petrus apostolus habebat et quod ipse pontifex Romanus solus est universalis Christi vicarius ... ». Clement VI, *Super quibusdam*, September 29, 1351: *RV 62*, fols. 89v-95r at fol. 90r; Raynaldus, ad ann. 1351, nn. 2-17 at no. 3; Déprez and Mollat, no. 2505. Concerning the development of the concept of *plenitudo potestatis*, see Robert L. Benson, *Plenitudo potestatis: Evolution of a Formula from Gregory IV to Gratian*: Studia Gratiana 14 (1967) 193-217; and Gerhart B. Ladner, *The Concepts of 'Ecclesia' and 'Christianitas' and their Relation to the Idea of Papal 'Plenitudo Potestatis' from Gregory VII to Boniface VIII*, in *Sacerdozio e Regno da Gregorio VII a Bonifacio VIII* (Miscellanea Historiae Pontificiae, 18), Rome 1954, pp. 49-77.

From recognition of the pope's supremacy flowed the papal role as ultimate judge of what constituted orthodox doctrine. As several letters pointed out, acceptance of papal supremacy meant the acceptance of Christian doctrine « as the Roman Church holds and teaches it »[23]. Clement VI stated the papal power even more bluntly when he wrote that « the Roman Church whose head is the Roman pope, is the only catholic [universal] church and in it alone is true salvation and the one true faith »[24]. Those who did not enter the fold over which the pope presides are doomed to wander in darkness, like sheep lost in the night[25].

Finally, membership in the true flock of Christ required acceptance of the Latin ritual in the administration of the sacraments. This emphasis on uniformity in ritual practices was another aspect of these letters that was rooted in the Gregorian reform. Early in his pontificate, Gregory VII (1073-1085) wrote to the king of Leon and Castile requesting him to impose the Latin rite on the churches in his kingdom. « May you, like the other kingdoms of the west and north, accept the order and ritual of the Roman Church—not those of Toledo nor any other but of that Church which was founded by Peter and Paul ... »[26]. The use of the ritual used in the pope's own church in Rome was to be the symbol of the links between every church throughout the world with the pope and, therefore, with the true flock of Christ.

Because unity of ritual had become the external sign of subordination to the pope, the use of a different liturgy was necessarily the sign of rebellion against Christ's vicar. When Rome insisted on the use of the Latin rite by those schismatics who did return to the fold, it did so in order to symbolize the fact of reunion in every parish church. In the letters contained in Vatican Register 62, discus-

[23] « ... quam ad Nos et sacrosanctam Romanam ecclesiam matrem omnium fidelium et magistram fidemque catholicam sine qua salus non est alicui geritis quodque in eadem fide prout eam dicta Romana ecclesia tenet et predicat desideratis instrui et confirmari percepimus evidenter ... ». Benedict XII, *Serena facie*, June 13, 1338: *RV 62*, fols. 32r-32v at fol. 32v; *Acta Benedicti XII*, no. 25, pp. 44-48 at p. 44; VIDAL, no. 1869. « ... quod sicut sacrosancta Romana ecclesia mater fidelium omnium et magistra tenet et docet ... ». Clement VI, *Inter cetera*, September 1, 1351: *RV 62*, fols. 97v-98r at fol. 97v; RAYNALDUS, ad ann. 1351, nn. 20-21 at no. 20; DÉPREZ and MOLLAT, no. 2490.

[24] « ... quod eadem ecclesia Romana cuius summus Pontifex est Papa Romanus est sola catholica et in ea sola est vera salus et una vera fides et unum baptisma et vera remissio peccatorum ... ». Clement VI, *Super quibusdam: RV 62*, fol. 89v; RAYNALDUS, ad ann. 1351, no. 3.

[25] « ... ut tu et eadem Armenie ecclesia non in tenebris sed in luce ad illas pure et simpliciter respondentes effecti lucis filii illius luminis veri de lumine ... omnem hominem venientem in hunc mundum illuminat ... ». *Ibid.: RV 62*, fol. 89v; RAYNALDUS, ad ann. 1351, no. 2.

[26] *The Correspondence of Pope Gregory VII*, ed. EPHRAIM EMERTON, New York 1932; reprint ed., 1966, lib. 1, no. 64, p. 29. Gregory VII was less willing to allow the use of languages other than Latin in the liturgy than many of his predecessors had been and than many of his successors would prove to be: see CYRIL KOROLEVSKY, *Living Languages in Catholic Worship*, trans. Donald Attwater, London 1957, p. 85.

sion of the need for uniformity of ritual was emphasized in several places. John XXII sent the Armenians a letter of instruction concerning the proper administration of the sacraments of confirmation and extreme unction, stressing the need for the Armenians to follow the Roman rite in these matters [27]. When Benedict XII wrote to the Mongol khans about extending imperial protection to missionaries and their converts, he specified that he was requesting this for those « churches, monasteries and chapels in which the works praising God are performed according to the ritual and practice of the Roman Church » [28]. Infidel rulers, like Christian ones, were expected to support the papacy's efforts to insure uniformity of ritual everywhere.

The constant repetition of the phrases which Boniface VIII and his thirteenth century predecessors used to describe the unity of the Church in the letters of fourteenth century popes demonstrates that the fourteenth century popes thought of themselves and their mission in the same way as the thirteenth century popes had done. They did not narrow their range of vision to the small world of Avignon, nor did they see themselves in a lesser role than the universal role of an Innocent III or Boniface VIII. In rejecting the particular application of the theme of ecclesiastical unity which Boniface VIII had made in regard to the kingdom of France, his fourteenth century successors continued to assert the same general claims to universal authority that he had made in *Unam sanctam.* It is instructive to realize that *Unam sanctam* was eventually included in an unofficial collection of decretals, the *Extravagantes communes* which was published in its final form in 1503 and later included with the other volumes that comprise the *Corpus iuris canonici* [29]. In spite of what *Meruit* may seem to say, Boniface VIII's formulation of the papacy's claims to universal responsibility for the souls of men continued to inspire his successors.

---

27 « ... et nos quidem qui ... gerimus vices eius in terris salutem animarum in cunctis nationibus divinitus humilitatis nostre cure commissis accuratius exquirentes ad unitatem omnium in orthodoxe fidei veritate sine qua salus esse non potest et in ecclesiasticorum consonantia rituum desideranter afficimur et quanto sincerius delectamur in unione huiusmodi tanto nimirum intentius quamlibet in illa dissidentiam detestamur ... ». John XXII, *Salvator noster: RV 62,* fol. 21r; *Acta Ioannis XXII,* p. 105.

28 « Nos tam ex hiis quam de missione nunciorum ipsorum admodum nobis grata tibi referentes gratiarum uberes actiones magnitudinem tuam rogamus attentius et hortamur, quatenus benevolentiam et favores huiusmodi erga prefatos Alanorum principes et alios christicolas in eodem Imperio commorantes continuare pro nostra et ecclesie predicte reverentia velit tua sublimitas et augere, et ut antistites et religiosi catholici et christiani alii ecclesias basilicas et oratora in quibus iuxta ritum et morem supradicte Romane ecclesie divine laudis peragantur officia, et offeratur pro delictis et peccatis populi hostia salutaris ... ». Benedict XII, *Celsitudinis tue,* June 13, 1338: *RV 62,* fols. 30r-30v at fol. 30v; Wadding, 7: pp. 249-250 at p. 249; Vidal and Mollat, no. 1864.

29 Concerning the development of these decretal collections, see Le Bras, pp. 252-256; Ourliac and Gilles, p. 138.

## 2. Practice — The Powers of the Missionaries

The general concept of the papacy's responsibility for all men as the fourteenth century popes expressed it was that which *Unam sanctam* had summarized, a view which the thirteenth century popes and canonists had formulated. The practical applications of these general principles appeared in several letters addressed to missionaries and papal legates who were sent to the various infidel and schismatic peoples [30]. Like the letters which presented the papal view of its responsibilities, the letters to missionaries were also derived from thirteenth century models.

The basic instructions for missionaries were contained in the bull *Cum hora undecima*, a bull that Gregory IX had first issued in 1235 and that was reissued in an expanded version during the remainder of the thirteenth century by several other popes. Although both Clement V and John XXII reissued the bull in the early fourteenth century, Vatican Register 62 contains only the version which John XXII issued in 1321. This was virtually identical with the expanded version of the one that Innocent IV had issued in 1245 and which Alexander IV, Urban IV, Nicholas IV, and Benedict XI had subsequently reissued [31].

The opening lines of the bull reflected the Apocalyptic tradition which was strong among the Franciscans in the early years of the Order's establishment [32]. Gregory IX and the other popes who reissued the bull reminded the missionaries that « since the eleventh hour has come in the day given to mankind ... it is necessary that spiritual men [possessing] purity of life and the gift of intelligence should go forth with John [the Baptist] again to all men and all peoples of every tongue and in every kingdom to prophesy because, according to the prophet Isaias, the salvation of the remnant of Israel will not occur until, as St. Paul says, the *plenitudo gentium* enters first » into the kingdom of heaven [33]. The task of the mis-

---

30 There is a useful survey of medieval missionary activity in Kenneth Scott Latourette, *A History of the Expansion of Christianity* (7 v., New York, 1937-1945), v. 2, *The Thousand Years of Uncertainty*, New York 1938.

31 The various editions of *Cum hora undecima* have been published by the Pontificia Commissio ad redigendum Codicem Iuris Canonici Orientalis: Fontes, ser. 3 (Vatican City): *Acta Honorii III (1216-1227) et Gregorii IX (1227-1241)*, ed., Aloysius L. Tăutu (1950), no. 210, pp. 286-287; *Acta Innocentii PP IV*, no. 19, pp. 36-42; *Acta Alexandri P.P. IV* (1254-1261), ed. T. T. Haluščynskyj and M. M. Wojnar (1966), no. 38, p. 73; *Acta Urbani IV, Clementis IV, Gregorii X (1261-1276)*, ed., Aloysius L. Tăutu (1953), no. 7, pp. 26-28; *Acta Romanorum Pontificum ab Innocentio V ad Benedictum XI (1276-1304)*, ed. F M. Delorme and A. L. Tăutu (1954), no. 79, pp. 142-144; no. 110, pp. 184-185; no. 153, pp. 252-255; *Acta Ioannis XXII*, no. 48, pp. 94-98. Clement V's version of the bull is in the *Bullarium Franciscanum*, 5: no. 84, p. 35.

32 Concerning the place of apocalyptic thinking in the early history of the Franciscans, see E. Randolph Daniel, *The Franciscan Concept of Mission in the High Middle Ages*, Lexington, Kentucky 1975, pp. 76-100.

33 « Cum hora undecima sit diei hominibus, ut exeant ad opus usque ad mundi

sionaries was to fulfill Christ's injunction to preach the gospel to all men so that the process of salvation might be completed as the Apocalypse described it. They were to strengthen those Christians whose faith was weak, to correct the false doctrines of heretics and to bring the non-believers to the fold. In order to facilitate the work of the missionaries, Gregory IX granted them a number of special privileges, including the right to hear confessions anywhere, to absolve excommunicates, to dispense converts from various kinds of irregularities, probably referring to minor impediments to marriage, and generally to ease the way to the fold for those outside of it [34].

When Innocent IV reissued *Cum hora undecima* ten years later, he gave it the form which it was to retain, save for some minor additions and modifications, in the later reissues of the bull. The difference between Innocent IV's version of the bull and that of Gregory IX lay in the amount of specific detail which was added. The new version spelled out the powers of the missionaries more precisely. In the first place, the salutation of the later version listed eighteen peoples to whom the Franciscans and Dominicans were sent, in addition to being sent generally to preach to the Saracens and pagans. The list included the various schismatic peoples of the East, Greeks, Bulgarians, Georgians, and Armenians. Reflecting perhaps Innocent IV's personal interest in the Asian mission, the letter also mentioned missionaries concerned with the Nestorians, Alans and the peoples of India, probably a reference to the Nestorians of the Malabar coast. Finally, the letter made reference to friars working in Africa among the Ethiopians and Nubians as well [35].

The body of the letter retained the apocalyptic opening that Gregory IX had used, but went on to clarify the precise nature and extent of the powers granted to the missionaries. Where the earlier

---

vesperam deputati et illud Apocalypsis eulogium cito credatur cum matris Ecclesiae consolatione complendum, videlicet oportere viros spiritualis vitae munditiam et intelligentiae gratiam cum Iohanne sortitos populis et gentibus, linguis regibusque multis denuo prophetare, quod non sequitur reliquiarum Israel per Isaiam prophetata salvatio, nisi iuxta Paulum Apostolum prius introeat gentium plenitudo ... ». *Acta Honorii III ... et Gregorii IX*, p. 286.

34 « ... per exhortationem vestram converti ad unitatem christianae fidei cupientes, recipere, baptizare ac aggregare filiis Ecclesiae sacrosanctae, audire confessiones, iniungere poenitentias salutares, sed et cum consilio dioecesanorum, si catholici et praesentes fuerint, excommunicatos, iuxta Ecclesiae formam, absolvere, cum irregularibus in illis casibus in quibus solent Legati Sedis Apostolicae dispensare et eos, qui quomodolibet a fide vel unitate Romanae Ecclesiae discesserunt, si redire voluerint ... satisfacere pro commissis, reconciliare et ab anathematis vinculo, quo tenentur, absolvere valeatis ... ». *Ibid.*, p. 287.

35 « Dilectis filiis fratribus de Ordine Fratrum Minorum in terras Saracenorum, Paganorum, Graecorum, Bulgarorum, Cumanorum, Ethyoporum, Syrorum, Iberorum, Alanorum, Gazarorum, Gothorum, Zicorum, Ruthenorum, Jacobinorum, Nubianorum, Nestorinorum, Georgianorum, Armenorum, Indorum, Mesolitorum aliarumque infidelium nationum Orientis seu quarumcumque aliarum partium proficiscentibus ... ». *Acta Innocentii PP. IV*, p. 36.

letter referred to « irregularities » from which the friars could dispense converts, Innocent IV specified certain irregularities connected with the reception of holy orders among schismatic clergy which might impede their reconciliation with Rome. The irregularities involved were technical ones, such as the age at which orders had been received. The pope assumed that the proper form of ordination had been employed so that schismatic clergy who submitted to Rome could be allowed to continue as priests [36]. Innocent IV's letter also considered the question of irregularities connected with marriage law. Schismatics or infidels who had contracted marriage within the degrees of consanguinity or affinity that were forbidden by canon law, but not forbidden by natural law, that is the third and fourth degrees, were not to be held to the provisions of the Church law that required dispensation before entering into such a marriage [37].

John XXII's reissue of *Cum hora undecima* repeated Innocent IV's version almost verbatim. It is ironic that John XXII continued to open the letter with the apocalyptic language of the thirteenth century Franciscans when his problem with the extreme wing of the Franciscan order is recalled [38]. The list of regions and peoples to whom the missionaries were sent remained the same, except for the omission of the Ethiopians and Syrians [39]. The additions included two new provisions of some interest. Those who visited the churches of the friars in the missionary lands and who went to confession could receive the same indulgence as did those who went on crusade. The second clause allowed the friars to hold property in spite of Boniface VIII's constitutions on the matter [40].

---

36 « Vobis praeterea dispensare liceat ... qui post susceptionem sacrorum ordinum vel in gradibus vel casibus a divina minime lege prohibitis matrimonia contraxerunt, remaneant in eisdem et hii, qui ad Ecclesiae catholicae redierint unitatem, ut inter suos habitent eisque communicent nec non, quod clerici nationum ipsarum, publice ad oboedientiam Sedis apostolicae redeuntes, gaudeant privilegio clericali ». *Ibid.*, p. 38

37 « ... et illis, qui de gentibus vel scismaticis noviter sunt conversi, dandi licentiam, ut uxores suas, cum quibus in gradibus a lege divina non prohibitis contraxerunt, valeant retinere ». *Ibid.*

38 MOLLAT, *The Popes at Avignon*, pp. 15-17; DANIEL, pp. 88-89.

39 There is another difference in the lists, but this may be a clerical error. Where Innocent IV's letter referred to missionaries working « in terras ... Mesolitorum », John XXII's letter reads « in terras ... Moclitorum ». John XXII, *Cum hora undecima*, October 23, 1321: *RV 62*, fols. 7r-8r at fol. 7r. The *Acta Ioannis XXII* has « in terras ... Mochlitarum », pp. 94-95; MOLLAT, no. 16102.

40 « ... vobis et cuilibet vestrum vere penitentibus et confessis illam indulgentiam presentium authoritate concedimus quam proficiscentibus in terre sancte subsidium sedes apostolica concedere consuevit, ac nichilominus ... omnibus vere penitentibus et confessis qui ecclesias et loca fratrum dicti vestri ordinis in partibus premissis constructa et in posterum construenda ... Centum dies de iniunctis eis penitentiis misericorditer relaxamus ... concedimus ut in Civitatibus ... ad habitandum domos ac loca quecunque de novo recipere seu hactenus recepta mutare aut ea venditionis ... aut cuiusvis alienationis titulo in alios transferre ... non obstante prohibitione felicis recordationis Bonifacii pape viii ... ». *Ibd.*: *RV 62*, fol. 8r; *Acta Ioannis XXII*, p. 97.

The development of the bull *Cum hora undecima* reflected the debt of the popes at Avignon to their thirteenth century predecessors for guidance in directing missionary activities. There is no indication that the three-quarters of a century of dealing with the schismatics and infidels gave the papacy any greater insight into the nature of the problems of missionary work than Innocent IV had possessed. In his turn, Innocent IV had relied upon the work of his predecessors. The treatment of marriage law in *Cum hora undecima* for example was derived from a decision which Pope Innocent III (1198-1216) had made concerning the marriages of Moslems in the Holy Land who became Christians. In the decretal *Gaudemus*, Innocent III had outlined the concessions that could be made with regard to marriage law in order to make the process of conversion easier. Marriages within the ecclesiastically forbidden degrees were to be accepted as valid without first obtaining a dispensation. Altough the various reissues of *Cum hora undecima* did not refer specifically to *Gaudemus*, other similar letters did, making it clear that Innocent III's decretal was the basis for the clause in the missionary bull[41]. Thus, when the popes at Avignon wanted to instructed missionaries on their responsibilities, they had at hand a thirteenth century model which they did not choose to modify in any significant way.

When missionaries in the field requested guidance from the papacy about specific problems which they faced, they generally received letters based on *Cum hora undecima*. In the East, for example, the friars encountered clerics whose priestly ordination or episcopal consecration seemed to have been irregular. Because of the need to encourage the reconciliation of schismatics, the missionaries were authorized to accept them as priests or bishops, presumably with the understanding that the questions about their consecration or ordination were of a minor technical nature and not matters of substance[42]. Those clerics whose ordinations were clearly invalid would, of course, require re-ordination.

John XXII faced a similar problem in the process of reuniting the Lithuanians and Ruthenians to the Church. A thirteenth century Lithuanian ruler, Mindaugas (1240-1263) had become a Christian only to relapse into paganism. Two papal legates sent to Lithuania in the fourteenth century went armed with a letter similar to *Cum hora*

---

[41] Concerning *Gaudemus* and the interpretation of it which the canonists made, see JAMES MULDOON, *Missionaries and the Marriages of Infidels: The Case of the Mongol Mission*: The Jurist 35 (1975) 125-141; see also, JOHN T. NOONAN, Jr., *Power to Dissolve*, Cambridge, Mass. 1972, pp. 347-359.

[42] John XXII, *Datur eis auctoritas*, October 3, 1333: *RV 62*, fols. 28v-29r; RAYNALDUS, ad ann. 1333, no. 42; MOLLAT, *Lettres communes*, no. 63877. This letter has the same salutation as *Cum hora undecima* and consists of a series of excerpts from that bull that deal with the status of schismatic clerics.

*undecima*, but which was not identical to it, outlining their powers and responsibilities. Here again, the emphasis was upon reconciling clerics with the Church and with accepting as valid marriages in the ecclesiastically forbidden degrees [43].

In spite of the numerous restatements of papal policy, the question of the marriages of infidels and schismatics continued to concern the papacy. In a memorandum written in 1333, John XXII discussed the problems which arose from the marriages of Christians with schismatics or infidels. Such marriages occurred where Christians lived in lands where infidels or schismatics predominated [44]. Missionaries had reported that many of these Christians were lost to the Church and had accepted the beliefs of their spouses. The pope declared that the terms of *Gaudemus* were to be followed in such cases so that as many as possible of these marriages could be recognized as valid, thus allowing the partners to enter or to return to the fold. No attempt was made to broaden the terms, however, beyond those which Innocent III had authorized [45].

During the reign of Benedict XII, the issue of polygamous marriages emerged as a consequence of the renewed interest in the mission to Asia. In a letter to the chiefs of the Alans, the pope mentioned that polygamy was forbidden [46]. A second or third marriage could take place only after the death of one partner. Here again,

---

43 « ... quod clerici nationum ipsarum publice ad dicte sedis obedientiam redeuntes gaudeant privilegio clericali ... Sit etiam vobis facultas eis qui de scismaticis ad unitatem ... fidei ... quod uxores suas cum quibus in tertio vel quarto gradu consanguinitatis vel affinitatis contraxisse noscuntur, dum in scismate permanerent, in uxores licite valeant retinere ». John XXII, *Exultamus: RV 62*, fols. 14v-16r; THEINER, *Vetera monumenta Poloniae*, 1: no. 290, pp. 190-92, at p. 191.

44 « Sane pro parte dilectorum filiorum fratrum ordinis predicatorum in terras sarracenorum paganorum ... coram nobis et fratribus nostris ... Cardinalibus in consistorio fuit expositum quod nonnulli predictorum orientalium et Aquilonarium infidelium nationum qui ad fidem catholicam dictorum fratrum predicationis et operationis ministerio seu alias sunt conversi pro eo quod in gradibus a lege divina non prohibitis matrimonia contrahere nequeunt absque dispensatione sedis apostolice speciali, a fide catholica et devotione ecclesie totaliter recedentes cum hereticis et sarracenis sepius per contubernium copulantur, propter quod ipsi et eorum proles proh dolor spiritualiter pereunt et multarum inde sequuntur pericula animarum ». John XXII, *Super gregem*, October 4, 1333: *RV 62*, fols. 25v-26r; *Acta Ioannis XXII*, no. 140, pp. 260-262 at pp. 260-261; MOLLAT, *Lettres communes*, no. 63878.

45 « ... taliter respondemus quod in favorem presertim christiane religionis et fidei fideles huiusmodi sic matrimonialiter copulati vel in posterum copulandi iuxta constitutionem felicis recordationis Innocentii pape III ... que incipit Gaudemus, in matrimoniis ipsis dictis impedimentis non obstantibus libere possunt et licite remanere coniunctim ». *Ibid.*: *RV 62*, fol. 26r; *Acta Ioannis XXII*, p. 261.

46 « De matrimonio vero tenet, quod nec unus vir plures uxores nec una mulier simul habere permittitur plures viros, soluta vero lege matrimonii per mortem alterutrius coniugum, secundas et tertias deinceps nuptias successive licita esse dicit, si impedimentum canonicum ex causa alia non obsistat ». Benedict XII, *Serena facie*: *Acta Benedicti XII*, pp. 46-47. In *RV 62*, this letter is abbreviated and reference is made to a similar letter of John XXII (fol. 32v), but the compiler did not further identify the letter to which he referred. The abbreviated version repeated the doctrinal points made in Benedict XII's letter, but it did not contain the disciplinary points such as those concerning marriage which are found in the full letter.

the papal response to a missionary problem was the solution which Innocent III had proposed almost a century and a half earlier. In the decretal *Gaudemus*, Innocent III had stated that the New Testament prohibited polygamy because Christ had spoken of there being « two in one flesh, not three or more »[47]. The pope admitted, however, that God must be able to authorize polygamy (and divorce) because the patriarchs of the Old Testament had practised polygamy and had been divorced, apparently with divine approbation[48]. Later canonists followed Innocent III's lead on this but failed to expand upon his conclusions[49]. In an interesting refusal to admit that the pope had all the powers of God in such matters as a result of his *plenitudo potestatis*, the canonists did not grant the pope the right to accept polygamous marriages contracted by converts before their baptism. Apparently, their willingness to recognize the papal power to exempt converts from the rigors of the law concerning marriage within the forbidden degrees did not extend to plural marriage even though such marriages were not absolutely forbidden by divine law in their opinion.

The problem of individuals who claimed to be priests or baptized Christians also continued to concern the missionaries. John XXII dealt with this question in some detail. Because of the need to deal gently with the schismatics who were being reconciled, the pope stressed the need to be sympathetic to the claims of such individuals[50]. In these cases, conditional baptism or ordination was to be used. The pope added that in order to avoid giving scandal to the schismatic population that had been receiving the sacraments from these priests, the usual ban against receiving all of the minor

---

47 « Verum absonum hoc videtur et inimicum fidei christianae, quum ab initio una costa in unam feminam sit conversa, et scriptura divina testetur, quod propter hoc relinquet homo patrem et matrem, et adhaerebit uxori suae, et erunt duo in carne una; non dixit: 'tres vel plures,' sed: 'duo,' nec dixit: 'adhaerebit uxoribus,' sed 'uxori' ». *Decretales*, 4.19.8. *Gaudemus*. Concerning the problem of polygamy, see MULDOON, *Missionaries*, pp. 129, 132-133, 138-141.

48 « Nec ulli unquam licuit insimul plures uxores habere, nisi cui fuit divina revelatione concessum, quae mos quandoque, interdum etiam fas censetur, per quam, sicut Iacob a mendacio, Israelitae a furto et Samson ab homicidio, sic et patriarchae et alii viri iusti, qui plures leguntur simul habuisse uxores, ab adulterio excusantur ». *Decretales*, 4.19.8. *Gaudemus*.

49 « *Sic et patriarchae* ... Abraham, Gen. XVI ... Iacob, Gen. XXIX ... Qui quatuor habuit, sed quando mos erat, crimen non erat ... ». HOSTIENSIS, *In quinque libros decretalium commentaria* (2 v., Paris 1512), 4.19.8. *Gaudemus*.

50 « ... habet siquidem pro parte vestra expositio in consistorio coram nobis et fratribus nostris facta quod de multis personis partium predictarum que ut presbyteri divina celebrarunt officia et pro talibus reputantur frequenter dubitari contingit, an iuxta formam ecclesie baptizati fuerunt vel non et an ordines rite receperint in quibus ut premittitur ministrarunt quodque si in ordinandis ipsis de novo interstitia temporum servarentur magnum scandalum inter populares, qui ab eisdem audierunt divina et sunt etiam eisdem confessi, posset verisimiliter generari ... ». John XXII, *Fidelium novella*, October 3, 1333: *RV 62*, fols. 26r-26v at fol. 26v; *Acta Ioannis XXII*, no. 139, pp. 259-260 at p. 259; MOLLAT, *Lettres communes*, no. 63877.

and major orders on the same day was to be lifted so that the re-ordination would occur as quickly as possible[51].

The compiler of Vatican Register 62 did not include any letters of missionary instructions from the reigns of Benedict XII and Clement VI. The obvious reason is that all such letters were virtually identical with the terms of *Cum hora undecima*, the most significant difference being that on occasion only part of the basic bull was reissued. Any later letters about missionary problems would receive the same basic response. Herein lay a fundamental weakness in the papal dealings with those outside the Church. Infidels and schismatics were simply lumped together indiscriminately as if the issues involved with the reconciliation of the latter were the same as those involved in the conversion of the former. The failure to distinguish between infidels and schismatics, as well as the failure to distinguish between primitive societies, such as that of the Mongols, and a sophisticated society such as that of the Byzantines, meant that the papacy had only a very vague conception of the peoples to whom the missionaries were being dispatched. No special provisions were made for the unique problems that each society posed for the friars sent to it. Furthermore, the papacy does not appear to have attempted to reformulate the basic letters for instructing missionaries in the light of the experience of missionaries[52]. The repeated use of Innocent III's decretals on the marriages of those outside the Church illustrated the fundamental difference between him and his successors in the fourteenth century. Innocent III had responded to specific questions raised by bishops who were involved with concrete problems and gave a concrete answer which fitted the situation as it had been presented to him. The tradition of canonistic commentary did not further develop Innocent's approach to the problem of dealing with potential converts, it only repeated it, thus placing the popes of the fourteenth century in a rigid posture when dealing with potential converts.

---

[51] « ... ut omnes et singulos partium predictarum de quibus dubitatur an fuerint baptizati vel non baptizare iuxta provisionem iuris in huiusmodi casu adhibitam ... omnes minores quam sacros ordines statutis temporibus aliquo tamen intervallo in huiusmodi sacris ordinibus recipiendis et conferendis propter eorum reverentiam observato si sine scandalo fieri possit, alioquin omnes una eadem die simul prefatos ordines sacros et minores pro huiusmodi scandalo evitando ... dicendo si ordinatus es rite non te reordino set si nondum ordinatus es te ordino ad sacros Ordines antedictos ... ». *Ibid., RV 62*, fol. 26v; *Acta Ioannis XXII*, pp. 259-260.

[52] It is true that two of the letters discussed here did mention the presentation of the missionaries' reports to the pope and his court, but this seems to have been at best a *pro forma* exercise. The papal responses in these cases do not indicate any changes in the position taken by the papacy in the situations that the missionaries described. The papal replies seem to have been automatic responses to situations that were, from the papal viewpoint, similar to earlier cases. Therefore, it was possible to use copies of the letters that had been sent on the earlier occasions.

## II

## THE PLIGHT OF EASTERN CHRISTENDOM

### 1. The Schismatic Kingdoms

The front line of defense against the infidels who were advancing on Europe from the East in the thirteenth and fourteenth centuries consisted of the schismatic Byzantine Empire and the schismatic kingdoms of Georgia and Armenia [1]. The secular and the ecclesiastical leaders of these states were the recipients of letters designed to bring them back into union with the Latin Church. The major theme of these letters, as the compiler of Vatican Register 62 saw it, was the conflict that existed between the two fundamental goals of papal policy in the East, the defense of the Christians against the infidels and the reunion of the schismatics with the Latin Church. The latter goal was the primary one so that the advance of the Tartars and the Turks could be seen as an act of divine providence to be used as a lever in forcing the return of the schismatics.

The Georgian kingdom received the least attention in these letters. The Georgians were of course included in the salutation of the reissued versions of *Cum hora undecima*, but Vatican Register 62 included only one letter sent to them alone. In this letter, *Cum simus*, John XXII instructed the Georgians in the basic truths of the Catholic faith. The theme was the unity of the true faith from which the Georgians had become severed [2]. The political fate of the Georgians had already been sealed. They were subjected to the Mongols with no immediate hope of rescue, so the papal letter did not hold out any hope of military aid from the West. The papacy saw in the inclusion of the Georgians within the Tartar sphere of domination at least one useful factor, the possibility of using the western contacts with the Georgians as a base for making further contacts with the Tartars. From this base, additional missionaries could be sent into the regions that the Tartars controlled. This letter, it should be pointed out, was another case in which a letter from the thirteenth century was refurbished for use in the fourteenth century.

---

[1] The general state of the eastern Christian kingdoms in the late thirteenth and the fourteenth centuries has been surveyed most recently in *A History of the Crusades*, gen. ed., KENNETH M. SETTON; v. 2, *The Later Crusades, 1189-1311*, ed. ROBERT L. WOLFF and HARRY W. HAZARD, 2nd ed., Madison, Wisconsin 1969; and v. 3, *The Fourteenth and Fifteenth Centuries*, ed. HARRY W. HAZARD, Madison 1975. The best introduction to the attempts to revive the crusades in the fourteenth century is AZIZ S. ATIYA, *The Crusade in the Later Middle Ages*, 2nd ed., New York 1965.

[2] « Cum simus super apostolice sedis speculam constituti vehementer dolere cogimur et turbari cum a capite suo membra quedam videamus esse divisa sueque divisionis dampnum tamquam mortificata non plangere nec sentire ... qui ecclesiam scindunt occidunt animas parvulorum ... » John XXII, *Cum simus: RV 62*, fol. 5v; *Acta Ioannis XXII*, pp. 89-90.

In the spring of 1245, Innocent IV had sent the same letter to the ruler of the Bulgarians in order to secure the return of his kingdom to the Latin Church [3].

The register contained a much larger number of letters dealing with the fate of the Armenian kingdom, the fate of which was not yet irrevocably determined. A series of four letters from the seventh year of John XXII's pontificate provided a dramatic picture of the deteriorating state of the kingdom. One of these letters, addressed to the entire Christian world at large, described the effects of a combined Moslem-Mongol attack on the Armenians. The sultan of Babylon who was leading the Moslems was described as a second pharaoh in the evils which he was inflicting of God's people [4]. The countryside was being devastated and the population killed or driven off. The very corpses of the dead were dug up by the invaders in a search for buried treasure, so wicked and greedy were the invaders [5]. The leaders of the Armenians had written to the West seeking aid from the pope in their hour of need [6]. The pope authorized a crusading indulgence for all who would go to the aid of the besieged Armenians as well as for the Armenians themselves [7]. Unfortunately, the most the pope himself could do was to send a letter of sympathy to the Armenians [8].

During the next pontificate, Benedict XII took a stronger stand against the errors to which the Armenians adhered. The King of

---

[3] Innocent IV, *Cum simus*, March 21, 1245: *Acta Innocentii PP. IV*, no. 20, pp. 43-46.

[4] « Soldanus Babilonie velut secundus nequitia pharao cuius cor contra dei erat populum induratum et Turchi licet eos graviter hactenus diutius afflixissent, quia christianis alia terra solida ultramarina preter Armeniam non remanserat ... Idem Soldanus cum Tartaris qui dudum per Centum annos Armenorum amici extiterant ... ». John XXII, *Dum mentis nostre aciem*, December 22, 1322: *RV 62*, fols. 9r-11v at fol. 9r; RAYNALDUS, ad ann. 1322, nn. 33-39 at no. 33; MOLLAT, *Lettres communes*, no. 18090. The *Acta Ioannis XXII*, no. 65a, pp. 123-125, contains only a small portion of this letter.

[5] « ... iam defunctis cum eorum exhumaret corpora, sepulchra violaret depredaretur tumulos ut nuda relinquerentur monumenta, sicut et viventium peculium rapuit, supellectilem spoliavit ... ». *Ibid.*: *RV 62*, fol. 9v; RAYNALDUS, ad ann. 1322, no. 34.

[6] « ... venerabiles fratres Archiepiscopi et Episcopi ac Carissimus in Christo filius noster Leo Rex et dilecti filii nobiles viri Ossinus Comes Curchi et gubernator, ceterique Barones ac populus Regni Armenie nobis per suas litteras et nuncios lacrimabiliter intimarunt ... ». *Ibid.*: *RV 62*, fol. 9r; RAYNALDUS, ad ann. 1322, no. 33.

[7] « Et ut vos ad transfretandum succurrendum et subveniendum prefatis Armenie regnique Cypri fidelibus possitis eo libentius et ferventius animari ... omnibus qui infra annum ... contra Soldanum et alios infideles in succursum et auxilium Regnorum Armenie et Cypri predictorum in personis propriis et expensis accesserint ... veniam indulgemus que proficiscentibus in terre sancte subsidium concedi per sedem apostolicam consuevit ... ». *Ibid.*: *RV 62*, fol. 11r; RAYNALDUS, ad ann. 1322, no. 39. In addition, see John XXII, *Inter alia*, December 20, 1322: *RV 62*, fol. 8v; *Acta Ioannis XXII*, no. 65, pp. 122-123; MOLLAT, *Lettres communes*, no. 18098.

[8] « Sic vobis et commissis huius populis contra ipsos adversarios persequentes ex alto victoria sic de celo veniens fortitudo et peccatorum cordibus directis ad deum eius misericordia ineffabilis adfecit formidines hostium, et pie conferat temporum gaudia tranquillorum ... ». John XXII, *Non dubitamus*, April 1, 1322: *RV 62*, fols. 11v-12v at fol. 12r; MOLLAT, *Lettres communes*, no. 18097.

Armenia, Leo V, had sent a mission to the papal court requesting aid in the struggle against the Moslems. The papal response was to insist that the Armenian king first see to the reform of the Armenian Church. Benedict XII admitted the seriousness of the military situation facing the Armenians, but he declared himself to be more concerned with reports about the « detestable errors which are held there by many people and which are preached there against the Catholic faith »[9]. If these reports were true, he argued, the Latin West could not send military aid to the Armenians, presumably because to do so would be to confirm the schismatics in their errors. It was first necessary that Leo V cause these errors to be eliminated from the church, so Benedict XII sent back with the embassy a list of 147 errors of doctrine, the *Fides Armenorum,* which he asserted were held by the Armenian Church[10]. In this way, the king could see clearly the points at issue between the two churches and bring the Armenians into line with the Latin Church. The pope wanted the Armenians to hold a council immediately to deal with the points in the *Fides Armenorum* so that all the clergy of the country could be informed of what was needed if military aid from the West was to be forthcoming. If the Armenians did return to the fold, « the enemies of the faith will not overcome them » the pope promised[11]. In a separate letter to the Catholicos of the Armenian Church, the pope pointed out that if he and his fellow prelates would accept papal primacy and all that it entailed, they could be welcomed back with open arms and would receive papal support in their struggle for survival[12].

The solution to the schism between the Latin and the Armenian

---

9 « Cumque ipsi oppressiones molestationes et afflictiones varias tibi fili carissime Regno et regnicolis tuis illatas ab infidelibus et que inferuntur iugiter exponentes a nobis subsidium super hoc humiliter postularint, eis duximus respondendum ... quod tam in maiori quam in minori Armenia nonnulli execrandi errores tenentur a multis et dogmatizantur ibidem contra fidem catholicam quam tenet, docet et predicat sacrosancta Romana ecclesia mater omnium fidelium et magistra ». Benedict XII, *Quamvis dilecti filii: RV 62,* fols. 34r-34v; *Acta Benedicti XII,* p. 114.

10 *RV 62,* fols. 100r-120r; *Acta Benedicti XII,* pp. 119-155. The Armenian response to the papal position is given in the *Articuli Armenorum cum responsionibus eorum,* in the *Acta Benedicti XII,* pp. 160-234. Concerning the *Fides Armenorum,* see GAY, pp. 9, 140-144.

11 « Tenemus quidem indubie quod si tui regnicole clerici et laici fidem predictam non impugnarent erroribus sicut nonnulli faciunt ut prefertur, sed eis expulsis omnino eam tenerent firmiter ut prefata Romana mater ecclesia tenet eandem, nequaquam adversus eos prevalere possent ipsius hostes fidei etiamsi aliunde quam a divine potentie dextera et seipsis auxilium non haberent ... ». Benedict XII, *Quamvis dilecti filii: RV 62,* fols. 34v-35r; *Acta Benedicti XII,* pp. 115-116.

12 « Sciturus quod si tu ac prelati et subditi partium predictarum hec adimpleveritis recognoscendo effectualiter eiusdem ecclesie Romane primatum, nos et sedes apostolica vobis paterne caritatis et dilectionis amplexibus occurrentes erga vos reperiemur et propitii continue in gratiis, favoribus et auxiliis opportunis ». Benedict XII, *Dudum ad audientiam,* August 1, 1341: *RV 62,* fols. 35r-35v (incomplete text); *Acta Benedict XII,* no. 56, pp. 117-119 at p. 118; VIDAL and MOLLAT, no. 3150.

churches was not as simple as Benedict XII's letters would seem to suggest it was. A council was held by the Armenians, but the assembled clergy denied that the Armenians actually held the beliefs attributed to them. They placed the blame for these accusations on an exiled bishop who had poisoned the papacy against the Armenian Church[13].

The response of the Armenians to Benedict XII's charges only reached Avignon in the reign of his successor, Clement VI. He found the situation in Armenia even worse. In a letter to the Armenian hierarchy and clergy, Clement VI warned the Armenians not to fall victim to the erroneous beliefs of the Fraticelli who were seeking converts from among the unsuspecting Armenians. These wicked heretics were wolves in sheep's clothing seeking to carry off the souls of the Lord's sheep[14]. The bishops were reminded that if the heretics proved persistent and resisted the efforts of the spiritual authorities to eliminate the threat they posed to the souls of the Armenians, then the bishops should call upon the secular arm for assistance[15]. The important point was to eliminate this new threat to the union of the two churches before it was too late.

The situation in Armenia continued to worsen, however, as the infidel armies continued to overwhelm the Armenians. King Constantine who succeeded Leo V wrote to the kings of France and England for support, but they refused to send any[16]. The discouraged ambassador who had delivered these letters visited Avignon on his return journey where he received a letter from Clement VI to Constantine. The pope gave the beleaguered king some theologically sound advice that could only have been cold comfort to him. The pope observed that the salvation of the soul was more important than the security of the body. Although the West was not able to

---

13 Gay, pp. 140-141; Atiya, p. 270.

14 « Habet namque fidedigna multorum licet displicibilis admodum et infesta relatio quod nonnulli pseudo religiosi sub pelle ovina voracitatem gerentes lupinam in Armenia maiori Imperii Persidis et aliis orientalibus et ultramarinis partibus ... ». Clement VI, *In amara trahimur,* May 29, 1344: *RV 62,* fols. 57v-58r at fol. 57v; Raynaldus, ad ann. 1344, n. 8 (the first few lines are ommitted); Déprez, Glénnison, Mollat, no. 873. In his introduction to this letter, Raynaldus identified these heretics as Fraticelli.

15 « Sed vos fratres Archiepiscopi et Episcopi per vos et alios quos ad hoc duxeritis deputandos eos solerter et fideliter perquirentes ubicunque reperti fuerint si prout et quando opportune fieri poterit capiatis et carceribus mancipetis ipsosque secundum statuta canonum corrigatis et etiam puniatis invocato ad hoc si necesse fuerit auxilio brachii secularis ... ». *Ibid.: RV 62,* fol. 58r; Raynaldus, ad ann. 1344, no. 8.

16 « ... Constantius miles et nuncius tuus lator presentium ad nos et sedem apostolicam destinatus quem et litteras tuas nobis presentatas ... grate recepimus expositis nobis per eum ... benigne audivimus ... ad Carissimos in Christo filios nostros Philippum Francie et Edwardum Anglie Reges Illustres litteras tuas deferre ... ». Clement VI, *Dilectus filius nobilis,* September 26, 1347: *RV 62,* fols. 86v-87r; Raynaldus, ad ann. 1347, no. 29 (only part of the letter); Déprez and Mollat, no. 1493.

provide the necessary assistance the king had requested, Clement VI nevertheless suggested that the king continue to struggle so that the « fog of error and schism might be blown away » with the result « that the light of the Catholic truth might shine ». If this effort at elimination of error succeeded, he informed Constantine, « you shall rule and guide your subjects not only in temporal affairs but lead them to eternal life as well », thus linking once again the reunion of the two churches with the possibility of military aid to Armenia [17].

In spite of the papal desire for reunion and the Armenian need for western assistance which the end of the schism seemed to promise, the Latin and Armenian churches remained apart. In 1351 Clement VI wrote again to the Catholicos seeking his submission. The response of the Armenians to the *Fides Armenorum* which had reached the West during Clement's reign had been rejected. Clement now sent yet another statement of Christian doctrine to the Armenians seeking their acceptance of the papal definition of what constituted true doctrine. The range of topics covered in this letter was a wide one, spanning both points of essential doctrine, such as the nature of Christ, and points of discipline, such as the use of the Latin calendar of saints' feast days. The fundamental point which Clement VI stressed was the need for the Armenians to adhere closely to the papal mode of practicing the Christian faith [18].

Because of the failure of the papacy to win over the Catholicos, Clement VI wrote to King Constantine encouraging him to impose the reunion on his people. The pope hoped that the king would require the Catholicos to respond to the papal questions about the beliefs held by the Armenians so that all Armenians, led by the Catholicos, would be reunited with the Latin Church, the true flock of Christ [19]. The pope placed the blame for the continuance of the schism on those in the Armenian church who refused to discuss the schism sincerely and to seek its end [20]. If the king would do as the

---

17 « ... quod omnis erroris et scismatis de partibus ipsis fugata caligine lumen catholice veritatis effulgeat tuque ipsos subditos tuos non solum temporaliter regas et dirigas, sed eis ad eterne vite gaudia salubriter prebuisse ... ». *Ibid.: RV 62,* fol. 87r; RAYNALDUS, ad ann. 1347, no. 29.

18 « ... tu et ecclesia Armenorum que tibi obedit creditis et tenetis, promittitis tenere et dicitis tu et tota ecclesia Armenorum tibi obedientium, quod eadem ecclesia Romana cuius summus Pontifex est Papa Romanus, est sola catholica et in ea sola est vera salus et una vera fides et unum verum baptisma et vera remissio peccatorum ... ». Clement VI, *Super quibusdam: RV 62,* fol. 89v; RAYNALDUS, ad ann. 1351, no. 3.

19 « Cupientes quod ipsi Catholicon et Armeni in eadem vera fide solidius roborati antiqui hostis qui primum scisma suscitavit in celo confutatis fraudibus et temptationibus superatis verum lumen catholice veritatis agnoscerent et unitati eiusdem Romane ecclesie aggregati ... ». Clement VI, *Sicut ut credimus,* September 14, 1351: *RV 62,* fols. 95v-96v at fol. 95v; WADDING, 8: pp. 60-62 at p. 60; DÉPREZ and MOLLAT, no. 2498.

20 « ... et Armenos alios non in veritatis simplicitate sed fictione quadam ipsius fidei negotium prosequi ymo quod detestabilius est et amplius deploramus, commu-

pope requested, he and his people would obtain « not only spiritual blessings but temporal ones as well ». To support the last point, Clement informed King Constantine that 6000 florins drawn from the papal treasury were available to the king or his agent at Cyprus [21].

In spite of the continuous efforts to achieve the reunion of the two churches, the movement failed. The theological differences were only part of the problem. Papal insistence on unity of ritual antagonized the Armenians because, as one scholar pointed out, the papal position did not take into account the national character of many of the ecclesiastical practices [22]. To the missionaries from the West, the only rule for determining orthodoxy was full and complete agreement with the Latin ritual. Without this sign of union, there was no way to distinguish between the Armenians who were reconciled with the Latin Church and those who remained in schism. In addition, the papacy was not able to provide significant military support for the Armenians. The refusal of Edward III and Philip VI to respond to the Armenian call for help meant that any papal assurances notwithstanding, the West was not going to come to the aid of the Armenians, whether they remained schismatics or returned to the fold. To the natural resentment of the Armenians to the papacy's willingness to use the dire situation facing Armenia was added the even greater resentment which the papal inability to provide the promised aid must have caused.

The manner in which the papacy dealt with the Armenians and Georgians was only an extension of the way in which the papacy had dealt with the Byzantine Empire for the past three centuries. The papal willingness to take advantage of the Moslem advances in the East to force the return of the schismatic Byzantines had a long history. The parallel development of the Moslem advance and the Gregorian reform movement placed the Byzantines in a difficult position because western aid came to be linked with reunion of the churches. During the fourteenth century, the popes at Avignon had to deal with the lingering bitterness which the conquest of Constantinople by the crusaders in 1204 had caused. The bitterness came not only from the conquest itself but from the callousness with which the westerners used the plight of Constantinople for their own ends [23].

---

nicatam eis per legatos eiusdem sedis salutarem doctrinam ipsius fidei in contemptum et derisum habuisse firmiter asseverant ... ». *Ibid.: RV 62,* fol. 96r; WADDING, 8: p. 61.

21 « ... pro certo sciturus quod nos qui salutem tuam et tui subditi populi in hac parte prosequimur et simpliciter querimus te Regnumque tuum non solum spiritualibus gratiis sed et temporalibus favoribus atque subsidiis disponimus prestante Domino multipliciter confovere. Quod ut ex nunc aliqualiter sentias de pecuniis apostolice camere Sex milia florenorum in Regno Cypri tibi seu procuratori tuo mandavimus exhibere ». *Ibid.: RV 62,* fols. 96r-96v; WADDING, 8: pp. 61-62.

22 GAY, p. 137.

23 The Fourth Crusade and its aftermath have been the subject of extensive scholarly analysis. Useful introductions to the issues involved can be found in: EDGAR

The letters in Vatican Register 62 reflect the main outlines of the problems which the Avignon popes faced in dealing with the Eastern Empire. Several distinct problems were involved. The fundamental one was the question of whether the physical security of Constantinople could be separated from the question of ecclesiastical reunion. The existence of pretenders to the Latin throne of Constantinople was a second problem. Could, or should, the papacy reject the concept of the Latin Empire as a sign of good faith in dealings with the East? Finally, the papacy had to face the fact that the only western states with a strong interest in the fate of the eastern Mediterranean were the merchant states of Genoa and Venice whose goals were conflicting ones. If any crusade was to be successful, however, the support of these states was essential.

In what no doubt was an unconscious gesture, the compiler of Vatican Register 62 framed the volume in terms of the papal dilemma over the Byzantine Empire. The first three letters concern the attempt of Charles of Valois to seize the eastern throne. His claim was based on his marriage to the heiress of the Latin emperors of Constantinople. The volume ends with letters from the Byzantines and the Armenians concerning the possibility of Church union. For the papacy, the primary goal was reunion and the consequent salvation of the souls of the lost sheep in the East. The problem was whether Charles of Valois or the Palaeologi could achieve the primary goal of papal policy as well as insure the defense of Constantinople against the Moslems.

Charles of Valois's claim to the throne of Constantinople came through his marriage to Catherine de Courtenay, the heiress to the claims of the last Latin Emperor, Baldwin II, who had died in 1273 [24]. Attempts to retake the Eastern Empire had gone on regularly since the ouster of Latins from Constantinople in 1261. Charles of Anjou, King of Naples and Sicily, had attempted a reconquest until the reunion of the churches that the Council of Lyons had achieved in

---

H. McNeal and Robert L. Wolff, *The Fourth Crusade*, in Setton, *History of the Crusades*, 2: pp. 153-185; Robert L. Wolff, *The Latin Empire of Constantinople, 1204-1261, ibid.*, pp. 186-233; Jean Longnon, *The Frankish States in Greece, 1204-1311, ibid.*, pp. 235-274. The most recent appraisal of the Fourth Crusade in the context of papal policy is Kenneth M. Setton, *The Papacy and the Levant (1204-1571)*, v. 1, *The Thirteenth and Fourteenth Centuries*, Philadelphia 1976, pp. 1-26. Two useful bibliographical articles are: Donald E. Queller and Susan J. Stratton, *A Century of Controversy on the Fourth Crusade:* Studies in Medieval and Renaissance History 6 (1969) 238-252; and Donald E. Queller and Gerald W. Day, *Some Arguments in Defense of the Venetians on the Fourth Crusade*: American Historical Review 81 (1976) 717-737.

[24] The claims of Charles of Valois to the throne of Constantinople have been reviewed recently from various perspectives. For his plans as seen in Constantinople, see Angeliki E. Laiou, *Constantinople and the Latins: The Foreign Policy of Andronicus II, 1282-1328*, Cambridge, Mass. 1972, pp. 52-54; and Deno J. Geanakoplos, *Byzantium and the Crusades, 1261-1354*, in Setton, *History of the Crusades*, 3: pp. 27-68 at pp. 42-44. For another perspective, see Setton, *The Papacy and the Levant*, 1: p. 164.

1274 ended the justification for his efforts. The subsequent failure of this reunion paved the way for Charles of Valois's effort at retaking Constantinople [25].

In the eyes of Clement V, the reconquest of Constantinople was a suitable goal for crusaders so he called for a crusading tenth to finance Charles of Valois's campaign. In a letter to the collectors of the tenth in Sicily, the pope explained that Michael VII (1260-1282) Palaeologus and his son Andronicus II (1282-1328) were schismatics so they were legitimate objects of a crusade [26]. The goals of the crusade were the noble ones of bringing back to the fold sheep that wicked rulers had led astray and of reinstituting the lawful ruler at Constantinople [27].

In another letter, Clement V described Andronicus II as the «self-styled emperor of the Greeks» [28]. This particular description went back to the late twelfth century when the canonist Huguccio had argued that the *translatio imperii* by which Pope Leo III (795-816) had crowned Charlemagne as Roman emperor meant that the Greek ruler at Constantinople was no longer the true emperor. In his opinion, the eastern emperors had lost their right to the title by becoming schismatics [29]. As schismatics, the eastern emperors were no longer capable of performing the basic function of the Christian empire, the defense of the Church against its enemies, so the pope had the right to transfer the title to a ruler who could perform those functions. A later canonist remarked in a commentary

---

[25] Concerning the various attempts at ecclesiastical reunion during the fourteenth century, see M. VILLER, *La question de l'union des églises entre Grecs et Latins depuis le concil de Lyon jusqu'à celui de Florence, 1274-1436*: Revue d'histoire ecclésiastique 17 (1921) 260-305, 515-532; 18 (1922) 20-60; LAIOU, pp. 308-329; GEANAKOPLOS, *Byzantium and the Crusades*, pp. 47-68.

[26] « ... more vigilis apostolice dirigimus considerationis intuitam ac intuemur Imperium inclitum Constant. a cultu dicte fidei qui vigere solebat ... Illudque per quondam Michaelem Paleologum dum vixit et post eius obitum per Andronicum eius filium, eiusque complices et fautores scismaticos ... ». Clement V, *Dum ad universas*, June 3, 1307: *RV 62*, fols. 1r-2v at fol. 1r; *Regestum Clementis papae V*, ed. the Benedictines of Monte Cassino (9 v. in 7, Rome 1885-1888), no. 1755.

[27] « ... de illo remedio per quod ad fidem reduci valeat antedictam vias et modos libenter exquirimus opemque ac operam promptis studiis exhibemus, unde cum dilectus filius nobilis vir Carolus Comes Andegaven. cuius mentem huiusmodi negotium persequi ratione uxoris sue Carissime videlicet in Christo filie nostre Catherine Imperatricis Const. Illustris, ad eiusdem recuperationem Imperii offerat se potenter velle intendere ... ». *Ibid.: RV 62*, fol. 1r.

[28] « Andronicum Paleologum qui Grecorum Imperatorem se nominat ... ». Clement V, *Andronicum Paleologum*, June 3, 1307: *RV 62*, fol. 4r; *Regestum Clementis papae V*, no. 1759.

[29] « *augustorum* ... unus enim solus debet esse imperator. regulariter. ut VII.q.I. in apibus. nec constantinopolitanum credo esse imperatorem set potius hereticum et schismaticum cum ecclesiam romanam non recognoscat caput sibi ». HUGUCCIO, *Summa*, Dist. 21, c. 7, *Nunc autem*, Pembroke College, Cambridge, *ms.* 72, fol. 130v. The problem of the two claimants for the imperial title is discussed in W. OHNSORGE, *Das Zweikaiserproblem im früheren Mittelalter*, Hildesheim 1947. Concerning the *translatio imperii*, see WERNER GOEZ, *Translatio imperii*, Tübingen 1958; and P. A. VAN DEN BAAR, *Die kirchliche Lehre der Translatio Imperii Romani*, Rome 1956.

on the decretal *Venerabilem* which concerned the imperial election that the ruler of Constantinople was no more the true emperor than the chess piece called a king was a real monarch [30]. In each case a label was used that bore no relation to reality. When Clement V referred to Andronicus II as a «self-styled emperor» he was simply repeating a stock canonistic phrase for such occasions.

In another letter Clement V gave some positive reasons for supporting Charles of Valois's campaign. He pointed out that Charles was a well-known and hardy warrior in the Church's behalf. Furthermore, the depth of Charles's desire to serve the Church will insure his perseverance in the work until he succeeds [31]. Finally, the pope observed that Andronicus II had failed to halt the Moslem drive to the West, a failure that could have only the most dire consequences for the Latin West [32]. The military reputation of Charles of Valois was proof that once he captured Constantinople, the eastern bulwark of Christendom would be shored up again. In another passage, the pope suggested that the failure of Andronicus to defend his borders against the enemy was linked with the fact that he is a schismatic who had led many souls away from the flock of Christ [33]. The Moslem victories in the East were, therefore, divine retribution for the schism. Returning the Eastern Church to communion with the Latin Church would be a major step in insuring victory in this conflict.

By 1310 the attempt to make Charles of Valois emperor had largely collapsed. Andronicus II had even proposed a marriage between one of his own sons and Charles's daughter. Such a marriage might have ended the threat of yet another crusade against the East-

---

[30] « *transtulit.* sic ergo regimen mundi translatum est ad teutonicos nam etiam habent regimen romane ecclesie ... et sic patet quod imperium non est apud grecos licet largo nomine appellatur imperator grecorum ... sicut rex scottorum dicitur rex ... ». TANCRED, gloss on the *Compilatio Tertia,* Gonville and Caius College, Cambridge, *ms. 17,* 1.6.19., *Venerabilem* (*Decretales,* 1.6.34). *Rex scottorum* was a scribal error for *rex scaccariorum*; see GAINES POST, *Some Unpublished Glosses* (*ca. 1210-1214*) *on the 'Translatio Imperii' and the Two Swords*: Archiv für Katholisches Kirchenrecht 117 (1937) 403-429 at p. 408. For a brief discussion of such scribal errors, see CHARLES DUGGAN, *Twelfth Century Decretal Collections,* London 1963, pp. 9-11.

[31] « Scimus enim quod ab eiusdem Comitis primordio iuventutis exaltationem ecclesie et fidei predictorum velut eiusdem ecclesie spiritualis alumpnus promovere sollicite studuit assistens eidem ecclesie ... et in hoc dei negotium agi considerans ferventi animo, brachio potenti et prompto exercicio nullis parendo laboribus propriam et suorum exposuit personas pro defensione sepedicte fidei et ecclesie libertatis huiusmodi ... ». Clement V, *Plenis in domino,* March 10, 1307: *RV 62,* fols. 4r-5r at fol. 4v; *Regestum Clementis papae V,* no. 1768.

[32] « ... nam si quod deus avertat prefatum Imperium ad Turchos sarracenos et infideles alios qui assidue Andronicum prefatum impugnant devenire contingeret, grave discrimen et confusionem gravissimam reciperet Romana mater ecclesia totaque religio Christiana ... ». *Ibid.: RV 62,* fol. 4v.

[33] « ... per quondam Mychaelem Paleologum tempore quo vivebit et post eius obitum per Andronicum eius filium ipsorum que complices et fautores scismaticos et ab unitate Christiane fidei deviantes elevatis superbie cornibus in divine maiestatis offensa apostolice sedis iniuria et totius christianitatis opprobrio ... ». *Ibid.: RV 62,* fol. 4v.

ern Empire and achieved the reunion of the churches that the papacy desired. The marriage plan failed, however, when Charles married his daughter to Philip of Taranto, Prince of Achaia, and also a descendant of Charles of Anjou. The marriage linked the two western families with the strongest claims to the Latin Empire, the opposite of what the marriage plans of Andronicus II were expected to accomplish [34].

Although there was further activity involving reunion of the churches and the defense of the East in the succeeding years, the compiler of Vatican Register 62 did not include any documents concerning it until he included some materials from the last years of John XXII's reign. In 1333 two Dominican friars who had been working among the Alans in the Crimea returned to the West by way of Constantinople where they discussed the possibility of reunion with Andronicus III (1328-1341). The emperor gave them a message for the pope which led to a response from John XXII. The pope did not hesitate to remind the emperor that the fate of Constantinople depended on the reunion of the churches. The choice was between conquest by the Moslems or submission to Rome, for « unless this reunion be achieved great danger threatens the empire at Constantinople because the wicked Saracens whose evil plan for seizing the lands of the Christians are well known » are advancing rapidly [35]. If the Greeks would only abjure their erroneous beliefs, the Latin Church would receive them warmly and, presumably, assist them in their struggle. In a separate letter to the Patriarch of Constantinople and the emperor the pope encouraged them to work jointly to achieve the desired reunion [36].

During the pontificate of Benedict XII the question of reunion appeared again. In an enthusiastic letter to Andronicus III, the pope declared that « it is with great joy that we are given to understand that the Greeks desire to be reconciled and reunited with the holy Roman Church » and that the emperor had informed him « that all the Greeks unanimously desired reunion and reconciliation » [37]. Papal

---

34 LAIOU, pp. 237-242; SETTON, *The Papacy and the Levant*, p. 164.

35 « ... quodque nisi unio huiusmodi procuretur Imperio Constantinopolitano propter perfidos sarracenos quorum prava intentio ad exterminium nominis Christiani, et ad occupandum specialiter partes ipsas prout experientia facti docet ardenter aspirat magnum noscitur periculum imminere ». John XXII, *Pridem*, August 4, 1333: *RV 62*, fols. 24v-25r at fol. 24v; *Acta Ioannis XXII*, no. 135, pp. 251-252 at p. 252; MOLLAT, no. 60899.

36 « ... ad unitatem et obedientiam eiusdem sancte Romane ecclesie sine dilatione aliqua preparetis et ad ovile domini redeatis vestramque intentionem laudabilem in realem deducatis effectum ac a vobis quelibet scismata et errores, quibus diabolica fraude fuistis hucusque decepti, penitus abigatis ... ». John XXII, *Ad unitatem*, August 4, 1333: *RV 62*, fols. 25r-25v at fol. 25v; *Acta Ioannis XXII*, no. 136, pp. 253-254 at p. 254; MOLLAT, no. 60900.

37 « ... nos intellexisse letanter, quod Greci reuniri et reconciliari sancte Romane ecclesie affectabant, tu ad hoc respondisti, de voluntate Baronum ipsorum quod om-

and imperial representatives were to meet at Naples to complete the work of reconciliation. As usual, the pope reminded the emperor that temporal benefits would accrue to him and to his people in addition to the spiritual benefits they would receive when he led the empire back into the fold [38]. In a letter to the emperor's second wife, Johanna, the daughter of Count Amedeo V of Savoy, the pope pointed out that an infidel married to a Christian wife could be saved through his wife's efforts [39]. He hoped that the empress would take the point and assist her husband to make the right choice, so that the work of reconciliation would be successful.

During the pontificate of Clement VI the approach which the papacy took to the problem of defending the East changed, at least as far as the compiler of Vatican Register 62 was concerned. Rather than concerning himself with enthusiastic generalizations about reunion and the wondrous benefits which would flow to Constantinople once it was achieved, the letters of Clement VI concentrated on raising a new crusade to clear the Moslem pirates out of the Aegean as the first step in an eventual drive to push the enemy out of Asia Minor. At the same time, however, he did not give up entirely on the possibility of reunion. Like his predecessors, Clement VI was not above using the crisis facing Constantinople to force reunion on the unwilling Byzantines.

In 1343 Clement VI wrote to John V (1341-1391), a minor whose regent was his mother Johanna, reminding him that now a dual threat faced the Empire. Not only were the Turks bearing down on Constantinople, the Tartars were moving in that direction as well. The pope mentioned that western aid was available at a price. He hoped that the Byzantines « having thrown off the poison of that wicked and damnable schism » would be reconciled with the papacy [40]. To the usual remarks about the benefits to be derived from reunion, the pope added a rhetorical flourish that paralleled the ancient pagan arguments about the effects that conversion to Christianity had on the fate of the Roman empire. Clement observed that « as

---

nes greci unanimiter desiderabant fieri reunionem et reconciliationem ... ». Benedict XII, *Nuper: RV 62,* fol. 29v; *Acta Benedicti XII,* p. 28.

[38] « Ideoque tuam excellentiam attentius in domino exhortamur quatinus bona innumera spiritualia et temporalia que ex reunione et reconciliatione tua et Grecorum predictorum ad sacrosanctam Romanam ecclesiam ... poterunt provenire ... ». *Ibid.: RV 62,* fol. 29v; *Acta Benedicti XII,* p. 28.

[39] « ... cum ad id sacre scripture pagina te invitet dicente apostolo: vir infidelis salvabitur per mulierem fidelem ... ». Benedict XII, *Veniens pridem,* January 17, 1337: *RV 62,* fol. 30r; *Acta Benedicti XII,* no. 15a, pp. 30-31 at p. 30; Vidal and Mollat, no. 1200. The reference is to *1 Corinthians* 7, 13-14.

[40] « ... volentes indubie te tenere, quod si tu ac Grecorum clerus et populus reiecta infectione illius execrandi ac dampnandi scismatis quod eos dampnabiliter a sacrosancta Romana ecclesia matre omnium fidelium et magistra divisit ... ». Clement VI, *Magnificentie,* October 21, 1343: *RV 62,* fol. 44v; Raynaldus, ad ann. 1343, n. 12 (*Munificientiae*).

long as Greece kept itself devotedly one with the Roman Church its mother, the excellence of its learning flourished before all men »[41]. In another letter of the same date sent to the Byzantine nobility and people, the pope made a similar point. « There is », he declared, « a widespread popular opinion, and the recorded deeds testify to it, that when Greece was caressed within the embrace of the one Catholic Church it subdued its enemies victoriously and gloriously, towering over all the nations of the earth »[42].

In the next few years, Clement VI wrote again to the widowed Johanna, seeking Greek involvement with the papacy and with the maritime powers of the West. These letters did not deal with the problems of reunion. They served to introduce individuals who wished to serve against the Turks or to suggest policies that might be undertaken to protect the East. One of these letters introduced a French knight named Peter de Palude who had travelled to the East « for the defense of the faith and of the faithful »[43]. Two other letters concerned the fleet which the pope was organizing under the command of Humbert of Vienne in order to regain control of the Aegean for the Christians[44].

The letters which dealt with the defense of the East and the reunion of the schismatics with the papacy reveal several basic difficulties in the papal approach to the problem of defense. In the first place, the goal of reunion meant to the eastern Christians a repetition of 1204 and the imposition of Latin rite clergy and practices, a goal that the masses of the schismatic clergy and people opposed. In the second place, although the papacy could promise

[41] « Et utinam tua et populi grecorum perpenderet prudentia diligenter quod ex reunione huiusmodi preter commoda spiritualia que vobis affluenter provenirent exinde multa bona temporalia resultarent, nam ut communis et vulgaris habet narratio et antiqua gesta testantur, quamdiu Grecia sub devotione ac unitate ipsius ecclesie Romane se tenuit tamquam matris, pre aliis mundi nationibus scientiarum precellentia floruit et militari potentia victoriose prefulsit ». *Ibid.: RV 62*, fol. 44v; RAYNALDUS, ad ann. 1343, n. 12. The argument given here is similar to that which pagans made against Christians toward the end of the empire in the West, an argument that St. Augustine refuted: see *The City of God*, trans. JOHN HEALY, ed. R. V. G. Tasker (2 v., London, 1945), bk. 1, ch. 3, pp. 3-5.

[42] « ... vulgaris et communis opinio et antiqua gesta testantur quod cum Grecia in sinu eiusdem ecclesie unite ac catholice foveretur, victoriose et gloriose inimicos suos suppeditabat et hostes pre aliis mundi nationibus militari potentia et strenuitate armorum prefulgens et florens nichilominus scientiis litterarum aliisque variis decorata virtutum et donorum insigniis lucidius coruscabat in quo statu ... ». Clement VI, *Quot et quanto*, October 21, 1343: *RV 62*, fols. 46r-46v at fol. 46v; DÉPREZ, GLÉNISSON, MOLLAT, no. 470.

[43] « ... dilectus filius nobilis vir Petrus de palude miles ... qui de partibus Burgundie ... ad partes transmarinas pro defensione fidei et fidelium eiusdem fidei zelo accensus ... ». Clement VI, *Exposuit nobis*, March 6, 1345: *RV 62*, fol. 66r; DÉPREZ, GLÉNISSON, MOLLAT, no. 1529; see also, *Cum dilectus filius*, April 8, 1344: *RV 62*, fol. 67v; DÉPREZ, GLÉNISSON, MOLLAT, no. 1623.

[44] Clement VI, *Nuper dilectus filius*, June 15, 1346: *RV 62*, fols. 82v-83r; DÉPREZ, GLÉNISSON, MOLLAT, no. 2582: *Quia paterne*, June 15, 1346: *RV 62*, fol. 83r; DÉPREZ, GLÉNISSON, MOLLAT, no. 2583.

aid for the East, no pope was able to supply any significant amount of men or money to defend these kingdoms against the Moslems. Furthermore, the rulers of the great kingdoms in Europe showed little interest in renewing the crusades. The wars within Europe were more profitable than the crusades in the East, at least as far as the kings of England and France were concerned. This time the papal call for crusaders was greeted not with *Deus vult* but with silence.

## 2. The Moslem Threat

The Moslem threat to Christian Europe was the greatest threat to its survival and the oldest [45]. It is not hard to understand why so many of the letters in Vatican Register 62 dealt wholly or in part with the Moslems. Even letters which did not relate directly to the Moslems mentioned them in passing. Underlying the letters dealing with the Mongol mission for example was the hope that their conversion would mean a European-Mongol alliance against the Turks. The conquest of the distant Canary Islands may have been linked with the goal of outflanking the Moslems of North Africa in order to relieve the pressure on Europe.

The one theme that is not found in the letters concerning the Moslems is the hope that they could be converted. Although plans for their conversion did circulate in fourteenth century Europe, no echo of these plans is found in the letters in Vatican Register 62 [46]. Instead, the language of these letters is the language of the crusade. What adds to the pathos of these repeated calls for crusaders is that they were issued between the two greatest shocks which the crusaders in the East received, the fall of Acre in 1291 and the decisive defeat of the crusading army at Nicopolis in 1396.

The Moslems played only a background role in the letters taken from the registers of Clement V, John XXII and Benedict XII. The major themes in the letters from these pontificates were defense of

[45] In addition to the work of Atiya and SETTON *History of the Crusades,* v. 3, two important works that deal with the Christian image of the Moslems, an image which shaped Christian-Moslem relations, are: NORMAN DANIEL, *Islam and the West: The Making of an Image,* Edinburgh 1960; and R. W. SOUTHERN, *Western Views of Islam in the Middle Ages,* Cambridge, Mass. 1962. The most extensive discussion of the papacy' relations with the Moslems is in SETTON, *The Papacy and the Levant,* pp. 163-223.

[46] The missionary work of the fourteenth century is largely associated with the Franciscans. The most recent study of this missionary work, DANIEL, *The Franciscan Concept of Mission,* contains an extensive bibliography. The most famous individual missionary, Ramon Lull, an associate of the Franciscans, was one of the foremost advocates of peaceful conversion of the Moslems: see E. ALLISON PEERS. *Ramon Lull: A Biography,* London 1929; and J. N. HILLGARTH, *Ramon Lull and Lullism in Fourteenth Century France,* Oxford 1971. There is less material available on the work of the Dominican missionaries: see B. ALTANER, *Die Dominikanermissionen des 13. Jahrhunderts,* Habelschwerdt 1924.

Christendom by the reunion of the schismatics and the conversion of the Mongols. Defeat of the Moslems was secondary to the work of reunion and of conversion. Furthermore, these early letters stressed the internal divisions in Europe which were hindering the efforts to stop the Moslems. John XXII, for example, repeated the long-standing condemnation of those Christians who traded in war supplies with the Moslems. The ban against selling arms and materials such as lumber and food to the Moslems had been included in the *Decretales* with the insertion of a prohibition of the practice which Clement III (1187-1191) had issued [47]. John XXII condemned « the damnable greed of some Christians » who engaged in the trade in spite of papal fulminations [48]. In particular, he railed against merchants who used ports in Cyprus, itself a prime target in the Moslem advance into the Mediterranean, to engage in such trade. He pleaded with the king of Cyprus to halt the practice.

The letters in Vatican Register 62 suggest that the idea of a new crusade against the Turks was at a low ebb at the papal court. The table of contents for the register mentioned a letter of John XXII inviting Philip VI to go on crusade [49]. For some reason, the letter referred to was not inserted in the body of the register. From the dates of the letters in the register that precede and follow the point at which such a letter would have been inserted, it can be determined that such a letter would have been sent in 1332 or 1333, near the close of John XXII's pontificate. The first topic which the table of contents lists for the reign of Benedict XII refers to a letter addressed to Philip VI in which the pope excused the king from fulfilling his crusading vow. Again, no such letter was placed in the text, but there is a note at the place in the register where the letter should have appeared indicating where it was supposed to be placed [50]. The letter would seem to have been one which Benedict sent in March 1336 explaining why he had felt bound to release the king from his vow. « Is it not apparent in fact that England and Scot-

---

47 « ... nos tamen omnes illos excommunicationi supponimus, qui tam amplius cum Sarracenis mercimonium habuerint, vel per se, vel per alios navibus seu quocunque alio ingenio eis aliaque rerum subsidia seu consilia, quandiu inter nos et illos guerra duraverit, duxerint impendenda ». *Decretales*, 5.6.12., *Quod olim*.

48 « Quantas ruinas hactenus attulerit christicolis transmarinarum partium, quantosque dederit casus adversos ceca et dampnosa nonnullorum christianorum cupiditas, qui de Regno Cypri eiusque partibus exeuntes armaturas, mercimonia, et alias res prohibitas detulerunt et definerunt sicut displicenter audivimus sarracenis, penas, prohibitiones, et sententias a canonibus, statutis et constitutionibus sedis apostolice contra deferrentes seu mittentes talia sarracenis inflictas ... ». John XXII, *Quantas ruinas*, April 24, 1323: *RV 62*, fols. 13v-14r at fol. 13v; MOLLAT, *Lettres communes*, no. 18119.

49 « Scribit etiam Regi Francie pro passaggio ultramarino ». *RV 62*, fol. 1*v.

50 « Dispensat dominus papa Regi Francie super iuramento per eum prestito de passagio per eum faciendo ultra mare ». *RV 62*, fol. 2*r. The same statement appears in the text at fol. 29v, but no letter is given there.

land are in conflict, Germany upset, Tuscany and Lombardy, Apulia and Sicily in complete anarchy? »[51]. Should Philip persist in going to the Holy Land he would probably be defeated in any event. These comments received additional emphasis from the fact that the next brief entry in the register was a note saying that Benedict XII « wrote letters of consolation to the kingdom of Armenia about the invasion of the kingdom which the Saracens had begun »[52]. The compiler may have thought that these two brief headings would serve to make the point about the failure of the Latins to assist their brothers because they were too busy murdering each other. There was no need for him to include the letters themselves. As a result, Benedict XII concentrated his energies on seeking peace among the European nations preparatory to raising another great crusade. Without peace within Christian Europe, no serious crusade could be attempted, much less be successful.

Benedict XII did become interested in a new crusade around 1340, but the compiler of Vatican Register 62 did not include any letters from this period in his volume[53]. Instead, he began the story of the crusade with the pontificate of Clement VI. The focal point of this attempt to stop the Turk was the Aegean where the Christian rulers of several islands were under heavy pressure from Moslem pirates[54]. Clement VI appears to have believed that the reunion of the Greeks with the Latin Church was more likely to occur if the West could create a successful crusading force. These letters also suggest that he was more pragmatic in his approach to a crusade than his immediate predecessors had been. Rather than proposing a grandiose crusade with impossible goals, Clement VI proposed a limited effort which would rely heavily on the fact that the Italian city states had strong interests in the Aegean that they were willing to defend.

The first letter of Clement VI in Vatican Register 62 spelled out the pope's goals. The pope informed Martin Zaccaria, a Genoese merchant from the island of Chios in the Aegean who was to command the papal vessels in the proposed crusading fleet, of the need to renew the crusade. « The faithful in Romania and in other places and on the islands which are adjacent who are being attacked and mangled by the assaults and persecutions of the Turks » need the

---

51 Benedict XII, *Sane, fili charissimi,* translated in JENKINS, p. 24; RAYNALDUS, ad ann. 1336, nn. 43-45 at n. 44.

52 « Scribit Regine Armenie litteras consolatorias super invasione Sarracenorum contra Regnum Armenie per eos attemptata ». *RV 62,* fol. 2*r. A slightly different version appears in the text. « Scribit Regine Armenie litteras consolatorias super invasione Regni Armenie per sarracenos attemptata ». *RV 62,* fol. 29v.

53 « ... the pope fell back on his earlier policy of stimulating war against the infidel as a means of effecting peace among Christians ». JENKINS, p. 67; see also, GAY, p. 28.

54 ATYIA, pp. 291-297; SETTON, *History of the Crusades,* 3: pp. 59-61.

assistance of the Latin West[55]. Zaccaria would command the four galleys that the pope planned to supply[56]. The Venetians, the king of Cyprus and the Hospitallers would contribute the remainder. The pope's interests were to be represented by the exiled Latin Patriarch of Constantinople who was authorized to remove or to replace Zaccaria if he proved incapable of leading the planned crusade successfully[57]. In his letters to the participants in this new crusade, Clement VI stressed that the Moslems were not ordinary enemies. They « thirsted for the blood of Christians and they desired the extermination of the glory of Christianity »[58].

At the same time as the crusading fleet was being raised, Clement VI was writing to various figures in the Eastern Empire seeking their support for the proposed crusade. An embassy that John V Palaeologus had sent to treat with the papacy was present in Avignon so Clement VI took the opportunity to inform him of the plans[59]. The pope hoped that the news of this plan would encourage the Byzantines to look more favorably on the idea of ecclesiastical reunion. Similar letters stressing the importance of the reunion, though not mentioning the fleet, were sent to the leading nobles of the Eastern Empire, to the patriarch of Constantinople and the bishops of the East, and to various powerful individuals within the Empire[60].

---

55 « ... fideles in Romanie et aliis partibus et Insulis adiacentibus commorantes quos diris afflictionibus et persecutionibus Turchorum infidelium molestari et lacerari non sine mentis amaritudine audivimus ... ». Clement VI, *Commotis*, September 16, 1343: *RV 62*, fol. 40r; DÉPREZ, GLÉNISSON, MOLLAT, n. 404.

56 « Cum autem pro eodem subsidio quatuor galeas armatas et munitas decenter nostris et ecclesie Romane sumptibus et expensis tenendas illuc per unum annum continuum faciamus transmitti ». *Ibid.*

57 « Nos quatuor galeas sufficienter armatas ... parari fecimus et muniri dilecto filio nobili viro Martino Zaccarie ... experto in talibus earundem galearum nostrarum generali capitaneo ... si forsan dictum capitaneum amoveri ab officio capitaneatus huiusmodi vel deficere aut alio impedimento notabili detineri contigeret, tu alium Capitaneum quem ad hoc idoneum et sufficientem credideris auctoritate nostra quotiens oportunum extiterit ... ». Clement VI, *Erga christicolas*, September 16, 1343: *RV 62*, fols. 40r-40v; DÉPREZ and MOLLAT, no. 280; SETTON, *The Papacy and the Levant*, pp. 180, 186, 190-194.

58 « Non sine mentis amaritudine auditis dudum duris afflictionibus quas gens illa nationis Turchorum fetide christianorum sanguinem siciens et ad exterminum nominis christianitatis aspirans christicolis in Romanie et alis adacentibus insulis et partibus transmarinis in quibus catholice fidei viget cultus degentibus minus crudeliter et terribiliter intulit ... ». Clement VI, *Non sine mentis*, September 16, 1343: *RV 62*, fols. 41v-42r at fol. 41v; DÉPREZ, GLÉNISSON, MOLLAT, no. 411.

59 « Magnificentie tue literas per dilectum filium nobilem virum Philippum de sancto germano nuntium tuum ... benigne recipimus ... explicavit affectum magne devotionis et reverentie nobis et apostolice sedi obtuleris ac expressis diris oppressionibus ... quas gens illa nationis Turchorum fetide inimica fidei christiane ... tibi et populo grecorum intulit ... ». Clement VI, *Magnificentie: RV 62*, fols. 44r-44v; RAYNALDUS, ad ann. 1343, no. 12 (*Munificentiae*).

60 Clement VI, *Quot et quanto*: fols. 46r-46v: *Salvator noster*, October 21, 1343: *RV 62*, fols. 45r-46r; RAYNALDUS, ad ann. 1343, no. 15; DÉPREZ, GLÉNISSON, MOLLAT, no. 468; *Et si ut sacra*, October 21, 1343: *RV 62*, fol. 45r; RAYNALDUS, ad ann. 1343, no. 13 (incomplete); DÉPREZ, GLÉNISSON, MOLLAT, no. 467.

The Latin Patriarch of Constantinople was empowered to negotiate the anticipated reunion in addition to his other duties[61].

By the summer of 1343, Clement was able to inform the king of Cyprus that the fleet would assemble in the fall at Nigroponte[62]. The pope pointed out that as the kingdom of Cyprus lay in the direct line of Turkish expansion, the king should be very anxious to cooperate in this venture that would be of immediate benefit to him and to his subjects[63]. The Angevin ruler of Sicily received a similar letter in the hope of arousing his support for the campaign[64]. In another letter, the queen of Sicily was asked to encourage her husband to support the crusading effort because even if « the power of those pagans is not yet present in those regions their power may grow » eventually and become a direct threat to the security of Sicily[65]. The pope added that he had a special interest in the fate of Sicily because it was a papal fief. As a good vassal the king should defend it for the papacy[66].

Finally, Clement VI circularized the West in order to obtain widespread support for the planned crusade. These letters stressed the wickedness of the Turks and the need for Christians to halt their advance before they overrun Europe[67]. To encourage popular feeling against the Turks, the pope described the horrors which would attend a Turkish conquest. In language that would have been more

---

61 « ... venerabili fratri nostro Henrico patriarche Constantinopolitano apostolice sedis legato aliqua imposuerimus super hiis et per nos vel ipsum legatum sint ad partes illas persone alique super tractanda reunione huiusmodi destinande ... ». Clement VI, *Cum nos qui licet*, October 21, 1343: *RV 62*, fol. 46v; DÉPREZ, GLÉNISSON, MOLLAT, no. 471.

62 « ... et quod omnes galee huiusmodi in festo Omnium sanctorum proximo futuro conveniant apud insulam Nigripontis ... ». Clement VI, *Ex relatione*, August 8, 1343: *RV 62*, fol. 48r; DÉPREZ, GLÉNISSON, MOLLAT, no. 332.

63 « ... considerans quantum tibi Regno et subditis tuis si dictorum paganorum ferocitas ulterius invalescat ... » *Ibid.*

64 « Cum igitur sciamus excellentiam tuam erga fidem catholicam et defensionem ipsius interne caritatis zelo et ardore fervere ac infidelium eosdem impugnantium ... ». Clement VI, *Quantum feritas illorum*, August 8, 1343: *RV 62*, fols. 48r-48v at fol. 48v; DÉPREZ, GLÉNISSON, MOLLAT, no. 333.

65 « ... carissima filia, debes diligenter attendere quod si paganorum predictorum quod absit in partibus illis potentia cresceret et audaciam peramplius insenirit (?) ... ». Clement VI, *Filia benedictionis et gratie*, August 8, 1343: *RV 62*, fols. 50r-50v at fol. 50r; DÉPREZ, GLÉNISSON, MOLLAT, no. 338.

66 « ... Regno Sicilie quod a nobis et cclesia Romana tenes in feudum ... ». *Ibid.*

67 « ... non sine amaritudine mentis accipimus quod gentes illorum infidelium paganorum que vulgari lingua Turchi vocantur ... ad extinctionem catholice fidei anelantes collectis sue viribus nationis ... cum maxima quantitate lignorum navalium armatorum in partibus Romanie et aliis locis fidelium convicinis eisdem christianorum fines per mare fuerunt ingressi et in christianos et loca ac insulas eorundem attrociter sevientes per mare discurrerunt hactenus et non desistunt discurrere incessanter, dampnificantes et depopulantes loca at insulas christianorum partium earundem ipsasque incendio miserabili supponentes ». Clement VI, *Insurgentibus*, September 30, 1343: *RV 62*, fols. 52r-53v at fols. 52r-52v; DÉPREZ, GLÉNISSON, MOLLAT, no. 433. In addition, see *Gustamus amaritudinis calicem*, December 1, 1343: *RV 62*, fols. 55r-57r; DÉPREZ, GLÉNISSON, MOLLAT, no. 559.

fitting for launching a massive crusade, the pope described the Turks as seeking the extinction of the Christian faith and that they had gathered vast amounts of men and arms to insure their success. They had caused havoc in their advance, wiping out the Christian population wherever they passed. The few survivors of the Turkish victories had been sold into perpetual slavery and forced to deny their faith[68]. The letter spelled out the plans which the pope had laid for halting the Turks and requested financial assistance from all Christians to make them possible. The pope said that this was the first step in a program designed « not only for aiding and assisting those Christians but also for the exalting of the Catholic faith »[69]. A crusading tenth was levied for a three year period in order to pay the costs of the expedition.

The initial results of the campaign in the Aegean justified Clement VI's efforts. In October 1344, the fleet took the city of Smyrna and the pope announced the victory in a series of letters to various western Christian leaders. While the victory might not have been the « glorious victory » which the pope called it, it did offer some hope to those Christians who may have believed that Christian arms were bound to fail in any contest with the Moslems in the East[70]. Clement hoped that the initial success in Smyrna would be followed up by greater Christian interest in the crusade.

The most likely sources of the men and funds which a large scale crusade would require were the kingdoms of France and England. Even though French interest in the crusade had declined since the end of the thirteenth century and even though the English found the wars in France more attractive than crusading in the East, Clement VI attempted to arouse them with the report of the victory at Smyrna. Perhaps he was recalling the success which Urban II had in calling the first crusade by pointing out the need for western Christians to come to the aid of their brothers in the East. In the letter to Edward III, the pope asked that he and his fellow monarchs put aside their domestic wars and turn that energy to a new crusade[71]. Like Benedict XII, Clement VI clearly recognized that peace

---

68 « Et quod nephandius est, christianos eosdem in predam abducunt et subiciunt orribili et perpetue servituti vendentes eos ut animalia, ipsosque ad abnegandum fidem catholicam compellentes ... ». Clement VI, *Insurgentibus: RV 62*, fol. 52v.

69 « ... igitur assidue cogitamus quando et qualiter negotium ipsum ad dei laudem et gloriam et non solum ad defensionem catholice fidei et professorum eiusdem, sed etiam exaltationem ipsius feliciter prosperetur et pro feliciori prosequtione ipsius decimas reddituum et proventuum ecclesiasticorum in certis terris ... ». *Ibid.: RV 62*, fol. 52v.

70 « Spiritualis gaudii per nos ex felicibus rumoribus nobis noviter nunciatis concepti, de quadam gloriosa victoria ... ». Clement VI, *Spiritualia gaudii per nos*, December 23, 1344: *RV 62*, fol. 62v; DÉPREZ, GLÉNISSON, MOLLAT, no. 1351.

71 « Rogamus itaque serenitatem Regiam et attentius in Domino exhortamur quatenus que quanta et qualia principes catholici ad eiusdem dilatationem fidei ac sue salutis et honoris augumentum possent agere hiis temporibus, si guerris et dissen-

within Europe was a prerequisite to any successful crusade. In another letter, the pope appealed to the pride of the English and French monarchs. Because they were the pre-eminent Christian rulers they above all others should be anxious to lead European society in the crusade[72]. The pope indicated that the Hundred Years War was preventing the two monarchs from playing their rightful role at the head of Christian society[73]. Similar letters went to Philip VI and to various members of his family in an attempt to win French support[74]. Curiously, these did not explicitly mention the role of the Hundred Years War in hindering French participation in the crusade. They did, however, indicate the important role which France would play in the reconquest of the East from the Turks.

The deaths of the three leaders of the army that had captured Smyrna, Zaccaria, the Latin Patriarch and the Venetian Pietro Zeno, during a subsequent military engagement in January 1345 darkened the glow of the earlier victory. They died in an attempt to expand their initial success into the conquest of the region around Smyrna, an effort which ended in a significant victory for the Turks whose army surrounded the crusader-held city[75]. In a letter to another legate in the East, Clement provided a gloomy picture of the state of Christendom at that point. He noted that Benedict XII had hoped for peace among Christian nations in Europe so that a united Europe would face the Turks and eventually defeat them[76]. Even on the border with the advancing Turks, he observed sadly, the Christians continued to fight among themselves oblivious to the threat which the Turks presented to their very existence. In Greece, for example,

---

tionibus suis cessantibus ... ». Clement VI, *Dudum afflictionibus variis*, February 1, 1345: *RV 62*, fols. 66r-67r at fol. 66v; RAYNALDUS, ad ann. 1344, nn. 4-6 at no. 6; DÉPREZ, GLÉNISSON, MOLLAT, no. 1462.

72 « Cum autem inter ceteros reges et principes orthodoxe fidei professores, tu amantissime fili et carissimus in Christo filius noster Philippus Rex Francie illustris potentiores et eminentiores reputemini, non indigne ... ». Clement VI, *Misse nobis hiis diebus*, March 18, 1345: *RV 62*, fols. 66r-67r at fol. 66v; DÉPREZ, GLÉNISSON, MOLLAT, no. 1582.

73 « O fili dilectissime, quam foret redemptori nostro placibile quamque christianitati expediens ac catholicis regibus et principibus apud deum meritorium et inter homines honorabile testaretur, veritas et fama celebris predicaretur, si omissis guerris et dissentionibus in quibus non sine maxima dei displicentia et offensa, ac animarum evidentibus periculis, sanguis illorum funditur, quos redemit preciosissimi cruoris effusio corporis Iesu Christi ad pacis et veritatis concordiam in qua delectatur altissimus, convertentes placabiliter corda sua adversus illos qui deum blasfemant Christianitatis vilipendunt ... ». *Ibid.*: *RV 62*, fol. 66v.

74 Clement VI, *Per litteras dilecti*, March 25, 1345: *RV 62*, fol. 67r; DÉPREZ, GLÉNISSON, MOLLAT, no. 1596; *Negotium transmarinum*, April 10, 1345: *RV 62*, fol. 70v; DÉPREZ, GLÉNISSON, MOLLAT, no. 1638; *Dudum attendentes quod*, April 10, 1345: *RV 62*, fols. 70v-71r; DÉPREZ, GLÉNISSON, MOLLAT, no. 1639.

75 ATIYA, pp. 295-296.

76 « ... Benedictus papa .XII. predecessor noster diligenter attendens quod licet inter fideles ubique optanda sit pacis unitas et fovenda ... ». Clement VI, *Dudum felicis recordationis*, April 1, 1345: *RV 62*, fols. 69v-70r at fol. 69v; DÉPREZ, GLÉNISSON, MOLLAT, no. 1608.

Duke Walter and the mercenaries of the Catalan Grand Company were quarreling over possession of the Duchy of Athens[77]. The Turks were taking advantage of these internal problems to press their advance into Europe[78]. Clement instructed the legate to work for the settlement of the conflict between the duke and the Catalans so that the Christians would be in a better position to halt the Turks[79].

In addition to the wars between Christians which were blocking a concentration of Christian military might against the enemies of Christendom, Clement VI also had to face the problem of conflict within the crusading forces. Men who had begun the crusade filled with zeal for the faith had begun to quarrel among themselves[80]. On all sides, the pope saw signs that even with an initial success in battle European Christians were not about to rush forward with spirits high in yet another attempt to stop and eventually drive back the Turk.

In spite of the loss of the crusade's leaders, Clement VI did not cease his efforts to inspire a crusade. He appointed Humbert of Vienne (1312-1355) to command the papal forces in place of Martin Zaccaria[81]. The problems which the new commander had to face were great. The civil war in the Byzantine Empire between John Cantakuzenos and the empress-regent Johanna was making the defense of the East even more difficult. As usual, Humbert, the papal agent in the East, was instructed to seek the reunion of the churches,

77 « ... dissentiones et guerre que in partibus Romanie propinquis et vicinis Turchis infidelibus et persecutoribus fidei orthodoxe olim inter dilectum filium nobilem virum Galterum ducem Athenarum et predecessores suos ex parte una et illos qui de societate magna Romanie se vocant ex altera ... ». *Ibid.* See also, Kenneth M. Setton, *The Catalan Domination of Athens, 1311-1388*, Cambridge, Mass. 1948.

78 « ... velut divisi et suis exausti facultatibus propter guerras et dissentiones predictas, minus potentes et fortes prefatique Turchi hoc videntes et sentientes, audatius et presumptuosius irruebant et irruerant infideles predictos ... ». Clement VI, *Dudum felicis recordationis: RV 62*, fol. 69v.

79 « ... circa hoc tractabilem benivolum et benignum, volens quod inter ipsum ducem et illos de societate predicta super reformatione pacis et concordie huiusmodi tractaretur ... ». *Ibid.*

80 « ... reputamus ut illi qui zelo dei et fervore accensi fidei contra Turchos ... ad partes se conferunt Transmarinas vitatis quibusvis dissentionum et rancorum odiis in pacis et caritatis vinculo persistentes ... Sane cum sicut intelleximus quandoque contingat quod aliqui ex peregrinis eisdem ... ad rixas rancores et odia invicem seu cum aliis provocantur nos de tue devotionis sinceritate quam te habere ad talia sedanda dampna et scandala fidedignis assertionibus percepimus in domino confidentes ut talium Venetiis existentium rixas dissentiones et discordias sedare, ipsosque ad concordiam viis et modis honestis et licitis revocare ... ». Clement VI, *Expediens admodum reputamus*, May 4, 1345: *RV 62*, fols. 74v-75r at 74v; Déprez, Glenisson, Mollat, no. 1682.

81 « Cum nos dilectum filium nobilem virum Ymbertum dalphinum Viennen., nobilitate preclarum, potentia preditum, virtutibus insignitum, et fidei fervidum zelatorem ac nobis et ecclesie Romane carum multipliciter et acceptum capitaneum sancte sedis apostolice et ducem exercitus christianorum contra Turchos fidei catholice inimicos auctoritate apostolica fecerimus ... ». Clement VI, *Cum nos dilectum filium*, August 1, 1345: *RV 62*, fol. 77r; Déprez, Glénisson, Mollat, no. 1861.

but it is difficult to see what he could reasonably be expected to accomplish in that sphere[82]. Humbert's military goal was the possession of the island of Chios for use as a base from which to operate his fleet. In addition, he hoped to obtain the support of the Catalan Grand Company[83]. In order to obtain their support, however, it was necessary to have Clement VI lift the excommunication which he had imposed on the Company[84]. All of Humbert's plans came to nothing in the end. In 1349 he gave up the world in order to become a Dominican friar.

Although Vatican Register 62 contained a number of letters relating to Clement's efforts at sponsoring a crusade, the number of letters is out of proportion to the success that he actually achieved. The conflicts within western Europe, within the Byzantine Empire and within the crusading army itself all contributed to the failure of the crusade. Smyrna remained in Christian hands until 1402 when the Tartars led by Tamerlane seized it[85]. No great crusade followed upon the news of the initial victory. The Hundred Years War continued to occupy the kings of France and England, deafening them to papal calls for a new war in the East.

Towards the end of the register, the compiler included some additional letters which dealt with the fate of Armenia, demonstrating to his readers what the failure of western rulers to help their brothers in the East eventually caused. The Mamelukes had invaded that unfortunate country once more and the pope sought to assist the people in their plight by seeking western aid for them. The Venetians, the king of Cyprus and the papal legate in the East each received letters requesting them to aid the Armenians[86]. The pope

---

[82] « Porro super credentia quam prefato nuntio sicut ipse nobis retulit ad te dederunt dilecti filii nobiles viri ... circa reductionem seu reunionem eiusdem imperatricis ac Grecorum ecclesie catholice procurandum volumus quod quantum poteris et expedire videris ac fructum exinde posse prodire conspexeris ... ». *Tanto iocundiori*, June 15, 1346: *RV 62*, fols. 80v-82v at fol. 81v; RAYNALDUS, ad ann. 1346, nn. 64-65 at no. 64 (incomplete); DÉPREZ, GLÉNISSON, MOLLAT, no. 2581.

[83] « ... ut carissime in Chrito filie nostre Iohanne Imperatrici Constantinopolitan. illustri insulam de Chio tibi et unioni valde necessariam velit ob favorem fidei accomodare usque ad triennium retentis ... ». *Ibid.*: *RV 62*, fol. 81r.

[84] « Cum autem sicut habet expositio supradicta, ipsi desiderantes redire ad sancte matris ecclesie unitatem ac prestare satisfactionem quam potuerunt pro premissis humiliter supplicaverint ac supplicent ad hec de benignitate apostolica se admitti ... et ipsi eisdem interesse valeant interdictum relaxari predictum vel saltem predictas excommunicationis et interdicti sententias per nos usque ad alicuius temporis spacium de quo nobis videbitur expedire de gratia speciali suspendi ut interim via satisfactionis tractari ... ». Clement VI, *Nuper expositum extitit*, June 15, 1346: *RV 62*, fols. 84r-85r at fol. 84v; DÉPREZ, GLÉNISSON, MOLLAT, no. 2590.

[85] ATIYA, pp. 298-300.

[86] Clement VI, *Occurrunt frequenter*, September, 1347: *RV 62*, fol. 86r-86v; RAYNALDUS, ad ann. 1347, no. 18; DÉPREZ and MOLLAT, no. 1482; *Dilecti filii nobilis*, September 26, 1347: *RV 62*, fol. 86v; C. KOHLER, *Lettres pontificales concernant l'histoire de la Petite Arménie au XIVe siècle*, in *Florilegium ou Recueil de travaux d'érudition dédié à M. le marquis Melchior de Vogüe*, Paris 1909, pp. 303-327 at p. 323; *Dum anxie cogitamus*, September 26, 1347: *RV 62*, fol. 86v; DÉPREZ and MOLLAT, no. 1492.

also wrote to the kings of France and England about the situation, but to no avail [87]. He could only respond to the Armenian call for aid by encouraging the reunion of the Armenian Church with the Latin Church [88].

The picture of the state of Christian arms in the wars with the Moslems that Vatican Register 62 contains was not entirely bleak. In two letters to Genoa, Clement VI praised the work of Alfonso XI (1312-1350) in pushing back the Moslems of Spain [89]. The pope praised the Genoese for their support of the king. At the same time, he complained that some Genoese merchants were trading in arms and other military supplies with the enemies of Alfonso XI, a trade that should be stopped [90].

In the long run, Clement's narrowly based approach to the crusade was not a great deal more effective than the efforts of his predecessors had been. His efforts proved that western European leaders had little interest in the crusade any more. The most heartbreaking part of the effort must have been the knowledge that Christians were continuing to supply the enemy with arms and equipment even as the Moslems advanced into Europe itself along the southern flank.

## III

## CONVERSION OF THE INFIDELS

### 1. The Mission to the Tartars

The best known example of peaceful contact with the world beyond Europe in the Middle Ages was the series of missionary journeys which Christopher Dawson labelled the Mongol Mission [1].

87 « ... benigne audivimus et intelleximus diligenter asserens se ad carissimos in Christo filios nostros Philippum Francie et Edwardum Anglie Reges illustres litteras tuas defferre ac eis aliqua exponere pro tui parte debere contulit ad eos ... ». Clement VI, *Dilectus filius nobilis: RV 62*, fol. 87r; RAYNALDUS, ad ann. 1347, no. 29.

88 « Rogamus itaque ... quod omnis erroris et scismatis de partibus ipsis fugata caligine lumen catholice veritatis effulgeat, tuque ipsos subditos tuos non solum temporaliter regas et dirigas, sed eis ad eterne vite gaudia salubriter prebuisse ... ». *Ibid.*

89 « Alfonsus Rex Castelle et Legionis illustris devotionis et affectionis favorem quem ad exterminum inimicorum fidei christiane ac ipsius fidei exaltationem et dilationem habuit ... percepimus sarracenos yspaniarum partium potenter aggressus et ad eos conculcandos modis et de suis finibus propellendos ... ». Clement VI, *Carissimus in Christo filius*, June, 1349: *RV 62*, fols. 87v-88r at 87v.

90 « Ceterum ne aliquos ex subditis aut servitoribus nostris ad deferendum sarracenis arma vel alia queque prohibita dampnanda prorsus ambitio captandi lucri temporalis ... ». *Ibid.: RV 62*, fol. 88r.

1 *The Mongol Mission*, ed. CHRISTOPHER DAWSON, London 1955; reprinted as *Mission to Asia*, New York 1966. The sources for the Franciscan aspects of the missionary effort can be found in *Sinica Franciscana*, ed. ANASTASIUS VAN DEN WYNGAERT (5 v., Quaracchi and Florence 1929-1954), 1: *Itinera et relationes Fratrum Minorum saeculi XIII et XIV*. Translations of many of the texts in *Sinica Franciscana* are available

From the first of these missions, that of John of Plano Carpini whom Innocent IV dispatched from the Council of Lyons in 1245, to the last mission which set out in 1370, there was a continuous tradition of papal contact with the Mongol (or Tartar) Khans and their Christian subjects. The Mongols provided a two-fold problem for the papacy. On the one hand, they posed a direct military threat to eastern Europe and to Asia Minor. On the other hand, the papacy and various missionaries were tantalized by the dream of converting them to Christianity, followed perhaps by a grand alliance between Europeans and Mongols against the Turks. The letters in Vatican Register 62 dealt only briefly with the threat which the Mongols posed to European society and were focused instead on the possibility of converting them to Christianity.

The possibility that the Mongols would become a major threat to the Christian world appeared in a letter of John XXII concerning the fate of Armenia. He argued that for a hundred years the Mongols and the Armenians had lived at peace. Now, however, in 1322. the Mongols were allying themselves with the Turks to attack the Armenians[2]. In doing this, the Mongols were of course doing precisely the opposite of what the papacy had envisaged for them. The pope may have believed that strong Christian support for the Armenians would cause the Mongols to reconsider their relations with the Turks.

The other region in which the Mongol advance remained a significant threat to Christians was northeastern Europe where Poland and Hungary remained under constant pressure from Mongol armies. Benedict XII, one of whose major goals was peace, wrote to Usbech (1312-1340), the khan of the Golden Horde that occupied Russia, asking that he end his wars with Poland and Hungary. The pope recognized that the causes of the conflicts along the border with Hungary and Poland were not necessarily the fault of the Mongols. Benedict XII hoped that if these Christian kingdoms attacked the Golden Horde, the khan would inform him so that he might be

---

in Dawson and in *Cathay and the Way Thither*, ed. HENRY YULE, rev. by HENRI CORDIER, 4 v., London 1913-1916. The basic introduction to the literature of the Mongol Mission is the *Biblioteca bio-bibliografica della Terra Santa et dell'Oriente francescano*, ed. GIROLAMO GOLUBOVICH, 19 v., Florence 1906-1948. The basic book on the Mongol Mission, to which all modern research is indebted, is G. SORANZO, *Il Papato, l'Europa christiana e i Tartari*, Milano 1930. A briefer, but more recent introduction to papal interest in the Asian mission, a volume that also brings Soranzo's bibliography up to date, is I. DE RACHEWILTZ, *Papal Envoys to the Great Khans*, Stanford 1971. Other basic works include: PAUL PELLIOT, *Les Mongols et la papauté*, 3 v., Paris 1923; and A. C. MOULE, *Christians in China Before the Year 1550*, London 1930. There is an interesting discussion of the response of Europeans to the appearance of the Mongols: CHARLES W. CONNELL, *Western Views of the Origin of the 'Tartars': An Example of Myth in the Second Half of the Thirteenth Century*: Journal of Medieval and Renaissance Studies 3 (1973) 115-137.

2 « Idem Soldanus cum Tartaris qui dudum per centum annos Armenorum amici extiterant ... ». John XXII, *Dum mentis*: *RV 62*, fol. 9r; RAYNALDUS, ad ann. 1322, no. 33.

able to bring the conflict to a speedy end through negotiation[3].

The major aims of fourteenth century papal contact with the Tartars were the protection of missionaries and their converts and the conversion of the leaders of the Mongol world. Although there had been missionary activity in Asia continuously since the mid-thirteenth century, it had never flourished greatly[4]. Niccolò and Maffeo Polo discovered this when they sought friars to return to China with them in answer to the Great Khan's request for 100 wise men to teach him the learning of the West. Only two Dominicans were willing to begin the journey, and they went only part way before returning home again[5].

The letters in Vatican Register 62 that concern the Mongol Mission fall into three groups. The first group of letters were those of John XXII in 1333 in which the pope announced the appointment of a new archbishop of Peking to the leaders of the Mongol empire. The second series of letters were those which Benedict XII wrote in 1338 in response to a request by Christians living in the Mongol Empire for a bishop. The final letters were also sent by Benedict XII, this time in 1340, to Usbech, the leader of the Golden Horde who had sent a mission to Avignon. All of these letters demonstrate that European Christians believed that peaceful relations were possible with the Mongols and that hopes for their conversion to Christianity continued to encourage the papal court to show interest in the work of missionaries in the East.

The starting point for discussing the Mongol Mission that the compiler of Vatican Register 62 selected, the appointment of a certain Friar Nicholas as archbishop of Peking in 1333, is a curious one. The see itself had been established by Clement V in 1307 in response

3 « Et insuper cum sicut intelleximus inter tuos ac Carissimorum in Christo filiorum nostrorum Ungarie et Polonie Regum illustrium officiales et subditos in confiniis Imperii tui et Regnorum Regum predictorum quandoque suscitari contingat dissentiones et guerras, ex quibus strages hominum lapsus rerum, et animarum amarius deploranda pericula subsequuntur, velit tua sublimitas ab invasione Regnorum predictorum desistere quia si Reges predicti inferrent tibi vel tuis iniurias indebitas vel offensas, et id nobis duxeris intimandum hec per Reges ipsos precabimur facere quantum cum deo poterimus tibi et tuis rationabiliter emendari ». Benedict XII, *Letanter et benigne*, August 17, 1340: *RV 62*, fols. 33r-33v at fol. 33v; WADDING, 7: pp. 269-270 at p. 270; VIDAL, no. 2853.

4 Although there were continuous missionary contacts with the East, few converts seem to have been made. The missionaries who went to Asia probably exaggerated their successes in order to attract additional friars to the work. For example, John of Monte Corvino stated that he had baptized 6000 converts and would have baptized even more if it had not been for the opposition of the Nestorian clergy: see DAWSON, p. 225. In the sixteenth century, the Jesuit missionaries were careful to publish material which would stimulate continued interest in their missionary efforts in Asia: see DONALD F. LACH, *Asia in the Making of Europe:* v. 1, *The Century of Discovery*, Chicago 1965, p. 317.

5 *The Book of Ser Marco Polo the Venetian Concerning the Kingdoms and Marvels of the East*, ed. HENRY YULE, rev. ed. HENRI CORDIER (3rd ed., 2 v., London, 1926) 1: pp. 13-14, 22-3.

to two letters which arrived in the West from John of Monte Corvino (1247-1328?), a Franciscan friar who had been sent to the East by Pope Nicholas IV (1288-1292)[6]. After various adventures, he reached Peking shortly after the death of Kublai Khan in 1294. This was a particularly unfortunate time to arrive because Kublai Khan who had shown a great deal of interest in European Christians, as Marco Polo noted in his book about his own travels in Asia, was succeeded by rulers who did not have any such interest. Furthermore, although the way to Asia was known to anyone who was interested in making such a trip, John of Monte Corvino spent most of his first dozen years alone in Peking. In 1305 and again in 1306 he wrote to his brethren in the West, informing them of his existence and the state of his missionary endeavors. In his letters he said that he had made many converts and that if it had not been for the opposition of the Nestorian clergy who resented his activities he would have made many more. The lack of any assistance in this work for many years and his advancing age moved him to write to the West seeking co-workers who would carry on this work[7].

The arrival of Monte Corvino's letters in the West must have come as a surprise after so many years of silence. Clement V responded to the friar's request for assistance by appointing him archbishop of Peking and sending several friars to work with him[8]. In terms of the number of clerics involved, the mission in China reached its peak in the early years of the fourteenth century.

In spite of the importance of John of Monte Corvino in the history of the Mongol Mission, Vatican Register 62 makes no mention of him or his associates at this point. Instead, the register dealt with the mission to China only in connection with the appointment of Friar Nicholas as archbishop of Peking, apparently to succeed Monte Corvino, in 1333. The letters, which were addressed to the Great Khan and to various other Tartar leaders, introduced Nicholas as a learned and virtuous man whom the pope had selected from among the ranks of many such men for the office of archbishop of Peking[9]. He would be assisted by a group of friars whom the pope was dispatching at the same time.

---

[6] WADDING, 6: pp. 77-82; WYNGAERT, *Sinica Franciscana*, 1: pp. 345-355; DAWSON, pp. 224-231. The only book length study of Monte Corvino is ANASTASIUS VAN DEN WYNGAERT, *Jean de Monte Corvino, O.F.M., premier évêque de Khanbaliq (1247-1328)*, Lille 1924.

[7] « Now I have been alone in this journeying without a confessor for eleven years, until there came to me Brother Arnold ... more than a year ago ... Moreover I have baptized about 6,000 persons there up to the present ... And if it had not been for the aforesaid slanders I might have baptized 30,000 more ... ». DAWSON, p. 225.

[8] RAYNALDUS, ad ann. 1307, nn. 29-39; WADDING, 6: pp. 76-77, 102-113.

[9] « Ecce igitur nos qui tuam et totius Regni tui salutem perpetuam sincera in domino dilectione zelamus ... cupimus provenire, ut hec faciliter et efficiter succedere valeant per misericordiam summi pastoris, venerabilem fratrem nostrum Nicolaum Archiepiscopum Cambaliensem Ordinis fratrum minorum professorem, virum quidem

The letter that accompanied Friar Nicholas and that was to introduce him to the Great Khan reflected the optimism about the possibility of converting the Mongols. Such optimism seems to have been a staple of curial rhetoric about the mission even if the reality of the situation was very different. The pope explained that word of the khan's interest in Christianity had reached him and that such interest was a credit to him[10]. If only the khan would act upon this interest in Christianity to become a baptized Christian, the pope assured him that eternal life would be his[11]. The sending of Friar Nicholas was described as a sign of the paternal interest which the pope had in the salvation of the Tartars. In his capacity as vicar of Christ, the pope was sending these friars just as Christ had sent his disciples to preach to the whole world[12]. Because the Mongols had long experience of Christianity through the Nestorians who were found throughout the Mongol empire, the pope was careful to point out that the khan should accept and protect those Christians who professed the doctrines that « the Roman Church, the teacher and mother of all those who believe in Christ, teaches, preaches and believes » for outside of that Church « there is no salvation »[13]. The pope expressed the hope that the words of the Franciscan would so move the khan that he and his subjects would be converted to the Christian faith.

In a letter to another Mongol ruler, the pope explained the friars' mission to the infidels in more detail. As all men belonged to the flock of Christ, the missionaries were to preach and instruct all men so that they might receive baptism and be readied for eternal life. This applied especially to « all those others who dwell outside

in devotione ac fide catholica fervidum, eminenter in sacra scriptura peritum, expertum in opere ac sermone, virtute comitiva stipatum, fama preclarum, a nobis ex multis bonis et ydoneis Religiosis, electum ... ». John XXII, *Accedit ad tue magnitudinis*, October 1, 1333: *RV 62*, fols. 26v-27[1]v at fol 27[1]v; *Acta Ioannis XXII*, no. 138, pp. 255-258 at p. 256; Mollat, *Lettres communes*, no. 63873.

10 « ... sicut fame preconium et fidedignorum relationis affatus ad apostolatus nostri audientiam perduxerunt, tu iactans tuum in dominum cogitatum, et promereri cupiens aput eum, christianis, in Regno et terra tui dominii commorantibus et aliis indigenis ad fidem orthodoxam conversis et in ea neophitis mansuetudinem favoris impendis, et benignitate favorabili tractas illos ... ». *Ibid.*: *RV 62*, fols. 26v-27[1]r; *Acta Ioannis XXII*, p. 255.

11 « ... aput maiestatem Regis regum eternam, qui potens est salvare rationalium et mortalium animas, si credideris in eum et baptizatus fueris legemque susceperis et impleveris, christianam requiem impetres sempiternam ... ». *Ibid.*: *RV 62*, fol. 27[1]r; *Acta Ioannis XII*, p. 256.

12 « ... ut ipse ac dicti fratres collaterales eidem more sanctorum apostolorum, qui dispertiti ore dominico, et spiritus sancti gratia illustrati serendo [ferendo] verbum dominicum cuncta mundi climata prout eis ascripta fuerunt peragrarunt coniunctim et separatim ... ». *Ibid.*: *RV 62*, fol. 27[1]r; *Acta Ioannis XXII*, p. 256.

13 « Hec est enim fides recta ... diffudit et divulgavit, usque ad terminos orbis mundialis, et quam dicta Romana ecclesia, mater cunctorum christifidelium et magistra docet, predicat, atque credit, extra quam non est penitus ulla salus ... ». *Ibid.*: *RV 62*, fol. 27[1]r; *Acta Ioannis XXII*, p. 256.

of the catholic and apostolic church and wander about in darkness »[14]. Nicholas had come to bring light into the darkness of unbelief. The pope asked that the ruler receive the missionary and listen to his message[15].

Finally, in a letter addressed generally to the Mongol people, the pope introduced the band of missionaries and explained his interest in the salvation of the Mongols. Again, he hoped that the people would listen to the teaching of the friars and enter the true fold reserved for Christ's flock[16].

After Friar Nicholas and his companions had left for Asia, papal interest in this work appears to have declined. The compiler of Vatican Register 62 made no further mention of this mission until 1338. In that year, an embassy arrived in Avignon from the Great Khan requesting that a successor to John of Monte Corvino be appointed[17]. The embassy consisted of representatives of the community of Alans who had been converted by Monte Corvino and a European identified as Andrew the Frank, probably sent to act as interpreter for the mission[18]. The Alans declared that John of Monte Corvino had died ten years earlier. Since that time they had been without the services of a priest[19]. They knew nothing of Friar Nicholas and his associates, suggesting that the mission had never reached the East[20].

---

[14] « ... nos ... in vicariatus officium pro eodem domino nostro Iesu Christo, eo disponente gerimus super terram tuam et ipsius Regni salutem zelantes in domino, qui te omnesque alios extra catholicam et apostolicam ecclesiam existentes, et in tenebris ambulantes, ad conversionem suamque veram lucem expectat, ad te dictumque Regnum aliasque circumpositas regiones et partes, ad predicandum tibi et gentibus earum verbum dominicum ... ». John XXII, *Deo vivo*, October 1, 1333: *RV 62*, fols. 271v-272r at 272r; *Bullarium Franciscanum*, 5: no. 1039b, pp. 557-558 at p. 557; Mollat, *Lettres communes*, no. 63874.

[15] « Eapropter magnitudinem tuam attente rogamus, et hortamur in domino deo nostro, per quem vivis et regnas, quatenus pro eius reverentia et honore, qui te ad ymaginem suam creavit, et permittit multitudini gentium imperare, et ad cuius imperium solvitur omnis caro, prefatos Archiepiscopum et fratres cum ad te idemque Regnum pervenerint, vultu sereno recipias, et a subditis tuis recipi iubeas ... ». *Ibid.*: *RV 62*, fol. 272r; *Bullarium Franciscanum*, 5: pp. 557-558.

[16] « ... exigente officii nostri debito tenemur, et totis desideriis affectamus omnem humanam creaturam extra sanctam Romanam ecclesiam existentem, fideique christiane insciam et deviam ab eadem dominici gregis inducere, ac reducere in ovile unire et reconciliare penitus ecclesie prelibate ». John XXII, *Salvator noster*: *RV 62*, fols. 272v-28v at fol. 28r; *Bullarium Franciscanum*, 5: p. 558, no. 1039d; Mollat, *Lettres communes*, 63875.

[17] de Rachewiltz, p. 187.

[18] « Nos mittimus Nuncium nostrum Andream Francum cum quindecim sociis ad Papam, Dominum Christianorum in Franchiam ultra septem maria, ubi sol occidit, ad aperiendum viam nunciis sepe mittendis per nos ad Papam, et per Papam ad nos ... ». This letter from Khan Togan Timur (1332-1370) introduced the embassy to Benedict XII: Wadding, 7: p. 247.

[19] « Hoc autem Sanctitati vestrae sit notum, quod longo tempore fuimus informati in fide catholica, et salubriter gubernati, et consolati plurimum per Legatum vestrum ... virum, qui tamen mortuus est ante octo annos, in quibus fuimus sine gubernatore, et sine spirituali consolatione, licet audierimus, quod providistis de alio legato, ille tamen nondum venit ». Letter from the Alans to Benedict XII: Wadding, 7: p. 248.

[20] Scholars are divided on the question of whether or not Friar Nicholas ever

Benedict XII responded to the Alans' request by sending a series of letters that introduced Friar Nicholas and that praised the khans for their interest in the souls of their subjects. The mission of 1333 was mentioned in only one letter, however, a letter to a lesser khan, Chansi, who ruled Turkestan. The khan was congratulated for having kindly received Friar Nicholas and his companions and for having extended his kindness to them [21]. According to the pope, the khan had allowed the missionaries to rebuild Christian churches which had fallen into disrepair and to build new ones. In addition, he was said to have allowed the missionaries to preach freely throughout his domains [22]. Benedict XII added that should the khan choose to send an embassy to the West to discuss the state of Christianity in his realm, he would be happy to receive it at the papal court [23].

The letters to the leaders of Turkestan suggest closer ties with them than with the other Mongol leaders and a greater knowledge of the state of Christianity there than elsewhere. In a letter addressed to two of Chansi's familiars, perhaps members of his court, Benedict XII referred to a plot of land which the khan had granted to a bishop of the Franciscan order, apparently Richard of Burgundy, for the construction of a church in the city of Armalech, near the modern city of Kuldja (Ining) in western China [24]. The pope indicated that he was aware that a church had actually been built on the site, suggesting closer contacts with Chansi's khanate than with other Mongol principalities. Similarly, he wrote to Usbech, Khan of the Golden Horde, about his having granted to unnamed Fran-

---

reached his destination. According to WYNGAERT, *Jean de Monte Corvino*, cited in *Acta Ioannis XXII*, p. 258, Nicholas eventually reached Peking where he died in 1368. MOULE, p. 197, argued that Nicholas did not reach there, an opinion accepted by RENÉ GROUSSET, *The Empire of the Steppes: A History of Central Asia*, trans. Naomi Walford, New Brunswick, New Jersey 1970, p. 319. According to DE RACHEWILTZ, p. 186, Nicholas travelled as far as Almaliq, a city near the modern city of Kulja in Sinkiang, but he did not get beyond there.

21 « ... et nichilominus sicut animo percepimus exultanti venerabilem fratrem nostrum [Nicolaum] Archiepiscopum, et dilectos filios fratres ordinis minorum dudum ad partes illas per felicis recordationis Iohannem Papam .XXII. predecessorem nostrum transmissos, recepisti favorabiliter et benigne, ad ipsos manum liberalem et munificam extendendo ... ». Benedict XII, *Leti rumores*, June 13, 1338: *RV 62*, fols. 31r-31v at fol. 31r; WADDING, 7: p. 251; VIDAL and MOLLAT, no. 1866.

22 « ... pro Dei reverentia concedendo licentiam reparandi destructas ecclesias et novas etiam construendi, et predicandi libere audire volentibus verbum Dei ... quatenus huiusmodi favores et gratias continuare velit tua sublimitas et etiam ampliare ... ». *Ibid.*: *RV 62*, fol. 31r; WADDING, 7: p. 251.

23 « ... libenter et amicabiliter reciperemus tuos nuntios, si ad nostram presentiam mitterentur, ut eos in personam tuam dulciter possemus alloqui ... et nichilominus nostros legatos vel nuncios ad tuam presentiam, partesque illas, ad propalandam viam salutis clarius proponimus ... ». *Ibid.*: *RV 62*, fols. 31r-31v; WADDING, 7: p. 251.

24 « ... unum fundum vestrum optimum cuidam Episcopo de ordine fratrum minorum in civitate Armalech deputato pro consolatione sua et christianorum ibidem degentium donatione libera concessistis, in quo ad laudem divini nominis satis pulchra ecclesia est constructa ... ». Benedict XII, *Letanter de vobis*, June 13, 1338: *RV 62*, fol. 31v; WADDING, 7: pp. 251-252 at p. 252; VIDAL and MOLLAT, no. 1867.

ciscans land for building a church in an unspecified city in his domains[25].

All the letters to the various khans stressed papal appreciation for the favor which they have shown Christianity. The letter to the Great Khan for example expressed special appreciation for his willingness to send the representatives of the Alans to the West. The pop added that he hoped the khan would extend his protection to persons in the Mongol Empire who followed the Latin rite[26]. Furthermore, Benedict requested the Great Khan to allow Christians to build churches and to preach freely throughout the empire. In his turn, the pope held out to the khan the hope of eternal life if he would only listen to the teachings of the missionaries and receive baptism[27].

The compiler of Vatican Register 62 also included a copy of a letter which Benedict sent Prince Fodim who led the Alan mission, encouraging him and his people to remain firm in the Christian faith. The letter informed the Alans of the request that the pope had made of the Great Khan to allow the Christians to practice their religion without interference. He hoped that the protection that the Great Khan would extend to Christians and the zeal of the Alans would eventually lead to the conversion of the Mongol Empire[28].

One element of the papal response to the mission of the Alans that the compiler did not mention was the sending of a papal legate back with them. The legate, John of Marignolli, arrived in Peking in 1342, having passed through Armalech where he had rebuilt a church and preached for a time. He remained there until 1347 when he began a return trip to the West that took him through India. He finally reached Avignon in 1353 where, presumably, he reported

---

25 « ... christianos fideles in tuo degentes Imperio favoribus et gratiis pro divina reverentia prosequeris opportunis, quodque fratribus minoribus in Imperio predicto morantibus, certum locum aptum et ydoneum in quadam Civitate que de novo edificatur favorabiliter concessisti ... ». Benedict XII, *Exultanti percepimus animo,* June 13, 1338: *RV 62,* fols. 31v-32r at fol. 31v; WADDING, 7: p. 252; VIDAL and MOLLAT, no. 1868.

26 « ... et hortamur, quatenus benivolentiam et favores huiusmodi erga prefatos Alanorum Principes et alios christicolas in eodem Imperio commorantes, continuare pro nostra et ecclesie predicte reverentia velit tua sublimitas et augere, et ut antistites et Religiosi catholici et christiani alii ecclesias basilicas et oratoria in quibus iuxta ritum et morem supradicte Romane ecclesie divine laudis peragantur officia ... ». Benedict XII, *Celsitudinis tue nuncios: RV 62,* fols. 30r-30v at fol. 30v; WADDING, 7: p. 249-50; VIDAL and MOLLAT, no. 1864.

27 « ... quod cum cognoscas veraciter, et lumen recipias fidei per quam in presenti habundanter replearis gratia et in futura vita eterne beatitudinis assequaris premium ... ». *Ibid.: RV 62,* fol. 30v; WADDING, 75 p. 250.

28 « ... ut tibi augeatur a deo meritum, ac nostram et dicte sedis gratiam et benedictionem acquiras uberius, solida continuatione persistens, Alanos et alios christicolas, partium illarum opportunis favoribus prosequaris et ut erga eos benevolentia Magnifici Principis Imperatoris Imperatorum omnium Tartarorum crescat iugiter et cultus divinus amplietur in eis partibus, fidesque catholica dilatetur, erga eumdem Imperatorem cui nos etiam super hoc scribimus ... ». Benedict XII, *Venientes nuper ad presentiam,* June 13, 1338: *RV 62,* fols. 30v-31r at fol. 31r; WADDING, 7: p. 250; VIDAL and MOLLAT, no. 1865.

on the state of Christianity in Asia. It is possible that his report discouraged further papal interest in the mission to Asia. Even as he left China, the uprisings that were to culminate in the ouster of the Mongols and the restoration of a native Chinese dynasty were beginning[29].

The final group of documents in this register that concern Asia dealt chiefly with papal contacts with Usbech, the leader of the Golden Horde. The immediate pressure of the Horde on the frontiers of Poland and Hungary posed a direct threat to these Christian kingdoms that caused the papacy to take a special interest in the fate of these Tartars. The khan sent two of his nobles and a Franciscan friar to Avignon in 1340. Benedict XII's response to this embassy was to repeat many of the same points that he had made in his letters of two years earlier to the East. He thanked Usbech for the favor that he had shown to the Christians and asked him to continue to give his special protection to those who followed the Latin rite[30]. He also reminded the khan that his Christian subjects were his most loyal subjects. The pope pointed out to Usbech that in a recent unsuccessful plot against the khan's life, only three Christians were involved. The remainder were all infidels. The discovery of the plot before it could be carried out seemed to the pope an act of divine intervention. Perhaps the khan should have accepted it as a sign of divine favor and received baptism[31]. The pope also wrote to the khan's wife and to his heir, emphasizing the spiritual advantages that accrue to those who enter the fold of Christ[32].

Perhaps buoyed by what might be seen as a good opportunity to

---

29 John de Marignolli, *Recollections of Travel in the East*, in *Cathay and the Way Thither*, 3: pp. 177-269 at pp. 211-212. See also, Grousset, pp. 341-342; de Rachewiltz, p. 196.

30 « Et ulterius exhortationibus et precibus nostris quibus christianos catholicos et Romane obedientes ecclesie, in tuo [imperio] degentes benivolentie tue commendavimus ... » Benedict XII, *Letanter et benigne: RV 62*, fol. 33v; Wadding, 7: p. 269.

31 « Praeterea quod, cum aliqui nequissimi homines, sceleris nefandissimi patratores, proditoriis et temerariis ausibus intentata tibi morte, te in tuo Palatio, igne supposito, nocturno tempore obsedissent, et Christianis praedictis falso imponere patrationem hujusmodi sceleris niterentur, tu divino auxilio feliciter ab hujusmodi periculo liberatus, et recordatus precum et exhortationum nostrarum praedictarum, ac impositionem praedictam esse falsam et calumniosam, Dei sapientia inspiratus, attendens praefatos Christianos, tamquam de hujusmodi scelere innocentes, tribus tantum exceptis, qui maligno seducti spiritu ... ». *Ibid.*; Wadding, 7: p. 269. This section of the letter was omitted in the copy inserted into *RV 62*.

32 « ... Christianos vero predictos opportunis favoribus, et benevolentiis habeas commendatos, ut ipse Deus, a quo bona cuncta procedunt, quique nullum bonum irremuneratum relinquit, te oculo pietatis irradiando, verae fidei lumine mentem tuam respiciat, et ad ea, quae sibi sunt placita, tuaeque saluti utilia, dirigat actus tuos ». Benedict XII, *Venientem nuper*, August 17, 1340: *RV 62*, fol. 33v; Wadding, 7: pp. 270-271 at p. 271; Vidal and Mollat, no. 2854. In addition, see Benedict XII, *Pridem ad nostram*, August 17, 1340: *RV 62*, fol. 33v; Wadding, 7: pp. 271-272; Vidal and Mollat, no. 2855. Both of these letters are represented in *RV 62* by brief headings that give the names of the recipients and the dates of the letters. The complete texts are in Wadding.

make a significant number of converts among the Tartars of the Golden Horde, Benedict XII took this occasion to write to the missionaries in the lands of the Tartars encouraging them to remain firm in their desire to preach the Gospel to the infidels [33]. At the same time, he warned them to keep closely to the teachings of the Latin Church and sent along with the letter a basic statement of Christian doctrine to insure that their converts adhered to the teaching of the Latin Church.

Optimism about the possibility of converting the Mongols was a significant part of the Mongol Mission. Although the numbers of actual converts from paganism or the number of schismatic Christians, of whom there was a large number in the Mongol Empire, who were reconciled with Rome was small, the occasional successes fired the missionaries' dreams. John of Monte Corvino's reconciliation of the Nestorian ruler of the Ongut Turks, a son-in-law of the emperor himself, must have struck the papacy and the missionaries as similar to the mass conversions that marked the advance of Christianity in Europe during the period of the barbarian invasions [34]. Monte Corvino also mentioned that he had made 6000 converts in Peking alone, a number which he claimed would have been much larger if it had not been for the strong opposition that his work received from the Nestorians [35]. John of Marignolli's visit to Peking may well have punctured the dreams of easy conversion of the masses of the Mongol Empire at which Monte Corvino hinted [36].

In spite of the failures of these missionaries to make any appreciable number of converts, friars continued to go in small numbers to various parts of the Mongol Empire. The well-known religious toleration of the Tartars, perhaps really only indifference to religion or fear of the unknown, made it easy for a missionary to travel throughout the East as long as the Mongols dominated Asia [37]. Asia under the Mongols was the only region outside of Christendom in the fourteenth century where missionaries could travel without requiring military protection. In spite of the border conflicts between various Christian states and their Tartar neighbors, the pa-

---

33 « ... ut in vobis inter nationes exteras constitutis non extinguatur eiusdem lucerna fidei, sed vehementius accendatur, ut quanto maioribus pressuris et tribulationibus vos contingit subici propter eam, tanto si constantes et perseverantes in ea fideliter fueritis ampliora et uberiora merita vobis exinde proveniant apud deum ... ». Benedict XII, *Supra gregem*, August 17, 1340: *RV 62, fols.* 33v-34r at fol. 34r; *Acta Benedicti XII*, no. 50, pp. 106-107 at p. 106; Vidal and Mollat, no. 2856.

34 Dawson, pp. 225-226.

35 *Ibid.*, p. 225.

36 de Rachewiltz, p. 197.

37 « In their superstitious awe of Heaven and of magical formulas, the Mongols felt it wise to conciliate not only their own shamans but also other possible representatives of the Divine — i. e., leaders of any cult who might conceivably be possessed of supernatural powers, such as Nestorian priests ... Buddhist monks ... Franciscan missionaries, or Muslim mullahs ... ». Grousset, p. 220.

pacy was inclined to seek peaceful relations with them whenever possible. In addition to the missionaries' experience with the Tartars and their willingness to allow missionaries to circulate throughout their lands, the papal attempts to seek peaceful relations with the Tartars reflected the thinking of canon lawyers on the possibility of such relations with infidel societies.

Most of the references in canon law to relations between Christian and non-Christian societies assumed armed conflict, an opinion that Christian experience with the Moslems helped to form. Nevertheless, the popes at Avignon and their staffs were aware that Innocent IV who as pope had initiated the Mongol Mission, had also in his capacity as a canon lawyer, considered the possibility of peaceful relations with non-Christian societies. Innocent IV took as his starting point for considering such relations a decretal of Innocent III, *Quod super his,* that concerned the vows which the crusaders took. Innocent IV raised the question of the right of Christians to deprive the Moslems of their lands. In the answer he distinguished between the lands which the Moslems had seized from Christians, such as Palestine, and those lands which they held elsewhere, which, he assumed, they had not taken in an unjust war. While Christians did have the right to retake the formerly Christian lands, they had no right to deprive the Moslems of their other territories [38]. He argued that all rational creatures had the right to govern themselves and to select their own rulers. The pope had no right to deprive infidels of their property and lordship simply because they were not Christians [39]. Innocent IV did, however, admit that papal responsibility for all men, both those within the Church and those outside of it, did provide a basis for a pope ordering Christian armies to deprive an infidel ruler of his office if he violated natural law [40]. Among the specific violations of natural law that he listed was the refusal of an infidel ruler to allow Christian missionaries the right to preach in his country [41]. Under such circumstances, the pope would be justified in requesting military aid from Christian rulers to protect

---

38 « Quod autem Papa facit indulgentias illis, qui vadunt ad recuperandam Terram sanctam ... Terra sancta iusto bello victa fuit ab Imperatore Romano post mortem Christi, unde licitum est Papae ratione Imperii Romani quod obtinet, illud ad suam iurisdictionem revocare, qui iniuste expoliatus est ... ». INNOCENT IV, *Commentaria,* 3.34.8., *Quod super his.* In addition, see MULDOON, *Extra ecclesiam non est imperium,* pp. 570-579.

39 « ... possessiones et iurisdictiones licite sine peccato possunt esse apud infideles, haec enim non tantum pro fidelibus sed pro omni rationabili creatura facta sunt ... non licet Papae, vel fidelibus auferre sua sive dominia sive iurisdictiones infidelibus, quia sine peccato possident ... ». INNOCENT IV, *Commentaria,* 3.34.8.

40 « ... bene tamen credimus, quod Papa, qui est vicarius Iesu Christi, potestatem habet non tantum super Christianos sed etiam super omnes infideles ... ». *Ibid.*

41 « ... tamen mandare potest Papa infidelibus, quod admittant praedicatores evangelii in terris suae iurisdictionis ... si ipsi prohibent praedicatores praedicare, peccant, et ideo puniendi sunt ». *Ibid.*

the missionaries in such a situation. The willingness of Mongol rulers to allow Christian missionaries to travel freely suggested that peaceful relations with infidels were actually possible along the lines that Innocent IV had outlined.

## 2. At the Opposite Ends of Europe

What makes Vatican Register 62 significant is not the fact that the compiler brought together texts which dealt with the Christian response to the major threat which the Turks and the Tartars presented Europe. These were well known threats, traditional causes for Christian concern with the borders of Latin Christendom. So too, the ambiguous response of Latin Christians to the plight of their schismatic brethren in the East was not unknown to the fourteenth century popes and their staffs. A small number of letters in Vatican Register 62 that concerned attempts to convert infidels at opposite ends of Europe, the Lithuanians in the north-eastern corner and the inhabitants of the Canary Islands at the south-western edge of Europe, underscore the theme of the register, the nature of the situation along the frontiers of Latin Christendom that stretched from the Baltic to the Atlantic. Admittedly, the absence of any documents directly concerning the North African shores of the Mediterranean is a curious omission. The importance which the island of Cyprus and the small Armenian kingdom, both of which faced the brunt of attacks by the Mameluke forces of Egypt, played in the register filled in at least some of the gap between the Canary Islands and the eastern frontier of Christendom. The compiler took a broad view of the frontiers that had attracted the attention of the various popes at Avignon.

The letters that were related to the attempts to convert the Lithuanians and the Canarians provide some insights into the difficulties which the papacy had in securing the conversion of small infidel societies along the edges of Europe that posed no military threat to European society. Examined in connection with the letters that concerned the major threats facing Europe, these letters illustrate one end of a spectrum of papal involvement in the frontiers that stretched from the fierce Turks to the little-known aboriginal Canarians.

The conversion of the Lithuanians presented a striking case of the way in which the papal desire to convert infidels to Christianity could collide with the territorial interests of neighboring Christian rulers. A Lithuanian state had emerged during the twelfth century. In the mid-thirteenth century, the leader of the Lithuanians became a Christian and received the title of king from Pope Innocent IV [42].

---

[42] Concerning the conflicts between the Lithuanians and their neighbors, the Teu-

The territorially large but structurally weak Lithuanian kingdom was an object of the expansionist interests of its neighbors. In a letter to Gediminas, the king of the Lithuanians (1316-1341), John XXII outlined the subsequent history of Lithuania. The original conversion of Mindaugas (1240-1263) had been only temporary. He and his subjects had relapsed into paganism « because of the cruel and wicked actions of the Master and the Knights » of the Teutonic Order who refused to allow the conversion of the Lithuanians to interfere with their desire for more land[43]. The continued attacks that the Knights made only added the Lithuanians' sense of grievance.

The pope's solution for the Lithuanian situation was to remind the people and their king that in spite of the injuries that the Teutonic Knights had inflicted upon them, they should see themselves as defenders of Christendom, not as its enemies. The Lithuanians had, after all, been Christians, so their rulers « should act as other Christian rulers act », defending Christendom from its enemies[44]. Gediminas had already begun to remedy the break with the papacy by allowing Dominican and Franciscan friars to operate within his realm so that the work of restoring the lost sheep to the fold could begin. The pope hoped that the king himself would return to the fold, leading the rest of his people behind him, reversing the action of his predecessor[45]. The pope also sent two legates to direct the missionary efforts.

In addition to offering the Lithuanians the opportunity for eternal salvation that Mindaugas had first accepted and then rejected,

---

tonic Knights and the Kingdom of Poland, see: M. Z. JEDLICKI, *German Settlement in Poland and the Rise of the Teutonic Order*, and O. HALECKI, *Casimir the Great*, in *The Cambridge History of Poland*, ed. W. F. REDDAWAY, J. H. PENSON, O. HALECKI, R. DYBOSKI (2 v., Cambridge, England 1941-1950) 1: pp. 125-147, 167-187; PAUL W. KNOLL, *The Rise of the Polish Monarchy*, Chicago 1972. The only book that deals with the conversion of the Lithuanians is JONAS TOTORAITIS, *Die Litauer unter dem König Mindowe*, Freiburg 1905, esp. pp. 124-132.

43 « ... quod quondam predecessor tuus Mindowe cum toto suo Regno fuit ad fidem Christi conversus, sed propter atroces et inimicabiles iniurias dilectorum filiorum Magistri et fratrum ordinis Theotonicorum sancte Marie Ierosolimitani, a fide huiusmodi recesserunt et in errorem pristinum sunt relapsi ... ». John XXII, *Missa nobis*, June 1, 1324: *RV 62*, fols. 16v-17v at fol. 16v; THEINER, *Vetera monumenta*, 1: no. 293, pp. 193-195 at p. 193; MOLLAT, *Lettres communes*, no. 20325. The papal letters refer to the Lithuanian rulers as kings and the letters that these rulers themselves wrote to western rulers also used the term king. Their actual title, however, was Grand Prince or Grand Duke: see the discussion in the *Encyclopedia Lituanica* (6 vols., Boston 1970-78), 2:362-365, Grand Prince. The same encyclopedia also has brief biographies of the Lithuanian rulers discussed here: Gediminas, 2:287-292; Kęstutis, 3:113-118; Mindaugas, 3:538-543.

44 « ... quod tu nequaquam christianos impugnas, tamquam fidem velis destruere christianam, sed defendis te ab inimicis tuis ut faciunt Reges et principes alii christiani ... ». *Ibid.*: *RV 62*, fol. 16v; THEINER, *Vetera monumenta*, 1: p. 193.

45 « ... et quod predicatorum [et] minorum ordinum fratres tecum habes quibus commisisti, et licentiam dedisti liberam ut baptizent, predicent, et informent christianum populum et etiam infideles, ut ad omnipotentem deum et dominum convertantur ... ». *Ibid.*: *RV 62*, fol. 16v; THEINER, *Vetera monumenta*, 1: p. 193.

John XXII promised to write to the Teutonic Knights informing them of the return of the Lithuanians to the Church. He indicated that this action should stop the attacks by the Knights and enable both sides to live at peace. In order to bring peace to the region as quickly as possible, the pope authorized his legates « to deal with every issue between you and the Master of the Knights and his Brothers in those lands which concerns the worship of God, the exhaltation of the faith, the honor of the apostolic see, the well-being of the Church, and the salvation of the souls and the bodies of the poor »[46]. Unfortunately, the pope and his legates were in no position to stop the Knights' drive which involved not religious issues but land[47].

John XXII did write to the Teutonic Knights as he had informed Gediminas he would. He informed them of his desire to end the strife between the Knights and the Lithuanians now that the lapsed Christians were on the verge of returning to the fold[48]. A major obstacle in the way of their return, however, was the treatment which they had received from the Knights. The Knights were ordered to cease their raids against the Lithuanians and to live at peace with them as befitted good Christians.

The instructions which John XXII sent to his legates in Lithuania covered a wide range of topics. The legates were told of Gediminas' wish for baptism and for the reconciliation of his people with the Church. According to the pope, Gediminas was prepared « to obey us in all things like other Catholic kings » once his differences with the Knights had been resolved[49]. The legates received a series of powers not unlike those provided in *Cum hora undecima* to speed up the process of reconciliation. In addition, John XXII sent a statement of Christian doctrine that the legates were to use in order to assure absolute fidelity to the doctrines of the Latin Church[50].

---

46 « Sed et memoratis Episcopo et Abbati dedimus in mandatis, ut omnia inter te dictosque Magistrum et Fratres, ac in dictis partibus agere studeant et tractare que ad cultum et laudem dei, exaltationem catholice fidei, honorem apostolice sedis, relevationem ecclesiarum, et pauperum animarum salutem et corporum pertinebunt ... ». *Ibid.*: *RV 62*, fol. 17; THEINER, *Vetera monumenta*, 1: p. 195.

47 Concerning the role of the Teutonic Knights, see: KNOLL, pp. 138-139.

48 « ... universitatem vestram rogamus, monemus, et hortamur attente, vobis in virtute sancte obedientie districtius iniungentes, quatenus postquam idem Rex fidem catholicam deo auctore susceperit, a molestiis dampnis et iniuriis inferendis eidem et hominibus Regni sui resipiscatis omnino, quin ymo teneri vos volumus cum eodem Rege et aliis personis illarum partium que ad fidem catholicam convertentur, fraterne et in pace vivere ... ». John XXII, *Pater luminum*, June 1, 1324: *RV 62*, fols. 18v-19r at fol. 18v; THEINER, *Vetera monumenta*, 1: no. 296, p. 196; MOLLAT, *Lettres communes*, no. 20328.

49 « ... quia paratus est nobis in omnibus sicut ceteri Reges catholici obedire, ac fidem recipere orthodoxam ... ». John XXII, *Exaltamus in domino*, June 1, 1324: *RV 62*, fols. 14r-16r at fol. 14r: THEINER, *Vetera monumenta*, 1: no. 290, pp. 190-192 at p. 190; MOLLAT, *Lettres communes*, no. 20322.

50 « ... vos ... ad partes illas ad evangelizandum dicto Regi et genti sue verbum vite, ac viam salutis eterne duximus destinandos, et ut articulos christiane fidei, dictis Regi et genti lucidius explanare et insinuare possitis, ipsos vobis presentibus

As was the case with similar letters to other missionaries, the papal letter stressed the notion of the Church's unity and the need to submit to the Latin Church in all matters including matters of ritual [51]. The reconciliation of the Lithuanians was complicated by the fact that in addition to those who had relapsed into paganism, the kingdom also included schismatics belonging to the Greek Church. These were the Ruthenians who had been conquered by the Lithuanians. The missionaries had to contend with the attraction which the Greek rite held for some of the subjects of Gediminas as well as re-converting the pagans in Lithuania. As a result, the legates were reminded that polygamy was forbidden, no doubt because it was a stock belief of the canonists that all infidels were polygamous, and also that unleavened bread must be used in the Eucharist, a reminder of the liturgical differences that separated the Latin and Greek churches [52].

In spite of John XXII's interest in the conversion of the Lithuanians, the work went slowly. The complete and prompt reunion of these lapsed Christians to the fold that the pope had envisaged in his letters did not occur. Twenty-five years later, Clement VI was still engaged in the work. This time the major stumbling block was not the Teutonic Knights but Casimir III (1333-1370), the king of Poland. A Polish army had invaded Lithuania in 1344 [53]. The pope reminded the king that the people whom he was attacking, the Duke Kęstutis and his fellow nobles, were Christians so they could not be attacked without risking papal disapproval [54]. At their baptism, the Lithuanians had been promised that their property and possessions would be secure from attacks by other Christians. The archbishop of Gniezno was ordered to send missionaries into Lithuania who would instruct the as yet imperfectly taught converts the rudiments of the faith [55]. Finally, Clement VI wrote to Duke Kęstutis

---

annotatos transmittimus, qui tales sunt. Credimus sanctam trinitatem ... ». John XXII, *Inter precipuos et precordiales,* Jume 1, 1324: *RV 62,* fols. 19v-20v at fol. 19v; THEINER, *Vetera monumenta,* 1: no. 298, pp. 197-198 at p. 197; *Acta Ioannis XXII,* no. 76b, p. 157 (incomplete); MOLLAT, no. 20330.

51 « Credimus sanctam catholicam et apostolicam unam esse veram ecclesiam in qua unum datur baptisma, et vera omnium remissio peccatorum ... ». *Ibid.: RV 62,* fol. 20r; THEINER, *Vetera monumenta,* 1: p. 198.

52 « Sacramentum eucharistie ex azimo conficit ipsa Romana ecclesia ... de matrimonio vero tenet quod nec unus vir simul plures uxores, nec una mulier simul habere permittitur plures viros. Soluta vero lege matrimonii per mortem alterius coniugum secundas et tercias deinceps nuptias successive licitas esse dicit ... ». *Ibid.: RV 62,* fol. 20r; THEINER, *Vetera monumenta,* 1: p. 198.

53 Concerning Polish-Lithuanian relations, see: KNOLL, pp. 136-138.

54 « ... eos dictosque populos postquam purificati unda sacri lavacri nostre fidei susceperint documenta intendimus prestante deo apostolicis communire presidiis, favoribus prosequi et auxiliis confovere ipsosque Kerstutim atque Germanos ac Heredes et successores eorum insignire titulo regio et Regalibus insigniis decorare iustique favoris presidio ipsos in eorum conservare iuribus et tueri ... ». Clement VI, *Magnificat anima nostra,* September 16, 1349: *RV 62,* fols. 88r-88v at fol. 88v; THEINER, *Vetera monumenta,* 1: no. 691, pp. 525-526 at p. 526; DÉPREZ and MOLLAT, no. 2066.

55 « ... fraternitati tue per apostolica scripta mandamus quatinus aliquos presbi-

assuring him that he and his people would be secure from attack and that additional clergy would be sent to Lithuania to speed the work of conversion[56].

The process of converting the Lithuanians encountered problems from the territorial desires of the neighboring Christian rulers. At the other end of Europe, the possibility of converting the pagan natives of the Canary Islands to Christianity was raised by a Christian ruler who apparently sought to create a domain for himself in lands which infidels occupied. In this case, the desire for land and the desire to make converts seemed to go hand in hand. The four letters concerning the Canary Islands from the pontificate of Clement VI announce the intention of Luis de la Cerda, a member of the house of Castile, to acquire the islands[57]. According to the pope, the prince's purpose in conquering these islands and installing himself as ruler of the native population was to « eliminate their wicked pagan error so that the glory of the divine name may be praised there and the beauty of the Catholic faith might flourish »[58]. The pope declared that he had created « Luis prince of those islands together with a grant of temporal proprietorship and lordship of those islands », a grant which was to be a hereditary one in Luis' family[59]. The justification for this action was that Luis de la Cerda came from a family long known for its interest in expanding the faith, presumably a guarantee that the conquest of the Canaries was being undertaken with the highest motives[60].

---

teros viros probos deum timentes et lege domini eruditos seculares vel regulares ... qui auctoritate nostra dictos duces ac alios Litvanos in eadem fide fideliter instruant, salubriter dirigant recteque informent et baptismatis renovent sacramento ... ». Clement VI, *Magnificat anima nostra*, September 16, 1349: *RV 62*, fols. 88v-89r; THEINER, *Vetera monumenta*, 1: no. 692, p. 526; DÉPREZ and MOLLAT, no. 2067.

[56] « ... quod sicut Carissimo in christo filio nostro Kazimiro Rege Polonie Illustri nobis intimante percepimus, vos cece paganitatis expurgatis erroribus et tenebris effugatis ad catholice fidei veritatem una cum subditis vobis populis concitis gressibus properatis ... Archiepiscopo gneznensi per alias nostras litteras damus expressius in mandatis quod ipse sacerdotes dei eruditos in lege domini ad vos cito mittere studeat ... ». Clement VI, *Gaudemus et exaltamus*, September 18, 1349: *RV 62*, fols. 89r-89v at 89r; THEINER, *Vetera monumenta*, 1: no. 693, pp. 526-527; DÉPREZ and MOLLAT, no. 2068.

[57] Concerning early European attempts to colonize the Canary Islands, see ROGER B. MERRIMAN, *The Rise of the Spanish Empire in the Old World and in the New* (4 v., New York 1918-1934; reprint ed., 1962), 1: pp. 142-166; and C. RAYMOND BEAZLEY, *The Dawn of Modern Geography* (3 v., Oxford 1897-1906; reprint ed., New York 1949), 3: pp. 428-429.

[58] « ... quod ipse ad acquirendas Fortunie ac quasdam alias Insulas in partibus Affrice consistentes et eidem adiacentes, ut ex illis eliminata paganei erroris spurcicia, divini nominis ibidem laudetur gloria et catholice fidei vigeat ... ». Clement VI, *Vineam domini sabaoth*, December 11, 1344: *RV 62*, fol. 61r; DÉPREZ, GLÉNISSON, MOLLAT, no. 1314.

[59] « ... eundem Ludovicum predictarum Insularum principem, cum concessione temporali proprietatis et dominii earundem sibi pro se suisque heredibus et successoribus facta sub certis modis, formis et conditionibus constituimus et deputavimus eumque insigniis dignitatis Principatus duximus ... ». *Ibid.*: *RV 62*, fol. 61r.

[60] « ... ipseque de stirpe ac domibus processit Regalibus, que circa cultum et

The compiler of Vatican Register 62 gave no reason for including the four letters dealing with the Canary Islands. While it might be attractive to consider the compiler as prophetic, seeing the islands as the starting point of European expansion westward, there is no basis for such a judgment. The list of those to whom the letters concerning the Canaries were sent suggests another reason for including these letters. The recipients of the letters included the kings of Aragon, Castile, Portugal, France and Cyprus, the city of Genoa, and Humbert of Vienne. Humbert of Vienne had at one time considered waging war against the Moors in Africa in conjunction with Luis de la Cerda[61]. The recipients of the letters announcing Luis' plans for the Canaries were precisely those which had a strong interest in Christian control of the Mediterranean. There is at least a hint that the conquest of the Canaries could be the base from which an invasion of Africa could be launched, rather in the way that the islands in the Aegean were to be used as a base for ending Turkish control of Asia Minor. In this case, the letters identified the Canaries as islands lying off the coast of Africa, a location which might have suggested to some observers the role the islands could play in a crusade. Nothing came of this first attempt to occupy the Canary Islands and both Humbert of Vienne and Luis de la Cerda turned their attention to other projects.

These letters concerning the Canary Islands derive some of their interest from the nature of the grant which the pope awarted to Luis de la Cerda. The compiler of Vatican Register 62 did not include the bull *Sicut exhibitae* of November 1344 in which Clement VI awarded the Canaries to the Castilian prince. In that letter, the pope granted the prince these islands with « *merum et mistam imperium et iurisdictionem omnimodam temporalem* ». The islands were to be a « *feudum perpetuum* » for Luis de la Cerda and his heirs. In turn they were to do liege homage to the pope and to his successors for the islands[62]. Although the letters to the various princes

dilatationem eiusdem fidei orthodoxe se devotis et fructuosis operibus consueverunt impendere, personarum spretis periculis, et expensarum profluviis non vitatis ... ». *Ibid.*: *RV 62*, fol. 61r.

61 Gay, p. 62. Humbert of Vienne received a copy of the letter *Cum inter cetera*, December 23, 1345: *RV 62*, fols. 61v-62r at fol. 62r; Déprez, Glénisson, Mollat, no. 1348. Copies of this letter were also sent to the king and queen of France and to the king and queen of Sicily: *RV 62*, fol. 62r.

62 « ... tibi et haeredibus tuis, et successoribus catholicis ac legitimis, et in devotione ipsius Romanae ecclesiae persistentibus, tam masculis quam foeminis in feudum perpetuum de fratrum nostrorum consilio et assensu, ac apostolicae plenitudine potestatis sub modo, forma, tenore, conditionibus, et conventionibus contentis praesentibus, concedimus et donamus, teque praedicto feudo per sceptrum aureum praesentialiter investimus ... ac tu et ipsi singulis successoribus nostris Romanis pontificibus per vos vel procuratores vestros ad hoc legitime constitutos recognitionem et homagium ligium facere, et plenum vassallagium et fidelitatis juramentum praestare tenebimini juxta formam ... ». Clement VI, *Sicut exhibitae*, November, 1344; Raynaldus, ad ann. 1344, no. 39, 41.

did not mention that the islands were to be a papal fief, those who received the letters no doubt understood the papal grant as creating a fief.

Underlying the letters concerning the conversion of the Lithuanians and of the Canarians was a somewhat different theory about the nature of relations between the papacy and infidel societies than the theory that appeared in the letters to the Tartars. The letters concerning Lithuania and the Canary Islands suggest that Christians had the right to invade infidel societies simply because they were infidel societies. The implication is that just as there was no salvation outside the Church so too there was no legitimate political authority outside the Church. If this was in fact what the letters meant, it would mean that Clement VI did not subscribe to Innocent IV's views about the rights of infidels. If the pope had done so, he would have been able to justify his position by referring to the canonists who did not accept Innocent IV's views. The canonist known as Hostiensis, for example, a student of Innocent IV, did not accept his master's opinion in this matter and argued that since the coming of Christ, infidels no longer possessed legitimate political authority so that Christians could legitimately invade their territories [63].

In practice, however, Clement VI authorized the conquest of these two regions on the presumption that the natives would interfere with peaceful missionaries. There was no reason to assume that the Canarians would receive missionaries with any more kindness than other had done. The history of missionary efforts in the thirteenth and fourteenth centuries, with the significant exception of the mission to the Tartars, was one of infidel opposition to Christian missionaries [64]. The most striking difference between the situation in Lithuania and in the Canary Islands was that the Teutonic Knights and the King of Poland were ordered to stop all military actions against the Lithuanians once they had been converted while the Canaries were granted in perpetuity to the family of Luis de la Cerda. In the case of the Canaries, the eventual conversion of the natives was not apparently to bring about an end to Castilian rule.

---

63 « ... mihi tamen videtur quod in adventu Christi omnis honor et omnis principatus et omne dominium et iurisditio de iure et ex causa justa, et per illum qui supremam manum habet nec errare potest omni infideli subtracta fuerit ad fideles ... » HOSTIENSIS, *Lectura,* 3.34.8., *Quod super hiis.* In taking this position, Hostiensis was following a line of argument that had been developed by the canonist Alanus Anglicus around 1200 and was constantly quoted by canonists who desired to reject Innocent IV's views on the rights of infidels. See MULDOON, « *Nullum imperium extra ecclesiam* », pp. 560-561, 578-579.

64 Here again, the papal view of events seems to have been shaped by the earlier experience of Christian missionaries in Moslem lands. The Moslems were not sympathetic to such missionaries so the papal view generally assumed that infidel would attempt to block missionaries.

One explanation of the willingness of Clement VI to grant the Canaries to Luis de la Cerda in perpetuity may have been that the pope acted on the principle that the Donation of Constantine had given the pope dominion over all islands in the West, along with the other powers mentioned in the Donation. Professor Luis Weckmann has traced a line of such letters reaching back to the eleventh century which, he argued, provided a precedent for the grant of the Canaries as a fief [65]. A weakness in this argument is that although the letter which invested Luis de la Cerda with the Canary Islands is similar to earlier letters involving the grant of islands as fiefs, *Sicut exhibitiae* did not mention the Donation of Constantine as a basis for the papal action. In general, the Donation was not widely used by popes or canonists as a basis for actions which the papacy undertook. While it is not certain why the canonists avoided using the Donation as a basis for papal actions, it may have been due to a hesitancy to believe that the Roman emperors could lawfully make such a grant. As a result, the Donation of Constantine probably was not the basis for justifying the conquest of the Canary Islands. The assumption that the natives of the islands would prevent the landing of peaceful missionaries was probably of more importance in causing Clement VI to act as he did.

Furthermore, Luis de la Cerda's plan to conquer the islands did not depend on papal approbation, only on his desire to convert the natives. The pope appears to have accepted the Castilian prince as the *de facto* ruler of the islands and agreed to support his efforts. Seen in this light, the pope was acting in a manner consistent with his dealings in other societies. He dealt with those who ruled, such as Kęstutis in Lithuania, on the assumption that conversion would proceed more rapidly with the assistance of a ruler who was sympathetic to missionaries. As the goal of saving the souls of all men was the overriding consideration in papal thinking, it was logical to accept Luis de la Cerda as the ruler of the Canaries and act in conjunction with him for the souls of the natives. In the event that his conquest was successful, his assistance would be required in any case if the natives were to be converted. Thus, the conquest of the Canaries and the re-conversion of the Lithuanians were based on the same principle, the conversion of all men with the aid of their secular rulers. This principle was in turn also found in the commentary of Innocent IV on the decretal *Quod super his* and in the practice of earlier popes.

---

65 Weckmann's conclusions were strongly criticized when they first appeared in a review by C. J. BISHKO: Speculum 25 (1950) 306-311.

## CONCLUSION

The letters in Vatican Register 62 reveal a much wider range of papal interest in the world beyond Europe during the fourteenth century than scholars have generally recognized [1]. The letters not only dealt with the Tartars as some scholars have implied or only with infidels. Rather, as the compiler himself was careful to point out, the letters concern the people of *outre-mer* and schismatics as well as the Tartars and infidels. The salutation of *Cum hora undecima* spelled out the range of nations and peoples in whom the papacy was interested. Broadly speaking, these letters indicate that papal interest was concentrated on the reunion of the schismatic eastern Christians with the Latin Church and on defending them from the neighboring infidels. Converting the Mongols and raising a crusade against the Moslems were both directed toward this primary end. Even the inclusion of the letters from the remote corners of the European world, Lithuania and the Canary Islands, reflected the desire to outflank if possible the Moslem threat to the Christians of the East by converting the infidels who lived along the borders of the Moslem world and uniting them with European Christians in the great crusade to eliminate the Moslem threat permanently. This dream of a last great crusade continued to inspire Europeans until the end of the fifteenth century when it inspired Columbus [2].

Although the defense of eastern Christianity was a stated goal of papal policy, this goal conflicted with another announced papal goal, the reconciliation of the schismatics with the Latin Church. The conflict resulted from the fact that to the papacy the schismatics were enemies of the true Church just as the Moslems and the infidels were. The compiler underscored this fact by lumping together Tartars and Byzantines, schismatics and infidels in the opening lines of the register. All these peoples were *extra ecclesiam* and

---

[1] The striking contrast between the « open » society of the twelfth century and the « closed » society of the fourteenth century is the theme of FRIEDRICH HEER'S, *The Medieval World: Europe 1100-1350*, trans. Janet Sondheimer, London 1962. While this contrast is aesthetically attractive, allowing the author to contrast the intellectual and religious vitality of the earlier era with the stultified condition of European religious and intellectual life in the later era, it also may not be an accurate picture of the fourteenth century. Heer describes the age of the Avignon papacy as the time when « the papal church put on the armour of stone walls whose chilly angularity symbolized the triumph of undeviated correctness and of overweening dominion » (p. 277). The existence of *RV 62*, however, suggests that this view of the Avignon papacy as encased within a stone and mortar cocoon is exaggerated.

[2] See, for example, Columbus's own statement of his purposes in the prologue to his *Journal of the First Voyage*, in *Journals and Other Documents on the Life and Voyages of Christopher Columbus*, trans. and ed., SAMUEL ELIOT MORISON, New York 1963, pp. 47-48. Elsewhere, Professor Morison says of Columbus, he « belonged to an age that was past » as well as being « the sign and symbol of this new age ». MORISON, *Admiral of the Ocean Sea*, Boston 1942, pp. 5-6.

therefore enemies of the Latin Church. Because the spiritual salvation of the schismatics was more important than protecting them from the Moslems, the papacy offered to help the schismatics only if they returned to the true Church. The three hundred years of gradual decline of the Eastern Empire in the face of the Moslem advance was seen as a series of warnings to the Byzantines to end the schism before it was too late. The same held true for the kingdom of Armenia. The letters speak of the need for western Christians to aid their brothers in the East, but there is always the assumption that these brothers have been reconciled with the Church. In one sense, the schismatics were even more wicked than the Moslems or the Tartars. Infidels only attacked the Body of Christ from the outside, but the schismatics mutilated that Body by their act of schism. By tying the offers of military aid to ecclesiastical reunion, the papacy only exacerbated the already bitter feelings which the schismatic populations of these nations had toward the papacy. This was especially true of the Byzantine population that recalled the sack of Constantinople in 1204 and had a living reminder of that event in the existence of the French pretenders to the Latin Empire. The paradoxical nature of the papal relationship to the schismatics is found at the very beginning of the register with Clement V's grant of a crusading tenth to aid those who would fight with Charles of Valois to re-establish the Latin Empire at Constantinople. In these three letters the internal contradiction of the papal policy in the East stood out clearly.

The position of the papacy within Europe was equally paradoxical. The popes at Avignon attempted to end wars between Christian monarchs within Europe and to divert these martial energies to the crusade just as their predecessors had done or attempted to do. The fourteenth century popes were, however, even less successful in making peace than the popes of the thirteenth century had been. Edward III and Philip VI continued to struggle for control of France in spite of papal appeals to end the conflict. In northeastern Europe, the refusal of the Teutonic Knights and the king of Poland to halt their attacks against the Lithuanians endangered the fragile results of the missionary efforts in returning the lost sheep to the fold. Papal fulminations against these unprovoked attacks fell on deaf ears. Although the popes at Avignon continued to speak and act as if they could lead European society as their predecessors had done, they were in reality unable to win widespread support for their plans.

When seen as an integral whole, the letters in Vatican Register 62 recall Thomas Hobbes' words about the papacy as the ghost of the

Roman Empire seated upon its own grave[3]. The popes at Avignon continued to employ the language of their predecessors and to assert the same policies that a line of popes from Innocent III to Boniface VIII had developed. While the form of the thirteenth century papacy remained, however, the substance had been drained away. The language of universal power in which the letters were written had become ritual incantation, repeated by rote but lacking in vitality. To a very large extent, the response of the Avignon popes to problems connected with the infidels and schismatics along the frontiers of Europe were those first made by the popes during the first half of the thirteenth century.

The dependence of the fourteenth century popes on the work of their predecessors is not surprising. The lawyer-popes of the thirteenth century not only developed the policies which their successors followed, they also developed the institutional and educational structure which molded the ways in which later popes could respond to situations. This growth of the papacy's role as *iudex ominum* with the subsequent collection of the decisions of the papal courts, the decretals, so that law students could study them meant that those who aspired to serve the papacy studied the mind of the papacy and became indoctrinated with the legal principles of the thirteenth century popes. In addition, the existence of books of legal formulas to guide the clerks who drafted papal letters and the existence of the papal files meant that there was little need for hard-pressed officials to create new responses to situations. The past provided all the models that anyone could want. No doubt, the enormous growth in the volume of correspondence which routinely passed through the papal chancery as a result of the work of ecclesiastical centralization that had been in process for two centuries contributed to the willingness to use standard letters whenever possible. As a result, even though the popes of the fourteenth century had available to them the letters and reports of missionaries such as John of Monte Corvino and John of Marignolli, as well presumably as access to Marco Polo's book about China, the letters issued by the papacy showed no influence from these sources. Even the visit by the Alans to Avignon does not seem to have had an effect on the way in which the papacy looked at the problems of missionary work.

The policies that the letters in Vatican Register 62 advance generally failed. The popes failed to arouse Europeans to undertake another crusade, they failed to reconcile the schismatics of the East, they failed to convert the infidels. Although each of these failures can be understood in political terms, collectively they represent a

[3] THOMAS HOBBES, *Leviathan*, ed. Michael Oakeshott, Oxford 1957, Part 4, ch. 47, p. 457.

failure of ecclesiastical imagination as well as a failure of policy. The experience of a century of papal contacts with infidels and schismatics should have been sufficient to indicate that the goals which the papacy was pursuing with these peoples were not being achieved. The experience should have been the basis of a re-evaluation of papal initiatives. Yet, this did not happen. The papal court continued to deal with infidels and schismatics in precisely the same way that it had always done.

The significance of Vatican Register 62 does not lie only in what it says about the dependence of the Avignon papacy on the canonist-popes of the thirteenth century. The papal interest in those outside the Church with which the register is concerned went back to the eleventh century and continued on into the sixteenth century. The areas with which the register dealt, with the exception of the Canary Islands, had all been the subject of papal interest before Clement V had ascended the papal throne and were still of interest when Clement VI died. The letters in this register were part of five hundred years of papal experience. They form a sample not unlike a core that a geologist has drilled to determine the nature of the strata which exist in a particular region. They do not provide a complete picture of medieval papal dealings with the peoples along the frontiers of Christendom. What the letters do reveal is the condition of the various strata of papal relations with those *extra ecclesiam* in the first half of the fourteenth century as one man saw them. This particular core sample suggests that the papacy was no longer capable of giving direction to European society and was incapable of responding creatively to situations involving those outside the Church. In recent years, studies of the responses of sixteenth century philosophers and publicists to sixteenth century contacts with the natives of the New World have indicated that these responses reveal the same inflexibility and the same dependence on thirteenth century legal thinking that the letters in Vatican Register 62 reveal[4]. Analysis of the letters indicates that the ecclesiastical response to those outside the Church had become fixed long before the great expansion of Europeans overseas made relations between Christians and infidels a crucial issue in international relations. As a result, the papacy's role in international relations declined rapidly because the basis upon which the papacy presumed to act was not capable of dealing with the newly discovered lands.

This conclusion does not, however, mean that Vatican Register 62 was of no value, or is valuable only as another illustration of the increasing rigidity of papal thinking in the later Middle Ages. In its

4 See JAMES MULDOON, *A Canonistic Contribution to the Formation of International Law*: The Jurist 28 (1968) 265-279; and KENNETH J. PENNINGTON, *Bartolome de las Casas and the Tradition of Medieval Law*: Church History 39 (1970) 149-161.

own time, the existence of this register must have reminded popes and their staffs of the importance that the mission to the infidels and to the schismatics had played in the life of the Church. Coming as it did, when European society was becoming closed off from Asia because of the end of Mongol hegemony, and at a point when the situation of the Eastern Empire was very precarious, the compilation of missionary texts could have served to encourage flagging interest within the papal court. The reconciliation of John V Palaeologus with the Latin Church in 1369, and the dispatching of the last mission to the Mongols in 1370 may have been linked to the spirit behind the compilation of this register.

Papal involvement in the problems of those regions represented in Vatican Register 62 continued on into the fifteenth century because the problems remained unresolved. In the 1430's Pope Eugenius IV (1431-1447) wrestled with the conflicting claims of the Castilians and the Portuguese for control of the Canary Islands while attempting to consider the needs of the native population as well [5]. The pressures of the Teutonic Knights on the united lands of Poland and Lithuania continued into the fifteenth century when the Council of Constance was asked to resolve the issue [6]. Papal interest in arousing crusaders in defense of Europe continued although without much success. The most significant crusading achievement of the sixteenth century, the defeat of the Turks at Lepanto by a fleet that Pius V had raised, recalled Clement VI's successful efforts to raise a limited crusade.

The value of Vatican Register 62 lies in its position within the chain of experiences and documents which linked the first phase of European expansion, that which ended in the mid-thirteenth century, with the later one which began with Columbus' voyages. Between these two periods there remained concrete evidence of the possibilities for expansion that existed. The reports of missionaries and the tales of merchants kept the knowledge of the world beyond

---

[5] The condition of the native population of the Canary Islands was of great interest to the papacy in the fifteenth century. The papacy's interest in protecting the natives from exploitation foreshadowed the interest of missionaries and lawyers in the rights of the natives of the Americas in the sixteenth century. See D. J. Wölfel, *La Curia Romana y la Corona de España en la defensa de los aborigénes Canarios*: Anthropos 25 (1930) 1011-1083; and James Muldoon, *A Fifteenth-Century Application of the Canonistic Theory of the Just War*, in *Proceedings of the Fourth International Congress of Medieval Canon Law*, Vatican City 1976, pp. 467-480.

[6] On the debate between the representatives of the King of Poland and of the Teutonic Knights at the Council of Constance, see *The Council of Constance* (Records of Civilization, Sources and Studies, no. 63), trans. Louise Ropes Loomis, ed., John H. Mundy and Kennerly M. Woody, New York 1961, pp. 443-445. The writings of the canonist who presented the case of the Polish King at the council have been published together with an extensive, and too enthusiastic introduction. See Stanislaus Belch, *Paulus Vladimiri and his Doctrine Concerning International Law and Politics*, 2 v., The Hague 1965.

Europe which was gained in the first period of expansion alive until Europeans could act on it once more. Vatican Register 62, like the reports of Franciscan missionaries and the travellers' tales, formed part of the fragile bridge between the two stages of European expansion.

# VI

# JOHN WYCLIF AND THE RIGHTS OF THE INFIDELS: THE *REQUERIMIENTO* RE-EXAMINED*

THE *Requerimiento* was one of the most striking legal documents of the entire age of European overseas expansion. A long line of publicists and scholars from Bartholomew de Las Casas to Lewis Hanke have discussed, praised and condemned it.[1] The *Requerimiento* appears to illustrate more clearly than any other single document the combination of high-sounding motives, legal chicanery and brute force that made the Spanish conquest of the Americas possible. In recent years, there has been increasing emphasis upon examining the conquest in terms of the brute force involved and a decreasing emphasis upon the motives and the legalisms which the Spanish employed.[2] As one scholar

*I wish to express my appreciation to my colleague, Professor Keith Davies, for his advice and assistance in the preparation of this paper. The present paper is a revised and expanded version of one first read at the Ninth Conference on Medieval Studies at Western Michigan University, May, 1974.

[1]The most convenient introduction to the *Requerimiento* is Lewis Hanke, *The Spanish Struggle for Justice in the Conquest of America* (Philadelphia, 1949) 31-36. The text is in the *Colección de documentos inéditos relativos al descubrimiento, conquista y organización de las antiguas posesiones españolas de ultramar*, second series (Madrid, 1885-19 ) XX, 311-314. The standard English translation is that of Sir Arthur Helps, *The Spanish Conquest in America and its Relation to the History of Slavery and to the Government of the Colonies* 4 vols. (New York, 1856-1857) I, 358-361.

[2]The value of studies dealing with the legal theories which were employed to justify or to condemn the Spanish Conquest has been criticized and defended in a series of exchanges between two of the leading students of the colonial period. See Lewis Hanke, "More Heat and Some Light on the Spanish Struggle for Justice in the Conquest of America," *Hispanic American Historical Review* 44(1964) 293-340; and "A Modest Proposal for a Moratorium on Grand Generalizations: Some Thoughts on the Black Legend," *Ibid.*, 51 (1971) 112-127. In response, see Benjamin Keen, "The Black Legend Revisited: Assumptions and Realities," *Ibid.*, 49(1969) 703-719; and "The White Legend Revisited: A Reply to Professor Hanke's 'Modest Proposal'," *Ibid.*, 51(1971) 336-355. What is still lacking are studies which focus on the links between medieval legal theories about the rights of non-Christian peoples *vis-à-vis* Europeans and the theories (and the practice) of the sixteenth century. Such continuity was outlined in Frank Tannenbaum, *Slave and Citizen* (New York, 1947) and developed somewhat by Herbert S. Klein, *Slavery in the Americas* (Chicago, 1967). E.N. van

has said, the *Requerimiento* was but a "useless legalism," and, presumably, no longer worthy of serious attention.[3] In addition, scholars have generally agreed that the *Requerimiento* is thoroughly understood. Following Las Casas, they have asserted that it contained the legal opinion of the thirteenth century canon lawyer known as Hostiensis that infidels had no right to property or political jurisdiction. In medieval terms, that infidels, such as the inhabitants of the Americas, did not possess *dominium*. In recent years, scholars have asserted that those who defended the Indians against the conquerors, such as Las Casas himself and Francisco Vitoria, drew upon the opinion of Hostiensis' teacher, the canonist-Pope Innocent IV.[4] In this way, the *Requerimiento* and the related debate about the rights of the Indians has been placed within its proper position within the late medieval canonistic tradition.

Yet another discussion of the *Requerimiento* and its roots in the legal tradition might seem unnecessary. The Indians obviously had little interest in the subtlties of sixteenth century Spanish legal thought concerning the rights of the conquered, and the conquerors themselves seem, in practice, to have been little concerned with legal niceties. Such an opinion, however, rests upon two important assumptions which have not been adequately examined. The first is that the document is rooted in the Hostiensian theory of the inability of infidels to possess *dominium*. The second is that the primary purpose of the *Requerimiento* was to offer to the Indians a summary of Christian religious doctrine and political theory in order that by accepting the truths contained therein they might avoid the evils that would attend upon bloody conquest. The contention of this paper is that both of these assumptions are in error, and that the *Requerimiento* was in fact based on the theories of Innocent IV, and that

---

Kleffens, *Hispanic Law Until the End of the Middle Ages* (Chicago, 1969) is suggestive of what could be done by beginning with medieval Spanish law. All three writers stressed the importance of the Spanish legal tradition in shaping the conquest. More attention has been generally paid to the philosophical and theological traditions, usually with heavy emphasis upon the influence of Thomas Aquinas. What scholars have tended to overlook is that the bureaucrats who administered the conquest were generally trained as lawyers and that their writings, when examined closely, indicate the major role which canon and civil law played in their intellectual formation.

[3]Manuel Giménez Fernández, quoted in Juan Friede, "Las Casas and Indigenism in the Sixteenth Century," *Bartolomé de Las Casas in History*, eds. Juan Friede and Benjamin Keen, (DeKalb, Illinois, 1971) 127-234 at 149-150.

[4]The links of Las Casas and Vitoria with the medieval canonistic tradition and their acceptance of the Innocentian position on the rights of the infidels are discussed in: Kenneth J. Pennington, "Bartolome de Las Casas and the Tradition of Medieval Law," *Church History* 39(1970) 149-161; and James Muldoon, "A Canonistic Contribution to the Formation of International Law," *The Jurist* 18(1968) 265-279.

its primary purpose was to protect the Spanish government from the charge that the conquest was based on heretical principles. The specific heresy involved was that of John Wyclif whose opinion that possession of *dominium* depended upon being in the state of grace, an opinion similar to that of Hostiensis, had been condemned at the Council of Constance.

In order to understand the legal tradition on which the *Requerimiento* rested, it is necessary to recognize that three centuries of debate in canonistic circles about the rights of infidels preceded its composition. The essence of the problem was first raised by the Donatist heretics of North Africa in the fourth century. They asserted that the ability of a priest to administer the sacraments validly depended upon his being in the state of grace, not upon his proper administration of the ritual involved, as their opponent, St. Augustine argued.[5] Although the Augustinian view prevailed within the Church, the Donatist position occasionally reappeared when reformers despaired of reforming the institutional Church.[6] The doctrine's appeal lay in its call to abolish all ecclesiastical evils by the elimination of institutionalism itself which the reformers saw as the root of the evils. By the early thirteenth century, the opinion that sacramental power rested on grace had been expanded to include secular power as well. It entered the canon law tradition through the writings of Alanus Anglicus, a defender of the most extreme papal claims to power. He argued that at the birth of Christ all true authority, *dominium*, both spiritual and temporal, was transferred to Him.[7] He in turn transmitted it to St. Peter and to Peter's successors. Infidel rulers who, by definition, did not recognize Christ as the ultimate source of their power and the pope as the channel through which legitimate power comes, did not, according to this view, possess *dominium*. Such were only *de facto* rulers, not *de iure*.

The opinions of Alanus did not receive a great deal of attention at first. For the most part, the canonists were not interested in the status of infidels during the early decades of the thirteenth century. They were

[5]On Augustine and the Donatists, see Herbert A. Deane, *The Political and Social Ideas of St. Augustine* (New York, 1963) *passim*.

[6]The extreme supporters of the Gregorian reform of the eleventh century are occasionally identified as being Donatist in orientation: see Christopher Dawson, *Religion and the Rise of Western Culture* (New York, 1950; reprinted, Garden City, N.Y., 1958) 205. Gregory himself has also been charged with Donatism: see Norman Cantor, *Church Kingship, and Lay Investiture in England, 1089-1135* (Princeton, 1958) 124, 244.

[7]The significance of Alanus was first stressed by Walter Ullmann, *Medieval Papalism* (London, 1949) 10, 14 and *passim*. See also A.M. Stickler, "Alanus Anglicus als Verteidiger des monarchischen Papsttums," *Salesianum* 21(1959) 346-406.

primarily interested in Alanus' arguments as they affected the debate concerning the extent of papal power over secular rulers in Christian society. Canonistic interest in non-Christians was restricted to consideration of Jews and Saracens whose activities impinged upon Christian society in some way. Only after the middle of the thirteenth century did canonists begin to give serious attention to the status of the infidels. At that point, the beginning of contacts with the Mongols of Central Asia necessitated a fuller consideration of the place of the infidel societies within the scheme of international relations that existed within canon law.

Had the views of Alanus been widely accepted, there would have been no need to develop any new theory of Christian relations with the infidels. If Alanus was correct, then Christians were within their rights to attempt the conquest of any infidel society which they might wish to dominate simply because the infidels had no legal right to rule. The canonist who began the reaction to Alanus' opinion and asserted that all rational creatures, Christians and infidels alike, could possess *dominium* was also the pope, Innocent IV, who first initiated relations with an infidel society.[8] Innocent argued that while Christians had the right to wage war against the Moslems in order to recapture the Holy Land and other territories once Christian but presently in Moslem hands, they had no right to conquer other Moslem lands simply because the rulers were Moslems.[9] Fitting the crusades into the framework of the traditional theory of the just war, Innocent was arguing that the reconquest of the Holy Land was a just war of recuperation. Wars to gain other Moslem territories would be wars of aggression and therefore forbidden.

Having stated clearly the right of infidels to claim *dominium*, Innocent IV then went on to explain how this right was not an absolute one. In his view, the pope, though not a universal temporal ruler, did have a

[8]". . . possessiones et iurisdictiones licite sine peccato possunt esse apud infideles. haec. enim. non tamen pro fidelibus. sed pro omni rationabili creatura facta sunt, ut est praedictum. ipse.enim.solem suum oriri facit super bonos. et malos. ipse etiam volatilia pascit . . et propter hoc dicimus, non licet Papae.vel fidelibus, auferre sua, sive dominia, sive iurisdictiones infidelibus, quia sine peccato possident. . . ." Innocent IV, *Commentaria in quinque libros decretalium* (Turin, 1581) *ad* 3.34.8., fol. 176. For a further discussion of Innocent's views, see James Muldoon, "*Extra ecclesiam non est imperium:* The Canonists and the Legitimacy of Secular Power," *Studia Gratiana* 9(1966) 553-580.

[9]"Quod autem Papa facit indulgentias illis, qui vadunt ad recuperandam Terram sanctam, licet eam possideant Saraceni, et etiam inducere bellum, et dare indulgentias illis, qui occupant Terram sanctam: quam infideles illicite possident, hoc totum est ex causa, nam iuste motus est Papa, si intendit Terram sanctam,que consecrata est. . . . Item Terra sancta iusto bello victa fuit ab Imperatore Romano post mortem Christi, unde licitum est Papae ratione Imperii Romani, quod obtinet, illud ad suam iurisdictionem revocare, quam iniuste expoliatus. . . ." Innocent IV, *Commentaria ad* 3.34.8., fol. 176.

universal judicial and missionary responsibility. Within Christian society he judged men, even rulers, according to the laws of the New Testament and of the Church. Jews he could judge according to the laws of the Old Testament if the leaders of their communities did not enforce these laws. He could judge infidels if they sinned against the laws of nature which, he assumed, were clear to all men.[10] Among the actions for which an infidel ruler could be punished by the pope was the refusal to allow Christian missionaries to circulate freely in his lands. In this case, the natural right of men to circulate freely in peace and the divine mission of the Church to preach to all men combined to override the natural right of any society to govern itself free of outside interference.[11] For Innocent IV, there existed a hierarchy of rights so that the right to *dominium* can and must be subordinate to the Church's mission.

Although the opinion of Innocent IV appears to have become the predominant one among the canonists, it was not unchallenged. Innocent's student, Hostiensis, generally a follower of his master's opinions, took strong issue with Innocent on this issue. Following instead the arguments advanced by Alanus, Hostiensis rejected the argument that infidels could possess *dominium*.[12] In his opinion, the coming of Christ ended the priestly powers of the Jewish priesthood and, by analogy, the powers of non-Christian secular rulers as well. The only exception that he made was for infidel rulers who recognized that their *dominium* was derived from Christ through the mediation of the Church.[13]

No canonist seems to have recognized the Donatist implications of Hostiensis' argument that *dominium* rests on grace, although it might be argued that the failure of later canonists to follow this line of argument suggests that they suspected the danger. It was when the similar opinion of John Wyclif was examined and condemned at the Council of Con-

[10] ". . . sic per praedicta apparet, quod Papa super omnes habet iurisdictionem, et potestatem de iure, licet non de facto unde per potestatem, quam habet Papa, credo, quod si gentilis, qui non habet legem nisi naturae, si contra legem naturae facit, potest licite puniri per Papam. . . . Item Iudaeos potest iudicari Papa, si contra legem evangelii faciunt in moralibus, si eorum prelati eos non puniant. . . ." *Ibid.*

[11] ". . . tamen mandare potest Papa infidelibus. quod admittant predicatores evangelii in terris suae iurisdictionis, nam cum omnis creatura rationabilis facta sit ad deum laudandum . . . si ipsi prohibent praedicatores praedicare, peccant, et ideo puniendi sunt." *Ibid.*, fol. 177.

[12] ". . . mihi tamen videtur quod in adventu Christi omnis honor et omnis principatus et omne dominium et iurisditio de iure et ex causa iusta, et per illum qui suppreman manum habet nec errare potest omni infideli subtracta fuerit ad fideles translata. . . ." Hostiensis, *Lectura quinque Decretalium*, 2 vols. (Paris, 1512) *ad* 3.34.8., fol. 124.

[13] "Concedimus tamen quod infideles qui dominium ecclesie recognoscunt sunt ab ecclesia tolerandi: quia nec ad fidem precise cogendi sunt. . . ." *Ibid.*, fol. 125.

stance that the implications of what Alanus and Hostiensis had argued became apparent. At the Council, the problem of the relationship of power, both sacramental and civil, to grace was more than a theoretical quarrel among theologians. For the institutional Church, the argument that priestly power depended on the priest's spiritual state meant the dissolution of the Church as an institution. For secular rulers, the implications of this theory emerged when the conflict between the Teutonic Knights and the King of Poland over control of pagan Lithuania reached the Council. The Council acted as a lens which focused two long standing problems in such a way as to make the implications of the legal theories involved clear to everyone.

Among the forty five propositions contained in the works of Wyclif which the Council condemned as false and heretical was the opinion that "No one is a civil lord, or a prelate, or a bishop, while in mortal sin."[14] The defenders of both the papal and the conciliar positions at the Council could agree on the destructive effects of such an opinion on the institution which each camp sought to control. At the same time, it is also clear that the Council Fathers did not read Wyclif's works extensively in order to reach their decision to condemn the propositions. They relied on the list of statements which the supporters of the condemnation advanced. On the surface, then, it would appear that Wyclif's views would justify the conquest of an infidel society on the grounds that the rulers, being infidels, were by definition not in the state of grace. Just as

[14]"Nullus est dominus civilis, nullus est prelatus, nullus est episcopus, dum est in peccato mortali." Charles-Joseph Hefele and H. Leclercq, *Histoire des conciles*, 10 vols. (Paris, 1916) VII, part 1, 517. Wyclif expressed this opinion in various places in his works. The following extract is representative of his views: "Nota tamen quod nullum est civile dominium, nisi in iusticia evangelica sit fundatum; ideo peccans mortaliter non habet dominium pocius quam virgo perpetua habet paternitatem carnalem. . . ." John Wyclif, *De Civili Dominio*, 4 vols., eds. R. L. Poole and J. Loserth (London, 1885-1904) I, 21-22. Precisely what Wyclif meant by this statement is in dispute. One view is that he meant a man in the state of mortal sin "has neither political authority nor property in the full and proper spiritual sense, but he does not mean that he cannot have these in the ordinary or legal sense." R. W. and A. J. Carlyle, *A History of Mediaeval Political Theory in the West*, 6 vols. (London and Edinburgh, 1903-1936) VI, 60. The difficulty with accepting this argument is that Wyclif pairs civil and ecclesiastical *dominium* so that if, as he argues, mortal sin invalidates the sacraments administered by the sinful priest and he should therefore be removed, then secular power must likewise be invalidated by the sin of its possessor and he too should be removed from his office. On the other hand, it has been argued with equal firmness that his system places real value only on *dominium* which is based on grace. See, L. J. Daly, *The Political Theory of John Wyclif* (Chicago, 1962) 76. The difficulties involved in grasping the meaning of Wyclif's arguments have been summed up thus: "So carefully did Wyclif obscure the logical consequences his theories on dominion would have meant for the nobility that the duke [John of Gaunt], the notoriously immoral son of an equally immoral father, together with the vicious Percy, appeared as his champions at St. Paul's." Joseph Dahmus, *The Prosecution of John Wyclif* (New Haven, 1952) 18.

his arguments could be used to dissolve the institutional Church, so too they could be used to justify unlimited conquest. Indeed, a close reading of *De civili dominio* will provide materials which appear to prove that Wyclif intended to apply his arguments in this way. At one point, for example, he illustrated the argument that *dominium* is lost by mortal sin with a reference to the ouster of Adam and Eve from the Garden of Eden, suggesting that Christians, acting in the place of God, could dispossess infidels.[15]

On the other hand, Wyclif generally subordinated the goal of conquering the infidels to that of converting them. Apparently aware that others might use his arguments to justify conquests, he stressed that the salvation of souls, not the conquest of infidel bodies was the proper goal of Christians.[16] Rather in the fashion of Innocent IV, he argued that the use of force against infidel rulers was justified only if they refused to allow Christian missionaries to enter their lands.[17] Furthermore, in keeping with his avowed intention of advancing ecclesiastical reform, he advised that Christian rulers would do better to employ their arms in reforming the Church at home before marching off to conquer infidels under the banner of religion.[18]

In the final analysis, Wyclif's views on Christian-infidel relations were quite traditional and rooted in the just war tradition which justified wars of defense, not wars of aggression.[19] Furthermore, in a striking reversal

[15]"Confirmatur per hoc quod nullum civile dominium est iustum simpliciter, nisi in naturali dominio sit fundatum; sed nemo habet naturale dominium pro tempore quo peccat mortaliter; ergo nec civile dominium iustum simpliciter. Minor patet ex facto iudicis summe iusti, qui expulit primum hominem de paradiso post peccatum. . " Wyclif, *De Civili Dominio*, I, 37-38.

[16]"Obiciunt nempe nobis infideles convertendi quod sumus prevaricatores manifestissimi legis nostre, cum predicamus despeccionem temporalium ac aspiracionem caritativam et pacificam ad eterna; et tamen de facto nulla gens insistit ardencius circa civile dominium vel pro temporalibus fratrem suum contra caritatem perturbando persequitur. non ergo per rapinam temporalium sed instar Christi ac suorum discipulorum, per eorum renunciacionem sermone et opere convertimus infideles." *Ibid.*, II, 9-10.

[17]"Licet ergo militantibus pugnare contra ferales qui nolunt exhortacionibus vel Christi legibus conparere, eciam contra infideles sectas, supposito quod sacerdotibus ecclesie revelatum sit quod eorum exhortacione neglecta sint per corporalem gladium castigandi." *Ibid.*, II, 255.

[18]"Rex igitur invadens regna extera si corpus rebellat anime, debet primo corpus suum subicere, cum sit hostis periculosissimus dampni maximi de proximo versimiliter illaturus. . . Racio prima est quod rex ad beneficienciam sui et suorum est obligacior, secunda quia inpugnacio eorum de quibus rex habet curam specialem est periculosior. . . ." *Ibid.*, II, 244.

[19]For example, Book II, ch. 17 of *De Civili Dominio* which deals with the just war cites *Causa* XXIII of the *Decretum*, the basic canonistic source for the just war, extensively, more extensively in fact than the editor's notes would indicate. Although Wyclif is said to share in the strong antipathy of theologians to lawyers, both canon and civil, nevertheless he cites their material a great deal. On Wyclif's antipathy to lawyers, see Daly, *Political Theory of John Wyclif*, 96.

of the usual argument that Christ's birth radically affected the right of non-Christians to *dominium*, Wyclif argued that it was wrong to point to the wars of the ancient Hebrews as a model for wars of religion waged by Christians. The coming of Christ meant the end of such wars. The God of the Old Testament ordered His people to fight. Christ ordered His followers to love all men and to preach to them.[20]

The failure of the Council Fathers to consider Wyclif's thought in all its complexity becomes quite apparent when their treatment of John Hus is compared with their treatment of Wyclif. The zeal with which the members of the Council sought to accuse Hus of being a follower of Wyclif, even on points that Hus rejected, suggests that the Council Fathers were very alarmed about Wyclif's opinions and very anxious to see them destroyed. Although Hus' opinions, like those of Wyclif, came to the Council as a series of propositions, the Bohemian had the distinct advantage of being present and being able to point out that his opinions had been quoted inaccurately. This appears clearly in the debate about Hus' views on *dominium* when he specifically denied teaching Wyclif's doctrine "that a priest in mortal sin does not consecrate." In response to this charge, he suggested that if his critics would take the trouble to examine his writings, they would see that he had written that such priests administer the sacraments unworthily but validly.[21] In spite of this, members of the Council continued to charge him with believing that *dominium* rested on grace. Jean Gerson, for example, asserted that "the most pernicious error" in all of Hus' works was precisely this opinion. Matthew Spinka has argued that "Gerson hastily assumed that Hus shared Wyclif's view without taking the trouble to note Hus's qualification of it," a charge that in all probability can be leveled against all the Council Fathers.[22]

[20]"Et videat quare per idem non sequitur quod cerimonialia et iudiciali veteris testamenti debent hodie observari. Consideret secundo quod patres veteris testamenti secundum legem singulariter eis datam in funiculo distribucionis conversantes habuerint infideles undique circumseptos, quos auctoritate Dei tanquam eius adversarios precepti sunt aggredi. In novo vero testamento cum preceptum est evangelium predicari cuilibet creature et omnes homines diligi remittenda est iniuria cuilibet instar Christi, eum per hoc medium omnes gentes debent converti." Wyclif, *De Civili Dominio*, II, 249.

[21]Peter of Mladonovice, "An Account of the Trial and Condemnation of Master John Hus in Constance," *John Hus at the Council of Constance*, ed. Matthew Spinka (New York and London, 1965. Records of Civilization: Sources and Studies, LXIII) 87-234 at 171-172.

[22]Spinka, *John Hus at the Council of Constance*, 171, note 25. See also, Matthew Spinka, *John Hus, A Biography* (Princeton, 1968) 248-249, where he argues that Gerson's criticisms of the Church were essentially in agreement with those which Hus had expressed, but that Gerson simply accepted "the calumnies of Hus' enemies for truth" and thus failed to see the areas in which he and Hus were in agreement.

While the sensitivity of churchmen at the Council to the implications of what they considered, too simply perhaps, Wyclif's considered opinion on *dominium* obviously resulted from the fear that his doctrine, if accepted, would dissolve the institutional Church, laymen had a similar response to its implications for secular power. When Emperor Sigismund heard Hus say that the effect of mortal sin was to render a secular ruler unworthy before the throne of God, he responded that all men were sinners and, presumably unworthy to possess *dominium.*[23] For the Emperor this was obviously an unsatisfactory conclusion, one which could lead to the dissolution of all secular government.

The most extensive discussion of the problem of *dominium* at Constance came in connection with the debate over the conflicting claims of the King of Poland and the Teutonic Knights to Lithuania. In this arena the practical implications of the ideas about *dominium* which Alanus, Hostiensis, and Wyclif had advanced came into public view. The Knights claimed the right to control Lithuania on the basis of papal bulls which authorized them to convert these infidels to Christianity. The King of Poland's representatives argued that the conversion of the Grand Duke of Lithuania and the subsequent Union of 1386 which linked Poland and Lithuania under a single ruler ended the role of the Knights in Lithuania. Paulus Vladimiri, a noted canon lawyer who served as an advocate for the Polish position at Constance, asserted that the Knights' position rested on the condemned doctrine of John Wyclif concerning *dominium* because they assumed that the Lithuanians, being infidels, were incapable of possessing *dominium.*[24] In an extensive discussion of the theory that grace is necessary in order to have *dominium*, an essay which significantly is entitled *Opinio Hostiensis*, Vladimiri concluded with a firm restatement of Innocent IV's assertion that all men, even infidels, have the right to *dominium*.

> Infidelity is not inconsistent with *dominium*, because *dominium* and preferential status spring from human law, namely the *ius gentium*. The distinction between the faithful and the infidels is from divine law. Divine right,

[23]Spinka, *John Hus at the Council of Constance*, 202-203.

[24]Paulus Vladimiri, "Articuli contra Cruciferos," Stanislaus F. Belch, *Paulus Vladimiri and his Doctrine Concerning International Law and Politics*, 2 vols. (The Hague, 1965) II, 905-988 at 917. Belch's work is an aggressive attempt to demonstrate the significance of Vladimiri in the development of international law and the importance of the conflict between the Knights and the King of Poland in focusing his ideas on the subject. The position of the Knights has been recently defended by Erich Weise, *Die Amtsgewalt von Papst und Kaiser und die Ostmission besonders in der 1. Hälfte des 13. Jahrhunderts* (Marburg, 1971).

however, which is derived from grace, does not remove right, which comes from natural reason.[25]

For Vladimiri, the Hostiensian argument that with "the coming of Christ all jurisdiction, pre-eminence, honor, and *dominium* were transferred from the infidels to the faithful" led logically to the conclusion that "a war against infidels who do not recognize Roman *imperium* is always just and licit for Christians."[26] This was a conclusion which he could not accept, preferring instead to follow the *communis opinio* of the canonists which was that of Innocent IV. Vladimiri appears to have been the first lawyer to comprehend fully the political consequences of what Alanus, Hostiensis and Wyclif had argued.

Had the debate on *dominium* remained on the level of legal tracts, the Wyclifian implications of the Knights' position might not have become widely recognized. A war of words between supporters of the Knights and those of the Poles which culminated in a special commission of the Council to investigate the charges raised in the quarrel eventually gave wide publicity to the problem. A Dominican friar, Johannes Falkenberg, a supporter of the Knights, declared that the Poles and the Lithuanians were "heretics and shameless dogs who have returned to the vomit of their infidelity." In addition, the friar also claimed that the "King of the Poles, since he is a bad ruler, is an idol and all the Poles are idolators and serve their idol Jaghil."[27] In this barrage Falkenberg mixed various charges, at least one of which, the assertion that the Poles had lapsed from the faith, was a traditional argument for a just war.

Falkenberg's charges received a good deal of attention from the Council, resulting eventually in a series of tracts and statements by various individuals for and against the friar's position. One of his supporters noted, however, that the accusation of idolatry, if taken literally, would convict Falkenberg of accepting Wyclif's condemned views on *dominium*, something that the Dominican surely could not have intended.[28] Rather than justifying the war on the grounds that the Poles and Lithuanians were infidels and idolators, this writer eventually argued that the work of the Knights was analogous to the task of reconquering Spain, thus shifting the basis of the war to the traditional just war of recuperation.[29] As Vladimiri had noted elsewhere, this

[25] Vladimiri, "Opinio Hostiensis," Belch, II, 845-884 at 883.
[26] *Ibid.*, 864.
[27] *Acta concilii Constanciensis*, ed. Heinrich Finke, 4 vols. (Münster, 1896-1928) IV, 363, 365.
[28] *Ibid.*, 364.
[29] *Ibid.*, 403.

analogy was invalid because Lithuania, unlike Spain, had never been occupied by Christians in the past.[30]

Although the Council did not resolve the conflict between the Knights and the King of Poland which dragged on until 1446, the Council's commission to study Falkenberg's charges did reach a conclusion. In December 1417, the commission drafted a report which condemned Falkenberg's tract because it "contained many false, detestable and damnable [statements] which are against the faith and against good morals. . . ."[31] While not specifically accusing the Dominican of adopting Wyclif's teachings, it is reasonable to assume that among the doctrines which constituted "errors against the faith" in Falkenberg's tract were the Wyclifian implications which the tract contained.

The condemnation of Wyclif's opinions at Constance and the recognition that Hostiensis' opinions on *dominium* were identical with Wyclif's forced the canonists to follow the opinion of Innocent IV on *dominium* or face the threat of condemnation. While the obvious reason for this shift was the threat which the doctrines of Wyclif posed for the Church as an institution, the effect was to cause a major shift in the attitude which the lawyers would take toward infidel *dominium*. The result was the development and refinement of Innocent IV's justifications for Christian intervention in infidel societies. For the remainder of the fifteenth century, the canonistic tradition continued to hold to the position that infidels did possess *dominium* but that the pope's responsibility for the souls of men and his role as universal judge could require him to order the use of Christian arms against infidel societies. In addition, there emerged the argument that Christians also had a responsibility to civilize primitive peoples as well as to convert them.[32] The justifications for conquest thus acquired a positive tone, stressing the advantages, both spiritual and temporal, which the infidels would obtain from Christian domination.

l'expansion Portugaise au XVe siècle," *Revue d'histoire ecclesiastique* [48(1953) 683-718; 49(1954) 438-461; 51(1956) 415-453 and 809-836]48(1953) 715-17 at 715. For a full discussion of this letter and its place in the development of legal thought about the status of infidels, see James Muldoon, "A Fifteenth Century Application of the Canonistic Theory of the Just War," Proceedings of the Fourth International Congress of Medieval Canon Law (Toronto, August 21-25, 1972).

[30]Vladimiri, "Opinio Hostiensis," Belch, II, 878.

[31]*Acta concilii Constanciensis*, IV, 430.

[32]King Edward of Portugal raised this argument in connection with the conquest of the Canary Islands in 1436. According to him: "Has indomiti silvestres fere homines inhabitant qui nulla religione coagulati, nullis denique legum vinculis irretiti, civili conversacione neglecta, in paganitate veluti pecudes vitam agunt. Iis navale comercium, literarum exercicium, genus aliquod metali aut numismatis nullum est." The text is in Charles-Martial de Witte, "Les bulles pontificales et

This was the legal tradition within which Juan López de Palacios Rubios was operating when he, as is generally supposed, drew up the *Requerimiento*. It is a tradition of which those who have described the document as expressing Hostiensian views have been unaware or which they have misunderstood. The essence of the *Requerimiento* is that the Indians do indeed have *dominium*. The Spanish could not lawfully invade their lands until the document had been read to them. The message of the *Requerimiento* is that the Christian Church is responsible for them and that the natives must allow missionaries to preach the Gospel to them. If they refuse to allow this and to recognize the papal appointment of Ferdinand of Aragon and his daughter Joanna as their overlord so that the work of conversion could proceed smoothly, then the Spanish troops could move. Failure to heed the message of the *Requerimiento* provided a *casus belli* which the Spanish needed in order to legitimize their attack in terms of Innocent IV's opinion on infidel *dominium*. If infidels did not have *dominium*, there would be no need to prepare the *Requerimiento* and to engage in the ritual of reading it before an attack.

The misinterpretation of the *Requerimiento* stemmed from two errors, one concerning what Hostiensis' views on *dominium* really were, and the other concerning the purpose for which it was composed. Both of these errors can be traced to the writings of Las Casas whose opinions have gone unchallenged. Las Casas admitted to being puzzled by Palacios Rubios' willingness to authorize the Spanish conquest on the basis of the Hostiensian position which Las Casas realized was unacceptable theologically.[33] What Las Casas did not perceive was that both the Innocentian and the Hostiensian positions led inevitably to the justification of the right of conquest. The two opinions differed on the basis for justifying such conquest, but Innocent IV, no less than his student, essentially admitted the right of Christians to invade infidel societies. What Las Casas and those who have followed his lead have overlooked was Innocent's careful creation of a scale of spiritual priorities which the pope could invoke to override the *dominium* of infidels. Although Las Casas was familiar with the legal tradition and employed it in his battle with the Spanish government, he was not a trained lawyer. He was far more concerned with the goal of protecting the natives than with

[33]Bartolomé Las Casas, *Historia de las Indias*, 3 vols., ed. Agustín Millares Carlo (Mexico, 1951) III, 25-28. Francisco Vitoria, *De Indis et de jure belli relectiones* Washington, D.C., 1917; reprinted, New York, 1964) 121-122, argues that Hostiensian arguments were used to justify the conquest, although he did not say specifically that Palacios Rubios employed them or that they were to be found in the *Requerimiento*.

exploring the subtlties of canon law. As a result, he missed the crucial distinction between Innocent's opinion and Hostiensis'.

Las Casas missed the importance of the subtle distinction between the two legal opinions because he assumed that the basic purpose of the *Requerimiento* was to inform the Indians of the choices open to them on the eve of a Spanish attack. If this was the real reason for its composition, then the line of critics from Las Casas to Hanke who have been scandalized by the vision of *conquistadores* reading it to trees and empty villages or hurling it at the backs of fleeing Indians has a right to be scandalized.[34] On the other hand, there is no evidence that the Spanish government took any great steps to insure that the document was read carefully and that the natives had sufficient time to ponder their response before the troops attacked. In fact, the major purpose of the document was to protect the Spanish from the charge that they were basing the conquest on Wyclif's doctrine of *dominium*. The *Requerimiento* fits into the series of documents which the Spanish used to legitimize their various conquests, in Europe and overseas. The papal bulls dealing with the conquest of Navarre and the more famous ones which Alexander VI issued to the Portuguese and the Castilians in 1493, granting them each the exclusive right to direct the exploration, settlement and subsequent conversion of a specific region were legitimizing documents. They formed part of a legal tradition by means of which the papacy sought to direct and control European conquest and expansion, a tradition which reached well back into the Middle Ages.[35] The *Requerimiento* was an effort to prove to the papacy that the conquest of the Americas was proceeding along the lines that the papacy would approve. That is, the primary reason for the conquest, according to the *Requerimiento*, was to convert and to civilize the natives. It was not undertaken for base motives. In addition, the Spanish felt obliged to state that they were not denying the *dominium* of the Indians, that, like Innocent IV, they were acting because of the overriding obligation of Christians to spread the Gospel. In the early days of the conquest, before the Spanish hold on the Americas was assured, the government obviously feared that other European nations would enter into the Americas. The easiest way for them to do so legally would be to prove to the papacy that the Spanish

[34]Hanke, *The Spanish Struggle*, 34-35.

[35]Ferdinand the Catholic in particular was very sensitive to the need for legitimizing conquests. See Roger B. Merriman, *The Rise of the Spanish Empire in the Old World and in the New*, 4 vols. (New York, 1918-1934; reprinted, 1962) II, 345. Two more recent works have sought to analyze this legitimizing role of the papacy in more detail: Luis Weckman, *Las Bulas Alejandrinas de 1493 y la Teorí Política del Papado Medieval* (Mexico City, 1949) and de Witte, "Les bulles pontificales. . ."

were not living up to the terms of Alexander IV's bulls, or to prove that the Spanish were justifying their conquest on a doctrine which had been condemned as heretical. It is no coincidence that the *Requerimiento* gradually fell into disuse in the 1540's as the Spanish conquest was becoming secure and when the progress of the Reformation was making a mockery of papal claims to universal jurisdiction. Papal approbation was no longer a factor worth considering in the administration of the conquest.

The strongest argument against this interpretation of the *Requerimiento* is the existence of Palacios Rubios' tract on the right of the Spanish to the Americas, *De las Islas del Mar Océano.* In the introduction to the first printed edition of the text, Professor Silvio Zavala argued that this treatise demonstrates the Hostiensian position of Palacios Rubios.[36] Here again, he followed the argument of Las Casas without further examination of the legal tradition within which the work was written. In fact, Palacios Rubios made it clear in the treatise that the Indians did possess *dominium*, that infidelity was not a suitable grounds for dispossessing them, and that only for good and just cause could the Spanish invade their lands.[37] In another place, to the question of the effect of conversion upon infidel *dominium*, Palacios Rubios responded that as they possessed *dominium* before their conversion, so they would continue to possess it after conversion.[38]

What Palacios Rubios, following Hostiensis, did assert was that infidels possessed no lawful authority over Christians, a position widespread among the canonists and philosophers, although not universal.[39]

[36]"A fin de fundo este principio, tan decisivo papa las relaciones entre la Christiandad y los reinos de infieles, Palacios Rubios se apoya en la doctrine canónica del siglo XIII, o como diriá Las Casas, sigue 'el error de Ostiensis'." Juan Lopez de Palacios Rubios, *De las Islas del mar Océano*, intro. and ed. by Silvio Zavala (Mexico City, 1954) XC.

[37]"En virtud, pues, de estos tres derechos parece haberse introducido en cierto modo el dominio de las cosas. . . . Todo esto se refiere no sólo a los fieles, sino a los infieles. . . . Fieles e infieles poseen y tienen lícitamente la propiedad de las cosas, como abiertamente lo afirma Inocencio, al que siguen todos los demás, al comentar el citado capitulo 'Quod super his, De voto'. . . ."

"De lo anterior se infiere primeramente que los infieles no deben sólo por motivo de su infidelidad y sin mediar otra causa justa, ser privados de sus bienes, ni moverles guerra en que los Cristianos se apoderen de lo que poseen." *Ibid.*, 41-42.

[38]"Por tanto, el dominio que en común o en particular tenían, lícita y justamente, antes de convertirse y de quedar sometidos a vuestro poder, lo conservan hoy, porque al tornarse Cristianos y súbditos vuestros no lo perdieron, como en el capítulo anterior hemos dicho de su ingenuidad y libertad, pues los infieles son capaces para el dominio de las cosas y posesiones." *Ibid.*, 39.

[39]"De lo dicho resulta que el dominio de prelación o jurisdicción que los infieles pretenden tener sobre los fieles puede quitárseles por sentencia u ordenamiento de la Iglesia, poseedora de la autoridad de Dios, porque los infieles, por mérito de su infidelidad merecen perder su potestad sobre los que pasan a ser hijos de Dios. . . ." *Ibid.*, 115.

Innocent IV, for example, following a long standing canonistic position, argued that having infidels rule over Christians was an imprudent situation but not an illegal one.[40] At no point did Palacios Rubios deny the essential point in Innocent IV's argument, namely that infidels did possess ***dominium***. Rather than attacking this position directly, he undermined it by developing the various arguments which Innocent himself had used to explain the overriding responsibility of Christians for the conversion of infidels.[41]

Placed within the proper legal context, the *Requerimiento* takes on a somewhat different sense than the one scholars have generally attributed to it. Professor Hanke, for example, assuming that it contained the Hostiensian position on the rights of infidels, argued that its proponents "lulled the King's conscience" with it in order to justify the conquest of the Americas.[42] When looked at as embodying the Innocentian doctrine of the rights of the natives and the superior responsibility of Christians for the souls of infidels, and a document which was only one of a long line of documents designed not to lull but to legitimize, there remains no need to suppose that the composition of the *Requerimiento* was any less an integral part of the quest for legitimizing the conquest than the earlier papal bulls had been.

In a wider context, Hanke's "Spanish Struggle for Justice in the Conquest of America" was not a uniquely Spanish theme at all. The justice which the Spanish sought to achieve was derived from the medieval canonistic tradition which placed the pope at the head of a judicial pyramid. The secular rulers of the world were subordinate to him and served as his agents in achieving a just and orderly world. By accepting the responsibility for administering the program of conversion

[40]". . . fatemur tamen, quod si populi conversi essent, sed domini remanerent infideles, quod Papa bene posset domino infideli dominium er iurisdictionem dimittere super fideles, arg. 1. ad Thimo.6. in prin. dummodo Christianos non gravaret iniuste. Item propter periculum posset cogi dominus ad recipendum pretium vel commutionem. . . ." Innocent IV, *Commentaria*, 3.34.8., fol. 177.

[41]It is interesting to note that the *Requerimiento* is constructed along the general lines of two letters which Innocent IV addressed to the leader of the Mongols in 1245. These letters discuss Christ's incarnation and the subsequent responsibility of the pope for the souls of all men. This is not to say that Palacios Rubios was directly influenced by Innocent IV's letters in the writing of the *Requerimiento*. Rather, the similarity suggests that Palacios Rubios thought along the lines of Innocent IV because he was influenced by Innocent's views on *dominium*. The bulls are in the *Monumenta Germaniae Historica, Epistolae saeculi XIII e registis Pontificum Romanorum*, II, sel. G. H. Pertz, ed. C. Rodenberg (Berlin, 1887) 72-75. See also, C. Dawson, *The Mongol Mission* (London and New York, 1955) 73-76.

[42]Hanke, *The Spanish Struggle*, 35.

in a particular region, as the Spanish and Portuguese had done by the terms of Alexander VI's bulls, a Christian ruler was accepting a papal licence, one which could be removed if the terms of the grant were not fulfilled. What is most striking is that the Spanish and Portuguese monarchs were among the last European monarchs to seek papal legitimization for their expansionistic activities. The view of a papally directed society which underlay the *Requerimiento* and the related papal documents was clearly an outdated one, a view of the world which is usually said to have been laid to rest with Boniface VIII.[43]

Finally, the struggle over the rights of the infidels was linked, through the legal tradition, to the far more important problem of the nature of the Church. When the lawyers defended the right of infidels to *dominium*, they were not thinking primarily of the inhabitants of the Americas. They were thinking of the related problem of ecclesiastical dominium. If infidels could not possess *dominium* because they were in the state of sin, neither could sinful priests, a conclusion which obviously unacceptable. The easiest of all justifications for European conquest of the non-European world, the denial of rights to the infidels, was made unacceptable by the condemnation of Wyclif's opinions at Constance. The elaboration of subtle legal distinctions to justify such conquests was a direct result of the lingering effects of that condemnation. John Wyclif, who had so little impact upon contemporary Church theology and reform, shaped the path which the lawyers were to take on the problem of *dominium*. The condemnation at Constance meant that the opinion of Innocent IV, not that of Hostiensis, would be the basis of legal thinking on the rights of infidels.

[43]It is interesting to note that Palacios Rubios cited Boniface VIII's *Unam sanctam* in his discussion of the Spanish claim to the Americas (page 88). Yet, although this bull is generally understood as the most extreme assertion of papal claims to temporal power, a document which enshrined the theories of Alanus Anglicus according to Walter Ullmann (*Medieval Papalism*, 11), it is possible to interpret it differently, in the tradition of Innocent IV's views on the relation of the two powers. For this interpretation, see James Muldoon, "Boniface VIII's Forty Years of Experience in the Law," *The Jurist* 31(1971) 449-477.

# VII

# The Development of Group Rights

THUS far we have discussed minority rights in broad theoretical terms, focusing on modern statements of the issues involved and on examples of the problems that minority groups face in the modern world. Before moving to an extended discussion of the variety of situations in which minority groups find themselves in the modern political environment, a look at the historical development of minority group rights will be useful in order to appreciate the relative novelty of such ideas. The opinion that a minority within a society possesses special group rights has been a matter of political and legal concern only for the past two centuries. The reason for this is paradoxical. Until modern political thinkers, beginning with the philosophes of the eighteenth century, developed the notion of majority rule, there was no need to define minority rights at all because there was no perceived adversarial relationship between majority and minority that required resolution.[1] Likewise, the notion that a state should be the political expression of a culturally homogeneous society has been generally accepted only since the eighteenth century. As a result, until modern times there has been no reason to assert the unique claims of minority groups.

The assertion that the majority should rule and that the minority group (or groups) should conform to the will of the majority, ideas springing from eighteenth century political thought and first implemented by the French revolutionaries, remains, even in the twentieth century, a predominantly Western European idea. Elsewhere in the world, states exist that contain a variety of linguistic and cultural groups, often joined together only in a very fragile way and dominated by one of the minority groups that comprises the entire body. In this form of society there is no perceived adversarial relationship between the dominant minority and a dominated majority. The conflict is among the various minority groups, each one seeking the dominant position. The groups that have lost the struggle for domination do not see themselves as forming a majority that

**Originally published in *Minority Rights: A Comparative Analysis*, ed. Jay A. Sigler (Westport, Connecticut, 1983), pp. 31–66.** 

shares a common body of interests with the other minorities in the same position. Indeed, even within western Europe, where the modern notion of the homogeneous state developed, the theory has neever been totally implemented even in the smallest political unit. Even as the philosophes and the revolutionaries of the eighteenth century were bringing the concept into being, the early theorists of nationalism were beginning to emerge, and with them came the notion that the individual cultural and linguistic traditions of the various European peoples deserved to survive in the face of growing pressures to become assimilated into the majority culture.

The contemporary world generally recognizes that within any large society there are groups, usually linguistic, cultural, or religious, that do not accept the values of the majority of the population. These differences are not simply what are defined as political differences, reflected in the existence of political parties. Rather, these differences reflect distinct outlooks on life, codes of values, and unique customs and traditions that are threatened, implicitly or explicitly, by pressures stemming from the majority. Spokesmen for minority groups demand legal protections for their groups, ranging from official recognition of a particular religion, through the establishment of public schools using the minority language, to the creation of a regional homeland and a fixed share of political power guaranteed to members of the minority. Their claim is that the minority groups have a right to exist, and so they demand a heterogeneous society in place of the homogeneous society that the majority's pressure seems to demand.[2] In a sense they are demanding a return to the sociopolitical structure of pre-eighteenth century Europe. By the standards of modern political thought, these spokesmen are reactionaries, although they do not see themselves as such. Their call for the rights of groups echoes the criticism of majority rule made by eighteenth-century spokesmen for the traditional corporate groups that composed medieval and early modern European society.

*HISTORICAL BACKGROUND*

In general, the political theory and practice of the ancient and the medieval Western world did not deal with the issue of majority rights versus minority rights. The assumption upon which ancient and medieval societies operated was that a society consisted of a variety of groups that dwelled within its geographical borders but that the right to participation in political life did not automatically follow from birth within the borders. Even in the smallest Greek city-state, citizenship was a jealously guarded privilege enjoyed by only a small percentage of the total population, even though the unenfranchised members of the population were usually linguistically and culturally indistinct from those who were citizens. In the largest city-state, Athens, there were about 400,000 inhabitants in the midfifth century B.C., of these, about 168,000 men, women, and children were Athenian citizens, while 200,000 were slaves.[3] The remainder consisted of aliens, usually citizens of other cities, who were permanent residents of Athens.[4] Furthermore, although Athens had the reputation of granting citizenship comparatively easily to foreigners who were likely to make important contributions to Athenian life, by modern standards at least, citizenship was granted only rarely.[5] In addition, Athens was unusual in the comparatively high ratio of citizens to noncitizens. Contemporary Sparta, for example, had at most 10,000 citizens who ruled over a much larger population of slaves and free inhabitants.[6] The Spartans were able to dominate their subject population only by forming a garrison state whose members were constantly on the alert for signs of rebellion among the helots, the state slaves who did the manual labor in Spartan society.

Complete political equality existed within the body of citizens in a city-state. The fact of citizenship transcended economic and social barriers that otherwise differentiated the citizens of a city such as Athens. Equality was the product of a long history of internal political conflict, as Aristotle's *Politics* demonstrated.[7] It was also constantly threatened by those who preferred government by an even more limited segment of the population. Sparta was more egalitarian than Athens in that the citizens were economically and socially equal as well. Furthermore, they were required to live the greater part of their lives in barracks and to eat at communal tables.[8] While the Spartan citizens formed a body of equals, they did not view the helots and the resident freemen, the *perioeci*, as in any way their equals. One historian has described the helots as "socially and morally the most submerged class in all Greece."[9] The harsh military life-style that the Spartans adopted was rooted in the need to protect themselves from the helots. Elsewhere in Greece there was a general sense of Greek superiority. The barbarians, that is those who were not Greek in culture, were presumed to be naturally inferior to the Greeks. Aristotle was even able to argue that the Greeks were fit by nature to rule other men because of their innate superiority.[10]

The city-state form of government continued to flourish in the ancient world even after the rise of empires. The Roman Empire was essentially a federation of city-states at the apex of which was the city of Rome itself.[11] Each city-state that the Romans conquered retained its local governing elite and political structure. The conquering Romans recognized that the stability of their empire depended upon the cooperation of the conquered. As a result, the Romans won the support of those whom they defeated by making peace treaties that allowed local elites to continue governing in their traditional fashion with a minimum of interference from Rome.[12] As long as taxes were paid and Roman subjects did not wage war with one another or with Rome, the conquerors were satisfied. In addition, the Romans made slightly different treaties with neighboring states in order to prevent the development of a common body of grievances against the Romans. In other words, even the conquered did not form a majority in the sense of a body of people with a broad base of common interests that differentiated them clearly from the Romans. Rather, each conquered society's leaders saw themselves as sharing to some degree in ruling the empire and possessing a special relationship with the imperial government. Furthermore, the Romans held out full Roman citizenship as the ultimate reward for those who supported the conquerors, making the members of the local elites partners in the elite that ruled the entire empire.[13] When the Emperor Caracalla granted Roman citizenship to all freemen in 212 A.D., however, he did not create a democracy in which a true majority determined imperial policy. There remained a large number of slaves and other persons who were not citizens. Furthermore, real power within the empire remained in the hands of a small number of individuals who formed the imperial elite.[14]

Although the political history of the Middle Ages differed greatly from that of the ancient world, ancient and medieval political structures were similar in that power remained divided among a variety of local power centers rather than centralized as tends to be the case in the modern Western world. The cities of the western Roman Empire gradually disappeared or were markedly reduced in size from the fourth to the tenth century A.D. Only during the eleventh and twelfth centuries did cities and towns reappear as important political and economic units.[15] Elsewhere, political power devolved into a variety of hands and institutions during the same period, only to coalesce gradually into rudimentary kingdoms. Even within these kingdoms, no matter how small, kings shared power with a variety of groups and individuals. When medieval writers described the nature of a society, they tended to do so functionally. That is, they saw society as composed of three functional groupings, those who pray, those who fight, and those who labor.[16] These groups obviously did not reflect equality of numbers. The great bulk of the population labored, but political power was restricted to the groups that fought and prayed. Only gradually did a fourth group appear to claim a place within this functional structure. This occurred when the growth of trade and the rebirth of urban life on a significant scale gave rise to the bourgeoisie, the city dwellers who functioned as merchants and bankers.

The functional nature of the medieval political outlook appears most clearly in that most medieval of institutions, the parliament. While the particulars of such assemblies varied from kingdom to kingdom and from century to century, medieval parliaments shared certain characteristics. In the first place, the existence of such an assembly reflected the general assumption that a king required the advice of certain segments of the population if he wished to rule effectively.[17] He was bound to request advice from those who possessed power, by which was meant economic, military, or moral power. In England, for example, the early parliaments had representatives from the clergy, the greater nobility, the lesser nobility, and the wealthier urban dwellers. By the end of the thirteenth century, the clergy as a bloc had withdrawn from Parliament, to meet separately as the Clerical Convocation, leaving the bishops and abbots of some large religious houses to attend the House of Lords in their capacity as landlords and royal vassals, just as the secular lords did. The division of the Parliament into a two-house assembly led to the union of the lower ranks of the landholding, warrior class, represented by the Knights of the Shire, with the representatives of the chartered town, the burgesses. Although other parliamentary bodies had as many as four branches, or estates as they were often termed, the principle of functional, not numerical, representation persisted. In addition, each of these estates had its own laws and judicial practices. The clergy answered to canon law, merchants to the law merchant, and nobles to the laws and courts of their own estate. Magna Carta in 1215 demonstrated the importance of these various legal systems as they functioned in early thirteenth-century England.[18] The first chapter explicitly guaranteed the rights and privileges of the church, while chapter thirteen did the same for the city of London and "all other cities, boroughs, towns, and ports" as well. Individuals were to be tried by their peers because only a man's equals knew the laws that governed his behavior. "Earls and barons shall not be amerced except by their peers," while no "freeman shall be taken or imprisoned or disseised . . . except by the lawful judgement of his peers or by the law of the land."

Below the politically enfranchised segments of medieval English society, no undifferentiated mass existed that could be described as a majority in the modern sense. The numerical majority of medieval Englishmen existed legally within the various categories of the unfree or serf class. Each degree of serfdom had its own rights and obligations.[19] Furthermore, every feudal manor and village had its own laws and customs, which regulated the behavior of those who lived there. The establishment of shires administered by the sheriff, a royal official responsible for collecting royal revenue, overseeing military affairs, and administering justice, led to the linking of the basic units of local government, the village and the hundred, to royal government. Periodically, the sheriff, accompanied by travelling royal judges, visited each village and hundred to inquire into administrative and judicial matters.[20] One historian has described the result as "self-government at the King's command."[21] Local laws and customs, suitable for parochial interests, were eventually supplemented by the common law, which had general application, unlike local laws and customs, which were "particular, extraordinary, special."[22] The common law and the handful of royal officials who enforced it formed the framework of government within which the estates, the hundred courts, boroughs, and so on functioned. The king, the law, and the sheriff formed a coordinating layer, a dominant minority, that directed English society, a society composed of numerous distinct groups.

Although the English political structure was the only one to survive the end of the Middle Ages largely unchanged, it was not unique. Every other European kingdom was administered in roughly the same fashion as modern comparative studies of medieval government emphasize.[23] The major difference between the English experience and that of the continental kingdoms is that the medieval English system of government survived the general move to centralized government associated with the rise of absolutism in the seventeenth century. Even so, throughout the eighteenth century absolutist states, of which France was the best example, retained many distinctive legal practices and political privileges for inhabitants of particular regions or members of different estates.

With the Enlightenment of the eighteenth century, however, the notion that a society should be legally and politically homogeneous became widespread in intellectual circles. Instead of a patchwork quilt of estates, communities, and associations, each with its own laws and customs, the philosophes wanted uniformity and order. In a sense, the philosophes wanted to revive the ancient notion of citizenship with each person possessing the same political and legal status.[24] The French Revolution put the ideas of the philosophes into practice, at least in the initial stages of the Revolution. The Preamble to the Constitution of 1791 summed up the goal of the new government this way:

> The National Assembly . . . abolishes irrevocably the institutions which were injurious to liberty and equality of rights.
>
> Neither nobility, nor peerage, nor hereditary distinction of orders, nor feudal regime . . . any longer exists.
>
> Neither privileges nor exception to the law common to all Frenchmen any longer exists for any part of the nation or for any individual.
>
> Neither *jurandes* nor corporations of professions, arts, and crafts any longer exist.[25]

Although the revolutionaries did not create absolute equality overnight for all the inhabitants of France and although the status of citizen was not automatically granted to anyone born in France, the French Revolution pointed the way to the modern notion of political equality.

With the end of what the French revolutionaries termed the "feudal regime," the problem of minority rights gradually began to emerge concurrently with the concept of the national majority that claimed the right to direct society's destiny. In spite of increasing linguistic, cultural, religious, and economic pressures, some lesser groups within the overall society refused to accept the values and practices of the dominant majority. Nineteenth century romantic nationalists stressed the importance of preserving the cultures of these submerged groups that appeared on the way to extinction. With the calls to retain traditional cultures and dying languages, there also emerged calls for political structures that would defend the threatened ways of life.[26] At this point, the rights of minority groups became a public issue with the official majority position of assimilation being defined as oppressive of a minority's right to its own way of life.

One final point remains for discussion. What is a right? The entire issue of minority status is bedevilled by that one word. The contemporary meaning of the word *right* is the result of the philosophical, legal, and political debates of the seventeenth and eighteenth centuries. A recent textbook on American governmental policies concerning rights stated that "a claim which is recognized and accepted by authoritative decisionmakers (courts, legislatures, governors) can grow into a right. . . . A right does not exist, except as a moral abstraction, unless someone or some group is prepared to make a claim for its implementation. . . . In a nutshell a right is a valid claim."[27] This pragmatic definition avoids dealing with the problems involved in the long history of philosophic debate about the nature of rights. At the same time, we must recognize that this functional definition of what constitutes a right is a very modern approach to the question.

Before the eighteenth century, those who concerned themselves with these issues that we would view as rights issues, the lawyers, philosophers, and theologians, rarely spoke of rights, that is the rights or validated claims of individuals or groups. Generally, they described the existing social order, suggested remedies for abuses, and considered society as a whole within which individuals sought their moral well-being. The ancient Roman lawyers, for example, pointed out that according to natural law, all men were free and all property was to be held in common. In practice, however, according to the *ius gentium*, the law of nature that is the actual practice of mankind, slavery and private property existed and were part of the normal order of things.[28] While the lawyers concentrated their attention on the situation that actually existed, philosophers and theologians focused on the moral purposes of society and on the moral qualities that the virtuous ruler should possess, accepting as given the basic social order.

In part at least, ancient and medieval writers did not think in terms of individual rights as we understand them because they did not assume an adversarial relationship between the individual and society. Like Aristotle, they assumed that men were naturally social and political animals and that man's nature required that he live in community, as part of a group, in order to become a fully developed human being.[29] The realities of medieval life reinforced this view. To live outside of a well-organized group was to place oneself at the mercy of anyone or any group that was stronger. In the Middle Ages, the term "outlaw" literally meant the person who was outside of the protection provided by a group and its law. The freest person in medieval society, paradoxically to the modern mind, was the person who was enmeshed in the greatest number of legal relationships. The feudal system of government made this point very clear in the homage ceremony, which demonstrated before witnesses the contractual relationship that created mutual responsibilities for lord and vassal. The contract specified certain rights and privileges that each party possessed. The more such relationships into which a man entered, the more rights he possessed and the more protection he received. While the most obvious example of this sort of right was the possession of land, the fief, it extended to a wide range of other items as well. One could possess the right to hold a court and share in the fines it assessed, be exempt from a particular court's jurisdiction, collect a particular tax, or be exempt from being taxed.[30] One observer noted that in the Middle Ages an individual possessed not rights in the modern sense, broad claims rooted in a general sense of how the world should function, but a bundle of specific and concrete rights that could be added to or subtracted from according to circumstances.

During the eighteenth century, the philosophes completed the development of a new theoretical basis for understanding rights. Parallel with their rejection of the group as the basic unit of society, they stressed the rights of the individual without regard to his membership in any group. In the Declaration of the Rights of Man, the French Revolutionaries turned the philosophes' theories into political reality. The assumption that each and every individual possessed the same fundamental rights underlaid the Declaration. The purpose of government was to protect these rights. In one sense, this view continued the medieval concept of government as being contractual in nature. It was different, however, in that it assumed that each individual had precisely the same contract with the government, not a unique contract based on status differences. Instead of assuming that natural law referred to the general principles that directed a just society, the philosophes pointed to a natural law that guaranteed inalienable rights to individuals.

Because of the great changes in political theory and political practice that took place during the eighteenth century, it might seem that the medieval political scene would bear no significant relationship to the modern scene. This would seem to be especially true where the question of minority rights is involved because of the shift from the group to the individual as the basic unit of society and the bearer of rights. This assumption would not, however, be accurate. The issue of minority rights exists in the modern world precisely because the withering away of groups claiming distinctive status within a society has not occurred. By attributing rights to individuals, not to groups, eighteenth-century thinkers believed that they would effectively destroy groups as the loci of rights. What they did achieve was the destruction of certain kinds of groups; the clergy, the nobility, and the guilds being the most prominent of these. By the early nineteenth century, however, spurred on by romanticism and nationalism, new groups, usually cultural and religious groups, were demanding political and legal recognition from the dominant majority. In effect, these groups were asserting that the inalienable rights possessed by individuals also belonged to groups. The difficulty was that while the rights assigned to individuals were comparatively straightforward, life, liberty, and property as John Locke put it, the rights claimed by groups were often vague and even divisive, threatening the cohesive social and political order that the revolution had created. One group might demand political and legal protection for an agricultural way of life that faced extinction as national policy required industrialization and urbanization. Yet another group might insist upon the use of its own language, a minority tongue, in courts and public schools. In both cases, the wishes of the dominant majority for the society as a whole would be frustrated if the minorities had their way.

The modern problem of minority rights has some analogues with medieval society in a minority group's demand for political and legal recognition that differs in some important ways from the cultural life of the dominant majority. The analogy is not, however, with the medieval secular government, which, as we have seen, clearly recognized the right of groups to exist. The comparison must be to the medieval Christian Church. Like the modern nation-state, with its core of common values and beliefs expressed through the public schools and various other institutions, the medieval church was not simply an institution but a way of life that was the highest expression of human life. The medieval church provided a common core of beliefs that lay at the heart of society. As the nation-state asserts the superiority of its cultural values over all others, so the medieval church claimed that it alone possessed religious truth superior to all other religions. When a minority culture in a modern nation-state exempts itself from the claims of the dominant culture and demands recognition of its right to exist free of interference, it makes the same claims against the dominant culture that medieval heretical groups made against the claims of the Christian Church.

The comparison of the nation-state with the medieval church is difficult to accept at first because of the modern assumption that religion is a matter of private conscience, not a matter of public policy. In medieval Europe, however, as J. N. Figgis noted long ago, the

> state had one basis of unity denied to the modern [state]—religion. Baptism was a necessary element in true citizenship in the Middle Ages and excommunication was its antithesis. No heretic, no schismatic, no excommunicate has the rights of citizenship.[31]

Being a matter of public interest, religion was of concern to secular officials as well as to ecclesiastical ones. The result was the close and necessary relationship between the temporal and the spiritual powers that is often seen as characteristic of medieval Europe. Figgis described the relationship bluntly: "[In] the Middle Ages the Church was not a State, it was the State; the State or rather the civil authority . . . was merely the police department of the Church."[32] While this statement somewhat overstates the realities of medieval political life, it certainly reflects the way in which many medieval ecclesiastical thinkers saw the relationship between church and state. Secular rulers at least mouthed spiritual goals when they took coronation oaths in which they promised to protect the church from its enemies and to advance spiritual goals.

Religion, Catholic Christianity to be exact, played a role in medieval society that the national culture and language play in a modern society legally composed of individuals, not groups. As the medieval church employed the secular power to achieve its ends, so the modern nation uses the state as the vehicle for achieving its goals. For this reason numerous minority groups in the modern world have demanded the right to establish their own states so that not only the individuals who compose this group will survive, but that the distinctive national culture will also survive as something apart from the individuals who share it. Furthermore, both the medieval church and the modern nation represent not only the dominant groups in their respective societies, they were—and are—numerical majorities as well. In theory, of course, the power of the medieval church was attributed not to its majority status but to its essential truth. Likewise, modern nationalists often attribute spiritual value to the "spirit of the nation" that transcends sheer numbers. Thus, when the church or the nation faces opposition from a numerical minority, they see such opposition as a conflict not only between groups but between truth and error, an even more important issue. Thus, to a significant extent, the contemporary debate about minority political rights is quite similar to the medieval and early modern debates about religious toleration.

The question of religious toleration is one that is virtually unique to

Christianity and stems from its assertion that it alone possesses the truth about God and the meaning of human existence. Other doctrines are not only wrong, they are positively dangerous to spiritual health and well-being. Modern nationalism, sometimes described as a "secular religion," differs from medieval Christianity in that each nation occupies only a small part of the earth's surface and population, while the church claimed a universal mission and expected eventually to include all men everywhere.[33] In each case, however, the Christian and the nationalist asserts not only the superiority of his own values but the inferiority, not to mention the subversive nature, of competing values. Those who reject the language and culture of the nation-state are heretics in a secular sense.

*RELIGION IN THE ANCIENT AND MEDIEVAL WORLDS*

Generally speaking, the problem of the rights of religious minorities did not exist in the ancient world. Just as ancient political society consisted of a congeries of political units headed by a dominant minority, so too ancient religion was pluralistic. Each political unit had its own religion that symbolized its sense of community. In turn the political unit, such as the city-state, comprised various groups, associations, and families, each of which had its own divine protectors and related cults. In *The Ancient City*, Fustel de Coulanges described the city this way:

> Several tribes might associate together, on condition that the religion of each should be respected. The day on which this alliance took place the city existed.
>
> We must remark, also, that when the different groups became thus associated, none of them lost its individuality, or its independence. . . . In religion there subsisted a multitude of subordinate worships, above which was the established one common to all; in politics, numerous little governments continued to act, while above them a common government was founded.[34]

At the political apex of the Roman Empire was the emperor ruling over the network of conquered states. At the apex of the religious system was the goddess Roma who ruled over the conquered gods of the conquered peoples. Below the emperor, local governments continued to function in subordination to the Romans and so did the local cults. The city-state rulers saw no difficulty with the continued existence of a variety of cults associated with tribes, families, associations, and so on, as long as the members of these cults also participated in the public rituals honoring the city's patron deity. Likewise, the Roman emperors interfered little in the religious practices of the conquered peoples unless such practices meddled in the common worship of the Roman gods.

By some later standards, the ancient city was broadly tolerant in religious matters, just as it was in political matters. At the same time, this does not mean that the rulers of ancient cities were necessarily tolerant on principle in the way that modern liberal states profess to be. Ancient society recognized common religious practice as the fundamental element that unified diverse groups into a community with common goals and interests. It was simply natural, without further analytical elaboration, for groups to possess their own religious cults. While intellectuals occasionally theorized that there was but one god and that the various local cults reflected one or another aspect of this god's qualities, this was a minority opinion. Much more common was the belief that each people or nation had its own experience with the divinity that was then reflected in its formal religious practice. In a sense, the religious structure of a nation was identical with its political structure. Religion was the ultimate characteristic that differentiated one society from another. This meant that any group of people had a natural right to express its unity by whatever religious rituals and practices that were traditional among its members.[35] Describing acceptance of divergent religious practices as a natural phenomenon did not mean that ancient thinkers developed a theory of religious toleration based on comparative study of various societies. Neither does it mean that in the ancient world the concept of a right as a valid claim existed. Natural in this sense simply meant traditional or customary practices of any society that were considered the normal mode of behavior and expression for members of that society. Such behavior should be tolerated unless there was some specific reason for not so doing.

The major exception to the general Roman policy of religious toleration concerned the various mystery cults that entered the Roman world from Egypt and Asia. Unlike the traditional cults found in the city-states, cults that stressed external forms demonstrating the bonds linking the citizens together, the mystery religions stressed individual experience with the divine. The devotees engaged in practices designed to give the worshipper immediate contact with the god or goddess, not a communal experience stressing social unity. From the conservative Roman perspective, the cultists were engaging in bizarre practices that were abhorrent and even dangerous to the social order.

> Consider the sacred rites of the mysteries; you will find tragic deaths, dooms, funerals, mourning and lamentations of woebegone gods. . . . Shaven priests, mourning, bewailing, and searching . . miserable votaries beating their breasts. . . . These old Egyptian rites have now found their way to Rome, so that you may play the fool.[36]

Furthermore, the Romans feared religions whose adherents met privately rather than holding their ceremonies in public. Mystery cults often met after dark in wooded areas or in caves out of public view. Roman officials feared that such meetings signified the unwillingness of the cultists to open their beliefs to public scrutiny because behind the facade of religion they were actually hatching plots to subvert the empire. In 270 A.D., for example, the Roman government banned Manichaeism, a mystery cult that originated in Persia, Rome's long-time enemy to the east. One Roman observer described this cult as a "perverted doctrine" and another example of the Persian threat to Rome.

> We have heard that these men have but recently sprung up and advanced from the Persian people, our enemy, to this part of the world, where they are perpetrating many outrages, disturbing the tranquillity of the people and also introducing the gravest harm to the communities.[37]

The Romans banned Manichaeism because of its mixture of secrecy and potentially subversive activities, not because of any particular intolerance of the doctrines themselves. That is, it was the social and political consequences of Manichaeism that the Romans opposed.

Roman religious toleration was, however, a two-way street. The Romans expected that the peoples whom they conquered would accept the formal rituals of Roman civic religion as a sign of Roman domination. While most conquered societies were willing to add Roman gods to their local pantheons, not all were willing to do so. The Jews and then the Christians were the most notable exceptions to Roman expectations about reciprocal religious toleration. Both groups asserted that their cult alone was the one true religion. All others were false, thus making reciprocal toleration impossible. The Romans responded to the claims of these two groups in interestingly different ways that reflected Roman ideas about the nature of religious toleration.

Basically, the Romans tolerated what they perceived to be the strange and stubborn behavior of the Jews in refusing to accept the forms of Roman civic religion.[38] Although on occasions the Roman government did consider affronting Jewish religious sensibilities, the traditional Roman policy of seeing a religion as an integral part of a national culture won out. It is not quite accurate to say that the Romans believed that the Jews had a right to their religious customs, at least not a right in law. Neither would it be accurate to see the Romans as recognizing a valid claim of the Jews to practice their own religion even if it meant rejection of a Roman cult. What the Romans saw was a collection of practices and attitudes that were strange, even seemingly anti-social by Roman standards, but a collection of traditional national customs nonetheless.

What the Romans did oppose very firmly were Jewish attempts to assert political independence from Rome. The Romans were not at all tolerant of that sort of activity. Roman toleration of Jewish stubborness in religious matters was influenced by Roman awareness of the close links between Jewish religious and political life. A proposal to place a statue of a Roman god in the temple at Jerusalem as a sign of Roman domination was rejected when the Romans recognized that the political and military consequences of such an action would cost more than the effort involved was worth.[39] The destruction of Jerusalem in 70 A.D. by the Romans was not for religious reasons but for political and military ones. The Jews had rebelled, so the center of their cult was destroyed as punishment. Their religion, however, was not banned, so that Jews dwelling within the Empire continued to practice their religion.

Roman toleration of Jewish religious beliefs did have some limits. In the first century A.D., an imperial edict forbade Jews living outside of Palestine from making converts from among their non-Jewish neighbors. From the Roman perspective, this edict did not violate the tradition of religious toleration. It was, rather, the Jews who were violating traditional standards by proselytizing in order to add members to their religious community who were not part of the Jewish nation. In addition, the Romans feared the growth of any religious group whose membership transcended national boundaries. The only international group that the Romans encouraged was that composed of those, Roman and non-Roman by birth, who possessed full Roman citizenship with its important legal and social rights. Roman citizenship was held out as the reward for those among the conquered who collaborated with the conquerors. The men from various nations who composed this international elite shared common interests that contributed to the empire's cohesion. If the Jews were successful in their proselytism, they might create an international group that, in Roman eyes, could compete with the Roman citizens for control of the empire.

This Roman fear of religious doctrines that were not restricted to a single identifiable national group led the Romans to their eventual confrontation with the Christians. As the Roman experience with the Jews demonstrated, the Romans would tolerate unpalatable religious ideas as long as they were not subversive of the social order and restricted to a single group. When unpalatable ideas became linked to a religion that transcended national boundaries, then the Romans reached the limits of their toleration. The Christians, though Jewish in origin, insisted that their religious teaching was directed to all men, not simply to a small number of Chosen People. Furthermore, as if to underscore Christianity's universal message, the Christians had no cult center of their own, as the Jews and others did. Neither were they a nation because they had no land of their own. Furthermore, the Christians at the outset shared with the despised mystery cults a tendency to meet behind closed doors, thus conjuring up the traditional Roman fear of subversion by secret societies. In addition, Christian doctrinal absolutism, international membership, and strange beliefs all combined to make Christianity appear to be a dangerously subversive movement, one that did not fall into the category of tolerated cults. Finally, like the Jews, the Christians rejected participation in Roman civic cults, which demonstrated to the Romans exactly how wicked the Christians were.

At first the Romans could not distinguish the Christians from the Jews, and so the early Christians benefitted from the toleration accorded the Jews. The increasing number of converts from among the non-Jewish population of the Roman world, however, meant that the Romans eventually did come to distinguish the two groups and to single out the Christians as a potentially dangerous group. The Emperor Nero (A.D. 54-68) was even able to use the Christians as scapegoats on whom to lay the blame for the great fire that destroyed much of Rome in A.D. 64. The historian Tacitus wrote that the Christians were really convicted "not so much for incendiarism as for their anti-social tendencies."[40] What Tacitus meant was that the Christian refusal to join in the great public rituals of the civic religion struck their fellow Romans as a serious form of anti-social behavior and as such worthy of harsh punishment, lest others be encouraged to withdraw from society as well. Elsewhere, the Romans termed the Christians "atheists" because they denied the existence of the pagan gods whose cults were at the heart of the civic rituals.[41] From the Roman point of view, to deny the gods was not only a religious statement, it was a politically subversive one as well.

Until the middle of the third century, however, the Roman government interfered only occasionally with the activities of the Christians. As the threat of barbarian invasion from without and economic collapse from within grew, persecution of the Christians increased. The purpose of the persecution was political, not religious. The imperial government was anxious to strengthen the sense of loyalty to Rome that the traditional rituals of civic religion were designed to encourage. The imposition of emperor worship, a product of Roman expansion into the Middle East, was designed to do the same in those parts of the empire where ruler worship was common.

The Christians did not see civic religious practices and emperor worship as being public or political functions. They saw them as worshiping false gods. Like the Jews, the Christians were clearly not syncretic in their approach to religion and so appeared subversive of the Roman order. In addition, the Christians' refusal to participate in the civic religious ceremonies could not be seen as the peculiar custom of a particular nation because the Christians were drawn from all segments of the Roman world. In A.D. 303, when the Emperor Diocletian unleashed the most extensive persecution of Christians that the Roman world had seen, he did it for political reasons, not religious ones. His goal was to insure the survival of the Empire and, if necessary, by forced conformity, of all those who lived there. Forcing all the inhabitants of the Roman world to indicate their loyalty by requiring them to perform the rituals connected with emperor worship was, presumably, in Diocletian's mind, not an invasion of private religious conscience but only a necessary part of public behavior.[42] To demand that all his subjects perform some nominal ritual before his statue was of a piece with his edicting freezing wages and prices. Both actions were designed to stabilize Roman society even at the expense of making it rigid. Neither policy worked, however, so that when Diocletian retired in A.D. 305, he left an empire that was in worse condition than when he had taken office.

Following a period of civil war among a series of contenders for Diocletian's throne, Constantine assumed the imperial office and initiated a policy that, while superficially the reverse of his predecessor's with regard to religion, was in reality quite similar. In A.D. 313, Constantine issued the Edict of Milan that gave legal standing to the Christian faith and provided for the return of Christian property that had been seized under Diocletian's persecution.[43] Contemporary Christian apologists attributed Constantine's reversal of Diocletian's policy to his having had a religious experience on the eve of his final battle in the civil war. While such an explanation cannot be dismissed out of hand because divine intervention in human affairs was taken for granted in the Roman world, other explanations can also be advanced. Although the Christians formed only a minority of the Empire's total population, they were found in large numbers in the great trading cities of the Near East, the region that Constantine was most determined to protect. In that sense, Christianity may have appeared to Constantine as a well-organized group whose support might make the survival of the Empire easier. If granted legal status, the Christians would presumably be grateful and anxious to show their gratitude by wholeheartedly supporting the Empire against its enemies.[44] At the same time, it is important to realize that Constantine did not make Christianity the official religion of the Roman Empire, as is often believed. He only gave the Christians the same legal recognition that other cults possessed.

The legalization of Christianity was not a response to a claim to religious toleration that the Christians presented. It was a recognition of the role that they might play in the effort to maintain the Roman Empire in its time of crisis. At the same time, the Christians themselves had long asserted a claim to legal recognition. From the middle of the second century, Christian writers occasionally tried to point out to the government that they did deserve toleration. Their argument was not that religious toleration was a good thing, but that the Christians practiced precisely the virtues that the Romans themselves traditionally praised. Furthermore, the Christians also pointed out their loyalty to the empire.[45] Christianity was after all founded within the Roman Empire, and its leader was not associated with the Jewish groups that sought to overthrow Roman domination of Palestine. In addition, the Christians were not associated in any way with the various enemies the Roman Empire was facing.

During the remainder of the fourth century, the status of the Christian Church within the Empire gradually rose. By the end of the century, the Christian Church was the sole legal religion in the Empire. In A.D. 382 the last vestige of the old civic religion passed from the Roman scene when the statue of Victory, which had stood in the senate house, was removed by order of the Christian Emperor Gratian. For centuries senators had placed a bit of incense on the flame that burned continuously before the statue. Even Christian senators engaged in this practice until the emperor ordered the statue removed because of its identification with the ancient pagan religion.

The removal of the statue of Victory provided an opportunity for the surviving pagans to pose the question of the rights of a religious minority within a Christian society.[46] Symmachus, Prefect of the City of Rome, a pagan belonging to an ancient senatorial family, protested the emperor's action and contrasted the Christian and the pagan attitudes toward religion. He pointed to the antiquity of the Roman state and the apparent connection between the traditional Roman religion and the success of Roman arms. Furthermore, he wondered how the Christians could be so certain that theirs was the sole true religion.

> The divine mind has distributed different guardians and different cults to different cities. As souls are separately given to infants as they are born, so to peoples the genius of their destiny. . . . Since our reason is wholly clouded, whence does the knowledge of the gods more rightly come to us, than from the memory and evidence of prosperity? . . .
>
> We ask, then, for peace for the gods of our fathers and of our country. . . What difference does it make by what pains each seeks the truth?[47]

In response to Symmachus's plea for toleration, St. Ambrose, Bishop of Milan and an advisor to the emperor, presented the Christian view of the nature of religion and of its role in society. Like Symmachus, Ambrose was a member of an ancient Roman family that had played an active role in political life, and he had also been an imperial provincial governor before becoming a bishop. His credentials as a Roman, in other words, were as good as those of Symmachus. He can be presumed to have understood exactly what Symmachus was defending. As a result, his rejection of the prefect's position was not simply that of an unsophisticated Christian exulting in his religion's victory over the old Roman cult. In Ambrose's opinion, the wicked religious practices of Symmachus's ancestors and of his own as well were of no interest. He flatly rejected the ancient view that a variety of paths led to knowledge of the gods. There was only one god and one path to him. The other so-called paths to god were false and could not claim any right to exist in a Christian society. In other letters Ambrose asserted the independence of the church from secular authorities on the grounds that the church's spiritual mission was superior to the secular government's mission to maintain physical peace and order.[48]

Ambrose's rejection of Symmachus's arguments marked the beginning of a new approach to the question of religious rights. Symmachus and his fellow pagans continued to take the position that absolute religious truth could not be known so that toleration was a reasonable policy. The pagans stressed that a religion should be judged by its antiquity and by its political or social successes. Finally, Symmachus's apologia for the old ways reflected the traditional opinion that every people has a religion that reflects its unique historical experience. For a committed Christian, as Ambrose surely was, truth was not a matter of historical experience or imperial success. Truth was absolute and could be known by those who wished to know it. It was not subject to the kinds of tests that Symmachus mentioned. Being untrue, the traditional Roman cult was a danger to the spiritual well-being of the Empire's subjects and should be abolished. A Christian emperor would have to take a different approach to religion than his pagan predecessors had taken. Ambrose and those who followed his line of argument gradually reshaped the role of religion in society. Where religion had once been a means of identifying a particular society and then linking its individual members together through communal rituals, religion in the Christian era became a means of achieving individual salvation, with the secular power playing a significant, but subordinate, role in the work of salvation. Thus, while religious toleration could be seen as good and even necessary in pagan society because it enabled divergent peoples to live together in harmony, toleration in Christian society was wrong because it harmed the possibility of salvation for individuals. Christianity, in other words, reversed the roles of religion and the political order, making religious goals, not political ones, the primary end of human society. In so doing, it destroyed the traditional basis for religious toleration.

The victory of the Christian Church over Roman paganism was only one part of the great transformation, not to say revolution, in conceptions about government that occurred as Roman Christianity came to replace Roman paganism. The universal Christian religion replaced the hierarchy of local civic cults that had previously dominated the European religious outlook. At the same time, the universal Roman political order broke up to be replaced not by another universal political order but by the feudal order in which political power was widely decentralized. Attempts to maintain or to re-create the pagan Roman Empire as a Christian Roman Empire failed. The city-state was replaced by the manor, a small, self-sufficient agricultural unit, except in Italy where urban life remained in existence although on a much smaller scale. Baptism into the Christian Church, not Roman citizenship, became the badge of membership in medieval society. Membership in the church was a prerequisite for participation in public affairs. As a result, there was no problem about the political rights of those who were not members of the Christian Church—they had none. On the other hand, the question of the right of a religious minority to exist was a separate issue and one that required a more complex answer.

The nature of the medieval Christian response to the presence of nonbelievers within Christian Europe varied according to a number of circumstances. In the first place, Christianity took a long time to penetrate the religious and cultural fabric of the peoples who outwardly became Christians from the fourth to the tenth centuries in the wake of the barbarian invasion of Europe. Pagan religious practices, sometimes under a Christian veneer, continued to survive, especially in rural areas. In addition, there were Jewish communities of long standing scattered throughout Europe. Rome, for example, was the home of a Jewish community dating back to about 200 B.C. In Spain there was a large Muslim population composed of those who remained there as the Christians proceeded to reconquer the peninsula from the Arabs who had conquered it in the eighth century.

From the fifth century until the late eleventh century, the Christian Church lived at comparative ease with residual paganism, Judaism, and Islam. The pagans were gradually converted, at least nominally. As for the Jews, although Christian Spanish rulers had begun to persecute Jews and to limit their role in public life before the Arabs invaded Spain in the eighth century, early medieval society elsewhere was generally tolerant of Jewish religious practice, although not to the extent of allowing Jews the right to participate in political life. The Muslims who remained in Spain after the Christian reconquest were also allowed to practice their religion publicly, even though church leaders, especially in the thirteenth century, objected to the policy of religious toleration.[49]

Starting in the late eleventh century, however, European Christian attitudes began to harden against religious toleration. To some extent, this change appears connected with the crusading movement that began in 1095 A.D. in an attempt to restore the Holy Land to Christian hands. Not only were the distant Muslims seen as a threat, the Jews living in Europe were also identified in the popular mind as secret supporters of the Muslims. Attacks on Jews were especially noticeable in those parts of northern Europe where crusaders gathered to begin the journey to the Near East. Cologne, a major mustering point for crusaders, was the scene of one of the earliest of these attacks as potential crusaders gathered to travel down the Rhine.[50]

Ecclesiastical and secular rulers often, but not always, opposed these acts of violence, not because they believed that the rights of the Jews were involved, but because they disliked the random, unofficial violence involved or because they believed that baptism should not be forced upon the unwilling. In 1215, the Fourth Lateran Council of the church mandated distinctive dress for Jews and required that they reside within a designated region of the towns they inhabited. This was the origin of the ghetto.[51] In Church law, the Jews were allowed to live among Christians, admittedly under restrictive conditions. Some secular rulers would not even allow that much. Jews in northern Europe generally came under the special personal protection of the rulers. This protection could be lifted at any time and for any reason or for no reason. In 1290, Edward I of England ordered all Jews out of his kingdom, a decision that was not reversed until Oliver Cromwell formally invited them to return in the midseventeenth century.[52]

In Spain, where the largest concentration of Muslims living in the Christian world could be found, the condition of the Muslims was roughly equivalent to that of the Jews elsewhere. There were restrictions on their activities, and at least some attempts were made to restrict aspects of their religious life. Popes occasionally complained about the fact that in Spanish Christian cities the cries of the mullahs calling the faithful to prayer could be heard to the scandal of Christians. Nevertheless, the role of the Muslims in the economic and professional life of Christian Spain effectively insulated them from persecution. Here again there was no formal legal right to practice an alien religion. Toleration was a practical necessity, not a theoretical ideal. Limits or restrictions on the religious practices of Muslims and Jews were not perceived as an invasion of their right to religious freedom. Instead, the Christian position was that these religious practices, though tolerated for practical purposes, were always a potential danger to Christian souls.[53] Periodically, efforts were made to convert Jews and Muslims to Christianity. In that way, the skills of these peoples would not be lost to their Christian masters, but the danger to the souls of Christians would be eliminated.

Muslims and Jews presented one test of the Christian reaction to the nonbeliever. Heretics, those who were members of the Christian Church but who objected to one or another of its doctrines, provided another test. Here again, the eleventh century was an important turning point in Christian attitudes toward those who did not conform in matters of religion. Before the eleventh century, heresy was generally seen as an individual matter. Increasingly, however, it became a social issue as distinct groups of dissenting believers appeared who rejected Church doctrine and even advocated what amounted to radical social change. From being an individual posing a threat to the souls of his neighbors, the heretic was transformed into a sinister member of a subversive cult desirous of overturning the entire social order. Heretics of this sort generally accused the church of having abandoned the poverty of the early church in favor of an alliance with temporal wealth and power. Almost as if to prove the truth of the allegation, church councils in 1179 and 1215 issued decrees asserting the need for cooperation between ecclesiastical and secular officials in order to rid Christian society of those who wished to subvert its spiritual and its temporal well-being. It should be noted that the heretics themselves were not demanding toleration. They, like the dominant papally led church, believed that they possessed the truth and were as willing to persecute nonbelievers as was the pope whom they criticized.[54]

The most emphatic statement of the relationship that should exist between church and state in these matters appeared in a decree of the Fourth Lateran Council 1215: "Convicted heretics shall be handed over for due punishment to their secular superiors." A secular ruler who "neglects to fulfill the demand of the Church that he shall purge his land of this contamination of heresy" risked excommunication and even loss of office. The Christian ruler who was appointed to replace a recalcitrant heresy hunter "shall exterminate the heretics, possess the land without dispute and preserve it in the true faith.[55]

Secular rulers saw no difficulty with their assigned role as executioners of heretics. As early as the sixth century, Christian Roman emperors at Constantinople had issued legislation designed to eliminate heresy by eliminating the heretics. One law stated that at the very least it "is just to deprive of their worldly goods those who do not worship the True God."[56] Other laws ordered the death penalty for heretics. Although the implementation of these laws varied from reign to reign depending on the realities of Byzantine politics, the principle was clear—heretics had no rights at all, not even the minimal toleration that Jews and Muslims enjoyed.

The first medieval secular ruler in Western Europe to issue legislation concerning heretics was the Holy Roman Emperor Frederic II (1220-1250). Between 1220 and 1239 he issued a series of decrees for his various possessions that provided a scale of punishments for heretics ranging from public recantation of error to the death penalty. In 1231 he issued the Constitutions of Melfi for the administration of his southern Italian possessions. In the constitutions he asserted the secular ruler's responsibility for eliminating heresy and specified burning as the proper punishment for convicted heretics. The opening chapter of the constitutions explained the importance of eliminating heresy this way.

> Heretics try to tear the seamless robe of our God. . . . They are violent wolves, but they pretend the tameness of sheep until they can get inside the sheepfold of the Lord. . . . They are sons of depravity. . . . Therefore, we draw the sword of righteous vengeance against them. . . . We have decided in the first place that the crime of heresy and these condemned sects should be numbered among the public crimes as it was promulgated in the ancient laws. . . . Committed to the judgment of the flames, they should be burned alive in the sight of the people.[57]

These laws in turn became the model for similar decrees issued by other Christian rulers over the next two centuries.

The medieval blending of spiritual and temporal interests into a definition of what constituted the common good meant that there could be no justification for heresy. As Thomas Aquinas (1225--1274) put it, "if forgers of money or other malefactors are straightway justly put to death by secular princes, with much more justice can heretics . . . be not only excommunicated but also put to death."[58] The analogy is striking because it compares the coining of false money with its implication for the temporal economy with the impact of false doctrine on the spiritual economy.

During the thirteenth and fourteenth centuries, special church courts, the courts of the Inquisition, searched out and extirpated heresy in Europe. By the early fifteenth century, these courts had fallen into disuse because of their success in eliminating heresy. At the same time, however, secular rulers continued to be vigilant where heresy was concerned. In 1401, Henry IV (1399-1413) of England issued a statute ordering the burning of convicted heretics.[59] This was a reaction to the appearance of a movement associated with the ideas of the theologian John Wycliffe (1320?-1384). Like earlier reformers, Wycliffe had demanded a purified church, one that gave up its lands and political power. His insistence upon purging the church of its wealth was attractive to some, especially nobles, who hoped to benefit materially from the process of divestiture that Wycliffe proposed. On the other hand, Wycliffe's argument that sinners could neither administer the sacraments nor hold public office legitimately was less acceptable. Wycliffe's ideas were condemned by the church, first at a synod of English bishops and then by the Council of Constance (1414-1417).[60] Henry IV's statute on the punishment of heretics made it clear that Wycliffe's teaching had significant social and political implications that had to be checked. It was not only Wycliffe's theological ideas that were dangerous, it was the fact that his followers "made unlawful conventicles and confederacies, they hold and exercise schools . . . and, as much as they may, excite and stir [the people] to sedition and insurrection and made great strife and divisions among the people." These activities result in "not only the greatest peril of souls" but "many other hurts, slanders, and perils . . . which, God forbid, might come to this realm" unless the spread of heresy was halted.[61]

The medieval identification of heresy with social and political unrest found its greatest crisis in the sixteenth century as the Protestant Reformation produced large-scale heretical movements that possessed strong political and military support. At the beginning of the Reformation, the identification of the religious community with the political community was firmly in place. By the end of the Reformation, there was strong evidence that the two communities could be distinguished, though intellectual support for this opinion was still weak. Once the existence of two or more religious communities within a single political community became theoretically possible, the problem of minority rights became an important one for political and legal thinkers. community became theoretically possible, the problem of minority rights became an important one for political and legal thinkers.

Two events in the sixteenth century paved the way for reconsidering the relationship of minority groups to the larger society in which they lived. The first of these was the Protestant Reformation that ended the Roman Catholic Church's monopoly of religion in Europe. There emerged as a result a multiplicity of Christian denominations, each asserting that it alone possessed Christian truth and each possessing strong political support that prevented Catholic authorities from eliminating it. The second event was the discovery of the non-European world and the subsequent debate about the rights, if any, that indigenous peoples possessed in the face of their potential conquest by Europeans. These events did not, strictly speaking, concern majority-minority relations. The Reformation was a debate about religious truth, not a debate about religious toleration. The debate that broke out in sixteenth century Spain about the conquest of the Americas concerned the right of a Christian minority to conquer a non-Christian majority in the name of religion. Nevertheless, both of these events contributed at least indirectly to the development of modern theories of minority rights.

Protestants as well as Catholics in the sixteenth century believed in the absolute truth of their version of the Christian religion. In the opinion of the leading Protestant reformers, the problem with the dominant Catholic Church was not simply that individual churchmen were corrupt or immoral. Rather, Martin Luther, John Calvin, and the other preachers of reform declared that the Church of Rome was teaching false and perverted doctrine, which, if followed, would lead men to eternal damnation. Luther, Calvin, and their followers were not asserting their right to practice a competing version of Christianity, they were demanding that secular rulers act to reform the practice of the Christian faith within their realms under the direction of reformed clergy. Inasmuch as secular rulers had long accepted a role in securing the spiritual as well as the temporal well-being of their subjects, the call by the reformers to impose reformed religious practice in their lands was acceptable to many rulers. For a ruler who took his spiritual responsibilities seriously, the problem was not whether he should interfere in religious practice but what religious doctrines and practices he should impose on his people.[62]

An unforeseen and unintended consequence of the Reformation was the emergence of policies granting limited toleration for religious minorities. This was not due to a revival of ancient skepticism about religious truth, but because of the inability of a single religious denomination to dominate Europe as a whole in the way that the Catholic Church once did. Even within the individual European kingdoms, rulers found it impossible to eliminate minority religious groups completely. The rulers of France and Germany in particular found themselves forced to authorize limited religious toleration and even to extend political rights to members of minorities in order to maintain the integrity of their kingdoms. The choice was for some form of religious toleration, usually for only one religious minority, as the price for ending a destructive civil war.

The religious civil wars that broke out in Germany during the 1520s resulted in the first attempts to use religious toleration as a basis to resolve potentially destructive conflicts. After facing two serious wars that were closely linked to the religious crisis, the Knights' War in 1522 and the Peasants' War in 1524-1525, some of the German nobles met at Speier in order to develop a solution to the seemingly endless series of wars that the Reformation had spawned. The nobles who attended the meeting proposed as a temporary solution that each secular ruler within Germany be allowed to determine the religion to be practiced within his domain. This would mean that the king of Germany and Holy Roman Emperor Charles V (1519-1555), a staunch defender of the Catholic Church, could not legitimately interfere in the religious life of any of the approximately 300 political units that composed Germany unless that unit was a part of his own family's personal domain. This solution was based on traditional principles about the rights and privileges of the German nobles. Throughout the Middle Ages they had acquired for themselves much of the power that in other kingdoms remained in royal hands. In spite of a late fifteenth century attempt to provide at least some rudimentary institutional forms that would unify the 300 political units in Germany, the central authority was virtually nominal. In this case, the local rulers took upon themselves the traditional royal responsibility for the spiritual well-being of their subjects. The result was the policy of *cuius regio eius religio*, his land, his religion. The ruler of the land could choose the religion of his people.[63] Even this formula did not give unlimited freedom to the nobles to select a religion. The only allowable choices were Catholicism or Lutheranism.

After another series of wars in which neither Catholics nor Protestants were able to win the upper hand permanently, another meeting was held, this time at Augsburg in 1555, to seek a permanent resolution to the crisis. Here again, the *cuius regio eius religio* formula was accepted as the basis of a solution. This time, Charles V assented to the solution so that either Catholicism or Lutheranism could be imposed by a noble on his subjects with imperial blessing. No other forms of Christian religion were permitted to "enjoy their religious beliefs, liturgy and ceremonies as well as their estates and other rights and privileges in peace" within Germany.[64] The Peace of Augsburg was the result of political exhaustion, not the result of any growing awareness that religious minorities possessed rights that should be respected. The best evidence of the Peace of Augsburg's essentially intolerant substance was its explicit rejection of all religious denominations other than the two denominations, Catholicism and Lutheranism, that possessed significant political and military power: 'However all such as do not belong to the two above-mentioned religions shall not be included in the present peace but be totally excluded from it.[65] Even as the peace was being signed, Calvinism was beginning to make significant inroads in areas that had been Lutheran previously, thus paving the way for a new round of religious violence and requiring a new solution that would incorporate a third denomination.

In the long run, the fissioning of the Protestant movement during the last half of the sixteenth century undermined the Peace of Augsburg. The failure to develop a theory of society that would reconcile the conflicting claims of competing religions meant that the growing number of religious minority groups could only make the situation worse, possibly leading to even harsher efforts to repress heresy. In 1618, the Thirty Years War, a three-sided religious war in Germany engaging the Calvinists along with the Catholics and the Lutherans, broke out. The Thirty Years War became the turning point in the history of the role of religion in Western society.[66] Ostensibly, the war began as a religious war involving the three major denominations in Germany. During the course of the war, however, it became clear that the war had provided an opportunity for neighboring states, regardless of their religious position, to acquire land and power in Germany even at the expense of their coreligionists. The rulers of Denmark, Sweden, and, above all, France supported one or another party in Germany in order to advance their own political ends. Eventually this led to the Catholic king of France providing the bulk of foreign support for Protestant rebels against the Catholic Hapsburg rulers of Germany. The reason for this was that French political interests would be best served by a weak German monarchy. Inasmuch as the Hapsburg monarchs were Catholics, it was rational for French policy to support the Protestant nobles who were in rebellion against the Hapsburgs. In matters of foreign policy, the French government was distinguishing between religious and political interests. The focus was upon achieving political goals that would enhance the stature of France even if the results would be detrimental to the Catholic Church elsewhere. The Peace of Westphalia which ended the Thirty Years War settled the religious issue in a few words.

> The Reformed [Calvinists] are to have equal rights in Religion and other matters with the other states and subjects.
> . . . but besides the religions named [Catholic, Lutheran, Calvinist] above, no other shall be accepted or tolerated in the Holy Roman Empire.[67]

This peace, in other words, only gave legal recognition to those religious groups that were too strong to be destroyed. Persecution of small Protestant sects such as the Anabaptists continued in the lands controlled by the three legally recognized religions. The Anabaptists were unable to win recognition because they were often pacifists and therefore unwilling to use force in their own defense. Thus they were fair game for the stronger powers that saw persecution of heresy as their religious duty. In the final analysis, the Peace of Westphalia simply reiterated the approach to religious minorities and to religious toleration that had been used ineffectively in Germany for over a century. Religious toleration, if indeed that is even the term for it, was available only to those groups who possessed political and military might.

The series of religious wars in Germany made it increasingly clear that religion was becoming a divisive force in society instead of the unifying force it had once been. The problem was now how to deal with religion in this new context. The traditional Christian opinion that there was only one true faith and that it was the secular ruler's responsibility to insure its position in the state was no longer viable. As political reality revealed a wide variety of competing religions, each claiming the privileges and position of the medieval church, the secular rulers found themselves in an increasingly complicated dilemma. A handful of people on the fringes of the Reformation movement, such as the Anabaptists, proposed separating religion from government and allowing each man to worship as he pleased so long as he did no harm to anyone. This solution was not acceptable to Catholics or to most Protestants because they continued to believe that toleration was fundamentally destructive to the purposes for which government existed in a Christian society.

Although Germany had the worst outbreaks of religious violence, it was France that produced the most extensive discussions of a theory of religious toleration.[68] In addition to problems arising from the religious crisis of the sixteenth century, France was also undergoing serious internal conflict involving the various political, economic, and social subgroups that composed the kingdom and their relationship to one another and to the monarchy. More than any other kingdom in Europe, France reflected the complex nature of medieval social structure as it survived into the early modern world. The request for religious toleration in France came at the same time as the monarchy was making strenuous efforts to eliminate group autonomy in favor of national uniformity. By the midsixteenth century, France was the scene of a series of religious civil wars pitting the Catholic monarchs against the Huguenots, the French term for Calvinists. The Huguenots had strong support from among the ranks of the nobles and from the urban commercial class, two groups that the monarchy aimed at bringing under tighter control. Thus, when the Huguenots demanded religious toleration, they were demanding a kind of autonomy in religious matters that the kings were anxious to eliminate in other spheres of French life. The religious civil war was then given special urgency because of its implications for the future of the French kingdom. Would the kingdom be unified and centralized under the king or would it be decentralized with a great deal of power remaining in the hands of the nobles and the middle class? By the 1580s it was clear that neither side could win a complete victory over the other and that the only victor would be the king of Spain, who was gaining influence in France through his support of the Catholic party in the wars.[69]

Faced with the possibility that France might be significantly reduced in power as a consequence of the religious wars, a group of important public officials, both Catholics and Huguenots, began to develop a basis upon which the existence of the French kingdom, with a Huguenot minority within it, could be assured. This group, known as the *politiques*, was headed by Michel de L'Hôpital, chancellor of France. These men were important political figures who were in a good position to weigh the consequences of the continuation of the religious wars on the future of the kingdom as a whole. In their opinion, the religious claims that the wars incorporated undermined the purpose for which government was established, that is peace and order. L'Hôpital was pragmatic in his approach to toleration and to the issue of minority rights. As a traditional Christian, he was opposed to religious toleration because of its detrimental effects on the souls of the king's subjects. On the other hand, he and his fellow *politiques* concluded that when the spiritual ends of society cannot be obtained except at the price of destroying the very political structure that was necessary to insure the achievement of these goals, then the spiritual goals became unrealizable and therefore must be subordinated to the needs of public order and security.

With the accession to the French throne of King Henry IV in 1594, the ideas of the *politiques* became political reality. Henry IV had been a leader of the Huguenot party who, because of the biological accidents of royal life in the sixteenth century, became the leading heir to the French throne. Reputedly saying that "Paris is worth a Mass," he reconverted to Catholicism, the religion of his earlier years. This made it possible for him to accept the throne. His public return to the Catholic Church made him acceptable to the Catholics, while the Huguenots recognized the necessity of the reconversion and accepted it. As king, Henry IV issued the Edict of Nantes in 1598, granting a number of legal privileges to the Huguenots while maintaining the Catholic Church as the official state religion.

> The Catholic, Apostolic and Roman faith [shall] be restored and re-established in all those districts and places of this our Realm . . . in which its exercise has been interrupted, there to be freely and peaceably exercised.

In return for agreeing not to interfere with the practice of the majority's religion, the Huguenots, numbering about 10 to 15 percent of the French population, were granted permission to exist.

> We permit those of the so-called Reformed Religion to live and abide in all the towns and districts of this our realm . . . free from inquisition, molestation or compulsion to do anything in the way of Religion, against their conscience . . . provided that they observe the provisions of this Edict.[70]

Here again, the basis for toleration, that is, for granting the right to exist and to participate in public life, rested not on a theory of rights but upon acceptance of political reality. There were so many Huguenots and they could muster so much political and military might that they could effectively bring much of the kingdom's life to a halt if they were not granted legal recognition. Like the Lutherans in Germany, the Huguenots forced the government to grant them legal status as the price for their allowing public life to function uninterruptedly. Only the Huguenots in France benefitted from this grant, however. It was not extended to any other Protestant sect. Under Henry IV's successors, the rights granted by the edict and its accompanying acts were gradually whittled away until Louis XIV revoked the Edict of Nantes in 1685. The Huguenots were then required to convert to Catholicism or to emigrate. From the royal perspective, the revocation was designed not only to save the souls of the Huguenots, but also to eliminate a group that opposed royal centralization of power in France.

The experience of the Huguenots was a microcosm of contemporary

European ideas about the role of religion in society and about the role of minority groups. When Henry IV issued the Edict of Nantes, he was responding to an immediate crisis in a traditional manner, that is, granting legal privileges to a corporate body that could not be eliminated. The Huguenots were simply being treated as other such groups, the clergy, the nobility, various economic groups, and chartered towns were being treated. Even as Henry IV was doing this, however, the tide was running against the conception of a kingdom as a federation of groups, each with its own rights, privileges, exemptions, and status. Under Louis XIII (1610-1643) and Louis XIV (1643-1715), the monarchy embarked upon a policy of limiting the powers of those groups that posed a threat to royal control of the entire kingdom.[71] The power of the church had been significantly restricted in the early sixteenth century when Pope Leo X granted to King Francis I the right to make all major ecclesiastical appointments in France.[72] By the terms of this agreement, the Concordat of Bologna, even the decrees of church councils, such as the Council of Trent (1564), could not be published in France without royal permission.[73] The powers of the nobles were limited less directly. More and more nobles came to rely upon positions in the royal service and other forms of royal largesse for their income. To insure obtaining a share of royal money, a noble was forced to attend permanently upon the king. Louis XIV capped this development when he constructed the great palace at Versailles as a stage on which he produced, directed, and starred in a continual pageant that kept the nobles occupied while royal officials carried on the supervision of government at the local and regional levels, a task that the nobles had traditionally performed.[74]

During the eighteenth century, there was a reaction against this policy of reducing the powers of the interest groups in order to strengthen the power of the monarchy.[75] Groups and their interests flourished during the eighteenth century as a line of weak French kings was unable to continue the policy of exalting the monarchy at the expense of the groups. On the eve of the French Revolution, there was even what has been termed an aristocratic reaction against a century of royal attempts to control the nobility. The attempt to bring peace and order to France by controlling the groups that possessed rights and privileges that caused division within the kingdom and to replace these group loyalties with total reliance upon the king's personal willingness to rule justly, that is the policy of royal absolutism, ultimately failed. The groups were too well-entrenched and the tools available to the government too weak to make absolutism possible. What all these efforts did demonstrate was that groups, whether based on religion, economic position, or hereditary status, could be destructive of national unity, to use a modern phrase. Some new basis for constructing a society using a basic unit other than interest groups would be required.

The new basis upon which modern societies were to be built was the autonomous individual who possessed a body of rights rooted in natural law, rights that preceded the creation of the state. The purpose of the state in this theory is to protect the rights of the individuals who compose the society. The religious wars of the sixteenth and seventeenth centuries were not sufficient in themselves to force the development of a theory of individual rights. What gave added weight to the pressure to discover a new basis upon which to construct governments was the European encounter with quite different societies in the wake of Columbus's momentous voyage. By the middle of the sixteenth century, European intellectuals had begun to debate the legitimacy of the European conquest of the non-European world that was beginning. The issue boiled down to what, if any, rights did non-European societies possess in the face of European conquest. In raising this question, however, the intellectuals were asking fundamental questions about the nature of society and of government. The discovery of societies that functioned along lines different from European states when joined to the demand for reconsidering the nature of religion's role in European society meant that it was possible to construct theories of society that did not rely upon the European experience alone.

The problem of the rights of non-Christians *vis-à-vis* Christians centered on the question of whether or not the Christian Church's obligation to preach to all men transcended a society's right to exclude foreigners and to govern itself according to its own laws without any outside interference. According to this line of argument, Christians could not legitmately invade non-Christian lands simply in order to convert the inhabitants to Christianity. In general, however, the writers who took this position, recognizing the natural right of men to select their own rulers and to live as they saw fit, also tended to admit an important exception to the right of a society's members to live as they pleased. If these people lived according to laws and practices that violated natural law, then it was permissible for European Christians to conquer them, not to convert them, but to force them to abide by the natural laws that bound all men.[76] In practice, violations of the natural law meant that the people practiced cannibalism or had unacceptable sexual mores. Under these circumstances, a Christian invasion was justified in order to punish crimes against the natural order.[77] The underlying assumption here, of course, was the notion that all men know, or could know, a basic set of principles governing human behavior.

As Europeans encountered an ever widening circle of different societies, ranging from very primitive aboriginal peoples to the very sophisticated Chinese and Japanese societies, they found it necessary to reconsider their attitudes toward non-Europeans. In addition, once the process of reevaluating the rights of non-Christians began, it was not possible to stop further analysis of minority groups within Europe as well. If non-Christian, non-European peoples had certain rights to govern themselves that were rooted in natural law applicable to all men, how could it be denied that minority groups within Europe also possessed the same rights? The ultimate goal in this line of thought was the concept of a world order based not on religious principles but upon rational assumptions about the nature of man and society that all men could accept. In the seventeenth century, Hugo Grotius presented the European world with his *On the Law of War and Peace*, a discussion of an international legal order based on the "law of nature . . . comprising alike that which is so called in a larger sense, proceeding as it does from the essential traits inplanted in man." This "essential trait" comes from God who has "willed that such traits exist in us."[78] Grotius spoke in terms of rights as legal capacities, not the philosophical notion of natural individual rights as they came to be understood in the eighteenth century. Nevertheless, Grotius played an important role in the development of those later ideas.

During the eighteenth century, attacks on the existing European hierarchical social and political order, combined with a deeper awareness of the great variety of social and political orders that existed elsewhere and a revival of interest in the republican thought of ancient Greece and Rome, all contributed to further reconsideration of the nature of political life. One result was a view of society based on egalitarian assumptions. That is, eighteenth-century intellectuals concluded that all men are equal by nature and possess the same basic rights so that in a just society everyone would be equal before the law and in the realm of public affairs. In differing but related ways, the American Declaration of Independence and the French Declaration of the Rights of Man expressed this new approach to political life. For the Americans, it was "self-evident, that all men are created equal, that they are endowed by their Creator with certain inalienable rights," and that "to secure these rights, governments are instituted among men." The rights that individuals possess spring from nature itself, not from law or from historical experience. This statement was, of course, inconsistent with a number of aspects of American colonial life at that point, slavery and property restrictions on voting being the most obvious contradictions. Nevertheless, the American thinkers at least recognized the conflict between their theories and the political realities.

Developing an egalitarian society was easier for the American colonists than it was for the Frenchmen who led the revolution that ended the *ancien régime* in 1789. The American colonies did have the rudiments of a hierarchical society, but such a society was comparatively undeveloped. Above all, there were few groups that possessed traditional or legal rights in the way that such group rights existed in Europe. When the French revolutionaries came to the problem of creating a new society, they had first to destroy the remains of an old and well-entrenched society. The revolutionaries drew up a constitution that made all men legally and politically equal. Rights belonged to individuals without regard to what, if any, groups to which they belonged. Groups became private matters, not matters of public law. In effect, the state became the sole legal group to which individuals belonged. It also became the guarantor of the individual's natural rights.

Since the eighteenth century, the theory that society is composed of groups that are bearers of legal or civil rights has battled with the theory that the individual is the only bearer of rights and that the state exists only to protect these rights. The basic terms of this battle were set down by Edmund Burke in his *Reflections on the Revolution in France*. Burke argued that natural and civil rights were different. Furthermore, he also argued that the historical experience of a society cannot be summarily dismissed by a committee of constitution-writing intellectuals. Thus, the claims of long-standing groups to special status cannot be rejected out of hand.[79] To a great extent, Burke's criticism of the French revolutionaries was that they failed to appreciate human psychology, that the sovereign individual of their theories not only did not exist, he could not exist. The response of the French revolutionaries and those who subsequently accepted their views was that the state should form the individual who would then take up the burden of these individual rights. The public school, along with the body of common law and the sole officially recognized national language, was to be the means of creating the new man. The problem of minorities was then to be eliminated by a process of social homogenization.

The expectations of the French revolutionaries about the new man who would be the model citizen of the new society were frustrated in a variety of ways even before the century was over. The pressure on the subordinate groups within France was resisted. Under Napoleon the Christian religion that the original revolutionaries ousted in favor of the Cult of Reason was restored, along with religious toleration for Protestants and Jews. Napoleon even created a class of noblemen when he created the Legion of Honor to recognize merit. The greatest threat to the ideals of the Revolution came, however, not from a betrayal of its principles in France, but from their extension throughout Europe. Romantic nationalism, a result of revolutionary ideas about society, spread throughout Europe, encouraging every linguistic and cultural group to desire its own sovereign state in order to protect its unique way of life.[80] The subsequent history of European political life has revolved to a great extent around the conflict between theories of individual rights and the demands of groups that their rights be recognized as well.

## *NOTES*

1. The development of modern nationalism has led to the idea that a state is the political form that a nation, that is, a culturally distinctive people, takes in the

political order. Those who belong to the nation and share its culture and values form the dominant majority. Those who reject this culture and its values form the minority or minorities that are at odds with the majority. For a recent survey of nationalism and its effects, though without any discussion of majority-minority rights, see Boyd C. Shafer, *Faces of Nationalism: New Realities and Old Myths* (New York: Harcourt Brace Jovanovich, 1972). The standard older works on nationalism are: Carlton J. H. Hayes, *Essays on Nationalism* (New York: Macmillan, 1926); and Hans Kohn, *The Idea of Nationalism*, reprint ed., (New York: Collier, 1967).

2. Within Europe, the successor states of the Austrian and Ottoman empires in eastern Europe have had the most difficulty in reconciling the conflicting interests of minority groups. See Oscar I. Janowsky, *Nationalities and National Minorities* (New York: Macmillan, 1945).

3. N.G.L. Hammond, *A History of Greece to 322 B.C.*, 2d ed. (Oxford: Clarendon Press, 1967), p. 329.

4. Albert A. Trever, *History of Ancient Civilization*, vol. 1, *The Ancient Near East and Greece* (New York: Harcourt, Brace and World, 1936), p. 292.

5. Raphael Sealey, *A History of the Greek City States, ca. 700-338 B.C.* (Berkeley: University of California Press, 1976), p. 299.

6. Trever, *History of Ancient Civilization*, 1, p. 181.

7. Aristotle, *Politics and Poetics*, trans. Benjamin Jowett and Thomas Twining, reprint ed., (New York: Viking, 1957), pp. 25-41.

8. Ibid., pp. 46-47.

9. Trever, *History of Ancient Civilization*, 1, p. 181.

10. Donald Kagan, *The Great Dialogue: History of Greek Political Thought from Homer to Polybius* (New York: Free Press, 1965), p. 235.

11. Harold Mattingly, *Roman Imperial Civilization* (London: Edward Arnold, 1957), pp. 84-85.

12. Ibid., p. 96.

13. Albert A. Trever, *History of Ancient Civilization*, vol. 2, *The Roman World* (New York: Harcourt, Brace, 1939), pp. 52-53; 335-37.

14. Ibid., pp. 636-37.

15. Christopher Brooke, *Europe in the Central Middle Ages, 962-1154* (New York: Hold, Rinehart and Winston, 1964), pp. 78-79.

16. Edward Peters, *Europe: The World of the Middle Ages* (Englewood Cliffs, N.J.: Prentice Hall, 1977), p. 271.

17. For a general survey of the origins of parliaments, see Bertie Wilkinson, ed., *The Creation of Medieval Parliaments* (New York: John Wiley, 1972).

18. On the significance of the Charter, see James C. Holt, *Magna Carta* (Cambridge University Press, 1965); and his *Magna Carta and the Idea of Liberty* (New York: John Wiley, 1972). A copy of *Magna Carta* is to be found on pages 173-84 of the latter work.

19. See Austin Lane Poole, *Obligations of Society in the XII and XIII Centuries* (Oxford: Clarendon Press, 1946), pp. 12-34.

20. Bryce Lyon, *A Constitutional and Legal History of Medieval England*, 2d ed. (New York: W. W. Norton, 1980), pp. 59-82, 166-79, 274-78, 391-407.

21. Christopher Brooke, *From Alfred to Henry III, 871-1272* (New York: W. W. Norton, 1966), p. 74.

22. Frederick Pollock and Frederic William Maitland, *The History of English*

*Law Before the Time of Edward I*, 2 vols, 2d ed. (1898; reprint ed., Cambridge: Cambridge University Press, 1968), 1, p. 177.

23. Sidney Painter, *The Rise of the Feudal Monarchies* (Ithaca: Cornell University Press, 1951); Joseph R. Strayer, *On the Origins of the Modern State* (Princeton: Princeton University Press, 1970).

24. For a convenient introduction to European political life in the eighteenth century, see R. R. Palmer, *The Age of Democratic Revolution*, 2 vols. (Princeton: Princeton University Press, 1959, 1964), 1, pp. 27-84; see also, Paul Hazard, *European Thought in the Eighteenth Century* (New Haven: Yale University Press, 1954), p. 173.

25. John Hall Stewart, *A Documentary Survey of the French Revolution* (New York: Macmillan, 1951), p. 231.

26. August 4th decrees, Ibid., p. 107.

27. Jay A. Sigler, *American Rights Policies* (Homewood, Ill.: Dorsey Press, 1975), p. 5.

28. A. P. d'Entrèves, *Natural Law: An Introduction to Legal Philosophy* (London: Hutchinson University Library, 1951), pp. 23-26.

29. R. W. Carlyle and A. J. Carlyle, *A History of Mediaeval Political Theory in the West*, 6 vols. (Edinburgh: William Blackwood, 1903-1936), 5, pp. 441-45.

30. F. L. Ganshof, *Feudalism*, trans. Philip Grierson, 3d English ed. (New York: Harper & Row, 1964), p. 113.

31. J. N. Figgis, *Political Thought from Gerson to Grotius: 1414-1625*, reprint ed. (New York: Harper, 1960), p. 20.

32. Ibid., p. 5.

33. Hayes, *Essays on Nationalism*, especially essay 4, "Nationalism as a Religion," pp. 93-125.

34. Fustel de Coulanges, *The Ancient City*, reprint ed. (Garden City, N.Y.: Doubleday, 1956), p. 127.

35. This view of a religion's social function was articulated about the middle of the second century A.D. by a Roman writer named Celsus. See Ernest Barker, *From Alexander to Constantine* (Oxford: Clarendon Press, 1956), pp. 379-80, 431-32.

36. Naphtali Lewis and Meyer Reinhold, eds., *Roman Civilization: Selected Readings*, 2 vols. (New York: Columbia University Press, 1951, 1955), vol. 2, *The Empire*, p. 574.

37. Ibid., pp. 580-81.

38. Salo Wittmayer Baron, *A Social and Religious History of the Jews*, vol. 1, *Ancient Times*, part 1, 2d ed. (New York: Columbia University Press, 1952), pp. 244-45.

39. Ibid., pp. 218-19.

40. Tacitus, *The Annals of Imperial Rome*, trans. Michael Grant (London: Cassell & Co., 1963), 15.49, p. 354.

41. Jean Daniélou and Henri Marrou, *The Christian Centuries*, vol. 1, *The First Six Hundred Years*, trans. Vincent Cronin (New York: McGraw-Hill, 1964), p. 83.

42. Barker, *From Alexander to Constantine*, pp. 353-54.

43. A.H.M. Jones, *Constantine and the Conversion of Europe* (London: English Universities Press, 1949), pp. 85-87.

44. Christopher Dawson, *The Making of Europe*, reprint ed. (New York: Meridian Books, 1958), pp. 48-49.

45. Daniélou and Marrou, vol. 1, *The First Six Hundred Years*, pp. 90-93.

46. Edward K. Rand, *Founders of the Middle Ages*, reprint ed. (New York: Dover, 1957), pp. 14-21.

47. Brian Tierney, ed., *The Middle Ages*, 2 vols. (New York: Knopf, 1970), vol. 1 *Sources of Medieval History*, pp. 22-23.

48. Ibid., pp. 24-25.

49. Robert Ignatius Burns, *Islam Under the Crusaders* (Princeton: Princeton University Press, 1973); Joseph F. O'Callaghan, *A History of Medieval Spain* (Ithaca, N.Y.: Cornell University Press, 1975), pp. 462-66.
1975), pp. 462-66.

50. Hans Eberhard Mayer, *The Crusades*, trans. John Gillingham (New York: Oxford University Press, 1972), pp. 43-44.

51. Friedrich Heer, *The Medieval World, Europe 1100-1300*, trans. Janet Sondheimer (London: Weidenfeld and Nicolson, 1926), p. 255.

52. George Clark, *English History: A Survey* (Oxford: Clarendon Press, 1971), p. 311.

53. James Muldoon, *Popes, Lawyers, and Infidels* (Philadelphia: University of Pennsylvania Press, 1979), pp. 50-51.

54. Jeffrey B. Russell, ed., *Religious Dissent in the Middle Ages* (New York: John Wiley, 1971), pp. 10-11.

55. H. Bettenson, ed., *Documents of the Christian Church*, 2d ed. (Oxford: Oxford University Press, 1962), pp. 185-86.

56. Henry St. Lawrence Beaufort Moss, *The Birth of the Middle Ages*, 395-814, reprint ed. (London: Oxford University Press, 1963), p. 113.

57. *The Liber Augustalis or Constitution of Melfi*, trans. James Powell (Syracuse: Syracuse University Press, 1971), pp. 7-9.

58. Bettenson, *Documents of the Christian Church*, pp. 186-87. Concerning Aquinas's political ideas, see *Aquinas: Selected Political Writings*, ed. A. P. d'Entrèves, trans. J. G. Dawson (Oxford: Basil Blackwell, 1970).

59. Bettenson, *Documents of the Christian Church*, pp. 251-55.

60. For a discussion of Wycliffe's political ideas, see *The Political Theory of John Wycliffe* (Chicago: Loyola University Press, 1962).

61. Bettenson, *Documents of the Christian Church*, p. 252.

62. Both Luther and Calvin called upon the secular rulers to impose religious reform upon their subjects as a fundamental obligation of good rulers. See Roland H. Bainton, *Here I Stand: A Life of Martin Luther*, reprint ed. (New York: New American Library, 1955), p. 17; John T. McNeill, *The History and Character of Calvinism*, reprint ed. (New York: Oxford University Press, 1967), p. 127.

63. Hajo Holborn, *A History of Modern Germany*, 3 vols. (New York: Knopf, 1959), vol. 1, *The Reformation*, pp. 201-46.

64. Bettenson, *Documents of the Christian Church*, p. 301.

65. Ibid.

66. C. V. Wedgwood, *The Thirty Years War*, reprint ed. (London: Jonathan Cape, 1964), pp. 492-93.

67. Bettenson, *Documents of the Christian Church*, p. 304.

68. McNeill, *History and Character of Calvinism*, pp. 237-54; J. W. Allen, *A History of Political Thought in the Sixteenth Century* (London: Methuen, 1928), pp. 73-102, 280-342.

69. Allen, *A History of Political Thought*, pp. 292-96.

70. Bettenson, *Documents of the Christian Church*, p. 302; McNeill, *History and Character of Calvinism*, pp. 247-52.

71. W. H. Lewis, *The Splendid Century*, reprint ed., (Garden City, N.Y.: Doubleday, 1957), pp. 102-11.

72. H. G. Koenigsberger and George L. Mosse, *Europe in the Sixteenth Century* (New York: Holt, Rinehart and Winston, 1968), pp. 225-26; John B. Wolf, *Louis XIV* (New York: W. W. Norton, 1968), p. 365.

73. Pierre Janelle, *The Catholic Reformation* (Milwaukee: Bruce, 1963), p. 226.

74. Lewis, *The Splendid Century*, p. 148.

75. Palmer, *The Age of Democratic Revolution*, 1, pp. 439-65.

76. Geoffrey Bruun, *The Enlightened Despots*, 2d ed. (New York: Holt, Rinehart and Winston, 1967), p. 36.

77. Muldoon, *Popes, Lawyers, and Infidels*, pp. 10-11.

78. Hugo Grotius, *De Jure Belli ac Pacis Libri Tres*, trans. Francis W. Kelsey, et al., 2 vols. *The Classics of International Law* (Washington, D.C.: The Carnegie Endowment for International Peace, 1925), p. 14.

79. Edmund Burke, *Reflections on the Revolution in France*, reprint ed. (Indianapolis: Bobbs-Merrill, 1955).

80. J. L. Talmon, *Romanticism and Revolt: Europe 1815-1848* (New York: Harcourt, Brace and World, 1967), pp. 95-109.

# VIII

# Solórzano's *De indiarum iure:* Applying a Medieval Theory of World Order in the Seventeenth Century*

AMONG the more important consequences of the discovery of the new world were the various attempts to develop a general theory of international law and relations. Although Hugo Grotius (1583–1645) generally receives the credit for initiating this effort, in fact his masterpiece, *De jure belli ac pacis libri tres,* was only one of many volumes dealing with these issues that appeared in the sixteenth and the seventeenth centuries. Most of the books written on the topic of international law and relations in these centuries were written by Spanish authors, as a glance at the citations in Grotius's work will demonstrate. Indeed, one of the more striking differences between the Spanish response to the discovery of the new world and the response to the discoveries in every other European country was the desire of the Spanish monarchs to defend and legitimize the conquest of the newly discovered lands. The Spanish monarchs not only prefaced their claims to lands in the new world with ritual legal formulas, as did the kings of England in the headings of charters granting lands in North America to colonists, but also encouraged the creation of an extensive literature that dealt with the legitimacy of the conquest of the

* An earlier version of this paper was delivered at the International Congress on "A Member of Another Religion in Religious Law" held at the Hebrew University of Jerusalem and at the University of Haifa, April 27–30, 1987.

Americas. Limited though this work was to the narrow technical problem of the legitimacy of the Spanish conquest, it nevertheless provided a basis for the eventual development of broader theories of international law and relations.

From the very beginning of the conquest, there was what Lewis Hanke has felicitously termed "The Spanish Struggle for Justice in the Conquest of America," a serious effort to deal justly with the inhabitants of the Americas.[1] The Spanish theologians, philosophers, and lawyers who wrote on the conquest sought to guide the monarchs and their advisors as they sought to create policies for governing the new world. In the post–World War I era, especially in the United States, the literature of this struggle attracted a great deal of scholarly interest because of the implications of this debate for twentieth-century theories of international law and relations.[2] In the 1970s and 1980s, scholars engaged in the debate about the justice of war in the nuclear age have again occasionally turned to the Spanish critics of the conquest as part of the search for a historically based theory of the just war.[3]

The bulk of the scholarly attention devoted to this issue has focused on the period from 1492 to 1550, from the first of Columbus's voyages to the great debate at Valladolid at which Bartolomé de Las Casas and Juan Ginés de Sepúlveda debated the legitimacy of the conquest before the imperial court. One result has been an explosion of materials and of debate about this period of the con-

[1] The fundamental work is Lewis Hanke, *The Spanish Struggle for Justice in the Conquest of America* (Philadelphia, 1949; reprint, Boston, 1965).

[2] The work of James Brown Scott, an official of the Carnegie Endowment for International Peace, was central here. As editor of a series of texts in the history of international law, the *Classics of International Law* series, he arranged for the publication of the works of Victoria and Suárez that dealt with the legitimacy of the conquest of the Americas. In his own work, *The Spanish Conception of International Law and of Sanctions* (Washington, D.C., 1934) Scott praised, too highly in the opinion of his critics, the contribution of these and other sixteenth-century Spanish thinkers who dealt with the legitimacy of the conquest to the formation of international law, seeing them as important forerunners of Hugo Grotius. See James Muldoon, "The Contribution of the Medieval Canon Lawyers to the Formation of International Law," *Traditio* 28 (1972): 483-97. In a review of recent books dealing with Las Casas and with Sepulveda, T. Bentley Duncan took up Scott's cause, arguing that it "is up to Europeanists to explore those massive Spanish foundations that underlie the work of Grotius and Milton, of Locke and Edmund Burke, and even of Thomas Jefferson." See *Journal of Modern History* 50 (1978): 766.

[3] The most important work of this sort is that of James T. Johnson, *Ideology, Reason, and the Limitation of War: Religion and Secular Concepts, 1200–1740* (Princeton, 1975), and *The Just War Tradition and the Restraint of War: A Moral and Historical Inquiry* (Princeton, 1981).

quest, especially about Hanke's interpretation of the conquest as a struggle for justice.[4] Another result has been an increasing interest in the works of Las Casas and the publication of a series of his works in translation.[5]

There is some justification for focusing analysis on the period 1492 to 1550. It might seem that after the debate at Valladolid failed to resolve the question of the legitimacy of the American conquest, the issue was of no further interest or importance to Spanish thinkers. This attitude seems to have led James Brown Scott and some other scholars who have examined the Spanish writers of the later sixteenth century to see them only as predecessors of Hugo Grotius, rather than as both predecessors of Grotius and at the same time as part of a continuing Spanish tradition that was developing parallel with the theories of Grotius and his successors.[6] The linear version of the development of international law moved discussion of the issues raised by the conquest of the Americas away from Spain and toward the issues that were of interest to European merchants such as the Dutch. Interest in the rights of conquered peoples played a much smaller role in the work of these later thinkers than it had in the work of the Spanish thinkers.

---

[4] This debate, which goes back to the sixteenth century and is rooted in Las Casas's criticism of the Spanish treatment of the Indians, is usually seen in terms of the "black legend." For a survey of the issue, see Charles Gibson, *The Black Legend: Anti-Spanish Attitudes in the Old World and the New* (New York, 1971). For the debate about Hanke's views, see in particular Benjamin Keen, "The Black Legend Revisited: Assumptions and Realities," *Hispanic American Historical Review* 49 (1969): 703–19, and "The White Legend Revisited: A Reply to Professor Hanke's 'Modest Proposal,'" *Hispanic American Historical Review* 51 (1971): 336–55. For Hanke's response to his critics, see "More Heat and Some Light on the Spanish Struggle for Justice in the Conquest of America," *Hispanic American Historical Review* 44 (1964): 293–340, and "A Modest Proposal for a Moratorium on Grand Generalizations: Some Thoughts on the Black Legend," *Hispanic American Historical Review* 51 (1971): 112–27.

[5] These works began to appear in 1966 as part of a scholarly commemoration of the four-hundredth anniversary of Las Casas's death. The volumes already published include Las Casas, *In Defense of the Indians*, trans. and ed. Stafford Poole (DeKalb, Ill., 1974), Las Casas's response to Sepulveda's argument that the Indians were natural slaves according to Aristotle's definition. See also *Bartolome de Las Casas in History*, eds. Juan Friede and Benjamin Keen (DeKalb, Ill., 1971).

[6] Hanke, for example, ended his discussion of the legitimacy of the conquest with the work of Francisco de Toledo, Viceroy of Peru, 1569–82. A recent symposium at Salamanca dealt with these issues in the period from 1492 to 1573, virtually the same time frame that Hanke had employed almost forty years earlier. See *Actas del I simposio sobre la etica en la conquista de America, 1492–1573* (Salamanca, 1984). I wish to thank Dr. Antonio Garcia y Garcia of the Pontifical University of Salamanca for bringing the proceedings of this conference to my attention.

Nevertheless, the issue of the rights and status of the inhabitants of the new world continued to interest Spanish thinkers at least through the first half of the seventeenth century, if only because the Spanish overseas empire continued to develop in those decades. Although modern historians debate the question of whether or not the Spanish empire was declining in the seventeenth century, those who administered that imperial government were fully involved in dealing with traditional problems.[7] These problems included the continuing need to justify the conquest in legal and moral terms. Furthermore, the consequences of the conquest for the inhabitants of the Americas were much greater after 1550 than before, since the Spaniards moved from exploration and conquest to permanent settlement with its long-term implications for a population that was expected to provide the labor force for the colonial economy.

One figure who contributed to this continuing process of defending and legitimating the conquest of the new world was the Spanish lawyer and imperial official Juan de Solórzano y Pereira (1575–1654), whose *Disputatio de indiarum iure: sive, de iure iusta indiarum occidentalium inquisitione, acquisitione et retentione,* appeared in two volumes, the first in 1629, the second ten years later. In 1648, the work appeared also in a Spanish version, the *Política indiana.*[8] Although Solórzano has been neglected by twen-

[7] Concerning the scholarly debate on the condition of the Spanish empire in the seventeenth century, see J. H. Elliott, "The Decline of Spain," *Past and Present* 20 (1961): 52–75, and Henry Kamen, "The Decline of Spain: A Historical Myth?" *Past and Present* 81 (1978): 24–50.

[8] Juan de Solórzano Pereira, *Disputatio de indiarum iure: sive, de iusta indiarum occidentalium inquisitione, acquisitione et retentione* (hereafter cited in text and notes as *DII*), 2 vols. (Madrid, 1629–39). The work also appeared in a Spanish translation, *Política indiana* (Madrid, 1648). Solórzano's work remained in print through the eighteenth century and was reprinted in Madrid as late as 1776. The most recent edition is *Política indiana,* 5 vols. (Madrid, 1972). This edition includes a brief biography of Solórzano, an extensive study of the work, and a bibliography of works that deal with Solórzano and his thought. Although Solórzano's name and work are certainly not unknown to modern scholars, he has not received much attention outside of Spain even though Lewis Hanke described him as "one of Europe's greatest jurists in the seventeenth century" in his *The First Social Experiments in America* (Cambridge, 1935), p. 4. In Hanke's opinion, the *Política indiana* was the "most learned and the most detailed statement made during the seventeenth or eighteenth centuries on the whole complicated question of Spain's right to America and her method of operations there." See Hanke, *Aristotle and the American Indians* (Bloomington, Ind., 1959), p. 92. Most recently, the importance of Solórzano in the development of early modern thought on the nature of non-European societies has been discussed in Anthony Pagden, *The Fall of Natural Man*

tieth-century scholars, he was well known in his own day and on through the early nineteenth century. References to his work can be found in a number of writings, especially those dealing with the relationship between colonies and their mother country. For example, several pamphlets dealing with the controversy between England and its North American colonies on the eve of the American Revolution cited Solórzano's work.[9]

Solórzano's work is significant for several reasons. In the first place, it is neither the work of a priest who was an academic philosopher or theologian such as Francisco de Vitoria or Francisco Suárez, nor is it the work of a missionary such as Las Casas. Solórzano was a lawyer whose long career in the Spanish imperial service included eighteen years as a judge in the Audiencia of Lima (1609–27) and subsequently memberships on the Council of Castile and the Council of the Indies. As a result, when he came to discuss the legitimacy of the conquest, he did so from the perspective of someone who was actively involved in the work of consolidating that conquest. In the second place, Solórzano placed the conquest of the Americas within the broadest possible intellectual context. He began with the Bible and Aristotle, cited a number of medieval writers, ranging from theologians such as Augustine and Aquinas, to canon lawyers such as Gratian and Pope Innocent IV, Roman lawyers such as Baldus and Bartolus, and finally, he cited the work of those writers who sought to apply medieval legal and philosophical concepts to the newly discovered peoples of the Americas. In particular, he cited extensively the works of his countrymen, both predecessors such as Francisco de Vitoria, and contemporaries such as Francisco Suárez, Domingo Soto, Diego de Covarruvias, and Joseph Acosta. He also cited other leading contemporary political and legal thinkers such as Robert Bellarmine. Solórzano drew upon the widest possible range of materials in developing his treatment of the con-

(Cambridge, 1982), pp. 165, 194–98. See also Pagden's "Dispossessing the Barbarian: The Language of Spanish Thomism and the Debate over the Property Rights of the American Indians," in *The Languages of Political Theory in Early Modern Europe*, ed. Anthony Pagden (Cambridge, 1987), pp. 97–98.

[9] See James Otis, *The Rights of the British Colonies Asserted and Proved* in *Pamphlets of the American Revolution, 1750–1776*, ed. Bernard Bailyn (Cambridge, 1965) 1:438. See also the two treatises by James Abercromby written before the revolution but not published until recently: James Abercromby, *Magna Carta for America*, ed. J. P. Greene, C. F. Mullett and E. C. Papenfuse, Jr. (Philadelphia, 1986), esp. p. 199.

quest, so his work is of special interest not only to the student of the conquest itself, but also to the student of seventeenth-century Spanish intellectual life.

Because the *De indiarum iure* is a massive work, running to approximately two thousand columns of densely packed analysis, discussion, and citations, it is not easy to summarize Solórzano's treatment of the conquest in a brief space. Let us consider only one section of the book in order to appreciate the author's achievement. Solórzano devoted the second book of his first volume to the arguments about the legitimacy of the conquest of the new world. In doing this, he was placing himself in the line of writers, beginning with Pope Innocent IV (1243–54), who had framed the debate about Christian-infidel relations in terms of the legitimacy of conquering the lands occupied by infidels. During the mid-thirteenth century, two leading canon lawyers created an intellectual framework for considering the relationship between Christian and non-Christian societies. This tradition began with the commentary of Pope Innocent IV, who wrote a commentary on a decretal of his predecessor, Innocent III (1198–1216). The decretal, *Quod super his* (X.3.34.8) dealt with the vows taken by those who had agreed to go on crusade. Innocent IV took the opportunity that his predecessor's letter provided to consider the much broader question of the right by which the pope could call for a crusade against infidels who were not subject to a Christian ruler. On what basis could the pope justify the conquest of those outside the Church, he asked, taking from them their lands and their political power? Innocent IV argued that Christ's commission to his successor and vicar gave the pope responsibility not only for the spiritual welfare of those within the Church, but also for the spiritual welfare of those outside the Church, because Christ's mission was to all men, not to some. At the same time, Innocent IV did not argue that the pope was to apply the law of the Christian church equally to all men. Christians, including heretics and schismatics, were subject to ecclesiastical, that is canon, law. Jews were subject to their own law, which the pope could interpret and enforce if their leaders failed to do so. Infidels were subject to the natural law, and the pope could punish them for violating it. The assumption underlying this use of the term natural law was that the terms of this law were apparent to all rational men, and those who violated it did so knowingly and deserved to be punished. Although Innocent IV did not define the content of the natural law, he did point out that idolatry, the worship of man-made gods, was clearly a violation of that law because men were obviously made to worship one god.[10]

Although infidels were not to be judged according to canon law, they were subject to the Christian interpretation of what constituted natural law by virtue of being subject to the pope acting in his capacity as supreme judge of matters involving the natural law. As a result, infidels were clearly placed within the orbit of papal jurisdiction. Furthermore, Innocent IV recognized that all men possessed certain basic rights by virtue of their shared human nature. Infidels, Jews, and Christians had a right to possess property and political jurisdiction. Christians could not deprive infidels of property and jurisdiction simply because they were infidels. If Christians wished to conquer an infidel kingdom, they would have to justify it in terms of violations of the natural law by the infidel occupiers of the land in question.[11]

Innocent IV's theory that papal jurisdiction and the consequences that flowed from it extended to all men everywhere became the basis for justifying the Spanish conquest of the new world. Although canon lawyers continued to debate certain aspects of Innocent's argument during the succeeding centuries, they never denied that the pope was competent to judge the actions of infidels according to the terms of the natural law as he understood it.[12] Some canonists, however, went further than Innocent had done, denying that infidels could legitimately possess property and political jurisdiction at all; since the coming of Christ, these had been restricted to those who were in the state of grace. The most important canonist who held this position was Innocent's own student, Henry of Segusio, better known as Hostiensis, who argued that because infidels no longer possessed any right to property and jurisdiction, the conquest of infidel kingdoms by Christians was always legitimate.[13]

What differentiated Solórzano's discussion of the legitimacy

[10] James Muldoon, *Popes, Lawyers, and Infidels: The Church and the Non-Christian World, 1250–1550* (Philadelphia, 1979) pp. 6-15. The terms *ius naturale* and *ius gentium* and several variants were often used imprecisely in many of these discussions. For a brief introduction to the problems of definition involved, see A. P. d'Entreves, *Natural Law: An Introduction to Legal Philosophy* (London, 1951).

[11] The reconquest of Spain from the Muslims or the crusades to regain possession of the Holy Land were judged just wars of defence or recuperation because they involved lands that had once been possessed by Christians and lost to the Muslims as the result of unjust wars of aggression. See Muldoon, p. 6.

[12] Muldoon, pp. 118–19, 124–27.

[13] On Hostiensis's arguments, see ibid., pp. 15–17.

of the conquest from the more narrowly legal discussions that preceded his work was his use of the extensive literature about the new world that missionaries and explorers had produced. This literature described the inhabitants of the new world and their ways of life to European audiences, adding a new dimension to discussions that had previously dealt almost entirely with abstract legal issues.[14] Solórzano was able to compare the practices of contemporary American societies with the practices of the ancestors of seventeenth-century Europeans. He even compared the Indians' cruel practices with those of the ancient Hebrews and Romans. This comparative approach reflected not only the widespread availability of information about life in the new world, but also, no doubt, Solórzano's own years as a judge of the Audiencia at Lima as well. Running through his treatise is the theme that medieval canonistic theories about the relations between Christians and infidels and the contemporary sociopolitical realities of the new world can be reconciled. The ultimate goal would be the development of a general theory of Christian-infidel relations that brought to the canonists' abstract legal theory a new dimension of understanding based on both the contemporary Spanish experience in the Americas and the historical experience of early medieval Christian Europe.

Although the great bulk of Solórzano's work was devoted to defending the conquest's legitimacy, a reasonable position for an official of the Habsburg empire to take, he was quite willing, even anxious, to present all sides of the debate about the legitimacy of the conquest before drawing his final conclusions. As a result, the *De indiarum iure* contained a number of the arguments that those who opposed the conquest of infidel societies had raised over the centuries. Specifically, it considered the proposition that infidels who were not subject to the jurisdiction of Christian secular rulers were not subject to papal jurisdiction either. If the reader was to accept this argument, he would then be forced to conclude that self-governing infidel societies were not subject to invasion and conquest by Christian rulers acting under papal warrant. This line of argument, if accepted, would destroy the legal basis for the Spanish conquest of the new world.

---

[14] This abstract approach to the issues involved was typical of the work of theologians such as Victoria as well as the work of the canon lawyers. Solórzano used a number of contemporary descriptions of the new world but relied extensively on the important work of José de Acosta. See Pagden, *Fall of Natural Man*, pp. 149–50, 194, 197–99.

Solórzano's discussion of the arguments against the legitimacy of the conquest of the Americas appeared mid-way through the first volume of his work. The previous arguments had demonstrated the legitimacy of "the conquest of the Indians who, because of their sins against nature, their cruel sacrifices, and their idolatries" deserved to be conquered by Christians, a conclusion that "rests on [the work] of numerous important authors and authorities previously discussed" (*DII*, I.ii.xiv. para. 1). In other words, sixteen hundred years of Christian scriptural, theological, and legal writings provided a firm basis for justifying the conquest. This was not sufficient, however, to conclude the discussion. Training in Roman law had taught Solórzano that "there can be nothing certain among men that does not consider any doubt or any differences of opinion" before formulating a conclusion.[15] Numerous criticisms of the conquest of the new world had been raised and needed to be addressed before Solórzano could conclude his treatise. Furthermore, these objections were not frivolous in nature, nor were they simply the theoretical speculations of academic philosophers. These were the objections of "other most learned doctors . . . who, moved by arguments and considerations that are no less valid, offer the contrary opinion [about the legitimacy of the conquest] as the surer and the more true, expressly teaching that infidels who are not subject to Christian princes cannot be attacked, even with papal authority, however great the power of the tyrants under whom they live, the idols whom they serve, and however great the wicked and evil crimes against the natural law and reason that they allow."[16]

At the outset of this discussion, Solórzano posed the fundamental issue in a stark way, contrasting two conflicting goods. Citing a number of sources to support his argument, he asserted that Christians have no obligation "to disturb the natural and legitimate division of government and to exercise jurisdiction over alien and foreign people under the pretext of charity" (*DII*, I.ii.xiv. para. 13). In other words, the supernatural good, eternal

[15] *DII*, I.ii.xiv. para. 1. The phrase is from the *Corpus iuris civilis*, 2 vols. (Geneva, 1626), *Authenticae*, 4.23.44. *De Tabellionibus*.

[16] Ibid., para. 2. There was even a long tradition of criticizing the crusades as a means of obtaining the conversion of the Muslims and ending practices that were considered to be violations of the natural law. See Palmer Throop, *Criticism of the Crusade: A Study of Public Opinion and Crusade Propaganda* (Amsterdam, 1940). In recent years, there has been an attempt to revise Throop's conclusions. See Norman Housley, *The Avignon Papacy and the Crusades, 1305–1378* (Oxford, 1986), p. 230.

salvation that Christian preachers could bring to the infidels did not override the infidels' natural right to govern themselves and to possess their lands in peace.

To support the argument that infidel societies were not subject to papal judgment, Solórzano drew upon a variety of sources. These sources included two statements from Gratian's *Decretum* that canonists had often cited in medieval debates about the relationship between church and state. The first statement was from a letter of Pope Nicholas I (858–67); the second was from a letter of Pope John I (523–26).[17] Both letters emphasized the distinction between the jurisdiction of the spiritual power and that of the secular power. At the same time, these letters also emphasized the preeminence of the pope in all matters with the result that he possessed the right to interject himself into the secular sphere when spiritual matters were involved. In Solórzano's argument, these letters demonstrated that as the pope had no absolute right to intervene in the secular sphere, even in Christian societies, he most certainly had no right to do so in infidel societies.

Solórzano next offered the argument that the achievement of the highest spiritual good did not justify the commission of the smallest evil act, a point that St. Augustine had made long ago (*DII,* I.ii.xiv. para. 15). At this stage, Solórzano appears to have been suggesting that the waging of war for the purpose of insuring the salvation of infidels, or at least to insure that they stopped committing acts that violated the natural law, would itself be an immoral act that could not be justified in terms of the desired end. Moral ends, so this argument went, required moral means.

Finally, Solórzano repeated Bernard of Clairvaux's warning to his former student, Pope Eugenius III (1145–53): "Mastery over the world is not for the Vicar of Christ, the apostolic mission is" (*DII,* I.ii.xiv. para. 16). In this case, Solórzano was suggesting that by using force to seek the salvation of infidels, the papacy would corrupt itself and deflect the church from its proper role in the world. In effect, all of the arguments that the Spanish jurist presented in this section of his treatise emphasized the fundamental limitations on the papacy's jurisdiction and contained the warning that to exceed these limits could only undermine the papacy's moral position.

Having developed the argument that Christians have no right

[17] Ibid, para. 13. The references were to the *Corpus iuris canonici* (Lyon, 1614), *Decretum,* D.96.c.6, *Cum ad verum* and c.11, *Si imperator.*

or obligation to force non-believers to adhere to Christian definitions of a properly ordered society, Solórzano then raised the question of who, if not Christians, should punish those who harm God by governing tyrannically, by practicing human sacrifice, or by worshipping idols (*DII,* I.ii.xiv. para. 18). According to the line of argument he was developing at this point, the fact that the Indians committed these admittedly evil acts did not automatically authorize Christians to punish them on behalf of God. Echoing the words of Gamaliel to the council of Jewish elders when faced with making a decision about how to deal with Christ's first followers, Solórzano suggested that if God found the practices of the Indians offensive, he was quite capable of protecting his own interests and punishing them: "God Himself can easily, if He wishes, ward off those injuries and restrain those wicked men for what they have done, just as He has often done [before]."[18]

To support this argument, Solórzano cited a number of scriptural sources, though not the story of Gamaliel, the most important of which came from the letters of St. Paul. In Romans (12:17–21), Hebrews (10:24–31), and 1 Corinthians (5:9–13), the apostle to the gentiles admonished his readers to live at peace with one another and to avoid conflict within the Christian community. When faced with internal conflict, the Christians should shun association with troublemakers as long as they persist in behavior that unsettled the community. Exclusion from the community was the worst punishment that Christians could inflict on troublemakers. Furthermore, Christians possess power only over the members of their own community. Those who were not members of the community, regardless of the nature of their crimes, were not subject to Christian judgment and punishment. As St. Paul said: "What business of mine is it to judge those who are outside [the Christian community]? For those who are outside, God will judge. Cast out the evil ones from among you."[19] The conclusion of this line of argument, according to Solórzano, was that: "Foreigners . . . and those who are outside, that is, those who are outside of the Church, such as Jews, heretics and gentiles, are left to the divine judgment for punishment" (*DII,* I.ii.xiv. para. 22).

Solórzano then moved from a discussion of the relationship that existed between Christians and non-believers within small, voluntary, Christian communities, such as those described in the

[18] Ibid., para. 19. See Acts, 5:33–40.

[19] 1 Corinthians 5:12–13.

New Testament to a discussion of the relationship between Christians and infidels that existed in medieval Europe, where Christianity was the official, all-pervasive religion. This section of the discussion drew upon the work of the Spanish Jesuit Francisco Suárez to support the argument that the Christian church had no right to judge those who did not belong to the Church. In contrast to Innocent IV, Suárez and some other theologians discussed here limited ecclesiastical jurisdiction to those who had been baptized and were therefore members of the Church, thus continuing the arguments that St. Paul had first raised. As for the unbaptized: "Power over those who have not received the sacrament of Baptism . . . has not been given directly to the pope or to other prelates . . . only [power] over those who have submitted themselves to the Christian faith" (*DII,* I.ii.xiv. para. 24).

If, as Suárez argued, the Church possessed no direct authority over the unbaptized, then why, asked Solórzano, did Thomas Aquinas assert that "the rites of infidels are by no means to be tolerated by the Church" (*DII,* I.ii.xiv. para. 29)? Did this mean that Aquinas would authorize the Church to order a military campaign against an infidel society in order to eliminate infidel religious activities? By no means. According to Solórzano, Aquinas was referring to the situation of infidels living among Christians and under Christian rulers, a circumstance that enabled a Christian ruler to act on his own to eliminate infidel religious practices in his kingdom. A Christian ruler who determined that infidel "rites and the temples of their idols and the sacrifices [they performed] presented some difficulty for the Christian religion" could refuse to tolerate them in his kingdom (*DII,* I.ii.xiv. para. 29). The references that follow this discussion make it quite clear that Solórzano was referring to the situation in Spain, where Islam had been tolerated to a limited degree since the Middle Ages. The limited toleration of Jews and Muslims in medieval Spain had always rested on pragmatism, not principle. When the needs of the Spanish kingdoms required the labor and services of these non-believers, their presence was tolerated. From the late fifteenth century, the fear, real or imagined, that Muslims and Jews, even those ostensibly converted to Christianity, formed a potential fifth column that would support a Muslim invasion of Spain meant that the value of the contributions of the non-believers to the overall good of Spain was outweighed by the potential harm they could do. The point being made here was that Christian rulers, not the pope, were the officials responsible for decisions regarding infidel practices. Christian rulers possessed direct power over their infidel subjects, but the pope did not.

Obviously Solórzano was not discussing religious toleration in the terms of the twentieth-century discussion of toleration. Quite the reverse. Infidels could be tolerated, as he saw it, only in order that "we might be able the more easily to win them to Christ and lest even worse things and even graver scandals [than limited toleration] might arise" (*DII*, I.ii.xiv. para. 30). At the same time, Solórzano also pointed out that Christians need not avoid contact with infidels. Indeed, St. Augustine had pointed out that as Christ had mingled with publicans and sinners in order to reach them, so too contemporary Christians must not isolate themselves and avoid contact with infidels. Rather, it was necessary to mingle with unbelievers in order to teach them about Christ's message.[20]

So far, Solórzano's discussion about the relationship between Christians and infidels dealt with situations that bore little resemblance to the situation that existed in the new world. The inhabitants of the Americas were neither baptized Christians nor were they subject to Christian princes when the Spaniards first encountered them. It was, therefore, at this point that Innocent IV's argument about the subordination of the infidels to the natural law and the pope's role as judge of men's behavior according to that law became useful in Solórzano's discussion. Because this section of the treatise dealt with arguments rejecting papal claims to power over infidels, however, Solórzano dealt with what critics of the conquest saw as the dangers implicit in Innocent's argument.

In Solórzano's presentation of the scholarly criticism of Innocent IV's argument, the pope's claim to universal jurisdiction based on natural law had far-reaching consequences, so far-reaching that if the pope's argument were taken seriously, it would have results that were completely unacceptable to reasonable men. In the first place, if infidels were to be punished for sins against nature, that is for actions against the natural order such as unnatural sexual practices, then they must also be punished "for other actions which they perform against the natural law, such as theft, fornication, adultery, homicide, and, generally, for all kinds of similar sins" (*DII*, I.ii.xiv. para. 31). Although it might seem that such a position would be a reasonable one, given the universal nature of Christ's message and the pope's responsibility

[20] *DII*, I.ii.xiv. para. 30. The reference is to the *Decretum*, 23.4.17. *Ad mensam*.

for seeing to the preaching of that message, Solórzano argued that, in reality, the argument that the pope is obliged to punish infidels for sins against the law of nature "is absurd, however, since the pope neither can nor should wage war on this basis against either the barbarians and infidels, to whom it cannot easily be shown that these things are sins against the natural law nor even against Christians who sin the more seriously in these matters because of their knowledge" (*DII,* I.ii.xiv. para. 32–33). If the pope were to do as Innocent IV and his followers suggested, that is, to punish violators of the natural law everywhere, and if he were to "confiscate the lands of Christians for this reason and grant them to other princes, he would be enabled to change the governance of kingdoms daily since in every country there dwell numerous sinners" (*DII,* I.ii.xiv. para. 32–33). Furthermore, Solórzano pointed out the paradox involved in punishing those who have sinned against natural law while at the same time attempting to convert them to the teachings of Christ. It "would seem contradictory to persuade the infidels to accept the faith which grants them the remission of all their past sins and [at the same time] to wage war against them because of those same sins and to punish them by force of arms" (*DII,* I.ii.xiv. para. 37).

Finally, Solórzano even presented some arguments that suggested that the behavior and practices of the infidels that Europeans cited as a basis for invading and conquering them were widespread not only in the past but also in the contemporary world, yet these practices did not necessarily justify the conquest of the peoples who practiced them. Although Solórzano did not use the term at this point, his argument here reflects the notion of the *ius gentium,* the practices and customs contrary to the natural law that existed in human societies. If these practices were so widespread as to be in some sense natural, or at least common to all men at least at certain stages of their development, then they could not be simply condemned as evil and punished.[21] As he said, "in truth, the same crimes and even the less serious actions attributed to the Indians were formerly recorded of other nations and even today are recorded," yet we "never read that for this reason that war was waged against them" (*DII,* I.ii.xiv. para. 53). Solórzano then went on to outline the terrible crimes that characterized ancient societies, even ancient Hebrew society, the same crimes that characterized contemporary American societies. Furthermore, even though the ancient Hebrews were God's chosen people, they were not authorized to punish those of their neighbors who violated God's law unless God himself specifically ordered them to do so. The "sacred scriptures recount many wicked deeds of the Amorrites and other people of Palestine, things it cannot be claimed seem any more horrible than those done by the Indians, even by those who are known as the Caribs, the most cruel of the Indians. . . . And yet the Hebrews could not attack them because of these crimes unless there was an express command from the Lord" (*DII*, I.ii.xiv. para. 57).

Here again, Solórzano's argument led to the conclusion that if God wanted people punished because of their misdeeds, he could either do it himself or he could inform Christians or their leaders in a clear fashion of his wishes in the matter. As Solórzano had already pointed out, the Bible demonstrated that God could act directly in human affairs whenever he wished to do so. He did not need to rely on Christians acting on their own initiative to avenge him.

Furthermore, according to Solórzano, it was not only people in the ancient world who committed the evil deeds attributed to the Indians. He pointed out that while it was true that various ancient peoples practiced idolatry and human sacrifice, so too, "the Gauls, Franks, Germans, Britons, Lithuanians, Northmen, Danes, and other northern people" engaged in precisely the same practices, "barbaric custom[s] that ended not so long ago" (*DII*, I.ii.xiv. para. 88–89). Even the Spanish lawyer's own ancestors, "learning from and imitating the Phoenicians, Greeks, Carthaginians, and other nations, were accustomed to immolate large numbers of people, very often even their own sons" (*DII*, I.ii.xiv. para. 93).

Solórzano's historical argument, based as it was on a wide knowledge of both ancient descriptions of primitive societies and contemporary descriptions of the various peoples of the new world, suggests that given enough time and enough Christian teaching and good example, even the most barbarous of the new world peoples, the Caribs, would eventually reach a civilized and Christianized way of life. Time and patience, not war and conquest, were the keys to this end.

It is tempting to hear Solórzano's arguments about the legitimacy, or rather the illegitimacy, of the conquest of the new world with a modern ear, an ear accustomed to irony and skepticism.

---

[21] Although Solórzano did not explicitly employ the traditional distinction between the natural law and the law of nations here, this distinction is clearly implicit.

The arguments that God could avenge wrongs done to him if he chose to do so and that he did not need human beings to act in his name, even with papal approval, rings with irony. Likewise, to the modern eye, the sight of the descendants of the barbarian invaders of Europe, people accused of the most heinous crimes by the Romans and other observers, now, having become Christians, slaying infidel officials accused of the same crimes as their conquerors' ancestors, waging war, and conquering in the name of God—this sight to a modern observer is a classic example of moral irony.

Irony, however, is a very fragile, even personal, form of criticism and it is too easy for a modern, skeptical, ironic student of these events to see irony in the observations of one who, like Solórzano, was a contemporary of the events. When the learned Spanish judge presented the argument that God could, if he felt so inclined, avenge himself, he was not being ironic, only literal. He was, perhaps, accusing the supporters of the conquest of the sin of presumption, that is, of acting for God as if he could not act for himself, in effect making themselves gods. By pointing to the documented crimes of the early medieval ancestors of the seventeenth-century Spanish, he was, perhaps, cautioning them to be humble in the face of other, different peoples. To some extent, this section of Solórzano's work is a series of warnings about the dangers of pride and arrogance, faults which, if left uncorrected, could only hinder the stated goal of the conquest, the conversion and the moral reform of the Indians.

Solórzano himself of course did not accept the arguments against the legitimacy of the conquest of the Americas that he presented here, and he did not oppose the conquest of the new world. He was primarily interested in explaining to his readers the best arguments that could be made against it. Nevertheless, the arguments presented here provide a devastating attack on one fundamental premise of the conquest—the right, even the responsibility, of Christians to conquer infidel societies in order to eliminate practices that violated the natural law. In so doing, Solórzano undercut the foundations of Innocent IV's assertion that infidels were subject to papal jurisdiction by way of the natural law, so that a pope could authorize the conquest of the Americas. In a paradoxical way, the arguments that Solórzano presented in the *De indiarum iure* lead to the conclusion that the salvation of the Indians will occur only when infidels are removed from the jurisdiction of the law and are brought freely to the faith.

The significance of Solórzano's work has rarely been appreciated because it came too late to contribute to the great debate about the rights of the American Indians that marked the first five decades of the Spanish conquest of the Americas. Scholarly emphasis on the work of early critics of the Spanish conquest of the Americas has led to a corresponding neglect of later work dealing with the conquest. In addition, modern scholarly interest has focused on those who opposed the conquest; Solórzano supported it, making him less attractive to twentieth-century sensibilities.

The very existence of the *De indiarum iure* demonstrates, however, that the question of the conquest's legitimacy continued to trouble Spanish imperial officials almost a century after the great debate at Valladolid. The inability of those who participated in that debate to resolve all their doubts about the conquest's legitimacy did not mean that the issue no longer concerned Spanish thinkers and officials. Furthermore, Solórzano did not simply restate the traditional arguments for and against the legitimacy of the conquest. In the *De indiarum iure* he attempted to create a more broadly based theory of Christian relations with the infidel societies of the Americas based on the experience of the Spanish in the new world as well as on the traditional legal, philosophical, and theological arguments. At the same time, however, it is important to realize that his work did not itself lead directly to modern international law. Its importance lies in the attempt he made to link medieval legal theories about the rights of infidels and the responsibility of the Church to preach to all men with the immediate experience of the Spanish in the new world. He sought not to anticipate Hugo Grotius but to offer, so to speak, an alternative vision of Christian-infidel relations using traditional materials and reflecting the concerns of medieval missionaries. Grotius later employed many of the same materials but understood them in a quite different way.

IX

# THE CONQUEST OF THE AMERICAS

## THE SPANISH SEARCH FOR GLOBAL ORDER

DISCUSSION OF A CHRISTIAN GLOBAL ORDER appears comparatively late in Christian thought. Christians always took for granted the universal nature of Christ's message and obeyed His injunction to teach all nations. This did not, however, generate any formal theological or philosophical discussion of the nature of a Christian world order.

Indeed, because Christianity first emerged in conflict with the society around it, early Christians tended to think of the world as an arena within which believers battled unbelievers. Instead of seeing religion as a part of the overall social order, Christians often thought of their relation to the social order in terms of the conflict between Church and State. Conflict, not cooperation, was the usual Christian view of global order. Christians sought withdrawal from the world, not a role in shaping its direction.

Not until Christianity became a dominant force in European society during the Middle Ages did Christian thinkers begin to consider a positive role for Christianity in the global order. To the extent that medieval thinkers did consider the nature of a Christian world order, they often looked to an idealized Roman Empire. Since the pagans had created, if not a global order, then at least a structure, the Roman Empire, that included all the then-known civilized world, should not Christians be able to create a similar order based on the true faith? By 1200, the hope of creating a Christian world order based on the medieval Roman Empire was only a political fantasy indulged in by romantics. The rulers of the emerging national kingdoms within Europe had rejected any form of subordination to the Holy Roman Emperor other than granting him an honorific precedence (Ladner 1954). Lawyers began developing explanations of why territories once part of the ancient Roman Empire were no longer so (Post 1964: 453–482).

The development of these sovereign national kingdoms could lead inevitably to a kind of international anarchy. To counter such tendencies, a line of popes beginning in the mid-eleventh century began to assert papal headship of the increasingly politically Christian Europe. Although papal leadership in purely spiritual matters was never in dispute, the application of spiritual leadership to political situations was always a matter of debate, if not actual conflict. At the beginning of the thirteenth century, Pope Innocent III (1198–1216) attempted to reinforce the papal leadership role by advancing the policy of placing the pope at the heart of the several feudal hierarchies that formed the various national kingdoms of Europe. The policy of papal feudal overlordship went back to the eleventh century, but Innocent III was the first pope to employ it as a basis for a European Christian order. Innocent III's program for a European Christian order under papal leadership failed. Secular rulers rarely heeded papal calls for arbitration in political disputes unless it was clearly in their interest to do so. The everyday realities of medieval political life exceeded the papal power to do anything about them.

If the papacy was unable to impose its conception of order on Christian society, it should come as no surprise that it showed little interest in considering the nature of a global order. Such an order would require the papacy to deal with the schismatic Greeks at Constantinople, the Mongols who were assaulting north-eastern and central Europe, and the Moslems whose conquests bordered Christian Europe from the Middle East, along the North African coast and on into Spain. Beyond these immediate neighbors of Christian society were other, virtually unknown, infidel societies. Given the political situation in which medieval European Christians found themselves, it should be no surprise that they tended to conceive of relations with those beyond Europe in terms of the just war of defense.

During the mid-thirteenth century, however, there emerged a small indication of the way in which a Christian theory of global order might develop. In commenting upon a letter of Innocent III concerning the vows taken by crusaders, Pope Innocent IV (1243–1254) raised the question of the right by which the Church could authorize a war against the Moslems at all. Rather than focusing on the just war of defense as the keystone of a discussion of Christian-infidel relations, Innocent IV began by asserting the right of all men to organize societies and to govern themselves as they saw fit. As a consequence, Christians had no right to attack and seize the lands of non-believers simply because they were not Christians. In the case of the Holy Land, Christians could legitimately wage war to regain it because it was taken from its Christian inhabitants by the Moslems in an unjust war. Other lands that the Moslems occupied could not be seized because they were legitimately occupied by the Moslems. The same was true for other infidel societies as well. Social organization and government were the natural rights of all men and did not depend upon being in the state of grace (Muldoon 1979: 5–14).

To the extent that Innocent IV's argument supported the natural right of all societies to exist, presumably in peace, it provided a basis for determining how these societies could live together in some kind of harmony. He did not stop, however, however, at asserting the right of all societies to exist. He suggested a potential global order based on Christ's statement that He possessed other sheep not of this flock. Traditionally, the Christians were seen as Christ's flock with the pope acting as shepherd in the place of Christ. Christ's reference to His having other sheep meant to Innocent IV that those who were not members of the Church were nevertheless subject to the jurisdiction of Christ and therefore of His vicar, the pope. The consequence of this argument was that the pope had judicial authority over all men. He judged Christians according to Christian law, Jews according to Mosaic law and infidels according to the natural law (Muldoon 1979: 10–11).

Taking Innocent IV's arguments as a starting point, it would be possible to develop a theory of global order based on the papal obligation to judge all men according to the law that governed their behavior. Christian rulers would enforce papal decisions using armed force where moral suasion failed to achieve the goal of ending evil practices. The kind of order that this could engender would not be one with which modern western men would be comfortable. It would make European Christians the rulers of the entire world, at least in theory. Only those societies that lived according to the Christian conception of the natural law could live at peace with Christian societies. Infidel societies would exist at the sufferance of Christian society. The implications for Christian society itself are not all that comforting either. Innocent IV had no objection to employing the secular arm to repress heretics and schismatics, and he certainly did not see Jews and Moslems as full members of Christian states possessing and exercising the same rights as Christians. Innocent IV's conception of a global order is essentially a religious one.

In the long run, the most important contribution of Innocent IV to the development of a theory of global order acceptable in twentieth-century terms is his argument that all men have the right to organize and govern themselves as they see fit, subject to the principles of natural law. In a sense, his arguments echo Thomas Aquinas' (1970: 3–9) arguments about the natural right of men to organize and govern themselves, suggesting the extent to which natural law justifications for the social order were becoming widespread in the thirteenth century. Innocent IV's arguments were restated and employed by canonists and others for the next two centuries, but his ideas were not given further development and refinement. His assertion of the natural right of all men to govern themselves became the *communis opinio* among the canonists, gradually displacing the argument that *dominium*, the right to possess property and political power, was, since the birth of Christ, based on being in the state of grace. This would have meant of course that only Christians could legitimately possess land and power. If *dominium* depended upon being in the state of grace, then Christians, presumably being in the state of grace, could legitimately conquer the entire world and impose a Christian order on it (Muldoon 1979: 16–17). While Innocent IV did indicate that there were legitimate occasions when Christians could conquer infidel nations, he was clear that his theory was not a blanket invitation to world conquest and global order.

It was not until the sixteenth century that Christian thinkers began to consider the issue of political order on a global scale. The establishment of the Spanish overseas empire in the century following Columbus' voyages saw the parallel development of preliminary concepts of international order based on some kind of international law and also on the assumption that peaceful relations were possible between Christian and non-Christian societies. The fundamental reason for the development of these theories was that the peoples of the New World whom the Spanish were encountering did not fit the traditional mold that the theory of the just war provided for dealing with non-Christian societies. Unlike the Mongols and the Moslems who threatened medieval Europe, the inhabitants of the New World were at peace with Europeans, if only because they were separated from them by several thousand miles of ocean. For Europeans to deal with these people, it was first necessary that the Europeans sail overseas to encounter them. In those terms, if anyone was the aggressor, it was the European seaman who claimed possession of the New World for his king.

The Spanish discovery of the New World occurred in conjunction with what R. Trevor Davies ([1937] 1954: 280–284) has termed "The Golden Age of Spanish Scholasticism," the period in which Spanish intellectual life reached its peak and in which Spanish thinkers played a major role in shaping the European intellectual outlook. As a consequence, a great deal of attention was paid to the moral and legal implications of the discoveries. Furthermore, the imperial government was interested in justifying its control of the newly discovered lands. The result was what Lewis Hanke ([1949] 1965) termed *The Spanish Struggle for Justice in the Conquest of America*, an attempt to deal with the inhabitants of the New World justly, according to Christian teaching. While this struggle had a number of aspects, the basic issue was the nature of the relationship between the Spanish, Christian, Hapsburg Empire and the infidel societies of the Americas. Although the Spanish never claimed global domination, the territories over which they claimed jurisdiction certainly comprised the largest amount of territory ever ruled by a single ruler. As a result, Spanish thinkers were among the first to consider the problem of order on something approaching a global scale.

Two Spanish priests, the Dominican Francisco de Vitoria (1486–1546) and the Jesuit Francisco Suárez (1548–1617), were the pioneers of Spanish thinking on international law and relations. Numerous Spanish theologians, philosophers, and lawyers contributed to the effort in what became a major collaborative work that went on well into the seventeenth century. The work of these Spanish thinkers stands as a bridge between medieval thinkers, such as Innocent IV, and modern thinkers on international law, such as Hugo Grotius (1583–1645). The work of Vitoria and Suárez provided a foundation that enabled theorists to move from a medieval, religious basis for international law and relations to a modern, secular basis. In part, at least, the reason that Grotius's views on these issues were significantly different from the views of Innocent IV was that by the time the Dutch theorist was writing, he had the work of the Spanish thinkers to assist him in breaking from the narrow confines of medieval just-war thought and beginning the development of a broader basis on which to rest the relations among nations (Muldoon 1972).

Francisco de Vitoria began his discussion of global order with an analysis of the problems associated with the discovery and conquest of the New World. The question of the legitimacy of the conquest was important to the Spanish monarchs. For two centuries, Iberian rulers had engaged in the early stages of overseas exploration, sending ships down the coast of Africa, discovering the Atlantic Islands, and colonizing some of them, tasks that contributed to their ability to discover and colonize the Americas. This work was always done under papal license. Papal Bulls outlining Portuguese and Castilian responsibilities in the Atlantic Islands and along the coast of Africa go back to the fourteenth century. The papal letters outlined regions in which the Portuguese or the Castilians had responsibility for the conversion of the native population. Several popes had specified distinct spheres of spiritual jurisdiction for each kingdom, but because neither ruler could support missionary activity in the sphere of the other, these papal letters created not only areas of spiritual jurisdiction but of political and economic jurisdiction as well. The profits of these activities were to underwrite the cost of missionary activity.

The most famous of these papal bulls were those that Pope Alexander VI (1492–1503) issued following Columbus' first voyage. These bulls, subsequently modified, divided the newly explored regions of the Atlantic into Portuguese and Castilian spheres of missionary jurisdiction. The pope did not, as is often said inaccurately, simply arrogantly divide the world between the two Iberian powers, as if he had the right to deprive the infidels of their lands and power simply because they were infidels. Obviously he could not do that, and the Castilians and the Portuguese knew it very well. The pope as the universal shepherd, however, could authorize particular Christian rulers to support and maintain the work of missionaries and that is what Alexander VI's bulls accomplished (Muldoon 1978).

From the beginning the issue of the extent to which force could be used in pursuit of missionary goals arose. The theory of the just war was expanded to deal with these new situations. Under what, if any, circumstances could Christian rulers use troops in the course of fulfilling their responsibilities? During the first half-century of the conquest of the New World, the legitimacy of the work troubled a number of Spanish thinkers and public officials. In 1550, a conference was held under imperial sponsorship at Valladolid, at which both the defenders and the critics of the conquest were represented (Hanke [1949] 1965: 117–32).

The result of this conference was inconclusive, not because the government was uninterested in the moral and legal implications of the conquest but because the issues appeared to be so intractable. Although Vitoria was dead by the time that the Valladolid conference took place, and his discussion of the conquest of the New World did not appear in print until 1557, his ideas were well represented at the Valladolid conference through the presence of his students. As a result, Vitoria's ideas came to play a major role in the Spanish discussion of the legitimacy of the conquest and, in the long run, in the discussion of the possibility of a Christian global order.

The basis for Vitoria's ([1917] 1964) entire treatment of the Spanish presence in the Americas appeared at the beginning of his first *relectio*, an extended discussion, of what he termed the problem of the "Indians Lately Discovered." He opened the discussion with a line from the New Testament. "Teach all nations, baptizing them in the name of the Father and Son and Holy Spirit." (Matthew 28:19) This narrow statement of spiritual mission was the basis upon which Vitoria based his discussion of the Spanish occupation of the Americas.

The first question he posed sprang logically from this charge. Is it possible, he asked, that "the children of unbelievers may be baptized against the wishes of their parents...." (Vitoria [1917] 1964: 116) This issue then gave rise to a series of related questions: "By what right these Indian natives came under Spanish sway... What rights the Spanish sovereigns obtained over them in temporal and civil matters... What rights these sovereigns or the Church obtained over them in matters spiritual and touching religion...." In Vitoria's view, the presence of Spanish missionaries in the Americas could not be discussed without consideration of the political implications of that presence, as well as consideration of the spiritual responsibilties of the Church.

Furthermore, Vitoria's ([1917] 1964: 119) approach to the issue was more than theoretical. He was aware of the evils and injustices that the conquerors were inflicting on the Indians. Although he did not say so directly, the fundamental issue here was the issue of worldwide order. What were the implications for the political order of the Church's obligation to teach all men?

After considering a variety of arguments supporting the legitimacy of the conquest in this first discussion of the issues involved, Vitoria ([1917] 1964: 128) concluded that "the aborigines undoubtedly had true dominion in both public and private matters, just like Christians, and that neither their princes nor private persons could be despoiled of their property on the ground of their not being true owners." In terms of global order, this meant that non-Christians need not automatically fear conquest by Christians because Christians must recognize the legitimacy of infidel property and political rights. This conclusion would suggest the possibility of a global order consisting of autonomous societies that worked together in harmony based on their natural right to exist rather than on some religiously based principles.

The second of Vitoria's discussions of infidel rights dealt with the assertion that there was a single ruler who was at least *de jure* the lord of the world. If this argument was accepted, then there could exist a global order under a single ruler whose position would most likely rest on the ability of his armies to force those who rejected his claim to world domination to accept it by force. There were two traditional candidates for this role, the Holy Roman Emperor, in this case Vitoria's own sovereign, Charles I of Castile who was also the Holy Roman Emperor Charles V (1519–1555), and the pope.

Vitoria ([1917] 1964: 130–134) rejected all the arguments that lawyers and theologians had advanced in support of these claims. He admitted that Roman law did, in one place, describe the emperor as the *Dominus mundi*, the lord of the world, but he rejected that claim as being little more than a rhetorical flourish. In historical fact, as the Dominican pointed out, even when the Roman Empire reached its peak in the first century after Christ, it did not include all of the known world. The coming of Christ and the eventual Christianization of the Roman Empire made no difference (Vitoria [1917] 1964: 132).

Vitoria also gave short shrift to the claim that the pope was the *de jure* temporal head of mankind. Citing numerous authorities, including Pope Innocent IV, Vitoria pointed out that the pope had no right to claim such temporal power. Papal power was spiritual, not temporal. Vitoria ([1917] 1964: 146) was even skeptical of any papal claim to a kind of indirect power in temporal matters, denying Innocent IV's argument that the pope could order Christian secular rulers to punish infidels who violated the natural law. In this case, rather than following the opinion of Innocent IV, as he usually did, Vitoria looked to Thomas Aquinas for guidance. According to his thirteenth-century Dominican predecessor, "prelates have received power over those only who have submitted themselves to the faith." At this point, Vitoria appears to have had doubts about the possibility of knowing the natural law. This is not because the Indians were unintelligent but because of the inherent difficulties in knowing what it contained. In effect, Vitoria ([1917] 1964: 147) argued that natural law provided no basis for papal-based world order. If failure to accept Christianity did not justify conquering the Indians, their failure to understand the natural law did not either.

Vitoria's discussion of the conquest could lead one to conclude that the traditional arguments about conquest and the potential of those arguments for developing a theory of global relations were not relevant in the sixteenth century. The reader might well conclude that there was no basis for a global order, at least no just basis, only conquest. Vitoria did not, however, feel that way. Even though traditional arguments based on Roman imperial domination or on papal spiritual jurisdiction did not apply, Vitoria was able to develop other approaches to the issue, approaches that were more in line with the actual development of a world society, if not world order, approaches that were essentially secular in nature.

Having recognized the right of infidels to possess property and political power and having denied the existence of any papal right to order the punishment of those who violated the natural law, Vitoria went on to demonstrate a basis for armed Christian intervention in infidel societies. This argument was founded on a conception of world order. Christians and infidels alike possess a natural right to travel freely throughout the world, a right founded in "natural society and fellowship." As a result, the "Spanish have a right to travel in the lands in question [i.e. the Americas] and to sojourn there, provided they do no harm to the natives, and the natives may not prevent them." This right to travel freely is founded in "the law of nations (*jus gentium*), which either is natural law or is derived from natural law..." (Vitoria [1917] 1964: 151). Interestingly enough, the first example of this right to travel that Vitoria ([1917] 1964: 152) gave was not the obvious case of Christian missionaries. He pointed instead to the right of merchants to travel.

Should the Indians fail to act peacefully toward the Spanish merchants and travelers who have come to the New World, then, and only then, did the Spanish have the right to resort to defensive force in order to protect them. Resort to arms should be the last resort. If "reason and persuasion" fail to move the natives, argued Vitoria ([1917] 1964: 154) and if "the barbarians decline to agree and propose to use force, the Spaniards can defend themselves and do all that consists with their own safety...."

Only after determining the existence of a right to travel freely for the purpose of trade did Vitoria ([1917] 1964: 157) consider the situation of the Christian missionary. The answer to the question of the missionary's right to travel precisely paralleled the answer given in the case of the merchant.

> If the Indians...prevent the Spaniards from freely preaching the Gospel, the Spaniards, after first reasoning with them in order to remove scandal, may preach it despite their unwillingness and devote themselves to the conversion of the people in question, and if need be they may then accept or even make war, until they succeed in obtaining facilities and safety for preaching the Gospel.

In the final analysis, Vitoria provided some justifications for the Spanish domination of the New World, but these justifications were not the traditional religious ones. He seems to reveal a good deal of skepticism about arguments based on natural law, even though the justification that he does employ, the right to travel freely throughout the world, is rooted in the natural law by way of the *jus gentium*. Perhaps the difference is that while the natural law is an abstract concept, the law of nations dealing as it does with what men actually do, is evidence of widespread acceptance of a right to travel in peace. Within the Europe of Vitoria's time, the right to travel freely was widely accepted. Thousands of people went on religious pilgrimages each year. As far back as the thirteenth century, the Magna Carta contained a clause, chapter 41, that expressly protected foreign merchants travelling in England, indicating the importance of the right to peaceful travel (*Magna Carta* 1972: 179). If one combines Vitoria's views about the right of all men to self-government with his views about the right to travel freely and his opinion about "the natural society and fellowship" that characterized mankind, one would have some of the basic elements needed to construct a theory of global order. Such a global order would, however, be based on natural premises, not on religious or spiritual ones.

As Vitoria dominated Spanish thought on the problem of international law in the first half of the sixteenth century, so Suárez dominated it during the last half of that century and on into the seventeenth century. Suárez's work was founded on the work of Vitoria. At the same time, Suárez was also forced to consider some new aspects of international relations that his predecessor did not have to treat. One result of the changed circumstances of the world within which the Jesuit lived was that he had to consider the nature of relations between Catholic states and Protestant states, as well as to consider the older problem of relations between Catholic and infidel states. The problem of Catholic-Protestant relations had been only beginning when Vitoria died, but by the end of the century this issue became crucial to any Catholic theory of international order.

The permanent establishment of Protestant states posed a new problem for Catholic thinkers on international relations because, as heretics, Protestants were, according to canon law, subject to ecclesiastical punishment. In the sixteenth century, popes had ordered Protestant rulers deposed and released their Christian subjects from obedience to them. In 1570, for example, Pope Pius V (Bettenson 1963: 339) issued the bull *Regnans in excelsi*, declaring "we deprive the said Elizabeth of her pretended right to the realm [of England]...and we enjoin and forbid all and several the nobles etc....that they presume not to obey her and her admonitions, commands, and laws." This letter did not lead to the deposition of Queen Elizabeth I (1558–1603). Indeed it did not even lead to any significant opposition, Catholics even being very active in opposing the Spanish Armada in 1588. Nevertheless Pius V's bull posed a serious problem for Catholics and Protestants interested in the European political order (Allen [1928] 1960: 106). Could Catholics be loyal subjects of a Protestant ruler and could Protestants assure Catholic rulers that they would be loyal in spite of religious differences?

Suárez came to the issue of Catholic-Protestant relations by way of a work that Elizabeth I's successor, James I (1603–1625), published in 1609. His *Apologie for the Oath of Allegiance* as a defense of the legal requirement that all the English king's subjects take an oath of allegiance that included the words (Suárez [1944] 1964: v. 2, 705):

> I do further swear that I do from my heart abhor, detest and abjure, as impious and heretical, this [damnable] doctrine and position; that princes which be excommunicated or deprived by the pope, may be deposed or murdered by their subjects or any other whatsoever.

The *Apologie* required a Catholic response; and in 1613 Suárez published one, *A Defence of the Catholic and Apostolic Faith*, that dealt with, among other points, the issue of papal claims to supremacy over secular rulers. In a larger sense, Suárez dealt with the issue of whether a Christian secular ruler was or could be completely free of all subordination to the pope in temporal matters. Under this heading he considered the question of whether the pope was supreme in temporal affairs.

Suárez ([1944] 1964: v. 2, 669) began his discussion with the observation that some defenders of papal power, especially priests, had claimed that "in the whole Catholic Church there exists but one supreme temporal prince, who holds, *per se* and directly, supreme civil power over the entire Church; and that this supreme prince is the pope...." After discussing the basis for this assertion, Suárez ([1944] 1964: v. 2, 671) concluded "that Christian kings do possess supreme civil power within their own order" and they recognize "no other person...as a direct superior...." The consequence was that "there exists within the Church no one supreme temporal prince over that whole body, that is to say, over all the kingdoms of the Church...."

Having disposed of the notion that there was a supreme temporal ruler over all the Christian rulers of Europe, neither the pope nor the Holy Roman Emperor being able to claim such jurisdiction, Suárez went on to discuss the power of the pope to intervene in the operation of a kingdom even though he was not the temporal overlord of that kingdom. James I of England had criticized the papacy on this very issue, according to Suárez ([1944] 1964: v. 2, 685). If James I had his way, the pope would be deprived "of every remedy against heretical princes," a theory that Suárez associated with the thirteenth-century Italian political thinker, Marsilius of Padua (d.1343), whose *Defensor Pacis* was a wholesale attack on the theory that the Church could intervene in the secular order under any circumstances. Could there be a stable international order within Europe if the pope could legitimately call upon the Catholic subjects of Protestant rulers to rebel and to replace their heretical rulers with orthodox ones? The crucial issue for Suárez was not the papal right to declare a ruler a heretic. That was what Suárez termed "directive power." The dangerous part was the pope's claim to possess "coercive power," that is the power to impose sanctions, even calling for rebellion, in order to implement his "directive power."

Defining a ruler as a heretic, a spiritual matter clearly within the papal sphere of jurisdiction, obviously had important ramifications in the temporal order. As the Suárez ([1944] 1964: v. 2, 685) saw things, the pope did possess "coercive power over temporal princes who are incorrigibly wicked, and especially over schismatics and stubborn heretics," because without "this coercive weapon...directive force is inefficacious...." Suárez ([1944] 1964: v. 2, 689) went on to point out that throughout the history of the Church "the popes have certainly made frequent use of the said form of censure when opposing emperors and kings." As Suárez ([1944] 1964: v. 2, 699–700) saw matters, the papacy had an especially strong reason for insisting upon the right to employ coercive power against secular rulers when their actions warrant it.

He argued that: "The sins of princes—especially those sins which are opposed to the faith and to religion—are more pernicious [than the sins of other Christians]; for princes easily lead their subjects to imitate them, whether by their [bare] example, or by favors and promises, or even by threats and intimidation." The role of the pope then was to defend the subjects of "a bad king, and especially one who is schismatic and heretical" because such a ruler "places his subjects in grave danger of perdition...." Suárez ([1944] 1964: v. 2, 701) was careful to point out that "the pope has not power to punish an un-baptized and heathen king for infidelity or other sins," but, as in the case of a heretical or schismatic ruler, the pope could free such a ruler's Christian subjects "from their subjection to their ruler, on the ground that they are in evident peril of moral destruction."

So far, then, Suárez's views did not bode well for a religiously divided Europe. Ironically, his arguments would hold more promise for Christian-infidel relations than for the relations between Catholic and Protestant powers. As long as the pope claimed the right to order Catholic subjects of Protestant kings to rebel, there was no serious possibility of peaceful, orderly international relations within Christian Europe.

Turning finally to the specific oath that James I required of his subjects, Suárez ([1944] 1964: v. 2, 725) concluded that the oath was a wrongful assertion of the temporal power's superiority over the spiritual realm. In the first place, he argued, it is wrong to assert, as the oath does, "that the pope is not endowed with power to depose a heretical or schismatic king who is dragging or perverting his kingdom to the point where it will embrace the same schism or heresy." In the final analysis:

> ...it is implicit in the very substance of the oath...that a temporal king may even exact of his subjects a sworn belief in regard to those matters having to do with the doctrines of the faith and with the renunciation of heresies.... And all this is surely equivalent to declaring that a temporal king holds primacy in spiritual—or ecclesiastical—affairs.

In Suárez's terms, James I of England has simply arrogated to himself and other secular rulers the power to intervene in spiritual matters while condemning the pope for asserting the right to intervene in secular matters, thus turning the papal view of the right order of things upside down. From the perspective of international order, however, James I's position had much to commend it. If the secular ruler is to be the ultimate judge of religious matters within his own kingdom, then an internal order would exist within a kingdom. On the basis of this internal order an international order of sovereign nations could be erected without reference to religious belief. Just as the principle of *cuius regio eius religio* became the solution to the religious struggle within the Holy Roman Empire, allowing each principality's ruler to determine the religion of that constituent element of the Empire, thus ending the religious wars that had nearly destroyed Germany, an international order could be erected on the principle of *cuius regio eius religio* as well. The German rulers within the Empire were to ignore the pope when they agreed on the principle of *cuius regio eius religio* in the Peace of Westphalia (1648), and James I was already suggesting the possibility of creating an international order without the pope (Randle 1973: 379–92).

In this way, Protestant rulers could negotiate with Catholic rulers safe in the knowledge that the Catholics of their own kingdoms would not be ordered to rebel against them; and Catholic rulers could be assured that their Protestant subjects would not be encouraged to rebel either. As Suárez may well have recognized, what James I and his fellow monarchs were actually doing was to make religion a matter of personal devotion, subject to the needs of public order as determined by the ruler (Allen [1928] 1960: 292–96). If this could be done at the national level, there is, theoretically, no reason to doubt that it could work on the international level. This view of religion as a private matter subject to governmental limitation was contrary to the teachings of the Catholic Church and to most Protestant denominations as well. It was, however, a view of the place of religion in the public order that developed from the bitter experience of the religious wars that accompanied the Reformation.

In other writings, those dealing with the conquest of the Americas, Suárez considered in greater detail the possibility of peaceful relations between Catholic and infidels. He discussed this issue in a series of lectures on the theological virtues of faith, hope, and charity, giving an indication of where his priorities lay. While these lectures had been presented in the classroom over the years, they appeared in print only in 1621 and so they contained the most complete discussion of the nature of Christian-infidel relations in Suárez's work. One of Suárez's ([1944] 1964: v. 2, 739) lectures was devoted to the topic: "On the means which may be used for the conversion and coercion of unbelievers who are not apostates." Under this heading, he began with a consideration of the Church's claim to possess the right to preach everywhere without hindrance. On this point, reasonably enough, Suárez ([1944] 1964: v. 2, 740) concluded "that the Church has that power by which it may legitimately preach the Catholic faith everywhere and to all kinds of unbelievers."

In terms of international relations, of course, the central issue was not the right of the Church to preach, but, rather, the Church's right to employ force in the implementation of that right. Following Vitoria and others, Suárez ([1944] 1964: v. 2, 742) argued that "the Church has the right of defending its preachers, and of subduing those who by force and violence hinder or do not permit this preaching." Suárez supported this conclusion with a variety of arguments, some of which gave a slightly different twist to old arguments.

For example, one argument he employed to justify the use of troops where a ruler sought to prevent the entrance of missionaries was similar to an argument he had used to justify the use of force against Protestant rulers. In both cases he argued that a ruler who did not allow Catholic missionaries to enter his kingdom was doing an injury to his subjects and the Church therefore had a right to employ force to protect such a ruler's subjects from this kind of injury as well as to protect the right of its missionaries to preach freely. A ruler who prevented the entry of preachers "does the gravest injury to many who perchance might have been converted if they had heard" the Gospel (Suárez [1944] 1964: v. 2, 743).

Thus, the use of force is defensive in a twofold sense. It defends the Church's right to preach and the subjects' right to hear the Gospel. The second line of argument that Suárez employed to support his argument about the use of force involved comparing missionaries to ambassadors. As temporal governments have the "right of protecting...ambassadors and of avenging an injury if they are ill-treated," so, too, the Church has "this right with respect to her own ambassadors who are the preachers of the faith...."

Having demonstrated the Church's right to use force in the defense of missionaries and of potential converts, Suárez then turned to the question of who can exercise this right and under what circumstances. He concluded, reasonably enough, that the pope alone has the responsibility of defending the "universal rights of the church." No secular prince has the right to act in these situations without papal approval because this is a spiritual matter not a temporal one. Secular rulers would be required for the actual exercise of force in these cases because the Church is not allowed to use force. Again following Vitoria and his predecessors, Suárez ([1944] 1964: v. 2, 746) added that "the pope can distribute among temporal princes and kings the provinces and realms of the unbelievers...in order that they may make provision for the sending of preachers of the Gospel to those infidels, and may protect such preachers by their power, even through the declaration of just war, if reason and a rightful cause should require it." Furthermore, the pope has the power to "mark off specific boundaries for each prince" as did "Alexander VI in the case of the kings of Portugal and of Castile." In this way, the potential converts would in effect bear the cost of their own conversion.

In Suárez's ([1944] 1964: v. 2, 747) opinion, the purpose for papal demarcation of areas of missionary activity was to insure that the missionary efforts "should be conducted in an orderly manner" while also insuring that "peace among Christian princes" was maintained and that "the welfare of the people committed" to each ruler's care was assured. In this stage of the argument, Suárez provided some basis for a theory of global order under papal direction, an order resting on religious motives and European armies.

In connection with the problem of defending the right of the Church to protect the preachers of the Gospel and the right of subjects to hear that preaching, Suárez had assumed in the case he had previously used that the ruler and his subjects were at odds on the issue. What if the ruler and his subjects were agreed in their opposition to Christian missionaries, could the Church still insist upon its right to use arms to insure their admission and their safety? In responding to this point, a point of some significance in the modern world where rulers are elected and, therefore, presumably reflect their constituents' views, Suárez ([1944] 1964: v. 2, 756) returned to the right of travel provided by the *ius gentium*: "...I think that they may be forced to permit the preachers of the Gospel to live in their territories; for this tolerance is obligatory under the *ius gentium* and cannot be impeded without just cause." At this point, Suárez appears to have been echoing Vitoria's discussion of the natural human community that included all men who thus have the right to travel everywhere in peace and security. The right to preach the Gospel becomes, in this case, an application of this natural right.

In another part of these lectures, Suárez dealt with the argument that the pope has the right to act as universal judge, specifically raising the issue of whether the pope has the right to order the destruction of idols. The Spanish Jesuit noted here that it was important to distinguish between what the rulers of Christian kingdoms should do within their own kingdoms and what they should do regarding idols worshipped by those who were not subject to them in temporal matters. Within his own kingdom, a Christian ruler has the right, even the obligation, to eliminate pagan rites if they are contrary to natural reason. According to Suárez ([1944] 1964: 769) infidels who are not subject to Christian rulers, however, "cannot normally be forced to change their errors and their rites" because "the Church has no jurisdiction over the unbelievers in question, and that coercion or punishment without jurisdiction is unjust." As a result (Suárez [1944] 1964: v. 2, 769–70), "an infidel state, supreme in its own order," cannot "be punished by the Church on account of its crimes, even if those crimes are contrary to natural reason; and consequently, it may not be compelled to give up idolatry or similar rites."

Suárez ([1944] 1964: v. 2, 780–81) did consider one case in which an infidel ruler could be deprived of his office by the Church. This situation, an example used in similar discussions reaching back to the thirteenth century, involved a ruler whose subjects had become Christians while he remained an infidel. In such circumstances "the Church may indirectly deprive" the non-Christian ruler of his power over his Christian subjects "if the welfare or defence of the latter makes this necessary." Here again, the argument for papal intervention rested upon the Church's right to defend its members, rights, and interests everywhere. If it could protect the Christian subjects of Christian rulers from the tyrannical actions of such rulers, the Church could certainly protect its members who were the subjects of an infidel ruler who was acting against their spiritual interests.

At the same time, Suárez did not encourage rebellion or invasion under such circumstances. He advised the Christian subjects of a wicked infidel ruler to "change their domicile and pass over to the realm of Christian princes." If their infidel ruler "attempts to prevent his Christian subjects from thus transferring their domicile, he may be forcibly resisted by Christian princes, and justly subdued in war in defence of these subjects, because they are being deprived of their right which they wish to exercise," that is the right to travel freely from one place to another. Yet again, what might appear to others as a form of Christian aggression against an infidel ruler is, according to Suárez, simply another example of the just war of defense.

Finally, and only briefly, Suárez considered the nature of relations that should exist between Christians and non-Christians. The bulk of this discussion dealt with the nature of such relations when non-Christians lived within a Christian society and under a Christian ruler. Virtually all of Suárez's ([1944] 1964: v. 2, 787–95) discussion considered Christian-Jewish relations, an issue long-debated in Spain. The theme of this brief discussion was that Christians were to be careful in their intercourse with non-believers lest their faith be undermined. At this point, Suárez might have gone on to consider such relations on the international level, but he did not.

The death of Suárez coincided with the beginning of the end for Hapsburg and Spanish power. In the year following his death, the Thirty Years War (1618–1648) began. By the end of the war, the Spanish Hapsburgs were bankrupt; and the Austrian Hapsburgs retained the imperial title but at the price of seeing it reduced to a shell of itself (Holborn 1959: 361–74). Furthermore, the Catholic Church, having been battered by the Reformation, withdrew into itself, condemning the modern world but having nothing with which to replace it except, perhaps, a return to an idealized and romanticized Middle Ages.

As late as the nineteenth century, Pope Pius IX could issue the *Syllabus of Errors* ([1864] 1954: 282–85) in which he catalogued all the intellectual and moral evils of the modern western world. Even when Leo XIII began to engage the Church with the modern world and its distinctive problems, he could only do so through a medieval prism. He not only began to consider social issues in *Rerum Novarum*, but he had also earlier issued *Aeterni Patris* ([1879] 1981: 187). In that letter, Leo XIII stated that among "the scholastic doctors, the chief and master of all, towers Thomas Aquinas" who "is rightly esteemed the special bulwark and glory of the Catholic Faith." The work of Vitoria, Suárez, and their colleagues simply fell into disuse in Catholic circles after the Thomist revival of the twentieth century. As a consequence, the only Catholic thinkers who tried to come to grips with the problem of global order in the modern world have been neglected in Catholic philosophical work.

The value of Vitoria and Suárez in the task of developing an intellectual basis for a concept of world order was rediscovered in the twentieth century by James Brown Scott, a Protestant lawyer who was active in the Carnegie Endowment for International Peace's campaign for world peace through world law (Muldoon 1972: 486–490). Scott encouraged the publication of a series of works on the origins of international law which included selections from the writings of Vitoria and Suárez which, he argued, were important building blocks for the subsequent, and more highly regarded, work of Grotius and his successors. The list of authors in the series, *Classics of International Law*, illustrated one of James Brown Scott's major points, namely that while Catholic writers began the development of modern international law, the work was later taken over and transformed into modern international law as a result of the Protestant thinkers who were more capable of dealing with the modern world.

James Brown Scott's conclusions about Catholic thinking on the issues of international law and relations bring us to the end of this discussion of sixteenth-century Catholic thinking on these issues. On the basis of the discussion presented here, what can be said about the contribution of Catholic thought to the issue of global order? My conclusion is pessimism about such a contribution unless there are some significant developments in Catholic social and political thought. Any modern liberal theory of global order must be based on an acceptance of the pluralistic nature of the modern world and an acceptance of differing views of the moral basis of society. No one really believes that every single form of social behavior can or must be accepted and tolerated. One would have to be morally invertebrate, not liberal, to tolerate human sacrifice or *suttee*. It is also hard to believe that even the most liberal westerners would really accept polygamy or child marriage. The issue is not absolute toleration but, as the medieval writers made clear, the degree of toleration to be exercised. In practice, modern men tend to believe in a kind of modified law of nations, what people generally do, rather than in an abstract law of nature, a fixed notion of what they ought to do, something they have in common with the Spanish international writers of the sixteenth and seventeenth centuries.

Catholic thought, based on Aquinas's teachings, still rests on the natural law basis of order. In the modern, pluralistic world this means that Catholic thought is often at odds with contemporary values. In itself, that is certainly not a bad thing. The difficulty arises when Catholics seek to participate in pluralistic societies. To what degree can they participate and to what degree must they withdraw from participation? In the contemporary world, this often presents dilemmas for many American Catholics. On the one hand, for example, their bishops recently issued a pastoral letter very critical of nuclear arms. On the other hand, the bishops have also taken a strong anti-abortion position. What is the voter to do when faced with a choice between a candidate who supports legal abortion and opposes nuclear arms and a candidate who takes the opposite positions? As the political position of President Reagan demonstrated, this is a real and immediate dilemma, not some neo-scholastic *reductio ad absurdum*. Modern pluralistic societies present these dilemmas all of the time. If this sort of dilemma exists on the national level, what greater possibilities for such dilemmas must exist at the international level. At the moment, Catholic thinking does not provide any but the most general contribution to the development of global order. It does, however, provide a number of dilemmas.

If Catholic thinkers wish to contribute to the debate within a pluralistic world about global order, about nuclear weapons, about the economy, and about issues such as abortion, they will have to go beyond the work of Aquinas. This is not to denigrate Aquinas. He was indeed the greatest and most inclusive of Catholic thinkers, but his thought reflected the circumstances of his own world. Later figures, like Vitoria and Suárez, began the task of developing Aquinas's principles to meet new circumstances. If Catholic thinkers wish to deal with contemporary problems within a Catholic tradition, they should at least consider beginning with Aquinas but then moving on through the critics of Aquinas and to the sixteenth-century continuators of the Thomistic tradition. Vitoria and Suárez did, after all, begin to wrestle with the problem of co-existence with infidel societies, one of the fundamental issues involved in the development of the modern pluralistic global order.

If there is to be a reconsideration of Catholic thought on global order, indeed reconsideration of global order from virtually any perspective, there can be no better time than the present. The forthcoming celebration of the five hundredth anniversary of Christopher Columbus' first voyage will soon be upon us. Although medieval writers had begun the discussion of the nature of a global order in a rudimentary fashion, the issue had little practical significance until Columbus' voyages made the New World a part of the European consciousness. Once he had encountered the inhabitants of the Caribbean islands, Columbus began the discussion of global order. How were these people to be treated? Were they valid possessors of the lands that they inhabited? Was it the moral responsibility of the Spanish to baptize and Christianize these people? If so, could or should force be used to protect the missionaries who went to preach to the Indians? Did European Christians have an obligation to stop practices that violated the natural law? Was the conquest of the Americas justified in order to stop cannibalism and human sacrifice?

All of these questions touching upon the relations between the Christian Old World and the pagan New World emerged within a few years of Columbus' voyages. In addition to all the other consequences of Columbus' voyages, economic, social, political, biological, as Lewis Hanke ([1949] 1965: 1) pointed out, the conquest of the Americas also gave rise to "one of the greatest attempts the world has seen to make Christian precepts prevail in the relations between peoples."

There will be a number of commemorations of Columbus' first voyage in the next several years. There will be parades of tall ships, re-creations of Columbus' landing on one or another Caribbean island, and other such activities. For religious organizations, a fitting commemoration would be serious consideration of the moral consequences of that voyage and their implications for the contemporary world.

## References

Allen, J.W. [1928] 1960. *A History of Political Thought in the Sixteenth Century*. London and New York: Metheun and Barnes & Noble.

Aquinas, Thomas. 1970. *Aquinas: Selected Political Writings*, edited by A.P. D'Entreves. Oxford: B. Blackwell.

Bettenson, Henry (ed.). 1963. *Documents of the Christian Church*. 2nd ed. London: Oxford University Press.

Davies, R. Trevor. [1937] 1954. *The Golden Age of Spain*. London: Macmillan.

Hanke, Lewis. [1949] 1965. *The Spanish Struggle for Justice in the Conquest of America*. Boston: Little, Brown.

Holborn, Hajo. 1959. *A History of Modern Germany: The Reformation*. New York: Knopf.

Holt, James C. (ed.). 1972. *Magna Carta and the Idea of Liberty*. New York: John Wiley.

James, I. 1918. "Apologie." 71–109 in *The Political Works*, edited by C.H. McIlwain. Cambridge: Harvard University Press.

Ladner, G.B. 1954. "The Concepts of 'Ecclesia' and 'Christianitas' and Their Relation to the Idea of Papal 'Plenitudo Potestatis' from Gregory VII to Boniface VIII." *Mescellanea Historiae Pontificiae* 18:49–77.

Leo XIII. [1879] 1981. "Aeterni Patris." In *One Hundred Years of Thomism: Aeterni Patris and Afterwards*, edited by Victor B. Brezik, C.S.B. Houston: Center for Thomistic Studies.

Muldoon, James. 1972. "The Contribution of the Medieval Canon Lawyers to the Formation of International Law." *Traditio* 28:483–97.

_____. 1978. "Papal Responsibility for the Infidel: Another Look at Alexander VI's *Inter Caetera*." *Catholic Historical Review* 64:168–84.

_____. 1979. *Popes, Lawyers, and Infidels: The Church and the Non-Christian World, 1250–1550*. Philadelphia: University of Pennsylvania Press.

Pius IX. [1864] 1954. "Syllabus of Errors." In *Church and State Through the Centuries*, edited by S.Z. Ehler and J.B. Morrall. London: Burns & Oates.

Post, Gaines. 1964. *Studies in Medieval Legal Thought: Public Law and the State, 1100–1322*. Princeton: Princeton University Press.

Randle, Robert F. 1973. *The Origins of Peace*. New York: Free Press.

Suárez, Francisco. [1944] 1964. *Selections from Three Works*, edited by Gladys L. Williams, Ammi Brown, and John Waldron. New York: Oceana.

Victoria (Vitoria), Franciscus de. [1917] 1964. *De Indis et de Ivre Reflectiones*, edited by Ernest Nys. New York: Oceana.

# X

# Spiritual Conquests Compared: *Laudabiliter* and the Conquest of the Americas

POPE Adrian IV's bull *Laudabiliter* (1155) authorizing King Henry II of England to invade Ireland has played a significant role in the scholarly and political debates about the legitimacy of the English conquest of the Irish. While the bull's authenticity is now generally accepted, such was not always the case.[1] Debate has also centered on the right of the pope to grant Ireland, or any other country, to a Christian ruler. In the case of Ireland, there is also the question of whether or not the pope was accurately informed about conditions in Ireland by the representatives of Henry II who sought Adrian's approval for the invasion. In the early fourteenth century, a group of Irish chieftains even addressed a letter to Pope John XXII (1316-1334) in an attempt to explain to this successor of Adrian IV that Henry's representatives "made false and wicked representation" to the papal court so that the English pope, Adrian IV, "did, in fact, but unfairly, confer upon that same Henry" lordship of Ireland.[2]

For the most part, polemicists and scholars have discussed *Laudabiliter* only in terms of relations between England and Ireland. There has been less interest in the wider significance of Adrian's letter, in its relationship to other papal documents dealing with the conquest of nations that the papacy deemed in need of Christianizing or of reforming. A few scholars have suggested that Adrian's bull did have some significance beyond its role in English relations with the Irish, but no one has as yet followed up on those suggestions in order to determine how *Laudabiliter* fitted into the overall scheme of Christian European overseas expansion.

In 1949, however, a Mexican scholar, Luis Weckmann, suggested that *Laudabiliter* was more than an isolated example of the papal abuse of power. He suggested that it was but one in a line of papal bulls authorizing the conquest of islands by Christian rulers that stretched back to the eleventh century and that culminated in the fifteenth and sixteenth centuries when various popes authorized the Portuguese and the Castilians to occupy parts of Africa and the Americas in order to spread Christianity.[3] According to Weckmann, there were seventeen bulls, the most famous of which were the three bulls that Alexander VI issued in 1493 following the voyages of Columbus, that contained what he termed the "omni-insular doctrine," the theory that the pope had suzerainty over all islands. He argued that this doctrine was rooted in a phrase found in the Donation of Constantine which granted the pope control of all the islands in the West. The first use of this power, according to Weckmann, came in 1051 when Pope Leo IX issued the bull *Convenit* which concerned the disposition of a small island, Gorgona, a few miles off of the Tuscan coast. Twelve such bulls appeared before Alexander VI issued his three bulls a few months after Columbus returned home. The purpose of these bulls was not to divide up the world into Portuguese and Castilian spheres of influence, as some modern writers have stated, but to end the long series of border wars that the two kingdoms had been fighting throughout the fifteenth century by regulating access to the New World and to insure the spread of Christianity in these newly discovered regions under the sponsorship and protection of these Christian rulers. Two subsequent bulls, Julius II's *Ea quae* (1505) and Leo X's *Precelse devotionis* (1514), completed Weckmann's list.[4]

The list of papal bulls concerning the disposition of islands includes two letters concerning Ireland, *Laudabiliter* and Alexander III's *Quoniam ea,* one of three bulls that pope issued in 1172 following Henry II's visit to Ireland. According to Weckmann's schema the English conquest of Ireland fitted into a larger pattern of papal claims to power over secular rulers and, to some extent at least, the papal role in the conquest provided a model for subsequent papal involvement in European overseas expansion. Seen in this light, *Laudabiliter* was also clearly a significant part of the papal policy of aggrandizing itself at the expense of secular rulers by asserting suzerainty over them in a variety of ways.

Weckmann's argument is an attractive one in several ways. In the first place, it links a number of papal documents, issued over several centuries, into a coherent chain that underscores the methods used to create the powerful papal monarchy of the twelfth and thirteenth centuries. Furthermore, Weckmann has linked the conquest and conversion of the New World to the conquest and conversion of the Old World, thus emphasizing the traditional nature of the work in which Columbus, Ferdinand of Aragon, Isabella of Castile and Alexander VI were engaged. Finally, this line of argument specifically connects the English conquest of Ireland to the growth of papal power.

On the other hand, there is a good deal that can be said against Weckmann's argument. The first point to be made is that only two of the papal letters he discusses actually mention the Donation of Constantine. The others only refer to the disposition of islands, a phrase that he has taken as a reference to the Donation. A few phrases common to a handful of papal letters written over a span of five centuries are not enough to demonstrate a consistent, conscious policy based on a document, the Donation, that is not mentioned in most of the bulls.[5] Furthermore, modern scholars have demonstrated how rarely the Donation was employed by the medieval papacy to justify its activities.[6] While it is true that some Catholic scholars sought to demonstrate the authenticity of the Donation as late as the sixteenth century, popes rarely cited it.[7] From the eleventh century onward, the popes sought to exercise power over secular rulers by accepting kingdoms as fiefs and then granting them back to their rulers. Curiously enough, Leo IX, the pope who, according to Weckmann, was the first to exercise the "omni-insular doctrine," was the initiator of this policy when he received the submission of the Norman conquerors of southern Italy who sought to legitimize their holdings. Eventually most of the European kingdoms became papal fiefs so that by the beginning of the thirteenth century, an aggressive pope, such as Innocent III (1198-1216), could use his feudal overlordship to intervene in the political arena in such diverse areas as Naples and England.[8] He did not need the vague powers outlined in the Donation when he had feudal agreements in hand. Weckmann's argument, then, is too narrowly based to be convincing.

Yet, although the evidence that Weckmann presented to suppport his argument will not bear the weight of the edifice he has constructed upon it, he did make an important point about Alexander VI's famous bulls, namely, that they were derived from a long-standing papal policy and were not based on newly created arguments to justify the conquest of the Americas. Furthermore, he recognized that the claims contained in *Laudabiliter* were similar to those employed in the defense of the Spanish conquest of the Americas. Furthermore, Weckmann does not appear to have been aware of the use made of *Laudabiliter* in the sixteenth and seventeenth centuries by Catholic writers anxious to defend the papacy against the Protestants. Indeed, in these later centuries, Adrian IV's bull played a role in intellectual life that it had never had played before as both defenders of papal power and defenders of the Spanish conquest of the Americas sought historical evidence to support their positions.

A convenient way to see the role of *Laudabiliter* in the sixteenth and seventeenth centuries is to see how one defender of the Spanish conquest of the Americas employed it. In 1629, Juan de Solorzano y Pereira, a Spanish lawyer and imperial official, issued the first volume of a two volume defense of the conquest. His *Disputatio de Indiarum jure* was a massive survey of the theological, philosophical, legal, historical, and anthropological information that had emerged in the course of what Lewis Hanke has labeled *The Spanish Struggle for Justice in the Conquest of America.*[9] Solorzano discussed *Laudabiliter* in the second book of his first volume, in a chapter entitled "Concerning the temporal power of the Holy See. . . ." The purpose of the chapter was to bring to the reader's attention the fact that the powers asserted by Alexander VI in 1493 were not novel and had been exercised by various popes over the preceding centuries. Solorzano first discussed Alexander VI's bulls concerning the New World and then moved to a discussion of precedents for such action. He cited *Laudabiliter* and a bull of Calixtus III (1455-1458), *Dudum siquidem,* as precedents for the bulls of 1493.[10] Adrian IV's bull demonstrated that the pope had the right, indeed the obligation, to insure the preaching of the Christian faith everywhere, even over the opposition of local rulers. Calixtus III's bull demonstrated that the popes had long been active in resolving the disputes that had arisen between the Castillians and the Portuguese as these nations ventured further out into the Atlantic.

Solorzano's understanding of *Laudabiliter* grew out of the polemics of the contemporary religious wars. He obtained the text of the bull from Cardinal Baronius' *Annales Ecclesiastici* and published it in the course of his discussion.[11] On the other hand, he said nothing about the circumstances that gave rise to the bull. In his eyes, the first point to make about *Laudabiliter* was that it demonstrated the pope's power to grant control over a people to a Christian ruler and, in the second place, that the bull demonstrated the recognition of this power by Christian rulers, such as Henry II. Furthermore, he argued that the English had long paid an annual fee to the papacy in recognition that they held Ireland as a fief from the pope. Henry II and his successors were therefore the pope's vassals for Ireland. This argument led to the conclusion that Alexander VI exercised the same powers that Adrian IV had exercised and so Ferdinand and Isabella were lawful holders of the Americas as papal vassals.

Solorzano's analysis of *Laudabiliter's* significance reflected his lack of awareness about the bull's origins. In the first place, Adrian's bull made no mention of feudal obligations of any sort. The letter does mention the payment of Peter's Pence, "the annual tribute of one penny from every house."[12] This was a traditional payment that might have seemed part of the feudal order to Solorzano but not to Henry II. Furthermore, *Laudabiliter* dealt with a Christian society whose members were not living up to the standards of Christian behavior that the papacy upheld. What the pope required of Henry II was that he bring the principles of the Gregorian reform movement into

Ireland where, because of the isolation of the Irish from the mainstream of Christian life, outdated religious practices and corrupt morals required reforming. The justification for Henry II's invasion of Ireland had much more in common with William of Normandy's invasion of England in 1066 than it did with the Spanish conquest of the Americas. William had promised to bring the principles of the Church reform movement to England where the Anglo-Saxon Church had remained mired in corruption and outdated practices, at least as the Norman apologists saw matters.[13] Neither he nor Henry II invaded a country inhabited by infidels for the purpose of bringing Christianity to an unbaptized people, as the Spanish did in the sixteenth century.

The nature of the arguments that Solorzano presented and the sources that he employed to develop his arguments indicate why he had little interest in presenting the reader with an accurate picture of the circumstances surrounding the issuing of *Laudabiliter.* His major concern was to defend the pope's right to grant nations to Christian rulers, precisely the kind of papal power that the Protestants had been attacking for a century. If the papal grant of Ireland to Henry II was a valid exercise of papal authority, then too, presumably, was the grant of the Americas to Ferdinand and Isabella. The best support for the argument that the pope did have the right to grant lands was the recognition of this power by rulers such as those of England who retained Ireland for over four centuries on the basis of Adrian IV's grant.

In addition to giving the reader the text of *Laudabiliter* and a brief discussion of its meaning, Solorzano also provided his readers with references to a number of writers who had discussed that bull. These references indicated how and why *Laudabiliter* came to Solorzano's attention and why it was important to defenders of the papacy. The references fall loosely into three categories: legal theorists; twelfth- and thirteenth-century chroniclers; and sixteenth- and seventeenth-century Catholic writers, both historians and polemicists, who were actively involved in defending the papacy from the charges hurled against it by the Protestants.

For the history and significance of *Laudabiliter,* Solorzano appears to have relied on two important contemporaries, Baronius' *Annales Ecclesiastici* and Cardinal Bellarmine's treatise dealing with the assertions of King James I of England about the independence of the English kings from papal control. He does not appear, however, to have examined these sources any more closely than he had examined Adrian's bull itself. In introducing Adrian IV's bull to his readers, Baronius had argued that the pope had invited Henry II to enter Ireland "for the betterment of the state of religion" there.[14] He made no mention of Ireland as a papal fief, nor did he mention that any sort of annual payment was required that would suggest some form of feudal dues. Baronius further undermined the argument that Solorzano sought to make by observing that when Henry II landed in Ireland, the native archbishops and bishops held a council at which they accepted the invader and his heirs as their lords forever. In support of this, Baronius quoted from the chronicle of Roger of Hoveden(d. 1201?) written soon after the events described.[15] Had Baronius been so inclined, he could have added that, according to Hoveden, some Irish kings accepted Henry II as their lord as well.[16]

Baronius and his sources provided a picture of the submission of the Irish that did not support Solorzano's emphasis upon papal authority. The Irish leaders voluntarily accepted Henry II as their ruler, presumably making the conquest of the island easier because at least some of the native leaders favored it. Admittedly, they would not have submitted without a show of papal and English power, but, nevertheless, the submission was portrayed as a voluntary one. The situation in sixteenth-century America was quite different from that found in twelfth-century Ireland. The Amerindians were not Christians, even lapsed ones, and they did not submit voluntarily to Spanish domination. It is true that in the early years of the conquest of the Americas, the Spanish priests read a statement explaining to the Indians why they were there and outlining the Christian faith to them. This was to be followed by either the voluntary submission of the listeners to Spanish rule or by an attack on them by Spanish soldiers. This document, the *Requerimiento,* was largely a formality inasmuch as it was read in Latin or Spanish, languages with which the hearers were unfamiliar, and made no allowance for differences of opinion about the legitimacy of the Spanish presence in the Americas.[17] It was a ritual designed to avoid the charge that the Spanish were seeking to impose Christianity on an unwilling people. Theologians had long previously determined that forced conversions were not valid. By reading the *Requerimiento* to the native population, the Spanish were giving the people an opportunity to learn about Christianity and to accept baptism freely as well as to accept Spanish overlordship. Although the reading of this document does echo the statement about the Irish bishops calling a council and freely accepting Henry II as their lord, echoing the need for a voluntary submission, the similarities are probably coincidental and are derived from different circumstances.

Baronius' discussion of *Laudabiliter* raised another point that both supported the Spanish conquest of the Americas and, at the same time, criticized continued English possession of Ireland. The commentary in the *Annales Ecclesiastici* emphasized that the papal grant of Ireland to Henry II was designed to improve the state of Christian life there. As Solorzano's work documented at great length, the Spanish worked hard and long to convert the Indians to the true faith. The imperial government played an active role in supporting and maintaining missionary activities. These efforts justified continued Spanish control of the Americas. On the other hand, the English had rebelled against the pope and threw off Roman ecclesiastical control. As a result, they could no longer be said to be working for the spiritual improvement of Ireland so they no longer had any right to occupy the island.

The conclusion that the English no longer possessed any right to possess Ireland was not unique to the writings of Solorzano and Baronius. Cardinal Robert Bellarmine made much of the same argument and at greater length in a treatise he wrote disputing the assertion of King James I of England that the English kings were not subject to papal authority.[18] Solorzano had cited Bellarmine's work in support of his argument that *Laudabiliter* signified the granting of Ireland as a fief. While Bellarmine's argument did support Solorzano's position, the Cardinal's argument was not quite as simple as the Spanish lawyer made it appear. Solorzano may have even misunderstood Bellarmine's position and the significance of the evidence he presented.

To the claim that the kings of England had never been subject to papal authority, Bellarmine presented an outline of English history that specified royal acts of submission to the papacy. He began with King Ine of Wessex who sent money to Rome as tribute in 740, apparently a reference to Peter's Pence that Solorzano interpreted as a sign of feudal submission. In later years, Offa and Canute made similar payments. According to Bellarmine's version of English history, the climax of this process of close papal-English relations came in 1213 when King John surrendered his kingdom to Pope Innocent III and received it back again as a fief. Citing Matthew Paris' (1200-1259) chronicle, Bellarmine asserted that John had surrendered England and Ireland "with the consent of the barons" to the pope. In recognition of this enfeoffment, John and his successors were to pay 1000 marks of silver annually to the pope.[19] It is likely that it was this act of enfeoffment, six decades after Adrian IV issued *Laudabiliter*, to which Solorzano was referring when he described Ireland as a papal fief.

Having demonstrated that James I's predecessors had recognized papal overlordship for several centuries, a proof that appears to have encouraged confusing Peter's Pence with feudal dues, Bellarmine turned to *Laudabiliter*. He argued that Henry II's possession of Ireland rested on a conditional papal grant, the condition being that the English would see to the reforming of the Church in Ireland. According to the Cardinal, the English kings had observed this condition in only minimal fashion, suggesting that even if the English had remained faithful to Rome, nevertheless they could be deprived of Ireland because of their failure to do what the terms of the grant required.[20] When Henry VIII broke with Rome, the English lost their legal basis for retaining Ireland.

Bellarmine based his argument and his history of England on the writings of two Englishmen, William of Newburgh (1136-1201) and Nicholas Sander (ca.1530-1581), a Catholic priest who left England for the continent during the Reformation and who wrote a history of the Reformation in England, and on the work of an Italian humanist resident in England, Polydore Vergil (d.1555), who wrote a history of England for the Tudors. In the treatise directed against James I, Bellarmine cited these authors as the sources of his historical evidence.[21] A careful examination of the sources, however, indiates that Bellarmine either did not actually read them or that he was very careless in his citations. Furthermore, by pointing to Polydore Vergil's work, he was in fact providing evidence that could counter his argument. Polydore Vergil's history makes no mention of *Laudabiliter,* an omission that may well have been quite calculated. In 1541, when Henry VIII officially styled himself King of Ireland, he did so, in part at least, because "the irishmen of long continuance, hath supposed the royal estate of this land to consist in the bishop of Rome for the time being and the lordship of the kings of England here to be but a governance under the obedience of the same."[22] At the same time, Polydore Vergil could not deny some papal role in the English acquisition of Ireland. The result was that he chose to focus his attention on the series of bulls that Alexander III had issued after Henry II had first visited Ireland. These bulls, issued in 1172, confirmed Henry's occupation of the island. In addition, Polydore Vergil's version of the events surrounding the English entrance into Ireland stressed Henry II's interest in Ireland was a personal one, an interest not sparked by Adrian IV's bull. When the king landed in Ireland, the native bishops and chieftains explained to him that after their ancestors had been converted to Christianity, they surrendered themselves into the pope's hands. Subsquent Irish leaders reaffirmed this submission periodically.[23] The result was that the pope possessed lordship over Ireland by the voluntary action of the Irish themselves and, therefore, only he could authorize Henry II's possession of the island. Upon hearing this, King Henry promply sent representatives to the papal court to request papal authorization for transferring the lordship to Ireland from the papacy to the English. The pope did as requested on condition that the English reform the Irish Church and eliminate the abuses that had crept into the Church. This version of the English conquest of Ireland avoided the issue of papal authority by placing the responsibility for the lordship of Ireland on the Irish themselves. It was the enthusiasm of the newly converted Irish themselves, not any papal action, that was the basis for papal overlordship of Ireland. When Henry II asked Alexander III to surrender papal lordship over Ireland to him, as the Irish leaders had suggested, he was, in effect, receiving power from the Irish, not from the pope who held the office only at the request of the Irish. According to this line of reasoning, the Reformation would have no bearing on English possession of Ireland because it did not rest on papal grant but on the voluntary submission of the Irish. In terms of the argument that Bellarmine wished to advance, namely that a long line of English kings had recognized papal lordship, Polydore Vergil's argument was of little value because it reduced the papal role in the English acquisition of Ireland to that of an agent of the Irish people.

Bellarmine's use of his other sources for the history of England, William of Newburgh and Nicholas Sander, also casts some doubts on his knowledge of the materials he cited with such confidence. The section of William of Newburgh's chronicle that the Cardinal cited, Book III, chapter ix, only dealt with the situation in Ireland from the point at which Henry II left the island in 1172 up to 1186. This chapter referred the reader to an earlier chapter, Book II, chapter xxvi, which dealt with the English invasion of Ireland in 1170, but there was no mention of *Laudabiliter* or of Adrian IV.[24] A reader of William of Newburgh could conclude that the papacy had nothing to do with the English acquisition of Ireland. Bellarmine's reference to Nicholas Sander's history of the Reformation in England had nothing to do with the situation in Ireland and may indicate that the Cardinal confused two of Sander's works, neither of which he had actually seen.[25]

When Solorzano cited William of Newburgh, Polydore Vergil and Nicholas Sander, he appears simply to have taken the references from Bellarmine or from some source common to both of them. In either case, there is no evidence that he had any direct access to any of them. It is likely that the same can be said for the other works that Solorzano cited. That is, he would appear to have synthesized the contents of various contemporary works without investigating the sources which such works employed. It is important to recognize, however, that even if Solorzano and the writers upon whom he drew made errors in the citation of their sources, this does not minimize the importance, or the perceived importance, of *Laudabilier* in sixteenth- and seventeenth-century debates about the power of the papacy and about the legitimacy of the Spanish conquest of the Americas.

The use of *Laudabiliter* in the Reformation debate about the nature of the Christian Church and the place of the pope within it came from the use of historical evidence by both Catholics and Protestants in the sixteenth and seventeenth centuries when they sought to defend their positions in the war of polemics that accompanied the Reformation. Each party looked to the past to illustrate what it considered to be the right order of the Church. For Protestants, the true Christian Church was to be found in the *Acts of the Apostles* and in the *Epistles*. The era of the primitive Church came to an end gradually, between the time that Constantine legalized Christianity with the Edict of Milan in 313 and the time that the popes came to dominate the Church, a point usually identified with the pontificate of Gregory I (590-604).[26] About the only heroes that the Protestants could find in the history of the Church between Gregory I and Martin Luther were those whom the Catholic Church had persecuted as heretics.

For Catholics, the rise of the papacy signified a necessary stage in the development of the Church. Constantine and Gregory I paved the way for the line of popes who ruled the Church in the eleventh, twelfth and thirteenth centuries. It was the Church that Bellarmine and Solorzano sought to defend, if for rather different reasons. The Church in these centuries exercised great power, providing a model for what the Church should be. The history of the Church in the next two centuries, with the Avignon period of the papacy, the Great Schism and the conciliar movement threatening the power of the papacy, provided little comfort to writers like Bellarmine and Solorzano. For defenders of the Church, the fact that the papacy was obeyed by secular rulers for so long was proof that the papacy's claims to power were valid.

For Bellarmine, the validity of *Laudabiliter* was demonstrated by the fact that the English kings claimed Ireland for several centuries on the basis of Adrian IV's letter. Therefore, Protestant rulers who rejected papal authority should, logically, return any property and rights they acquired as the result of papal grant, something no such ruler would do.

While Bellarmine was anxious to defend the papacy's power in the face of Protestant attacks, Solorzano's interest was more limited. He was anxious to demonstrate the right of the Spanish to possess the Americas. The interests of writers such as Solorzano and Bellarmine coincided to the extent that the Spanish Empire in America rested for its legitimacy upon a papal bull. Solorzano was then committed to defending the power of the papacy, not for the sake of the papacy itself but because the Spanish king was an agent of the papacy in the exercise of the power in a specific situation. For each, *Laudabiliter* was a useful document, although each saw it in the light of his own particular interests. For Bellarmine, the papacy was a strong, independent institution, capable of issuing orders to secular rulers and expecting them to be obeyed. For Solorzano, the papacy was something else, a weaker institution, one that could authorize and legitimize actions, but not an independent power capable of ordering secular rulers about.

In the final analysis, Weckmann was correct in seeing *Laudabiliter* as part of the basis for justifying the Spanish conquest of the Americas, although not for the reasons that he offered. There is little evidence that Adrian IV's bull had any direct bearing on the bulls issued by Alexander VI in 1493. Furthermore, there is no evidence that the Donation of Constantine played a role in the development of theories of papal power. Once the conquest was well under way, however, with the coming of the Protestant Reformation, the Spanish were compelled to develop legal justifications for their empire. Conquest and possession were not sufficient. Defenders of the papacy and of those who exercised power in its name, reached back into the history of the papacy to find evidence to support their positions. *Laudabiliter* emerged as a useful tool in the defense of the papacy and of secular rulers who engaged in conquests under papal license. There was no continuous tradition of using *Laudabiliter* in the development of papal claims to grant territory to secular rulers. What appears to have happened in the sixteenth and seventeenth centuries is that Catholic writers, looking for evidence to support their view of the papacy's powers, reached back into the past and found documents such as *Laudabiliter* and situations such as the English conquest of Ireland that could be used to advantage in contemporary situations. This period saw, in effect, a revival of interest in the High Middle Ages, a conscious attempt to link the present with the particular period in the past and an equally conscious attempt to overlook evidence from the other period that would conflict with the position already taken. Solorzano and others like him were using *Laudabiliter* to advance their own interests in that same way that contemporary Puritan lawyers in England were using Magna Carta.

There was an irony in the way in which writers such as Solorzano, Baronius and Bellarmine used history and the existence of a continuing tradition of the acceptance of papal authority by secular rulers to justify the validity of that authority. Centuries earlier, faced with the charge that he was an innovator who was rejecting time-honored ecclesiastical customs and practices, Pope Gregory VII (1073-1085), one of the architects of the strong papacy that these writers were defending, declared that Christ had said: "I am the Truth and the Life," not "I am Custom."[27] It was the Protestants in the sixteenth and seventeenth centuries, the opponents of the strong papacy, who now declared that truth, not tradition or custom, was the fundamental issue at stake and it was the Catholics who defended custom and tradition as the standard for determining the validity of practices and institutions.

NOTES

[1] The standard text of *Laudabiliter* is in *Pontificia Hibernia: Medieval Papal Chancery Documents Concerning Ireland*, ed. M.P. Sheehy, 2 vols. (Dublin, 1962, 1965) 1:15-16. Concerning the question of the document's authenticity, see M.P. Sheehy, "The bull *Laudabiliter:* a problem in medieval *diplomatique* and history," *Journal of the Galway Archaeological and Historical Society* 29(1961) 45-70; and J.A. Watt, *The Church and the Two Nations in Medieval Ireland*, Cambridge Studies in Medieval Life and Thought, series 3, vol. 3 (Cambridge, 1970) 36-40.

[2] "The Remonstrance of the Irish Princes," in *The Expansion of Europe: The First Phase*, ed. James Muldoon (Philadelphia, 1977) 138-143 at 139. The original text is in John of Fordun,

*Scotichronicon*, ed. Thomas Hearne, 5 vols.(Oxford, 1722) 3:908-926. See also, James Muldoon, "The Remonstrance of the Irish Princes and the Canon Law Tradition of the Just War," *The American Journal of Legal History* 22 (1978) 309-325.

[3] Luis Weckmann, *Las Bulas Alejandrinas de 1493 y la Teoría Política del Papado Medieval* (Mexico City, 1949). He has also summarized his argument in two shorter pieces: "Alexandrine Bulls," (*New Catholic Encyclopedia*, 15 vols. (New York, 1967) 1:306; and "The Alexandrine Bulls of 1493: Pseudo-Asiatic documents," in *First Images of America: The Impact of the New World on the Old*, ed., Fredi Chiappelli, 2 vols. (Berkeley, 1976) 1:201-210.

[4] The Latin texts of these bulls, along with those of Alexander VI, can be found in *European Treaties bearing on the History of the United States and its Dependencies to 1648* (Washington, 1917), 5678, 107-117.

[5] A much more impressive argument about the reliance of Alexander VI on the work of his predecessors is to be found in Charles-Martial de Witte, "Les bulles pontificales et l'expansion portugaise au xv$^{e}$ siècle," *Revue d'histoire ecclesiastique* 48(1953)683-718; 49(1954)438-461; 51(1956)413-453 and 809-836; 53(1958)5-46 and 443-471.

[6] The most recent study on this topic is Domenico Maffei, *La Donazione di Cosantino nei giuristi medievali* (Milan, 1964).

[7] For example, Innocent III, one of the most aggressive developers of papal power cited the Donation only once although he was well aware of its existence and the possibilities it contained: see R.W. Carlyle and A.J. Carlyle, *A History of Mediaeval Political Theory in the West*, 6 vols. (Edinburgh and London, 1903-1936) 5:182-183. For sixteenth-century defenses of the Donation, see Donald R. Kelley, *Foundations of Modern Historical Scholarship* (New York, 1970) 98.

[8] Carlyle and Carlyle, 5:183-184.

[9] Juan de Solorzano y Pereira, *Disputatio de Indiarum jure: sive, de iusta Indiarum Occidentalium inquisitione, acquisitione, et retentione* (Madrid, 1629, 1639). Lewis Hanke, *The Spanish Struggle for Justice in the Conquest of America* (Philadelphia, 1949; reprinted, Boston, 1965).

[10] Solorzano, vol. I, lib. ii, cap. xxiv, para. 27 and para. 29.

[11] Caesar Baronius, *Annales ecclesiastici*, 12 vols in 4 (Cologne, 1609) 4:ad ann. 1159.

[12] *Pontificia Hibernia*, 16. There is a translation of *Laudabiliter* in *Irish Historical Documents 1172-1922*, ed. Edmund Curtis and R.B. McDowell (London, 1943; reprinted, New York, 1968) 17-18.

[13] David C. Douglas, *William the Conqueror: The Norman Impact Upon England* (Berkeley, 1964) 343.

[14] Baronius, ad ann. 1159. "... hic describemus ex codice Vaticano diploma datum ad Henricum Anglorum Regem, de rebus Hiberniae in meliorem statum religionis restitutis."

[15] *Ibid.*, ad ann. 1171. " hi omnes (inquit Rogerius) tam Archiepiscopi quam Episcopi receperunt sibi Henricum Regem Angliae et haeredes suos in Reges et dominos in perpetuum. "

[16] Roger of Hoveden, *Chronica*, ed. William Stubbs, Rolls Series, vols. 51, 52 (London, 1868-1871) 1:30.

[17] Concerning the *Requerimiento*, see James Muldoon, "John Wyclif and the Rights of the Infidels: The Requerimiento Re-Examined," *The Americas* 36 (1980) 301-316.

[18] Robert Bellarmine, *Opera*, 5 vols, in 4 (Naples: 1858-1860) vol. 4, part 2, "Apologia ad Librum Jacobi Magnae Britanniae Regis," 345-413 at 356.

[19] *Ibid.*

[20] *Ibid.*

[21] *Ibid.*

[22] State Papers, Henry VIII, 11 vols. (London, 1830-1852) 2:480, 3:278, 304, in *Irish Historical Documents*, 77.

[23] Polydore Vergil, *Polidori Vergilii urbanatis Anglicae Historiae* (Basle, 1534) 216-217.

[24] Bellarmine, 356. William of Newburgh, *Historia rerum Anglicarum, Chronicles of the Reigns of Stephen, Henry II, and Richard I,* ed. R. Howlett, 4 vols. (London, 1884-1889), Vol. I, II.

[25] Nicholas Sander, *De origine ac progressu schismatic Anglicani, libri tres* (Ingolstadt, 1585); *Rise and Growth of the Anglican Schism,* trans. David Lewis (London, 1877).

[26] Martin Luther, for example, saw "the papacy as the Antichrist. . ." He believed that "the Papacy as the Antichrist assumes eschatological proportions as a historical entity that has arisen since the death of the last bishop of Rome, Gregory I." John M. Headley, *Luther's View of Church History* (New Haven, 1963) 154-155.

[27] "Si consuetudinem fortassis opponas, aduertendum fuerit quod Dominus dicit: 'Ego sum ueritas et uita.' Non ait: 'Ego sum consuetudo', sed 'ueritas.'" *The Epistolae Vagantes of Pope Gregory VII,* ed. H.E.J. Cowdrey (Oxford, 1972) no. 67, p. 151. On the history of this phrase, see Gerhart B. Ladner, "Two Gregorian Letters on the Sources and Nature of Gregory VII [sic] Reform Ideology," *Studii Gregoriani* 5(1956) 221-242.

XI

# The Remonstrance of the Irish Princes and the Canon Law Tradition of the Just War*

The great sixteenth century debate about the rights of infidels that the expansion of European society overseas had generated among intellectuals, lawyers and humanitarians was the culmination of a lengthy process of development.[1] The intellectual roots of the debate reached back to the twelfth century. The framework within which the Spanish participants in the debate, men like Francis Vitoria and Bartholomew de Las Casas, functioned when considering the plight of the inhabitants of the Americas had been created by the canon lawyers of the thirteenth century. These medieval lawyers had been interested in the problem of relations between medieval Christendom and the peoples who lived along its borders. A fourteenth century compiler of papal documents concerning Christian contacts with the non-Christian world described the contents of his compilation as letters concerning the "affairs of the Tartars, the lands of *outre-mer,* of infidels, and of schismatics."[2] If one added to this the phrase "of heretics and Jews as well," one would have a complete list of the various kinds of people who existed outside the bounds of Christian society. To be *extra ecclesiam* it was not necessary to live outside the territorial bounds of Christendom.[3] Heretics, schismatics, Jews, and Moslems dwelling in Europe were as much outside the Church

---

* An earlier version of this paper was delivered at the Eleventh Conference on Medieval Studies at Western Michigan University, May, 1976.

1. The most recent survey of the literature concerning this development is James Muldoon, "The Contribution of the Medieval Canon Lawyers to the formation of International Law: A Bibliographical Survey," *Traditio* 28 (1972) 483-97. See also, Kenneth J. Pennington, Jr., "Bartholome de Las Casas and the Tradition of Medieval Law," *Church History* 39 (1970) 149-61.

2. Vatican Register 62, fol.1*r. This register and its significance are discussed in J. Gay, *Clément VI et les affaires d'Orient* (Paris, 1904) 8-9.

3. Concerning the notions of Christendom and of Europe, see Denys Hay, *Europe, the Emergence of an Idea,* 2nd ed. (Edinburgh, 1968).

as was the infidel who inhabited the most remote corner of Asia, Africa or the Americas. The problem of the infidel in the sixteenth century was a special case of the person *extra ecclesiam* with whom the medieval canonists and philosophers had concerned themselves.

At the heart of the debate about the rights of those outside the Church was the question of whether the pope could authorize Christian rulers to invade lands occupied by those who were not within the Church.[4] Christian rulers who desired to expand their dominions generally sought papal authorization to do so. From the late eleventh century through the sixteenth century, the stages of European expansion are marked by papal letters authorizing secular rulers to invade and occupy various lands on the grounds that those who presently occupy the lands were in some way undeserving. Furthermore, this line of papal bulls reflected the development of legal speculation about the rights of those *extra ecclesiam*. The curial officials who drafted the letters, as well as many of the popes themselves, were canon lawyers by training, so that papal letters reproduced the debates of the law schools about the rights of infidels. The bulls stand like surveyors' stakes marking off not only the stages of physical expansion but also stages of intellectual development.[5]

The related development of territorial expansion and intellectual interest in the rights of those on the border of Christendom came together in 1317 when Donald O'Neill, self-styled "King of Ulster," wrote to Pope John XXII concerning the English invasion of Ireland.[6] He sent to the pope a copy of the bull *Laudabiliter* which Pope Adrian IV had issued in 1155 authorizing the conquest of Ireland, and he included with it a critique of the bull which has subsequently become known as the Remonstrance of the Irish Princes.[7] The Remonstrance rejected the allegations about Irish

---

4. The best introduction to the problem of the just war is Frederick H. Russell, *The Just War in the Middle Ages,* Cambridge Studies in Medieval Life and Thought, series 3, no. 8 (Cambridge, England, 1975).

5. The line of bulls is outlined in Luis Weckmann, *Las Bulas Alejandrinas de 1493 y la Teoría Política del Papado Medieval* (Mexico City, 1949).

6. Concerning the invasion of Ireland, see: Michael Dolly, *Anglo-Norman Ireland,* Gill History of Ireland, vol. 3 (Dublin, 1972) 44-46, 54-81; J. A. Watt, *The Church and the Two Nations in Medieval Ireland,* Cambridge Studies in Medieval Life and Thought, series 3, vol. 3 (Cambridge, 1970) 35-41.

7. The two documents appear together in Johannis de Fordun, *Scotichronicon,* 5 vols., ed. T. Hearne (Oxford, 1722) 3:906-26. English translations of these documents are found in *Irish Historical Documents 1172-1922,* eds. Edmund Curtis and R. B. McDowell (London, 1943; reprinted, New York, 1968) 17-18 and 38-46.,

society contained in *Laudabiliter* and contained a series of complaints about the behavior of the English in Ireland. Although the pope does not appear to have answered O'Neill directly, he did send two letters concerning O'Neill's charges, one to King Edward II of England and one to the papal nuncios in England.[8] The result is a small file of letters illustrating the development of legal thinking about the right of conquest and the dilemma in which the papacy was beginning to find itself. Should the popes continue to be involved in the work of conquest and, if so, under what terms?

At first glance, it might seem strange that Ireland provided an illustration of the problems associated with expansion that came to a head in the sixteenth century. The Irish were, however, both within and without Christian Europe. While the Irish were at least nominally Christians, socially and economically they had a kind of society, tribal and pastoral, that had disappeared from the heartlands of European society before the twelfth century.[9] From the papal point of view, the Irish Church in 1155 required reforming in order to bring Irish religious practices in line with the reforms begun during the previous century, reforms associated with the pontificate of Gregory VII. The implementation of these reforms was hindered by the comparatively primitive nature of Irish society. That society in turn contributed to the creation of what the papacy saw as practices in need of reform.[10]

In order to appreciate the arguments contained in *Laudabiliter* and in the Remonstrance, one must realize that neither document described Irish society as it actually existed. Presumably Adrian IV's bull derived its description of Irish society from the English supplication for permission to invade the island.[11] Likewise, the Remonstrance was designed to appeal to the papacy by describing the society in terms that would convince Pope John XXII and his

---

8. *Vetera Monumenta Hibernorum et Scotorum*, ed. August Theiner (Rome, 1864), *Paternum morem*, no. 422, p. 201, and *Ecce filii*, no. 423, pp. 201-2.

9. ". . . Irish civilization in the tenth century probably still had much in common with that of the Gaulish Celts before the Romans arrived." A. J. Otway-Ruthven, *A History of Medieval Ireland* (London, 1968). 1. See also Edmund Curtis, *A History of Ireland*, 6th ed. (London, 1950) 49-50.

10. Watt, *The Church and the Two Nations*, 1-34.

11. There is an extensive literature about *Laudabiliter*, much of it concerning its authenticity. The problem is briefly outlined in Watt, *The Church and the Two Nations*, 36-40. The authenticity of the bull has been defended by M. P. Sheehy who has edited the definitive edition of the texts of medieval papal-Irish relations: *Pontificia Hibernica: Medieval Papal Chancery Documents concerning Ireland*, 2 vols. (Dublin, 1962-65). In addition, see his "The bull *Laudabiliter:* a problem in medieval *diplomatique* and history," *Journal of the Galway Archaeological and Historical Society* 29 (1961) 45-70.

advisors to withdraw the approval Adrian IV had given for the invasion of Ireland in the twelfth century. In both cases, the facts alleged were selected in accordance with what the writers thought would influence the pope to act favorably in their behalf. Even though the Remonstrance has the appearance of a cry from the heart of an oppressed people, it reveals a carefully constructed argument designed to impress the pope by framing the complaints about the English in terms of the canonistic discussion of the just war.

Although *Laudabiliter* was only a brief letter, it was, like most papal letters, tightly written; it contained a good deal of information and implied a great deal more. The contents of the letter may be divided into three parts: a brief description of Irish society; a statement concerning the basis on which the pope was acting; a blessing on the English endeavor.

In words probably derived from a letter sent by Henry II to the papal court concerning the proposed invasion of Ireland, Adrian IV described the Irish as "a rude and ignorant people." The goals of the English in Ireland were "to enlarge the boundaries of the Church, to proclaim the truths of the Christian religion . . . and to root out the growths of vice from the field of the Lord. . . ."[12] It would be easy to conclude from this that the Irish were pagans, not Christians, and that the English were proposing to bring Christianity to Ireland for the first time.

The stated justification for approving the English invasion, however, indicated that the Irish were indeed Christians, although they had lapsed from the faith.[13] Again apparently drawing on Henry II's letter, the pope declared that "Ireland and all islands on which Christ the sun of righteousness has shone, and which have accepted the doctrines of the Christian faith, belong to the jurisdiction of the blessed Peter and the holy Roman Church. . . ."[14] Adrian IV thus placed the conquest of Ireland within the framework of the Gregorian reform. The role of Henry II would be to insure that the reforms

---

12. Curtis and McDowell, 17-18. "In the conventional manner of papal letters which are replies to petitions or requests, it begins with a résumé of the petition itself." John Watt, *The Church in Medieval Ireland*, Gill History of Ireland, vol. 5 (Dublin, 1972) 31.

13. The English view of the Irish from the twelfth to the sixteenth centuries was largely shaped by the writings of Giraldus Cambrensis, an English cleric who visited Ireland in 1183 and 1185. He therefore possessed first-hand knowledge of the conquest and some experience of the Irish. See his *The Topography of Ireland* and *The Conquest of Ireland* in Giraldus Cambrensis, *The Historical Works*, trans. Thomas Forester, rev. and ed., Thomas Wright (London, 1909).

14. Curtis and McDowell, 17.

that the papacy sought would be achieved. The success of the reform movement had traditionally been linked to the ability of the popes to unite papal and royal interests. William of Normandy, for example, had invaded England in 1066 armed with a special banner blessed by the pope because he had promised to impose the papally sponsored reforms on the English Church which, he had informed the pope, was mired in corruption. The twelfth century invasion of Ireland was another example of the conjunction of papal and royal interests. In both cases, the secular ruler who proposed the invasion would no doubt have proceeded without papal authorization. Such authorization, however, provided legitimacy for the planned invasion, a useful adjunct, if not an absolutely necessary one. At the same time, the papacy hoped to see the fruits of the reform movement achieved in these lands, something that might be done without an invasion, but something that appeared more likely with the armed support that the invaders promised.

The reference in *Laudabiliter* to papal authority over all islands has also been understood in another fashion. A friend and secretary of Adrian IV, the noted humanist John of Salisbury, remarked that the award of Ireland to Henry II was based on the powers granted to the papacy by the Donation of Constantine.[15] This famous forgery dating from the eighth century purported to describe how Emperor Constantine (311-37) granted the western lands of the Roman Empire to Pope Sylvester I. The document listed a number of specific territories that the emperor transferred to the pope and also made reference in general terms to granting the pope imperial authority over all islands in the West. At the end of the eleventh century, Pope Urban II had issued letters concerning the disposition of certain islands in the Mediterranean in which he ascribed his power to dispose of the islands to the power over islands derived from the Donation.[16] Adrian IV's bull, however, did not specifically refer to the Donation, only to papal power over islands "on which Christ the sun of righteousness has shone," suggesting that only those islands which had been or still were Christian were subject to the power mentioned.

John of Salisbury, and modern scholars who have attributed Adrian's actions to the Donation, appear to be at odds with the canonistic tradition concerning the Donation's significance. Gratian

---

15. For John of Salisbury's remarks, see Watt, *The Church and the Two Nations*, 35. For the text of the Donation, see *Select Historical Documents of the Middle Ages*, ed. Ernest F. Henderson (London, 1925) 319-29. See also, Domenico Maffei, *La donazione de Costantino nei giuristi medievali* (Milan, 1964).

16. The texts of the two bulls are in Weckmann, 265-68.

did not include the text of the Donation in his basic compilation of canon law known as the *Decretum* (c.1140). The unknown scholar who completed Gratian's work by adding texts that the master had not included did add the Donation to the *Decretum*, but succeeding generations of canonists seem to have followed Gratian's lead.[17] The Donation was rarely glossed by the canonists and rarely cited in discussions of papal power.

The difficulty with using the Donation is not hard to see. If the basis for papal intervention in Ireland, or anywhere else, was the Donation, then the papacy would be restricted to exercising authority in the western lands of the Roman Empire. Indeed, if the Donation was the basis for papal action, Adrian IV could not have authorized English conquest of the Irish, because Ireland had never been part of the Roman Empire. Furthermore, while a literary figure such as John of Salisbury may have felt that the Donation was an adequate basis for papal action, the trained lawyers who were beginning to emerge as papal advisors may have had doubts about the legal right of an emperor to alienate half of his empire.[18] Even more important to the canonists was the fact that reliance on the Donation would mean that the papacy derived a significant part of its power from a secular power. Since one of the major propositions of the reform papacy was that God Himself was the source of papal authority and that ecclesiastical power was therefore superior to secular, Adrian IV and his advisors would not have been inclined to give ammunition to their secular opponents by using the Donation as a basis for papal action.

Thus, the chief argument in *Laudabiliter* was that the invasion of Ireland was justified to reform the Irish church. The Donation of Constantine is clearly secondary, if it is to be regarded as part of the argument at all. There is also a suggestion of a third argument in the assertion that the Irish were "a rude and ignorant people" and therefore the legitimate objects of papal authority.

Answers to all of these arguments are to be found in the Remonstrance of the Irish Princes, but the emphasis is markedly different. Some of the Remonstrance seems to assume the validity of *Laudabiliter* and charges the English with violations of its terms.

---

17. *Corpus iuris canonici*, ed. Emil Friedberg, 2 vols. (Leipzig, 1879-81). vol. 1, *Decretum*, D.96 c.14, *Constantinus*. Because this letter was not included by Gratian it is termed a *palea*. Concerning the *paleae*, see G. Le Bras, C. Lefebvre and J. Rambaud, *L'Age Classique, 1140-1378: Sources et Théorie du Droit*, Histoire du Droit et des Institutions de l'Eglise en Occident, vol. 7 (Paris, 1965) 100-14: R. W. and A. J. Carlyle, *A History of Mediaevel Political Theory in the West*, 6 vols. (Edinburgh and London, 1903-36) 2:209-13.

18. Carlyle and Carlyle, 2:213.

The Irish apparently hoped that the pope would act on these charges by putting pressure on Edward II with whom they were already at war. The Irish had previously announced the withdrawal of their allegiance to Edward II and had recognized as their king, Edward Bruce, the brother of the victor at Bannockburn in 1314.[19] Like the letters of William of Normandy and Henry II to the papacy, the Remonstrance announced a policy that had been decided upon and for which the petitioner sought papal approval.[20]

More important than the specific charges of English perfidy, however, was the part of the Remonstrance which suggested that the individual who drafted it was aware of current canonistic thinking on the problem of the just war. If the pope accepted these arguments, he would have been forced to recognize the illegality of the invasion of Ireland authorized in *Laudabiliter*. Canonistic theories of the just war played their major role in the brief history of the Irish and their coming to Ireland that opened the *Remonstrance*. The essence of this introductory material was that Ireland was a stable, well-ordered society ruled by a long line of native kings. The letter came from "Donald O'Neill, king of Ulster and by hereditary right true heir to the whole of Ireland, and also the under-kings and nobles and the whole Irish people. . . ."[21] The tribal, decentralized Irish society suggested in *Laudabiliter* was thereby transformed into what would appear to be a typical feudal kingdom. Such a picture of Ireland was designed to impress upon the reader that the Irish did not form some strange, primitive society that required civilizing at the hands of the English. The Irish were already civilized and organized in the usual European pattern.

The Remonstrance went on to describe the origins of the Irish people. They had come from Spain about 3500 years earlier led by three sons of Milesius. They occupied Ireland, which was uninhabited at that time, and from those men came a line of 197 kings in the direct line of succession. Donald O'Neill was the current descendant of the sons of Milesius. In the reign of King Legarius, the Holy Spirit inspired Pope Celestine to send St. Patrick to convert the Irish to Christianity. From that time, there had been 61 kings "of the same blood, without intervention of alien blood . . . kings that in temporal things acknowledged no superior" ruling "here

---

19. The war between England and Scotland that led to the decisive Scottish victory at Bannockburn with important effects for Ireland is discussed in Curtis, 94-100.

20. On the background of the Remonstrance, see Otway-Ruthven, 224-51. In addition, see J. A. Watt, "Negotiations between Edward II and John XXII concerning Ireland," *Irish Historical Studies* 10 (1956) 1-20.

21. Curtis and McDowell, 38.

uninterruptedly in humble obedience to the Church of Rome until the year 1170." The letter went on to catalogue the injuries that the English had inflicted upon the Irish, injuries that the invaders cloaked in "some show of religion."[22] The native population had been hunted down and tormented so that the Irish people whom the invaders "had promised to shape to good morals and to bring under laws" lost their "holy and dove-like simplicity" that in turn "has been surprisingly altered into a serpentine craftiness," the result of regular contact with the English.[23] The invaders in their turn justified their behavior by asserting "the heresy that it is no more sin to kill an Irishman than a dog or any other brute."[24]

For these reasons, the Remonstrance continued, the sovereign status of Ireland, the failure of the English to live up to the terms of *Laudabiliter,* and the fact that the English were heretics—the Irish acted to remedy their situation. Having been willing to be ruled directly by Edward II without the mediation of the English settled in Ireland, the Irish accepted Edward Bruce as their king because Edward of England had failed to answer their request for direct rule. Their only purpose was to save their lives and to protect their "law and liberty." Edward II "who calls himself lord of Ireland, and also the said kings his predecessors have wholly failed . . . to do and exhibit orderly government" in Ireland. No one can accuse the Irish of perjury in this refusal to obey the king of England "since neither we nor our fathers have ever done homage or taken any other oath of fealty to him or his fathers." The Irish have called upon Edward Bruce to lead them because "it is free to anyone to renounce his right and transfer it to another," so that "all the right which is publicly known to pertain to us in the said kingdom as its true heirs, we have given and granted to him by our letters patent" and we have "unanimously established and set him up as our king and lord. . . ."[25]

Thus of the three arguments which Adrian IV used in *Laudabiliter* to authorize the invasion of Ireland, the Remonstrance was largely directed at the third, the one barely suggested in *Laudabiliter,* that the Irish were "a rude and ignorant people" and therefore the legitimate objects of papal authority. That so much of the Remonstrance should be directed to this argument reflects not only the

---

22. Id., 38-39.
23. Id., 40-41.
24. Id., 43.
25. Id., 44-6. In reality, however, many of the Irish rulers had previously submitted to the English kings at various times. See, for example, the Treaty of Windsor in 1175 between Rory O'Conor, the High King of Ireland, and Henry II, in Curtis and McDowell, 22-4.

different perceptions of the English and the Irish but also the changes which took place in the canonistic theory of the just war between the twelfth and the fourteenth centuries.

The arguments that Adrian IV advanced indicated that the papal right to authorize the invasion of Ireland rested principally on the papal responsibility for the souls of Christians. The Irish, though backsliders, nevertheless remained members of the Church and as such remained subject to papal jurisdiction. The assertion that the Irish were "a rude and ignorant people" and therefore the legitimate objects of papal interest, however, suggests that even if the Irish had not originally been Christians, the pope could still have authorized the English invasion of Ireland because of the wicked practices in which the Irish engaged.

By the end of the twelfth century, an English canon lawyer, Alanus Anglicus, developed a theory of papal power that did not limit that power, as Adrian IV may well have assumed it was limited, to Christian people. St. Augustine had argued that heretical clerics had no power to impose coercive ecclesiastical sanctions, because they were severed from the true source of ecclesiastical power. Alanus took that argument and applied it to the political sphere. In his opinion, Christ, when He was on earth, held both spiritual and temporal power. These powers, symbolized by the two swords that Peter possessed, Christ then granted to Peter, His vicar on earth, and to Peter's successors, the popes.[26] Thus only those who recognize that their right to *dominium,* whether in spiritual or in temporal matters, comes from Christ through His vicar can lawfully claim to possess property and lordship. No legitimate political authority and no legitimate ownership of property existed *extra ecclesiam* any longer. Therefore, the invasion of a non-Christian society by Christians was always legal because the infidels were by definition usurpers of *dominium* that belonged *de iure* if not *de facto* to Christians. This opinion was later developed by Henry of Susa, known as Hostiensis, and through him became a part of the mainstream of canonistic thought by the end of the thirteenth century.[27]

This is not to suggest that Adrian IV's views about the right

---

26. Concerning the development of the theory of the two swords, see Gerhart B. Ladner, "The Concepts of 'Ecclesia' and 'Christianitas' and their Relation to the Idea of Papal 'plenitudo potestatis' from Gregory VII to Boniface VIII," *Miscellanea Historiae Pontificiae* 18 (Rome, 1954) 49-77 at 57-9: A. M. Stickler, "Alanus Anglicus als Verteidiger des monarchischen Papsttums," *Salesianum* 21 (1951) 346-406 at 362: Russell, 197-98.

27. The development of these ideas is discussed in James Muldoon, "*Extra ecclesiam non est imperium:* The Canonists and the Legitimacy of Secular Power," *Studia Gratiana* 9 (1966) 553-80.

of the pope to authorize the invasion of Ireland influenced Alanus Anglicus' theory that no legitimate authority existed outside of the Church. Rather, both Adrian IV and Alanus were engaged in a search to find the limits of papal authority. Although *Laudabiliter* did not directly address the question whether the pope could authorize an invasion of a land that was not at least vestigially Christian, it did suggest extending papal authority to include societies that were uncivilized.

During the first half of the thirteenth century, there emerged a theory of papal rights over infidels that went beyond the powers implied in *Laudabiliter* but stopped short of the views that Alanus and Hostiensis expressed. The canonist Sinibaldo Fieschi, Pope Innocent IV, argued that non-Christians did have rights to power and property that Christians could not infringe. Specifically, he argued that *dominium* existed within both Christian and non-Christian societies, so that Christians could not legitimately invade infidel societies without just cause. The fact that the possessors of the land were infidels was not in itself sufficient grounds for invasion and conquest. Pointing to the election of Saul as King of Israel, Innocent explained that all societies had the natural right to choose their own leaders and to rule themselves without outside interference. This right to select the ruler was part of the *dominium* that every society possessed. He added, however, that societies that did not adhere to the principles of natural law could be invaded and reformed, because even infidels were obliged to follow the precepts of natural law that were common to all men.

Innocent IV's remarks on the legitimacy of non-Christian government appeared in a commentary on a decretal that dealt with the vows taken by those who went on crusade.[28] His commentary raised the fundamental question of the right of Christians to deprive Moslems of their possession of the Holy Land and the right of the pope to authorize such a conquest. His answer to this question led to a discussion of the various kinds of just wars that Christians could wage. The Holy Land, for example, was a legitimate object of Christian warfare because the Moslems had taken it from its Christian masters without just cause, presumably as part of an unjust war of aggression. By virtue of his position as heir of the Roman Emperor, the pope possessed the right to authorize the restoration of the Holy Land to its rightful rulers, that is to Christian control. tion of the Crusade on his position as successor to the Roman

28. Innocent IV, *Commentaria Doctissimi in Quinque Libros Decretalium* (Turin, 1581) 3.34.8, *Quod super his*, fols. 176-77. See also Muldoon, "*Nullum imperium extra ecclesiam*," 572-79; and Russell, 198-203.

Emperor, because the Donation of Constantine only applied in the Innocent added that even if the pope could not base his authoriza-western part of the Empire, nevertheless the current Holy Roman Emperor could authorize such a conquest by virtue of his status as King of Jerusalem.[29] In such a case, the pope would be within his rights to encourage Christian warriors to support the emperor in his legitimate desire to regain what was lawfully his.

The discussion of the origins of government in Innocent IV's commentary may well be the reason why the writer of the Remonstrance went to the trouble of prefacing his text with a history of the Irish, a history that differed from the usual description of the Celts' coming to Ireland. Traditionally, the coming of the sons of Milesius was an heroic tale, telling of how they came not to an uninhabited island but to one occupied by the "semi-divine" Tuatha Dé Danann.[30] The result was a war of conquest ending in the subjection of the Dananns. In the light of Innocent IV's treatment of the right of all societies to govern themselves without interference, the story of the conquest of the island by the Milesians might well have seemed imprudent in a letter to John XXII, a canon lawyer who was presumably acquainted with the lawyers' treatment of the just war.[31] No one could complain about the O'Neill family's domination of Ireland, however, if the ancestors of the present ruler had taken possession of an uninhabited corner of the world. By then pointing to the long line of kings presumably chosen by the Irish to rule over them, the Remonstrance asserted the right of the Irish, like the ancient Israelites, to select their own rulers. The fact that each king peacefully succeeded his predecessor obviously was intended to convince the pope that far from being a barbarous and primitive people who might reasonably be presumed to be violating the laws of nature, the Irish were a stable, peaceful folk undeserving of an invasion designed to civilize them. Perhaps even more important was the fact that possessing the right to select their own rulers, the Irish were within their rights to choose Edward Bruce as their king.

Even the charge of heresy that the Irish leveled at the invaders

---

29. Innocent IV, 3.34.8, fol. 177. The Holy Roman Emperor, Frederick II had obtained the title King of Jerusalem by his marriage to Isabel of Brienne: see Thomas Curtis Van Cleve, *The Emperor Frederick II of Hohenstaufen: Immutator Mundi* (Oxford, 1972) 222-26.

30. Curtis, 1.

31. Innocent IV was one of the most famous lawyers of his day. John XXII, also a canon lawyer by training, ordered the compilation and publication of a number of papal decretals in a volume entitled the *Extravagantes* that is included in the *Corpus iuris canonici*.

would seem to stem from Innocent IV's commentary. Although the charge might seem to be a piece of exaggerated rhetoric, added merely for effect, it is quite possible to understand it in a serious fashion. The Irish accused the English of equating the killing of an Irishman with the killing of an animal, making the English innocent of murder.[32] If the English clergy had taken the position of Alanus that no legitimate authority existed outside the Church, then logically it would be no sin to kill an Irishman who refused to recognize English overlordship. Such a person would be a usurper and a Christian would be within his rights to deprive such a person of his possessions by force, even killing him if necessary.

Finally, the Remonstrance also appears to have been a response to the claim that the papacy could dispose of Ireland because of the Donation of Constantine. According to the author of the Remonstrance, Ireland, like the Holy Land, had never been a part of the Roman Empire. The Irish had never recognized any overlord in temporal affairs, so the Donation could not possibly apply to them. The only basis for anyone to assert authority over Ireland would be an ecclesiastical one. The writer provided a basis for asserting some kind of direct papal power over Ireland by describing St. Patrick as having come to Ireland at the order of the pope. In this way, the only ecclesiastical authority with power in Ireland would be the pope, not the archbishop of Canterbury, as the English had occasionally argued. The description of St. Patrick's coming even bears some similarity to the story of Pope Gregory I sending Augustine to England at the end of the sixth century, perhaps reflecting an Irish desire to assert a kind of ecclesiastical parity with the English.[33]

That the argument based on the Donation of Constantine should have received so little treatment in the Remonstrance indicates, perhaps, the lack of intellectual respectability of this argument in the early fourteenth century. We have already suggested that it is not even the major ground of *Laudabiliter*. That the major ground of *Laudabiliter*, church reform, should also have received such little treatment indicates how the focus of doctrine about the just war had shifted by the fourteenth century. Of course, the argument of Irish ecclesiastical independence does suggest a further argument, that the pope in the twelfth century should have ordered reform of the

32. Curtis and McDowell, 43.

33. Id., 39. On the claim of the archbishops of Canterbury to primacy over the bishops of Ireland, see Watt, *The Church and the Two Nations*, 6-10.

Irish church from within and not at the hands of the English. The charges of English perfidy, too, suggest an additional argument, that even if the pope may authorize an invasion from outside to reform the church in a given area, the English have not done what they were supposed to do under *Laudabiliter* and therefore the Irish are entitled to repudiate their lordship.

The Remonstrance stated that both in law and in fact the English presence in Ireland was unjustified. The letter had no effect, however, and the Irish do not even seem to have received a direct reply. The senders of the letter may have realized that there would be a few, if any, direct results from such a letter. After all, just as the English had not needed *Laudabiliter* to invade Ireland in the first place, so too the existence of a papal letter condemning their actions would not cause them to leave. The Remonstrance was part of a propaganda war, a search for the legitimization of the policy that the Irish had already begun. To a lesser extent, it may have been rooted in the belief that the pope could exercise some influence on the English and thereby mitigate the circumstances of the conquest.

The only known response to the Irish Remonstrance consisted of two letters that John XXII wrote, one to Edward II, the other to the papal legates in England who had transmitted the Irish letter to Avignon. The letter to Edward II asked that the king adhere to the terms of *Laudabiliter* and to punish those who had abused the terms of the bull. Since the Irish acceptance of Edward Bruce as their king had been based on the failure of Edward II to govern them well, presumably an improvement in English government in Ireland would encourage the Irish to submit to English control once again. Rather pragmatically, the pope argued that the failure of the English to come to terms with the Irish would eventually necessitate the expenditure of large sums of money in order to put down the major revolt that was likely to occur. If the English monarch would only correct the abuses now, however, any future Irish rebellion would clearly be an unjust war. On the other hand, the pope did not indicate any specific sanction that he would impose on the English if they refused to eliminate the abuses of the terms of *Laudabiliter*. He did hint that the failure of the English to heed the cries of the embittered Irish people might justify transferring control of Ireland from the English to some other people who would end the abuses and, eventually, complete the reform of the Church in Ireland.[34] The letter to the legates spoke in even more general

34. Theiner, no. 422, p. 201.

terms, stressing their responsibility for advising the English king wisely in this matter.[35]

In political terms, this small correspondence had no significance. The English remained in Ireland. Edward Bruce died in October 1318 doing battle with the English forces. Donald O'Neill was by then an exile in the hinterlands of Tyrone. Edward II's government remained in firm control of Ireland and John XXII issued a condemnation of Robert Bruce's government in Scotland, thus denying it the legitimacy that Bruce sought for it.[36] In an ironic turn of events, the leaders of the English government in Ireland sent to John XXII a counter-remonstrance abound 1331. This letter repeated many of the charges found in the letter from O'Neill. The Irish were even accused of being heretics.[37] The image that each side had of the other was clearly heartily reciprocated. There is little evidence that either side was willing to make any significant concessions toward the other in order to negotiate a settlement of the conflict.

The significance of these letters is not in their impact on the conflict between the English and the Irish in the early fourteenth century. Rather, the series of events outlined in the documents provide a model that papal involvement in the expansion of Europe was to follow from the fourteenth century to the sixteenth. In general, expansion was legitimized by the issuance of papal bulls. Complaints about the effects of European conquest of infidel societies came to be composed by Christians who argued, in terms of Innocent IV's ideas about the nature of the just war, that a particular conquest was illegal. In the early fifteenth century, representatives of the King of Poland argued before the fathers of the Council of Constance that the Teutonic Knights no longer had the right to expand in Lithuania because the Lithuanians had become Christians and no longer posed a military threat to Christendom. The lawyer who argued the Polish case explicitly based his arguments on Innocent IV's commentary that dealt with the just war.[38]

---

35. Id., no. 423, pp. 201-2.

36. Watt, "Negotiations," 3; Watt, *The Church and the Two Nations*, 188-89; Curtis, 98-9.

37. ". . . in eadem terra Hibernie pullulavit et pullulat heresis ac discentio inter Hibernicos, gentes indomitas, Dei et hominis inimicos, sacrilegos, incendiarios ecclesiarum. . . ." Letter from Edward II to John XXII in Watt, "Negotiations," 19.

38. Stanislaus Belch, *Paulus Vladimiri and his Doctrine Concerning International Law and Politics*, 2 vols. (The Hague, 1965) 1: 75.

In the sixteenth century, the major critics of the Spanish conquest of the Americas, the philosopher Francis Vitoria and the Dominican friar Bartholomew de Las Casas chose to criticize the conquest in the same terms.[39]

The response of the later popes to the criticisms of European conquests was not unlike that of John XXII. The attempts to correct the abuses of the later conquests went unheeded as had the cries of the Irish. Even when faced with arguments based on their own legal system, the popes failed to act other than to issue pious statements about the need of secular rulers to act responsibly toward the peoples whom they conquered and, hopefully, would convert to Christianity.[40] In the case of the Remonstrance, John XXII had good reason to believe that the Irish church would be brought into line with Roman reforms if the English remained dominant in Ireland, just as in the sixteenth century, when faced with the picture of the barbarous people of the Americas, the papacy concluded that the interests of Christianity and of civilization would best be served by a European conquest of the Americas. In both cases, the ultimate goals of papal policy, church reform and the conversion of the infidel, were too important to the papacy to leave to chance. The support of strong governments was deemed essential to success in both areas.

In the realm of practical politics, the support of Edward II was essential to a pope who was chronically short of funds and who required a political counterweight to the King of France. In the sixteenth century, the papacy required the support of the Spanish rulers in the face of the Reformation and the political, as well as the religious, unrest that followed. These issues were always limiting factors when the papacy was forced to take sides in the legal battles between the conquered and the conqueror.

Finally, no pope could do a great deal to stop or even to ameliorate the effects of the conquests. In the early fifteenth century the King of Portugal put the matter bluntly to Pope Eugenius IV. The pope had forbidden further Christian expansion in the Canary Islands because a number of bloody incidents between Portuguese invaders and communities of Christian converts had led to the deaths of many converts. The king presented several argu-

---

39. See note 1 *supra*.

40. Papal bulls authorizing the conquest of the Americas always insisted upon just treatment of the Indians, but the treatment accorded them was obviously not generally in accordance with the papal desires: see Lewis Hanke, *The Spanish Struggle for Justice in the Conquest of America* (Philadelphia, 1949; reprinted Boston, 1965) 1-3.

ments, stressing the important role that the Portuguese would play in the conversion and the civilizing of these very primitive people. In addition, he pointed out ominously that even if he as an obedient son of the Church heeded the papal prohibition against further expansion, this would only mean that men with baser motives, self-interested greed, would disregard the ban and there would be no one to stop them, least of all the pope. Authorizing the Portuguese to expand their domination over these islands was the one way in which the papacy might be able to protect the natives from exploitation.[41]

Thus, the legal battle between the English and the Irish during the early fourteenth century reflected the limitations of legal argumentation when faced with the needs of policy-makers. John XXII and his advisors were lawyers, but they were also policy-making officials who had to take legal theory and fit it into the context formed by political and ecclesiastical goals. Furthermore, legally trained policy-makers may well have been suspicious of the picture of Irish society that the Remonstrance painted and of the picture of the Americas that Las Casas painted. John XXII's staff might well have suspected that the author of the Remonstrance had retouched the picture of Irish history in order to win papal support. They may even have felt that legal arguments were being manipulated simply to fit the needs of Irish politics, not those of the Church. The same could be said of the arguments that Las Casas and other opponents of the Spanish conquest of the Americas presented.

From the twelfth to the sixteenth century, then, the papacy sought to deal with the dilemma that its various interests created. Being responsible for the conversion of all men, it was hard for any pope to refuse approval for a request to extend the Church in the wake of European expansion. Furthermore, papal political interests in Europe generally made it impolitic to antagonize major powers that might support the papacy in its battles within Europe. Finally, there was no evidence that the papal refusal to authorize expansion would in any way affect the course of events. This dilemma appears fully developed in papal relations with Ireland. *Laudabiliter,* the Remonstrance and the two subsequent letters of John XXII illustrate the problem and the inability of the papacy to develop a reasonable

---

41. Letter of King Duarte of Portugal to Eugenius IV, August, 1436, in Charles-Martial de Witte, "Les bulles pontificales et l'expansion portgugaise au xve siècle," *Revue d'histoire histoire ecclesiastique* 48 (1953) 683-718 at 715. This letter led to another discussion by canonists concerning the rights of infidels: see James Muldoon, "A Fifteenth Century Application of the Canonistic Theory of the Just War," *Proceedings of the Fourth International Congress of Medieval Canon Law* (Vatican City, 1976) 467-80.

solution to the problem. The fundamental theme that links the long chain of papal documents that dealt with the problems raised by European expansion is the difficulty in which the papacy found itself when attempting to reconcile political, legal and pastoral interests. If condemning expansion would have no effect on potential conquerors, was it better to acquiesce and to legitimize the conquest in the hope that the conquerors would listen to papal admonitions about treating the natives justly? Perhaps a strong stand rooted in moral principle would have been the answer. In any event, such an answer was not forthcoming. The Irish were the first in what proved to be a long line of people on the edges of European society who looked to the papacy for justice against their conquerors. Like all the others, the Irish were doomed to frustration.

# XII

## The Indian as Irishman

THE continuity between the reconquest of Spain during the Middle Ages and the Spanish conquest of the Americas is a staple of historical writing. Even without Roger B. Merriman's famous volumes, the links between the two stages of the Spanish Empire are clear.[1] The attitudes which motivated the Spanish to create their sixteenth-century empire and the institutions which they employed to direct it found their origins in the medieval Spanish tradition of conquest. This tradition, continuously modified by new situations, formed a unifying theme in Spanish history. Although scholars have long noted a similar continuity in the development of English expansion, it has received less scholarly attention.[2] The history of English colonial expansion from the Norman Conquest, through the settlement of Wales and Lowland Scotland, the leap across the Irish Sea, and the eventual thrust into the Scottish Highlands served to develop the attitudes and the institutions which underlay English colonization in the Americas from

1. From W. H. Prescott onward, a series of historians has subsumed the history of the Spanish Empire under the general theme which Merriman made explicit: *The Rise of the Spanish Empire in the Old World and the New*, 4 vols. (New York, 1918–1934). In recent years Professor Charles Verlinden has stressed the importance of continuity in colonization techniques: see *The Beginnings of Modern Colonization* (Ithaca, 1970).

2. The British Empire has so far lacked its Prescott or Merriman. *The Cambridge History of the British Empire*, 8 vols. (Cambridge, 1929– ), allots only parts of five chapters in the first volume to English colonization before 1600. Even A. P. Newton's *The Colonizing Activities of the English Puritans* (New Haven, 1914) does not see the connection between the Irish and the American colonizing activities. The work of David B. Quinn provides the best overall introduction to the problem of the relationship between the medieval and the early modern periods of English colonization, but his work deals only with the last phase of the medieval experience. His views are expressed most fully in his *England and the Discovery of America* (New York, 1974).

the sixteenth to the eighteenth centuries, just as the *reconquista* underlay Spanish overseas expansion in the same period.

In recent years scholars have begun to turn attention to the analysis of the links between the experiences which shaped English life and society on the eve of the movement overseas and the societies which the colonists created in the New World. The emphasis thus far has been upon showing how a particular attitude or institution which is known to have existed in England and to have influenced a particular group of colonists was modified or abandoned because of the group's experience in America. In this way Professor Edmund S. Morgan has been able to ask why the first settlers in Virginia were able to "spend their time bowling in the streets when their lives depended on work" and to answer by discussing the attitudes toward work which contemporary Englishmen possessed and the understanding of the Indian way of life which they derived from Spanish descriptions of the Americas.[3] In similar fashion, by examining the attitude of East Anglian Puritans to Stuart military policy, and their conception of the covenant, T. H. Breen has been able to illustrate the gradual transformation which occurred in their attitude toward the place of the militia in society as they found themselves in need of armed force against the Indians.[4] In these cases the frontier served as a catalyst in the process of transforming English attitudes and institutions.

The purpose of this paper is to examine how one group, the Puritans of Massachusetts Bay in the seventeenth century, viewed the Indians, and how the policy which the Puritans developed for dealing with the Indians gradually changed during the course of experience on the frontier. It is important to realize that the first colonists came equipped with ideas about primitive peoples and how they should be treated. The colonists expected to meet inhabitants of the Americas and were prepared to deal with them. English colonists had available to them the experience of the Spanish in the Americas, experience that was widely published and readily available. They were also aware of the medieval and contemporary experience of the English in Ireland. It was the

3. Edmund S. Morgan, "The Labor Problem at Jamestown, 1607–18," *American Historical Review* 76(1971):595–611 at 596.

4. Timothy H. Breen, "English Origins and New World Development: The Case of the Covenanted Militia in Seventeenth Century Massachusetts," *Past & Present* No. 57 (November 1972):74–96.

"Wild Irish," fellow-Europeans, not the inhabitants of some far distant land, who provided the Englishman with his stereotype of primitive and barbarous society.[5] When, therefore, the colonists came to deal with the Indians, they did so in the light of English experience in Ireland. Although the similarity between the Irishman and the Indian might seem far-fetched to the modern eye, it was quite reasonable to the sixteenth- and seventeenth-century observer. As one official wrote, in terms applicable to the Indian but actually describing the Irish, they "wanted neither wit not valour" but they lacked the basic institutions and skills of civilized people. They "did neuer builde any houses of Bricke or stone (some few poor Religious Houses excepted)" before Henry II's invasion in 1170. Furthermore they did not "plant any Gardens or Orchards, Inclose or improve their lands, liue together in setled Villages or Townes, nor made any prouision for posterity." In a word their whole way of life was "against all sense and reason."[6] The Irishman with his long, flowing hair, outlandish clothing of skins or roughly woven cloth, and unintelligible language was as exotic a crea-

5. Current scholarship dealing with the issue of slavery in the Americas has tended to argue that the Indians and Negroes were treated alike because the colonists perceived them in the same terms. According to Winthrop Jordan, "Indians too seemed radically different from Englishmen, far more so than any Europeans. They were enslaved, like Negroes, and so fell on the losing side of a crucial dividing line. It is easy to see why: whether considered in terms of complexion, religion, nationality, savagery, bestiality, or geographical location, Indians were more like Negroes than like Englishmen. . . . Why were Indians, as a kind of people, treated like Negroes and yet at the same time very differently?" *White Over Black* (Chapel Hill, 1968), p. 89; see also p. 29. In addition, see David B. Davis, *The Problem of Slavery in Western Culture* (Ithaca, 1966), pp. 176–81. The residents of seventeenth-century Massachusetts, however, do not appear to have compared the Indians to Negroes but to Irishmen or to other European types of savages. Howard M. Jones, *O Strange New World* (New York, 1964), pp. 167–79, does stress the importance of the English in Ireland, but only discusses the Tudor period and omits any discussion of the previous four centuries of English experience in Ireland.

6. Sir John Davies, *Discovery of the True Causes Why Ireland was never Entirely Subdued* (London, 1612; reprinted, Shannon, 1969), pp. 169–70. The importance of the experience in Ireland upon the shaping of English attitudes is discussed at length in various writings of David B. Quinn. In particular see his *The Elizabethans and the Irish* (Ithaca, 1966) and his earlier works: *The Voyages and Colonizing Enterprises of Sir Humphrey Gilbert*, 2 vols. (London, 1940); *Raleigh and the British Empire* (London, 1947); "Ireland and Sixteenth Century Expansion," *Historical Studies* 1(1958):20–32. Similar views have also been expressed by A. L. Rowse in *The Expansion of Elizabethan England* (New York, 1955). The most recent expression of this view is that of Nicholas Canny, "The Ideology of English Colonization: From Ireland to America," *William and Mary Quarterly* 30(1973):575–98.

ture in the streets of London as a native of China or America would have been.[7]

Because of this long-standing identification of the Irishman with the barbarian, writers who wanted to describe the Indians to European audiences often compared the Indians to the Irish. According to David B. Quinn, by 1588 there existed among the English "a pattern of referring North American Indian practices to those of the Irish."[8] Crucial to this comparison was the belief that Indians were white men whose dark color was the result of outdoor living combined with the practice of decorating the body with various kinds of dyes.[9] To John Smith the deerskin robes which the Indians wore did not differ much "in fashion from the Irish mantels."[10] Even the geopolitical situation of the Indians resembled that of the Irish. Richard Hakluyt argued that North America and its inhabitants could be used to outflank the Spanish Empire in much the same way as the Spanish used Ireland and supported Irish rebellions against the English.[11] Finally it is worth noting that the first active promoters of American colonization, the Gilberts and Walter Raleigh, had turned to North America only after the failure of their attempts to settle in Ireland.[12] It was, then, only natural for early explorers and settlers to view the Indians in terms derived from the experiences of the English in Ireland. In order to understand the initial Puritan attempts to deal with the Indians, it is first necessary to understand how the English perceived the Irish and how they dealt with them.

The literature concerned with the relations of the colonists with the Indians has generally overlooked both the place of the "Wild Irish" in

7. When Shane O'Neill visited London in 1562 to make his submission, he appeared "with a guard of ax-bearing galloglasses, bareheaded, with curled hair hanging down, yellow surplices dyed with saffron or man's stale[urine —ed.] long sleeves, short coats, and hairy mantles. Whom the English people gazed at with no less admiration than nowadays they do them of China and America." William Camden, *History*, cited in Quinn, *Elizabethans*, p. 153.

8. Quinn, *Elizabethans*, p. 23.

9. John Smith, *The Generall Historie of Virginia, New-England, and the Summer Isles* (London, 1624; reprinted, Ann Arbor, 1966), p. 30. See also Alden T. Vaughan, *New England Frontier: Puritans and Indians 1620–1675* (Boston, 1965), pp. 42–43.

10. Smith, *The Generall Historie*, p. 32.

11. Richard Hakluyt, "Discourse of Western Planting," *The Original Writings and Correspondence of the Two Richard Hakluyts*, ed. Eva G. R. Taylor, 2 vols. (London, 1935), 2:241.

12. Quinn, *Elizabethans*, p. 111.

the formation of English attitudes toward the Indians and the policies which the colonists developed to deal with them.[13] On the one hand there are those who simply assert that Europeans generally had such contempt for non-Europeans from the beginning that the only policy they could pursue was one of subordinating or destroying them.[14] On the other hand, there are those who subscribe to Alden Vaughan's argument that the Puritans "followed a remarkably humane, considerate, and just policy in their dealings with the Indians."[15] Yet

13. Lewis Hanke's *The Spanish Struggle for Justice in the Conquest of America* (Philadelphia, 1949) remains the most extensive study of European attempts to understand the Indian and to place him within a European moral-legal framework. A convenient survey of current scholarship on the problem of the status of the Indian in North America with emphasis upon the modern period is Wilcomb E. Washburn, *Red Man's Land / White Man's Law* (New York, 1971). In addition see Wilbur Jacobs, *Dispossessing the American Indian* (New York, 1972). Explanations of why the English colonists treated the Indians as they did tend to be general in nature. For example Washburn stated that "the tradition of Indian subordination and inferiority in America society . . . was latent in the civilization of Europe, a heritage of her Christianity and of her classical past." Washburn, *Red Man's Land*, p. 3. In an earlier essay, however, he had pointed to one institution developed on the Irish frontier which was later employed in America (the royal land grant). He did not proceed further with this line of investigation to consider other kinds of relationships between the Irish and the American frontiers. See Wilcomb E. Washburn, "The Moral and Legal Justifications for Dispossessing the Indians," in James M. Smith, ed., *Seventeenth Century America* (Chapel Hill, 1959), pp. 15–32. Yasu Kawashima, who has focused attention on the legal status of the Indian in colonial Massachusetts, has also failed to see any earlier experience of English colonization being brought to bear on the status of the Indian. See his "Legal Origins of the Indian Reservation in Colonial Massachusetts," *American Journal of Legal History* 13(1969):42–56; and "Jurisdiction of the Colonial Courts over the Indians in Massachusetts, 1689–1763," *New England Quarterly* 42(1969):532–50. The parallels between the Praying Towns and treatment of the Irish has also been overlooked. See the recent study by Neal Salisbury, "Red Puritans: The 'Praying Indians' of Massachusetts and John Eliot," *William and Mary Quarterly* 31(1974):27–54. Richard Slotkin, *Regeneration Through Violence. The Mythology of the American Frontier, 1600–1860* (Middletown, 1973), p. 42, has noted the parallel between the Praying Towns and the policy of the Puritans in Ulster toward the Irish but does not deal with older practices.

14. "It did not take many years before the white man's religion and his lust for land, which was almost religious in its fervor, clashed with the Indian's quite different notions. Considered to be heathens, the Indians were fair game for bloodthirsty missionaries, such as Cotton Mather who extolled the burning alive of a townful of Indian men, women, and children. The passion to acquire land led to more conflicts, and an obscene and bloody conquest that was to go on for more than three hundred years began." Robert Burnette, *The Tortured Americans* (Englewood Cliffs, 1971), p. 12.

15. Alden T. Vaughan, *New England Frontier*, p. vii. His views have been strongly criticized as being too sympathetic to the Puritans. See the review by Theodore B. Lewis, Jr., in *William and Mary Quarterly* 23(1966):500–502.

neither side in the debate has examined the roots of the attitudes and policies which they assert the colonists possessed and implemented.

From the beginning of English penetration into the Celtic lands there emerged stereotypes of the Welsh, Scots, and Irish.[16] In the case of the Irish, even the papal bull of 1155 which authorized Henry II's invasion described the natives as a lawless and vice-ridden people. The responsibility of Henry II was to see to "the extension of the boundaries of the Church . . . the restraint of vice . . . the correction of morals and . . . the implanting of virtues" and "to imbue that nation with good morals."[17] This picture of a primitive society steeped in vice appeared some years later, embellished and expanded, in Gerald of Wales' writings on Ireland. Forced to admit that the Irish had long since been converted to Christianity, Gerald described them as wonderfully "ignorant of the rudiments of Christianity" as well as a "most filthy race, a race sunk in vice," and given to "treachery more than any other nation." To illustrate his argument, he told the story of one primitive Irish community encountered by some English sailors. The long-haired natives, dressed in animal skins, lived on a diet of meat, fish, and milk and were amazed at the sight of bread and cheese.[18] Through the sixteenth century, the picture which Gerald drew remained the key to the English view of the Irish. Even Holinshed's *Chronicles*, which was "the most important work" of the late sixteenth century concerning Ireland, included Gerald's works.[19]

While the English characterized the Irish as wild and barbarous, they did not assume that such behavior was innate. The general opinion was that the Irish were essentially like the English and could become civilized. It was the Irish way of life that made them wild, not any racial or biological cause. As a result, English laws dealing with the treatment

16. W. R. Jones, "England Against the Celtic Fringe: A Study in Cultural Stereotypes," *Journal of World History* 13(1971):155–71; and Edward Synder, "The Wild Irish: A Study of Some English Satires Against the Irish, Scots, and Welsh," *Modern Philology* 17(1919–1920):687–725.

17. Adrian IV, *Laudabiliter*, in Edmund Curtis and R. B. McDowell, eds., *Irish Historical Documents 1172–1922* (London, 1943), pp. 17–18. The literature concerning this bull, much of it concerned with its authenticity, is discussed in J. A. Watt, *The Church and the Two Nations in Medieval Ireland* (Cambridge, 1970), pp. 36–40.

18. Giraldus Cambrensis, *The Historical Works*, ed. Thomas Wright (London, 1905), pp. 139–40.

19. Walter J. Ong, "Spenser's *View* and the Tradition of the 'Wild' Irish," *Modern Language Quarterly* 3(1942):561–71 at 562.

of the Irish took as their goal the conversion of the Irish to the English way of life. The Statutes of Kilkenny (1366) summed up the first two hundred years of English experience with the Irish. Irish historians have generally condemned the Statutes as racist in nature.[20] If by racist one means a policy which assumes biological inferiority, the Statutes of Kilkenny are not racist. What they condemn is not the Irish as a people but the way of life they follow. It is cultural not racial inferiority that is involved. The purpose of the Statutes was to prevent English settlers from succumbing to the lure of the Irish way of life and becoming, as was later said, "more Irish than the Irish." The Statutes forbade the selling of war horses or arms to the Irish, and forbade the English inhabitants from dressing or living in Irish fashion. The English were also forbidden to allow their children to be raised in Irish fashion lest they identify themselves with the Irish rather than the English.[21] Such regulations are typical of the laws which a minority group dwelling within an alien society makes in order to retain its group identity. The laws were directed not at the native Irish but at the so-called "degenerate English" who had gone native and thereby weakened the colony by depriving it of their military support. An Irishman who wished to have the protection of English law and who agreed to adopt the English way of life could do so.[22]

During the sixteenth century, the English sought to reverse the decline of the state of the colony. The importance of the new policy was illustrated by Henry VIII's assumption of the title King of Ireland in 1541. The essence of the Henrician policy was to bring the native Irish under royal control by having the native chiefs surrender their power to the crown and receive it back again. The policy of "surrender and re-grant," if successful, would have weakened and eventually destroyed the tribal structure by transforming the chief into a royal vassal deriving his power from the king, instead of a leader selected by tribal election.[23] In addition, this policy received reinforcement from pressures on the Irish to change their way of life. At least some of the

20. Modern Irish historians have often compared the Statutes with *apartheid*, an interpretation which is rejected by J. N. Watt, *The Church and the Two Nations*, p. 200, n. 4.

21. Curtis and McDowell, *Irish Historical Documents*, pp. 52–59 at 53.

22. Curtis and McDowell, *Irish Historical Documents*, pp. 46–47, Edward II's order authorizing the Irish to be admitted to English law in 1321. See also J. A. Watt, *The Church and the Two Nations*, pp. 130–31, 160.

23. Edmund Curtis, *A History Of Ireland* (6th ed., London, 1950), pp. 168–73.

"surrender and re-grant" agreements included clauses requiring the chiefs to refrain from using their Gaelic titles, "to use the English habits and manner," to "bring up their children after the English manner, and the use of the English tongue," and to put such of their "lands as shall be meet for tillage, in manurance and tillage of husbandry," and, finally, to build houses for the farming population.[24] This policy failed as did similar efforts in later years.

The failure of the English to conquer and colonize Ireland successfully in the sixteenth century produced two important results. In the first place, it generated an extensive literature devoted to analyzing the Irish situation and to proposing solutions to the problem. In the second place, it forced potential colonizers to look farther afield, eventually to America, for a land suitable for their purposes. It seems logical to assume that those who sought other regions to colonize would have read not only the literature which enthusiastically promoted American colonization, but also to have read some of the material concerning the failure to colonize Ireland successfully in order to avoid making the same mistakes.

The literature dealing with the failure of the Irish conquest often came from the pens of English officials who had long experience in Ireland. While their views on the best way of securing the conquest varied, they are based on first-hand knowledge of the situation. All of these writers assumed the superiority of the English way of life. They also assumed that this way of life held out obvious attractions to many of the Irish, so that if the English were careful to present their way of life at its best, the Irish would be attracted to it and force would not be necessary. When, in 1531, for example, Sir Thomas Cusack pointed out to the Privy Council the obstacles blocking successful colonization of the island, he cited the native Irish fear that the invaders planned to "banish them, and put them from their lands forever."[25] He argued, however, that this only showed how the Irish misunderstood the English intention. In his opinion the opposite was true. He would have the English extend to the Irish English property law so that the lower classes of the Irish would be enabled to own their land and be secured

24. Agreement Between the Government and MacGilpatrick (1543), Curtis and McDowell, *Irish Historical Documents*, pp. 106–7 at 106.

25. Sir Thomas Cusack to the Privy Council (1541), *Irish History from Contemporary Sources*, ed. Constantia Maxwell (London, 1923), pp. 114–15 at 114.

from the arbitrary exactions of their chiefs. If the natives were given letters patent granting true ownership of their land, they would stop supporting the chiefs who kept them poor and would support the English.

Although other writers were less optimistic than Cusack and were inclined to see the problem as more complex than he did, nevertheless they, like Cusack, saw the problem as being one of culture not of biology. To Edmund Spenser the essential problem was the semi-nomadic character of Irish life. In his opinion history and observation of the contemporary world proved that those who follow a pastoral way of life and live off their cattle are uncivilized and warlike. On the other hand, once such peoples settle down to an agricultural existence, they become peaceful and civilized. The purpose of conquering the Irish was then to force them to settle down in order to rise to a civilized level of existence.[26] Spencer identified the Irish with the Scythians described by ancient historians.[27] Their long hair was a "Scithian abuse" as was the Irish practice of keening or wailing over the dead.[28] The entire pastoral way of life was Scythian.[29] It was, therefore, the mission of the English, like the ancient Romans, to conquer the barbarians in order to bring them the benefits of law and of civilization.[30] Failure to civilize such barbarous peoples had serious consequences. The Romans fell before the onslaught of barbarous nomads and, by implication, so might the English in Ireland unless the Irish were conquered. The barbarian was dangerous not only in military terms, however. The civilized life is a fragile one, and dwelling among barbarians often transforms civilized men into savages. In Ireland the original Norman invaders had, for the most part, "degenerated and growen allmoste meare Irishe yea and more malitious to the Englishe than the verye

26. ". . . For loke into all Countries that live in suche sorte by kepinge of Cattle and youe shall finde that they are bothe verie Barbarous and vncivill, and allsoe greatlye given to warr." Edmund Spenser, *Works*, ed. E. A. Greenlaw *et al.*, 10 vols. (Baltimore, 1932–1957), 9:217.

27. "... FFor from the sundrie manners of the nacions from whence that people which now is Called Irishe weare derived some of the Customes which now remaine amongest them haue bene firste fetched . . . ffor not of one nacion was it peopled as it is but of sundrie people of different Condicions and manners But the Chiefest which haue firste possessed and inhabited it I Suppose to be Scithians. . . ." Edmund Spenser, *Works*, 9:82.

28. Edmund Spenser, *Works*, 9:102, 105.

29. Edmund Spenser, *Works*, 9:97–98.

30. Edmund Spenser, *Works*, 9:179–80, 229.

Irishe themselves."[31] The "degeneration" of the English Spenser attributed to the practice of "fosteringe and marryinge with the Irishe."[32] The practice of fostering children in Irish fashion meant that English children were raised in Irish families, speaking Irish and perceiving themselves as Irish, thus falling away from the English way of life.

Writing about two decades after Spenser, Sir John Davies, attorney general for Ireland, saw the Irish problem in terms quite similar to Spenser's, suggesting that by the early seventeenth century there existed a body of information about the Irish colony and its problems upon which all those interested in the problem could draw and to which they could add. For Davies the essential problem was the nature of the Brehon law which the Irish used.[33] In his opinion it did not secure either the persons or the property of the Irish. If the English would but inform the Irish of the protection given by the Common Law, they would readily leave their old way of life.[34] In practice, however, even though many Irish did perceive the advantages of the Common Law, the English often refused to admit Irishmen to its blessings, and so the Irish turned away from the English.[35] Like Spenser, Davies pointed to the Romans as the model which should be followed in this as in so many other regards.[36] The success of the Romans was due to the exten-

31. Edmund Spenser, *Works*, 9:96.

32. Edmund Spenser, *Works*, 9:119.

33. "For, if wee consider the Nature of the Irish Customes, wee shall finde that the people which doth vse them, must of necessitie bee Rebelles to all good gouernment . . . they were little better than Canniballes, who doe hunt one another. . . ." Sir John Davies, *Discovery of the True Causes*, pp. 165–66.

34. "For heeretofore, the neglect of the Lawe, made the English degenerate, and become Irish; and now, on the other side, the execution of the Law, doth make the Irish grow ciuil, and become English." Sir John Davies, *Discovery of the True Causes*, p. 272.

35. "Notwithstanding, it is euident by all the Records of this Kingdome, that onely the English Colonies, and some few Septs of the Irishry, which were enfranchised by special Charters, wer admitted to the benefit and protection of the Lawes of England; and that the Irish generally, were held and reputed Aliens, or rather enemies to the Crowne of England; insomuch, as they were not only disabled to bring anie actions, but they were so farre out of the protection of the Lawe, as it was often adiudged no fellony to kill a meere Irish-man in the time of peace." Sir John Davies, *Discovery of the True Causes*, p. 102.

36. "But the Romaine State, which conquered so many Nations both barbarous and Ciuill; and therefore knewe by experience, the best and readiest way of making a perfect and absolute conquest, refused not to communicate their Lawes to the rude and barbarous people, whom they had Conquered. . . ." Sir John Davies, *Discovery of the True Causes*, pp. 124–25.

sion of their law to those whom they conquered. Davies praised James I for extending the law to all Irishmen. If this was followed up by enforcing the laws against living and dressing in Irish fashion and by insuring that the Irish send their children to English schools, "we may conceiue an hope, that the next generation, will in tongue & heart, and euery way else, become English; so as there will bee no difference or distinction, but the Irish Sea betwixt vs."[37]

Cusack, Spenser, and Davies represent but do not exhaust the mass of information on colonization available in sixteenth- and seventeenth-century England. They seem to reflect the general opinion about the Irish, that is, that the Irish "did indeed have a nature amenable to civilization" and only needed to have that nature cultivated. They lacked the capacity to transform themselves, so that the English "who were cultivated in those arts which the Irish lacked" and who "had a right to Ireland by virtue of conquest" had therefore the right to impose "English customs and laws" upon them.[38]

It was in this intellectual climate that the Puritans began to plan their settlement in Massachusetts Bay. Serious planning appears to have been a hallmark of the Puritan assault upon New England, which was, as S. E. Morison has pointed out, "founded consciously, and in no fit of absence of mind."[39] A great deal of preliminary planning took place in order to insure the safety of the migration. One must, therefore, suppose that a colonization society so anxious to do the job right as to send out a preliminary party in 1629 to explore the region in advance of the main body would also be well aware of the literature regarding previous colonies and their experiences.

The best evidence of the thoughtful way in which the Puritans planned their colony in Massachusetts is to be found in the writings of two of the founders of the colony, John White and John Winthrop. White's *The Planters Plea*, a propaganda piece designed to soothe the doubts of those who were considering the move, raised the obvious question, Why not plant a colony in Ireland? White responded with great realism. "Ireland is well-nigh sufficiently peopled already, or will

37. Sir John Davies, *Discovery of the True Causes*, p. 271–72.
38. Walter J. Ong, "Spenser's *View*," pp. 564–65.
39. Samuel Eliot Morison, *Builders of the Bay Colony* (2nd ed., rev., Boston, 1958), p. 3.

be in the next age."[40] Such an answer was somewhat disingenuous, as it overlooked the fact that the native Irish and the "degenerate English" were not only numerous, they stood firmly in the way of any English expansion, as the historical record made clear. As John Winthrop observed in his much shorter private record of his feelings about the proposed colony, the recent plague that destroyed the Indian population along Massachusetts Bay was a sign that Divine Providence was guiding the Puritans to settle there. According to Winthrop the natives should welcome the English because they would help to replenish the population.[41] Massachusetts Bay was an ideal location because it lacked that which made settlement in both Ireland and Virginia difficult, if not impossible: a large native population.

The Puritans also argued that colonization should lead to the conversion of the remaining natives to Christianity. While it is true that conversion of the natives was a standard part of the formal rhetoric of any letter patent authorizing colonization, nevertheless the Puritans appear to have taken this responsibility seriously. John White, for example, squarely faced the argument that the Indians were descendants of Noah's accursed son Cham (or Ham) and therefore not suitable subjects for conversion. To agree with this would render useless any missionary efforts and perhaps even justify extermination of the natives. He denied that this was so, but even if it were true, it would not prevent the need for missionary efforts.[42] Some years later, John Winthrop recorded the reappearance of such a belief in some quarters and its rejection by the magistrates of Massachusetts.[43]

These early writers did not enter into the controversy about the origins of the Indians except to deny their accursed status. The later writers who did give opinions on this topic often suggested that the

40. John White, *The Planters Plea. Or the Grovnds of Plantations examined, and vsuall Objections Answered* (London, 1630); reprinted in *Tracts and other Papers Relating Principally to the Origin, Settlement, and Progress of the Colonies in North America*, ed. Peter Force, 4 vols. (Washington, 1836–1846), 2:15–16.

41. Allyn B. Forbes, ed., *Winthrop Papers*, 5 vols. (Boston, 1929–1947), 2:113. On the intellectual background of the arguments for entering and taking the land, see Chester E. Eisinger, "The Puritans' Justification for Taking the Land," *Essex Institute Historical Collections* 84(1948):131–43.

42. John White, *The Planters Plea*, pp. 30–31.

43. John Winthrop, *Winthrop's Journal, "History of New England," 1630–1649*, ed. J. K. Hosmer, 2 vols., Original Narratives of Early American History (New York, 1908; reprinted, New York, 1953), 2:18–19.

Indians were the descendants of the ten lost tribes of Israel.[44] Here again, the Puritans found themselves seeking to classify the Indians within existing categories of peoples and then acting toward them on the basis of previous experience with similar peoples. As a result the work of settlement could be justified by White, as others previously had justified the conquest of Ireland, in terms of the Roman conquest of the ancient world. As the Roman had divine authorization to conquer the ancient Britons "that hee might bring Religion afterwards," so too the English could not bring to Christianity "those who are not subdued to the rule of Nature and Reason."[45] The spreading of English law and customs, therefore, provided the foundation upon which the Christian faith could build.

In addition to book knowledge of Ireland, the Winthrops also possessed first-hand knowledge of Ireland and its inhabitants. John Winthrop, Jr., had attended Trinity College in Dublin for two years (1622–24), while Emmanuel Downing, the elder Winthrop's brother-in-law, had been living there at the same time.[46] The possibility of settling in Ireland had even interested the senior Winthrop at one point.[47] When, at a later date, three wolfhounds and their handler were brought over from Ireland to Massachusetts, the younger Winthrop was expected to deal with the handler because he was reputed to know "the Irish condition."[48]

44. Alden T. Vaughan, *New England Frontier*, pp. 20–21. See also, L. E. Huddleston, *Origins of the American Indians: European Concepts, 1492–1729* (Austin, 1967).

45. John White, *The Planters Plea*, p. 6.

46. The only full-length biography of John Winthrop, Jr., is Robert C. Black, *The Younger John Winthrop* (New York, 1966). See also, Richard Dunn, *Puritans and Yankees* (Princeton, 1962), p. 60.

47. "Send me worde in your nexte how Mr. Olmstead and that plantation prospers. I wish oft God would open a waye to settle me in Ireland, if it might be for his glorye." John Winthrop to John Winthrop, Jr., April 20, 1623, *Winthrop Papers*, 1:281.

48. "You shall allsoe receiue in this shipp 3 woolfe doggs and a bitch with an Irish boy to tend them. for the doggs my m[aste]r hath writt sufficiently, but for the boye thus much. You have bin in Ireland, knowe partlie the Irish condition. this is a verie tractable fellowe and yet of a hardie and stout corage; I am perswaded he is very honest especially he makes great conscience of his promise, and vowe. . . . At this first comminge ouer he would not goe to church; nor come to prayers. . . . I hope with gods grace he will become a good convert. Converte gradatim. Sir, I dare boldlie saye it is as much honor for you to winn this fellowes soule . . . as to winn an Indians soule out of the Diuells clawes. . . ." Edward Howes to John Winthrop, Jr., August 5, 1633, *Winthrop Papers*, 3:134.

Because the leaders of Massachusetts Bay began with a conception of the Indian's place in the spectrum of uncivilized societies, they began with a preconceived notion of how to treat him. The assumption being that the Indians were like the Irish, it was logical for Winthrop and the others to presume that the techniques employed to deal with the Irish would work in Massachusetts for the Indians. Their touching belief in their ability to deal successfully with the Indians in spite of the well-known failures of English colonizing and civilizing efforts in Ireland rested on avoiding the errors made in Ireland. Winthrop argued that the failure of the previous colonial ventures was not because of the underlying policy which shaped them but because "their mayne end which was proposed was carnal and not religious." Their founders sought "profitt and not the propagation of religion." Furthermore, the people who made up the colonies were "a multitude of rude and misgoverned persons the very scumme of the land."[49] While this description obviously fit the inhabitants of Virginia as described by John Smith, it also described many of those Englishmen who went into Ireland.

For John Winthrop the work of transforming the Indian from his traditional way of life to the English one was not going to be difficult. Formal study of the existing literature about colonization and experience with the native Irish had indicated the mistakes made previously. By holding out to the Indians the advantages of English law, by educating them in English ways, and, finally, by converting them to Christianity, the Puritans would serve their religious mission and insure the security of the colony as well.

From the beginning of the colony the Puritans encouraged Indian chiefs to submit themselves to English control in return for protection from their enemies.[50] The treaties of submission, while like the Irish

49. *Winthrop Papers*, 2:114.

50. "This writing is to testify, That we Pumham, sacham of Shawomock, and Saconoco, sachem of Patuxet, etc., have, and by these presents do, voluntarily and without any constraint or persuasion, but of our own free motion, put ourselves, our subjects, lands and estates under the government and jurisdiction of the Massachusetts, to be governed and protected by them, according to their just laws and orders, so far as we shall be made capable of understanding them. . . ." John Winthrop, June 12, 1643, *Winthrop's Journal*, 2:125–26. On Puritan policy regarding the Indian tribes, see Alden T. Vaughan, *New England Frontier*, p. 155ff. Kawashima points out that the policy of extending the jurisdiction of Massachusetts Bay over the individual members of the

treaties of "surrender and re-grant," differed in one important aspect. The Indians were not obliged to adopt English ways, other than to accept English law. No doubt the reason for this was that the Irish treaties were based on the belief that the Irish were a conquered nation, while the Indian treaties were negotiated on a basis of peaceful mutual benefit. On the other hand, the Puritans could and did encourage the Indians to adopt English ways. A correspondent of the younger Winthrop advised him that the granting of distinctive European clothing to friendly chiefs would encourage potentially hostile chiefs to "be allured to loue and respect the English in hope and expectation of the like ...."[51] He also informed Winthrop of "an English written Accedence and grammer of such a rare method" which would be used for "the speedy bringinge of English and Indians to the perfect vnderstandinge of our tonge and writinge. ..."[52] The schools in Boston and Roxbury, according to the elder Winthrop, were to teach English and Indian alike, although the laws establishing schools made no specific mention of either group.[53] Harvard College also included Indians among its alumni from its earliest days. Its charter explicitly stated that the aim of the college was to "conduce to the education of the English and Indian youth of this country in knowledge and godliness."[54] Instruction in manual trades and agriculture was also proposed.[55]

The most famous aspect of this policy of acculturation was the estab-

---

tribes was part of a policy of "breaking up their tribal structure and confining them as groups to somewhat artificially established plantations or inducing them to come to live individually in the white communities": "Jurisdiction," *New England Quarterly* 42(1969):533. This was a logical policy to follow, given the long discussion of the bad effects of tribal organization on the Irish. As Davies and Spenser had observed, tribally organized people were, by definition, uncivilized.

51. Edward Howes to John Winthrop, Jr., March 26, 1632, *Winthrop Papers*, 3:74.

52. Edward Howes to John Winthrop, Jr., April 20, 1632, *Winthrop Papers*, 3:77.

53. John Winthrop, July 3, 1645, *Winthrop's Journal*, 2:224. The school laws of 1642 and 1645 can be found in *Documents of American History*, ed. Henry S. Commager (7th ed., New York, 1963), pp. 28–29.

54. Charter of Harvard College, May 31, 1650, in *American Colonial Documents to 1776*, ed. Merrill Jensen, *English Historical Documents*, vol. 9 (New York, 1955), pp. 558–59 at 558.

55. Richard Dunn, *Puritans and Yankees*, p. 131. It is rather curious that the English appear to have ignored the fact that the Indians were agriculturists. Most of the sources contain references to Indian gardens which provided the natives with food. The essence of the objection to describing the Indians as farmers was that the style of agricultural life which they followed enabled the men to wander from place to place for long periods of time.

lishment of the Praying Towns for groups of Indians who wished to become Christians. As the process of civilization logically preceded baptism, the General Court of Massachusetts Bay granted town sites to potential Indian converts. Regulations for the administration of such towns were also provided. The regulations for administering these towns stressed that the Indians must follow a settled agricultural way of life. Men who were "idle a weeke, at most a fortnight," were fined and each single man was "to set up a Wigwam and plante for himselfe, and not live shifting up and downe to other wigwams."[56] Again, like the Irish, the men were to cut their long flowing hair and the women were to dress in English fashion, keeping their breasts covered.

Evidence that the Puritans believed that the process of acculturation would go quickly and easily appears in Winthrop's *Journal*. Although his own knowledge of the difficulties involved in bringing the Irish to English ways no doubt served to keep him cautious, nevertheless he had concrete evidence that acculturation was possible for the Indians. Among the Indians whom he encountered in Massachusetts was one who had been kidnapped and taken to Europe where he served with Walter Raleigh. Having been returned to New England, he "was now turned Indian again."[57] In other words, the savagery and barbarism of the Indian were not innate but determined by his cultural environment. By returning to his original habitat, the Indian in question had found it easy to relapse, but had he remained in English surroundings, he would have remained English in manners. As a result, when John Winthrop

56. John Eliot, *The Daybreaking of the Gospel with the Indians, Old South Pamphlets* vol. 6, no. 143 (Boston, 1904), pp. 20–21. See also Ola E. Winslow, *John Eliot, "Apostle to the Indians"* (Boston, 1968). Alden T. Vaughan, *New England Frontier*, pp. 346–47, has printed the rules for governing the community of Praying Indians at Concord, Massachusetts, issued in January 1647. This list contained twenty-nine rules, some of which were not precise rules of behavior but rather exhortations to virtue, such as no. 11, "That they may labour after humility, and be not proud." Of the eight regulations listed by Eliot, five are essentially contained in the list of twenty-nine. What does not appear in the Concord list is the emphasis upon settling down in one place. In addition there was a curious ban on Indian games. Rule 20 stated: "Whosoever shall play at their former games shall pay 10s." According to Vaughan, among the Indian games was a kind of football played on a mile-long stretch of beach which lasted for several days and in which the participants wore war paint (50). The Statutes of Kilkenny forbade the English to play the Irish game of hurling, a game which is like field hockey, because of the injuries done to the players. See Curtis and McDowell, *Irish Historical Documents*, p. 54.

57. John Winthrop, *Winthrop's Journal*, 1:61.

saw an Indian chief dressed in English clothing and sitting at his table "where he behaved himself as soberly, etc., as an Englishman," he must have attributed the good manners he observed to the clothing and surroundings.[58] Cases such as these, and similar cases in Ireland, must have encouraged the English to believe in the eventual success of the acculturation process if only the efforts were firmly maintained.

Yet during the seventeenth century such acculturation did not occur on any large scale, either in Ireland or in Massachusetts. Neither native population made the move up the scale of social "evolution" that might have been expected. In both areas some elements of the native population consciously resisted acculturation. Catholic Irishmen saw in Trinity College, Dublin, a means of weaning the younger generation from its religion.[59] Among the Indians in Massachusetts, there appeared a spirit "pursuading them to forsake the English, and not to come at the assemblies, nor to learn to read."[60] Even in the Praying Towns there was a disturbingly large number of backsliders who found the English way difficult even with the supportive institutions of an organized community.[61] Also some chiefs saw the conversion of their subjects to Christianity as a threat to their own power.[62]

Finally the English feared both the Irish and the Indians from the very beginning. The desire to convert and to acculturate the natives battled with a strong fear of what could happen to a small body of colonists surrounded by barbarians. Even before the colonists had sailed for Massachusetts, instructions had been issued for dealing with the natives in order to avoid "the hurt that may follow through our

58. John Winthrop, *Winthrop's Journal*, 1:58, March 23, 1631.

59. ". . . they [the English] determined . . . to found a University in the capital of the Kingdom, in which they put heretical masters to teach their pestiferous doctrines, and uproot the desire of Catholics to cross the seas." Mss, Irish College, Salamanca, Spain, 1611–1620, cited in Constantia Maxwell, *Irish History*, p. 347. The same document also criticized the English for forcing the Irish to speak English.

60. John Winthrop, *Winthrop's Journal*, 1:260.

61. Alden T. Vaughan, *New England Frontier*, pp. 304–7.

62. ". . . and that thay [Indian chiefs] had a great fear to have ani of ther indians should be Caled or forsed to be Christian indians. thay saied that such wer in everi thing more mischivous, only disemblers, and then the English made them not subject to ther kings, and by ther lying to rong their kings." "A Relacion of the Indyan Warre, by Mr. Easton, of Roade Island., 1675," in *Narratives of the Indian Wars*, ed. C. H. Lincoln, Original Narratives of Early American History (New York, 1913; reprinted, New York, 1952), pp. 7–17 at 10.

much familiarities with the Indians."[63] As in the case of the Irish frontier, trade was to be carefully regulated and no arms were to be sold to them at all.[64] At the beginning of the settlement there was even a ban on Indian servants residing with English families without official approval.[65] While these regulations obviously protected the precarious situation of the colony in its early days, they also meant that Indian contacts with the English would be severely limited, and therefore the opportunities for the Indians to see the advantages of the English way of life decreased.

In addition the Puritans do not appear to have tolerated intermarriage. The romantic tale of Pocahontas and John Rolfe was not repeated in New England. According to Alden Vaughan, there is no record of any legal marriages between English and Indians in Massachusetts in the period 1630–1676.[66] The fame of Pocahontas obscures the fact that this marriage was exceptional, even in Virginia, and that she went to England, where she died. She made the transformation to being an Englishwoman and is shown in a contemporary picture in European dress.[67] Had the situation been reversed and had Rolfe gone native, the story might not have been so warmly received by contemporaries. Pocahontas had done as an Indian should do. Two centuries earlier the Statutes of Kilkenny had forbidden marriages with the Irish because of the effects on the English partner. While the savage and barbarous way of life was viewed as inferior to the English way of life, nevertheless the English realized that some Englishmen might prefer it. Ireland had lured a number of Englishmen into the Irish way of life, thus creating the "degenerate English" who had become the most dangerous enemies of the English government in Ireland. The fear of repeating the same situation in Massachusetts appears to have caused the Puritans to discourage, if not actually forbid by law, intermarriage. Because the Puritans considered the savage to be one whose way of life

63. First General Letter of the Governor and Deputy of the New England Company for a Plantation in Massachusetts Bay . . . , April 17, 1629, in *The Founding of Massachusetts*, ed. Edmund Morgan (Indianapolis, 1964), pp. 452–65 at 461.

64. First General Letter, p. 460.

65. Court of Assistants, Boston, March 1, 1630–1631, First General Letter, pp. 401–2 at 402.

66. Alden T. Vaughan, *New England Frontier*, p. 209.

67. See the picture of Pocahontas by an unknown British artist in J. T. Flexner, *American Painting: First Flowers of our Wilderness* (Cambridge, 1947), p. 13.

conditioned him to certain kinds of behavior, it was clear that, logically, should an Englishman choose to adopt Indian ways he would become a savage himself. Roger Williams complained of a man who had fled from Plymouth and had "turned Indian in nakedness and cutting of haire, and after many whoredomes, is there maried."[68] Another colonist, describing yet another settler who had fled to the woods to avoid punishment, lamented "that those that professe themselvs to be Christians, should be more barberous and wyld then Indeans."[69] Thus did a sea-change transform the old saying about the English who had become more Irish than the Irish.

Fear of the consequences of too much familiarity with the natives may even have contributed to the great efforts which the settlers of Massachusetts employed to rid themselves of Thomas Morton of Merrymount. The revels on the mount no doubt horrified the Puritans and the Pilgrims, but the constant harassment of Morton in his later, less successful, years is not easy to explain.[70] If, however, Morton's neighbors saw him not simply as a successful, if licentious, fur trader, but as the prototype of the degenerate Englishman in America, then their almost unreasoning hatred of him and his works becomes more intelligible. The Merrymount settlement attracted both Englishmen and Indians, male and female. Morton was apparently able to secure arms for the Indians. Could he have placed himself at the head of a mixed society? While he may not have had such ideas, the Winthrops, relying on their knowledge of Ireland, may have supplied the image. If life in a savage society had so corrupted the Normans in Ireland, why could not the same happen in Massachusetts? Morton had to go.

During the course of the seventeenth century the situation in both Ireland and Massachusetts worsened. The Puritan could easily see himself surrounded by savage papists and devilish savages. Just as the Puritan Englishman elaborated the "Black Legend" about the Spanish as a response to the continuous wars with Spain, so too, the failure to pacify and assimilate culturally the Indians and the Irish seems to have

68. Roger Williams to John Winthrop, December 10, 1637/1638, *Winthrop Papers*, 4:7.

69. William Coddington to John Winthrop, May 22, 1640, *Winthrop Papers*, 4:247.

70. Alden T. Vaughan, *New England Frontier*, p. 90, has summed up the situation neatly, pointing out that "the Merrymount episode belongs not in the realm of moral quibbling, but of interracial diplomacy."

led to a new myth, that of the fundamental inability of these peoples to rise to the English level of civilization.[71] In Ireland the savage rebellion of the 1640's brought Cromwell's troopers in to do the work of God by slaughtering large numbers of the Irish who had refused to accept the new order.[72] The pacification of Ireland by the sword and the subsequent removal of many of the natives from their lands may well have suggested something to the New England Puritans.

The outbreak of King Philip's War spelled the end of the attempt at acculturation in Massachusetts. Faced with a war against a powerful Indian leader, the Puritans gradually came to lump all Indians together, Praying and infidel alike. At the outset of the war, loyal Indians were resettled to places chosen by the colonists. Any Indian found "skulking" outside of the assigned area was presumed to be an enemy and could be killed on the spot.[73] The literature which the war spawned painted a terrible picture of the ferocious Indian warrior. Even the Praying Indians came in for extensive criticism, being in reality, as one writer said, not Praying but "Preying Indians" who "have made Preys of much English Blood."[74] The same writer also claimed that the English were unable to feel secure "because they cannot know a Heathen from a Christian by his Visage, nor Apparel."[75] From fearing that the Praying Indians might relapse into barbarism, the Puritans appear to have been led to doubt the possibility of fundamental transformation of the Indian

71. On the origin of the "Black Legend" see William S. Maltby, *The Black Legend in England* (Durham, 1971). On the problem of classifying non-European cultures in relation to European, see Margaret T. Hodgen, *Early Anthropology in the Sixteenth and Seventeenth Centuries* (Philadelphia, 1964), pp. 386–430.

72. ". . . the Irish were also to be punished as rebels and as 'papists,' and the fate dealt out to them was only possible to minds steeped in the story of the Jews and the Amalekites." Edmund Curtis, *A History of Ireland*, p. 252. The solution included arranging for 30,000 Irish soldiers to leave the country in order to join the Spanish and French armies, the sending of "thousands of common Irish . . . to the West Indies as practical slaves," and the transportation of the remainder of the native aristocracy west of the Shannon, leaving twenty-six of the thirty-two counties in undisputed English control. The remaining Irish in the twenty-six counties were to be used as a labor pool.

73. The order was made in a council held in Boston, August 30, 1675, in "The Present State of New-England With Respect to the Indian War," *Narratives of the Indian Wars*, ed. C. H. Lincoln, Original Narratives of Early American History, pp. 21–50 at 32–33.

74. *Narratives of the Indian Wars*, p. 49. The writer went on to add that "now they are all reduced to their several Confinements; which is much to a general Satisfaction in that Respect."

75. *Narratives of the Indian Wars*, p. 32.

personality. Mrs. Mary Rowlandson, a ransomed prisoner of the war, had no doubts that the possibility of acculturation was in vain. To her, all Indians were "atheisticall, proud, wild cruel, barbarous, brutish (in a word) diabolicall creatures."[76] She reserved her strongest criticism for the Christian Indians who had joined Philip. One is portrayed as so lacking in basic human feeling as to have betrayed his own father to the English for crimes which they both committed in order to save his own life. Another wore a necklace composed of the fingers of dead Christians.[77] In an unconscious parody of Puritan theological speculation, she said of another Indian that "his conscience was so tender and scrupulous" that he would not eat horsemeat until his brother showed him in the Bible where such was allowed. On the other hand this tender and scrupulous conscience was "as large as hell, for the destruction of poor Christians."[78] In recording the last days of her captivity, Mrs. Rowlandson summed up the efforts of the Puritans to bring the Indians to the English way of life. In a story reminiscent of Winthrop's description of the chief who dressed in English clothes and acted as a civilized man, she related:

> In that time came a company of Indians to us, near thirty, all on horseback. My heart skipt within me, thinking they had been Englishmen at the first sight of them, for they were dressed in English Apparel, with Hats, white Neckcloths, and Sashes about their wasts . . . but when they came near, their was a vast difference between the lovely faces of Christians, and the foul looks of those Heathens. . . .[79]

For Mary Rowlandson the attempt to civilize the Indians was bound to fail because they were fundamentally unable to rise above their savage way of life. Dressing them in English fashion and teaching them English ways only introduced them to new tools for them to employ in their barbarous activities. Environment could not overcome heredity.

With the end of King Philip's War, the Indians were dealt with in a manner which recalls Cromwell in Ireland. The Puritans killed or en-

76. "A Narrative of the Captivity and Restauration of Mrs. Mary Rowlandson," *Narratives of the Indian Wars*, pp. 109–67 at 116.

77. *Narratives of the Indian Wars*, p. 152.

78. *Narratives of the Indian Wars*, p. 152.

79. *Narratives of the Indian Wars*, p. 148.

slaved many of the Indians. The slaves were sent out of Massachusetts, often to the West Indies where they may have encountered the Irish, Scots, and Welsh whom Cromwell had sent there.[80] No doubt the policy of Indian removal was justified in terms similar to those used to justify Irish removal. As one contemporary wrote, should the Irish remain, "the English may degenerate, and turn Irish" as the "experience of former ages has urged."[81] Although Indians did remain in Massachusetts, by the mid-eighteenth century the Praying Towns had so declined that Englishmen gradually replaced the Indian population. Even though Cotton Mather writing in 1699 was still able to identify the Indians with Scythians, and therefore presumably held out some hope for them, this was an outdated view.[82] Although this earlier history was included in Mather's *Magnalia* as an appendix, Mather's final opinion on the Indians was that the Indians had been brought to America by the Devil to serve as an obstacle to the spread of Christianity.[83] While many people still hoped and worked for the acculturation of the Indian, the popular view was that he was irredeemably sunk in savagery. The same was true of the Irishman. The brutal wars of the seventeenth century provided concrete evidence of the wickedness and essential corruption of both groups. During the seventeenth century, Europeans who were creating the rudiments of anthropology were able to argue that many of the various primitive non-European societies existed "in a place in the hierarchical series of societies separate from and lower than European man but still higher than the animals."[84] The nineteenth-century caricatures of the Irish with simian features illus-

80. Alden T. Vaughan, *New England Frontier*, p. 319. Almost thirty years earlier Roger Williams had written to John Winthrop, Jr.: "It is said that after Cromwell had discomfited the Welsh, with 6000 he was forced to incounter 19 thousand Scots of whome he tooke 9000 prisoners etc. great store of Scots and Wellsh are sent and sold as slaves into other parts." Ca. December 3, 1648. *Winthrop Papers*, 5:287.

81. Vincent Gookin, *The Great Case of Transplantation in Ireland* (1655), p. 3, cited in Godfrey Davies, *The Early Stuarts, 1603–1660*, The Oxford History of England (2nd ed., Oxford, 1959), 9:165. In fact, this tended to happen in spite of a law forbidding Cromwell's soldiers from marrying Irishwomen, thus continuing the tradition of Englishmen becoming if not more Irish than the Irish, at least as Irish.

82. Cotton Mather, *Decennium Luctuosum*, in *Magnalia Christi Americana*, 2 vols. (Hartford, 1853, 1855; reprinted New York, 1967) 2:580–681 at 594.

83. Cotton Mather, *Decennium Luctuosum*, 1:42.

84. Margaret T. Hodgen, *Early Anthropology*, p. 414.

trate how far the process could go.[85] Even a people dwelling within the physical boundaries of Europe was not immune from being reduced to a subhuman status.

If, as this essay argues, the seventeenth-century experience of the English with primitive societies in Ireland and Massachusetts caused a fundamental change in their attitude toward such societies, it would be interesting to examine English-Indian relations in the other colonies in similar terms. To what extent did this experience influence later colonists? To what extent did different colonizing groups with different aims and assumptions base their policies toward the Indians on other aspects of the European experience of expansion and colonization which they brought with them? To what extent did the English derive their approach to the Indians from the Spanish experience and to what extent from their own experience in Ireland? Many factors obviously played a part in seventeenth-century English attempts to acculturate the Indians of America, but failure to completely "civilize" the natives according to strict English standards and preconceived notions gradually eroded what peaceful and constructive relationships had been established. Like the Irish of a century or two before, the Indians proved too great a threat to the English way of life, and the English attitude reverted to a position of intolerance and hatred toward those who would not bow to English values.

85. See, for example, the cartoons of Thomas Nast in Morton Keller, *The Art and Politics of Thomas Nast* (New York, 1968), plates 103, 104; and L. Perry Curtis, *Apes and Angels: The Irishman in Victorian Caricature* (Washington, 1971).

# INDEX


Abraham: IV 174–5, 180
Acosta: Joseph: VIII 33
Acre: V 162
Adrian IV, pope: X 174, 176–8, 180–82; XI 310–14, 316–18
*Aeterni Patris*: IX 81
Alans: V 144, 147, 159, 176–8, 192
Alanus Anglicus: I 560–61, 563, 565, 578; VI 303–6, 310; XI 317–18, 320
Alexander III, pope: X 175, 181
Alexander IV, pope: V 143
Alexander VI, pope: III 497; IV 168–70, 176, 181–3; VI 313–14, 316; IX 70, 79; X 175–7
Alfonso XI, Spanish king: V 171
Alius: I 568
Ambrose, St, bishop of Milan: I 567–8; VII 47–8
Amedeo V, count of Savoy: V 160
Americas, Americans: II 267–9, 271–2, 275–7; IV 183; VI 313, 315; VII 53, 61; VIII 29–33, 36–7, 41–2, 44; IX 69, 73, 83–4; XI 310, 323–4; XII 267–8, 270, 274
Anabaptists: VII 56
Andrew the Frank: V 176
Andronicus II, Byzantine emperor: V 157–8
Andronicus III, Byzantine emperor: V 159
*Annales Ecclesiastici*: V 132–3; X 177–80
*Apologie for the Oath of Allegiance*: IX 75
Aquinas, Thomas: II 265, 268–70, 274; III 491, 494; VII 52; VIII 33, 40; IX 68, 72, 82–3
Arabs: VII 49
Aragon, king of: V 132
Aristotle, Aristotelian: II 265, 268; VIII 33
Aristotle, *Politics*: VII 33, 38
Armenia, Armenians: V 130–32, 137, 139–40, 142, 144 150–55, 164, 170–72, 182, 191
Athens: VII 32–3
Augustine of Canterbury: XI 320
Augustine of Hippo, St: I 556–7; VI 303; VIII 33, 38, 41; XI 317
Augustus, Roman emperor: I 557
Babylon, sultan of: V 151
Baldus: VIII 33
Baldwin II, Latin emperor of Constantinople: V 156
Baronius, Caesar: V 132; X 177–80, 184
Bartolus: VIII 33
Belch, Stanislaus: III 495–7; IV 175
Bellarmine, Robert, cardinal: VIII 33; X 178, 180–84
Benedict XI, pope: V 143
Benedict XII, pope: V 129–31, 137, 139, 142, 147, 149, 151–3, 159, 162–4, 167–8, 172–3, 177–80
Bernard of Clairvaux: VIII 38
Boniface VIII, pope: II 268–9; IV 168; V 129, 133, 135–8, 142, 145, 192; VI 316
Breen, T.H.: XII 268
Brierly, J.L.: III 489
Bruce, Robert: XI 322
Bulgarians: V 144, 151
Burke, Edmund: VII 62
Byzantine Empire, Byzantines, Greeks: V 131, 139, 149–50, 155–7, 160–61, 165, 169–70, 190–91,

Cajetan, Thomas: II 269, 274
Calixtus III, pope: X 177
Calvin, John, Calvinism: VII 53, 55–6
Canary Islands, Canarians; IV 175–8, 180–81, 183; V 162, 182, 186–90, 193–4; XI 323
Cantini, J.A.: I 575–6
Canute, king of England: X 180
Caracalla, Roman emperor: VII 34
Caribs: VIII 43
Carlyle, A.J.: III 486
Casas, Bartolomé de las: IV 184; VI 301–2, 312–14; VIII 30–31, 33; XI 309, 323
Casimir III, king of Poland: V 185
Castile, king of: V 132
Catalan Grand Company: V 169–70
Catherine de Courtenay: V 156
Celestine, pope: XI 315
Ceuta: IV 176
Charlemagne: I 562: II 277; V 157
Charles I, king of Spain: II 270: IX 72

Charles of Anjou, king of Naples and Sicily: V 156
Charles of Valois: V 156–9
Charles V, holy Roman emperor: II 270; VII 54–5; IX 72
Childerich III, king of Franks: I 568; II 277
*Christianitas*: I 580
*Classics of International Law*: III 487–8, 490; IX 82
Clement III, pope: V 163
Clement V, pope: V 128, 130–31, 136, 143, 157–8, 162, 173, 191, 193
Clement VI, pope: V 129, 131, 133, 139, 141, 149, 153–5, 160–61, 164–71, 185–9, 193–4
*Clementinae*: V 128
Columbus, Christopher: IV 170, 181; VII 60; IX 68, 70, 83; X 175
conciliar movement: V 126; X 183
Concordat of Bologna: VII 59
Constantine, king of Armenia: V 153–5
Constantine, Roman emperor: I 567, 577; VII 46; X 182–3; XI 313
Constantinople: I 559, 562; V 130, 132, 140, 155–60; IX 66; VII 51
Constitutions of Melfi: VII 51
*Convenit*: X 175
*Corpus iuris canonici*: V 142
Coulanges, Fustel de, *The Ancient City*: VII 41
Council of Basel: IV 175–6
Council of Constance: III 484, 496; IV 175; VI 303, 305–6, 308–11; VII 52; XI 322
Council of Lyons (1245): V 172
Council of Lyons(1274): V 156–7
Council of Trent: VII 59
Covarruvias, Diego de: VIII 33
Cromwell, Oliver: VII 50; XII 286–8
crusade, crusader: I 575; II 272; V 132, 151, 155, 157, 162–71, 190, 194; VII 49–50; IX 67; XI 318
*Cum hora undecima*: V 143–50, 184, 190
*Cum secundum leges*: II 268,
*Cum simus*: V 150
*Cum venisset*: I 566
Cusack, Sir Thomas: XII 274–5, 277
Cyprus, king of, kingdom of: V 165–6, 170

Davies, Sir John: XII 276–7
Davis, R. Trevor: IX 69
Dawson, Christopher: V 171
*De civili dominio*: VI 307
*De Indis*: II 267; III 484
*De jure belli ac pacis* (On the Laws of War and Peace) [Hugo Grotius]: II 265; III 483, 486, 489–90, 494; VII 61; VIII 29
*De jure belli relectio* Francisco de Vittoria): III 490
*De las Islas del Mar Océano*: VI 314
Declaration of Independence: VII 61
Declaration of the Rights of Man: VII 38, 61
*Decretales*: IV 170, 173; V 129, 163
*Decretum*: I 556–8, 567–8, 570; IV 170; VIII 38; XI 314
*Defensor Pacis*: IX 76
Diocletian, Roman emperor: VII 45–6
*Disputatio de indiarum iure*: VIII 32, 34, 36, 44–5; X 177
*dominium*: I 574, 578; II 267–9; IV 171, 174, 183; VI 302–5, 307–16; IX 68; XI 317–18
Donation of Constantine: I 558–9, 573, 577; V 189; X 175–6, 183; XI 313–14, 320
Donatists: VI 303
*Dudum siquidem*: X 177

*Ea quae*: X 175
Edict of Milan: VII 46; X 182
Edict of Nantes: VII 58–9
Edward Bruce, king of Scotland: XI 315–16, 321–2
Edward I, king of England: VII 50
Edward I, king of Portugal: IV 179–80, 183
Edward II, king of England: XI 311, 316, 321–3
Edward III, king of England: V 155, 167, 191
*Eger cui levia*: I 575–8
Elizabeth I, queen of England: IX 74–5
England, king of: V 132, 153, 162, 170–71, 187; VIII 29
Enlightenment: VII 36
Ethiopians: V 144–5
Eugenius III, pope: VIII 38
Eugenius IV, pope; IV 177–80, 183, 184; XI 323
*Extravagantes Communes*: V 142
*Extravagantes Johannis Papae XXII*: V 128

Falkenberg, Johannes: VI 310–11
Ferdinand of Aragon: VI 312; X 175, 177–8
feudalism, feudal regime: VII 37–8
*Fides Armenorum*: V 152, 154
Figgis, J.N.: VII 40
Fourth Council of Carthage: I 571
Fourth Council of Toledo: I 571
Fourth Lateran Council: VII 50
France, king of: II 271; V 132, 153, 162, 170–71, 187; VII 55
Francis I, king of France: VII 59
Franks: II 277
Frederick II, holy Roman emperor: VII 51

French Constitution (1791): VII 36
French Revolution: VII 31, 36–8, 59, 61–62

*Gaudemus*: V 146–8
Gay, Jules: V 133
Gediminas, king of the Lithuanians: V 183–4
Genoa, Genoese: V 156, 171
Gentili, Alberico: III 485, 487
Georgia, Georgians: V 130, 132, 137, 139, 144, 150, 155
Gerald of Wales: XII 272
German, king, emperor: I 561, 566,
Gerson, Jean, theologian: VI 308
*Glossa ordinaria*: I 563, 570
*Glossa Palatina*: I 565
Gratian, Roman emperor: VII 47
Gratian, canonist: I 556–7, 567, 579; IV 170; VIII 33, 38; XI 313–14
Great Khan: V 173, 175–6, 178
Great Schism: V 126; X 183
Greeks: V 144
Gregorian Reform: V 130, 133–4, 155; X 177; XI 312
Gregory I, pope: X 183; XI 320
Gregory VII, pope: I 568; V 141; X 184; XI 311
Gregory IX, pope: I 571; V 128, 143–44
Gregory X, pope: V 127
Gregory XI, pope: V 131
Grotius, Hugo: II 265; III 483–95, 497; IV 184; VII 61; VIII 29–31, 45; IX 69

Hagar (Agar): IV 174–5, 180
Hakluyt, Richard: XII 270
Hanke, Lewis: III 492; VI 301, 313, 315; VIII 30–31; IX 69, 84; X 177
helots: VII 33
Henry II, king of England: X 174–5, 177–82; XI 312–13, 315; XII 269, 272
Henry IV, German emperor: I 568
Henry IV, king of England: VII 52
Henry IV, king of France: VII 58–9
Henry VIII, king of England: X 180–81; XII 273
heresy, heretics, heretical sects: I 556–7, 559, 567; II 267–8; IV 170; V 129, 130, 144
Hobbes, Thomas: V 191
Holinshed's *Chronicles*: XII 272
Holland, Thomas E.: III 485–7, 489, 493, 496
Holy Land: I 573–4; II 273; V: 130, 146, 164; VI 304; VII 49; IX 67; XI 318, 320
Hospitallers: V 165
Hostiensis (Henricus de Segusio, Henry of Segusio): I 556, 578–9; II 273; III 484, 48–86, 492, 495, 496–7; IV 172–5; V 188; VI 302, 305–6, 310–16; XI 317
Huguccio of Pisa: I, 558–60, 562–5, 569; V 157
Huguenots: VII 58–9
Humbert of Vienne: V 161, 169–70, 187
Hundred Years' War: V 129, 168, 170
Hus, John: VI 308–9

*imperium*, *imperator*, emperor, imperial: I 557–67, 573, 576, 578–9; II 269–72; V 135, V 156–60, 165, 191; VI 309; VII 33, 41, 45–9, 51, 54; VIII 32; IX 66–7, 69, 72, 75, 77; X 183; XI 314, 318–20; XII 270
Indians: IV 181; VI 302, 313; VIII 36–7, 43–5; IX 72–3, 84; XII 270–71; XII 280–89
Ine, king of Wessex: X 180
infidels, infidel society: I 555, 556, 574–5; III 484; IV 169, 171–7, 179–81, 183–4; V 129–30, 137–8, 142, 145–7, 148–50, 171, 179–82, 185, 188, 190–94; VI 302–7, 309–12, 314–16; VIII 34–8, 40–42, 44–5; IX 66–7, 69–71, 73–4, 76, 78–81; XI 309–10, 317–18, 322–3
Innocent III, pope: I 561–2, 566, 571–2, 579–80; II 271–2; IV 168, 171; V 128, 142, 146–9, 181; VIII 34; IX 66–7; X 176, 180
Innocent IV (Sinibaldo Fieschi), pope, canonist: I 555–6, 572–80; II 272–7; III 484–6, 495–7; IV 168; IV 170–75, 180–81, 183; V 127, 138, 143–6, 150, 181–2, 188–9; VI 302, 304–5, 307, 309–13, 315–16; VIII 33–5, 41–2, 44; IX 67–9; XI 318–20, 322
Innocent VI, pope: V 128, 131
*Inter caetera*: IV 168–70, 181–4
Isabella, queen of Castile: X 175, 177–8
Ishmael: IV 174, 180
Isidore of Seville, *Etymologies*: I 557

James I, king of England: IX 75, 77: X 178, 180; XII 277
Jews (Hebrews): I 556; II 268; IV 170, 172, 175, 181; VI 304–5; VII 43–5, 48–51, 62; VIII 34–6, 39–40, 42; IX 67–8, 81; XI 309
Joannes Andreae, canonist: IV 173
Johanna, wife of Andronicus III: V 160–61, 169
John Cantakuzenos: V 169
John I, pope: VIII 38
John of Legnano, canonist: III 487; IV 173
John of Marignolli, papal legate: V 178, 180, 192

John of Monte Corvino, archbishop of Peking: V 174, 176, 180
John of Plano Carpini: IV 170, 172; V 172
John of Salisbury: XI 313–14
John V Paleologus, Byzantine emperor: V 131, 160, 165 194
John XXII, pope: V 128–31, 136–9, 142–3, 145–8, 150–51, 159, 162–3, 172–3, 183–5; X 174; XI 310–11, 321–4
John, king of England: V 129: X 180
Julian the Apostate, Roman emperor: I 567–8
Julius II, Pope: X 175

Kestutis, duke of the Lithuanians: V 185, 189
King of Jerusalem: I 573
King Philip's War: XII 286–7
Kublai Khan: V 174

L'Hôpital, Michel de: VII 57
Ladner, Gerhard: I 580
*Laudabiliter*: X 174–84; XI 310–16, 318, 320–21, 324
Laurentius Hispanus: I 563
League of Nations: III 489, 491, 492, 494
legitimate, legitimacy: I 553–6, 558–9, 561, 563–4, 567–73, 575–80; II 267, 268–9, 275; III 484; VII 60; VIII 30, 35, 37, 43; IX 68–9, 71
Leo III, pope: V 157
Leo V, king of Armenia: V 152–3
Leo IX, pope: X 175–6
Leo X, pope: VII 59; X 175
Leo XIII, pope: IX 81
Leon and Castile, king of: V 141
*Liber Sextus*: V 129
Lithuanians, dukes of: V 132
Lithuanians, Lithuania: IV 175–6, 181; V 146, 182–6, 188–91, 190–91, 194; VI 306, 309–11; VIII 43; XI 322
Lombards: I 562,
Louis XIII, king of France: VII 59
Louis XIV, king of France: VII 59
Luis de la Cerda: V 186–9
Luther, Martin, Lutheranism: VII 53, 55–6, 58; X 183

Magna Carta: VII 35; IX 74; X 184
Major, John: III 492
Malabar coast: V 144
Mamelukes: V 170, 182
Manichaeism: VII 43
Marsilius of Padua: IX 76
Martin V, pope: IV 176
Mather, Cotton: XII 288
Matthew Paris, chronicler: X 180
Mattingly, Garrett: II 265–6
Merriman, R.B.: III 492; XII 267
*Meruit*: V 136, 142
Michael VII, Byzantine emperor: V 157
Mindaugas, king of the Lithuanians: V 146, 183
Mollat. G.: V 127
Mongols: I 580; IV 170–73; V: 130, 132, 138, 142, 149–51, 162–3, 171–3, 175–81, 190, 194; 304; IX 66, 68
Moors: V 187
Moreau-Reibel, Jean: III 494–6
Morgan, Edmund S.: XII 268
Morison, S.E.: XII 277
Morton, Thomas, of Merrymount: XII 285
Moslems (Muslims): I 573, II 272–3; IV 173–4, 176; V 130, 146, 151–2, 155, 158–60, 162–5, 167, 171, 181, 190–91; VI 304; VII 51; VIII 40; IX 66–8; XI 309, 318

Napoleon, emperor of France: VII 62
Nero, Roman emperor: VII 45
Nestorians: V 144, 174–5, 180
Nicholas I, pope: VIII 38
Nicholas IV, pope: V 143, 174
Nicholas V, pope: IV 181
Nicholas, Friar, Archbishop of Peking: V 173–7
Nicopolis: V 162
Nubians: V 144
Nussbaum, Arthur: III 493–4
Nys, Ernest: II, 265; III 483–90, 493–6

O'Neill, Donald, King of Ulster: XI 310–11, 315, 319, 322
Offa, king of Mercia: X 180
Oldratus de Ponte, lawyer: IV 173–5, 180–81
*On War, Reprisals, and the Duel*: III 487; IV 173
*Opinio Hostiensis*: VI 309
Oppenheim, L.: III 486

Palacios Rubios, Juan López de: VI 312, 314–15
Palaeologi: V 156
Parry, J.H.: III 492
Pastor, Ludwig: V 127
*patriciatus*: I 560,
Patrick, St.: XI 315, 320
Paul, St: I 570: V 143; VIII 39–40
Peace of Augsburg: VII 55
Peace of Westphalia: VII 56; IX 77
Pepin, king of the Franks: II 277

*Per venerabilem*: II 271,
Peter's Pence: X 177, 180
Peter, St, pope: I 561; V 135; VI 303; XI 312, 317
Petrarch: V 126
Philip Augustus, king of France: V 129
Philip of Taranto, prince of Achaia: V 159
Philip the Fair, king of France: V 133, 135–6
Philip VI, king of France: V 155, 163–4, 168, 191
philosophes: VII 36
Pius V, pope: V 194; IX 74–5
Pius IX, pope: IX 81
Pocahontas: XII 284
Poland, king of: III 484; IV 175; V 132, 188; VI 306, 309, 311; XI 322
*Política indiana*: VIII 32
*politiques*: VII 57–8
Polo, Maffeo: V 173
Polo, Marco: V 192
Polo, Niccolò: V 173
Polydore Vergil, historian: X 181–2
Portugal, king of: V 132
Post, Gaines: I 554
Praying Towns: XII 282–3, 286, 288
*Precelse devotionis*: X 175
Puritans: XII 268, 271, 277–82, 284–7

Quinn, David B.: XII 270
*Quod super his*: I 572, 575–8; II 272, 274–6; III 486; IV 171–2, 180; V 181, 189; VIII 34
*Quoniam ea*: X 175

Raleigh, Sir Walter: XII 270, 282
Raynaldus, Odorico: V 126
*Reflections on the Revolution in France*: VII 62
*Regnans in excelsi*: IX 74
Regout, Robert: III 494–6
*Requerimiento*: VI 301–3, 312–16; X 179
*Rerum Novarum*: IX 81
Richard of Burgundy, Franciscan, bishop: V 177
Rolfe, John: XII 284
*Romanis pontifex* (Eugenius IV): IV 180
*Romanis pontifex* (Nicholas V): IV 181
Rome, Roman, Romans: I 557, 559–60, 562, 567, 573; II 270; VII 33–4, 37, 41–9, 51; VIII 36–7, 44; IX 72, 75, 77; XI 314–20; XII 276, 279
Rosselli, Antonio: IV 180
Rowlandson, Mary: XII 287
Rufinus, canonist: I 569
Ruthenians: V 146

Sander, Nicholas, historian: X 181–2
Saracens: II 268; IV 170, 174; V 144, 159, 164; VI 304
Sarah, wife of Abraham: IV 174–5
schism, schismatic: I, 559, 567; IV 170; V 129–31, 136–9, 141, 144–8, 150–52, 154–5, 157–8, 161, 163, 180, 182, 185, 190–93; VII 40; VIII 34; IX 66, 68, 76–7; XI 309
Scott, James Brown: III 486–94, 496; VIII 31; IX 82
Scythians: XII 275, 288
Sepúlveda, Juan Ginés de: VIII 30
*Sicut exhibitae*: V 187, 189
Sigismund, holy Roman emperor: VI 309
Smith, John: XII 270, 280
Solórzano y Pereira, Juan de, Spanish official: VIII 32–45; X 176–80, 182–4
Soto, Domingo de, Spanish theologian: III 490; VIII 33
Spain, king of: II 277
*Spanish Struggle for Justice in the Conquest of America*: III 492; IX 69; X 177
Sparta: VII 33
Spenser, Edmund: XII 275–7
Spinka, Matthew: VI 308
Statutes of Kilkenny: XII 273, 284
Stickler, Fr. Alfons: I 557, 579
Suárez, Francisco: II 266; III 484, 488, 492, 493; VIII 33, 40; IX 69, 75–83
*Summa Omnis qui iuste*: I 567
*Syllabus of Errors*: IX 81
Sylvester I, pope: XI 313
Symmachus, prefect of Rome: VII 47–8
Syrians: V 145

Tacitus, Roman historian: VII 45
Tamerlane: V 170
Tancred, canonist: I 562–3
Tartars: V 138, 150, 160, 170–75, 179–82, 188, 190–91, XI 309
Teutonic Knights: III 484; IV 175; V 183–5, 188, 191, 194; VI 306, 309–11; XI 322
Theiner, Augustin: V 126
Thirty Years' War: VII 55–6; IX 81
*translatio imperii*: I 561; V 157
*Treatise on War, Reprisals, and Duels*: III 487
Treaty of Tordesillas: IV 183
Turks: V 150, 160–64, 166–9, 171–2, 182, 187

*Unam sanctam*: V 133, 135–8, 142–3
Urban II, pope: V 167; XI 313

Urban IV, pope: V 143
Urban V, pope: V 131
Usbech, khan of the Golden Horde: V 172–73, 177, 179

Vanderpol, A.: III 485–91, 493, 496
Vaughan, Alden: XII 271, 284
*Venerabilem*: I 561–3, 566; II 271; V 158
Venice, Venetians: V 156, 165
Vittoria, Francisco de (Francisco Vitoria, Francis Vitoria): II *passim*; III 484–6, 488–97; VI 302; IX 69–74, 78–80, 82–3; XI 309, 323
Vladimiri, Paulus: III 484, 495–7; IV 175, 184; VI 309–10

Wadding, Luke: V 126, 133
Walter, duke of Athens: V 169
Weckmann, Luis: III 497; V 189; X 174–6; 183
White, John, *The Planters Plea*: XII 277–9
William of Newburgh, chronicler: X 181–2
William of Normandy, king of England: X 178; XI 313, 315
Williams, Roger: XII 285
Winthrop, John: XII 277–82, 285
Witte, Charles-Martial de: III 497
Wright, Herbert F.: III 490
Wyclif (Wycliffe), John, English theologian: VI 303, 305–11; VII 52

Zaccaria, Martin, Genoese merchant: V 164–5, 168–9
Zachary, pope: I 568
Zavala, Silvio: VI 314
Zeno, Pietro, Venetian crusader: V 168

For Product Safety Concerns and Information please contact our EU representative GPSR@taylorandfrancis.com Taylor & Francis Verlag GmbH, Kaufingerstraße 24, 80331 München, Germany

**Batch number: 10704002**

Printed by Printforce, the Netherlands